Ethics and the A Priori

Over the l
about the 1
and the rel
we give of

This lo
Smith's ess
vating reas
internal ar
compulsic
moral real
normative
of moral
and cogni

Collec
interest t

Michael

7 MAY 2025

For Jeremy, Julian, and Samuel

Ethics and the A Priori

SELECTED ESSAYS ON MORAL PSYCHOLOGY AND META-ETHICS

MICHAEL SMITH

Princeton University

CAMBRIDGE
UNIVERSITY PRESS

PUBLISHED BY THE PRESS SYNDICATE OF THE UNIVERSITY OF CAMBRIDGE
The Pitt Building, Trumpington Street, Cambridge, United Kingdom

CAMBRIDGE UNIVERSITY PRESS
The Edinburgh Building, Cambridge CB2 2RU, UK
40 West 20th Street, New York, NY 10011-4211, USA
477 Williamstown Road, Port Melbourne, VIC 3207, Australia
Ruiz de Alarcón 13, 28014 Madrid, Spain
Dock House, The Waterfront, Cape Town 8001, South Africa

http://www.cambridge.org

First published 2004

Printed in the United States of America

Typeface Bembo 10.5/13 pt.   *System* LATEX 2$_\varepsilon$ [TB]

A catalog record for this book is available from the British Library.

Library of Congress Cataloging in Publication Data

Smith, Michael (Michael A.)
Ethics and the a priori : selected essays on moral psychology and meta-ethics / Michael Smith.
p.   cm. – (Cambridge studies in philosophy)
Includes bibliographical references and index.
ISBN 0-521-80987-8 – ISBN 0-521-00773-9 (pb.)
1. Ethics. I. Title. II. Series.
BJ1031.S63   2004
170–dc22   2003065394

ISBN 0 521 80987 8 hardback
ISBN 0 521 00773 9 paperback

Contents

Preface   *page* ix
Sources   xi

   Introduction   1

Part One Moral Psychology

1   Internal Reasons   17
2   The Incoherence Argument: Reply to Schafer-Landau   43
3   Philosophy and Commonsense: The Case of Weakness
    of Will (co-authored with Jeanette Kennett)   56
4   Frog and Toad Lose Control (co-authored with
    Jeanette Kennett)   73
5   A Theory of Freedom and Responsibility   84
6   Rational Capacities   114
7   On Humeans, Anti-Humeans, and Motivation: A Reply
    to Pettit   136
8   Humeanism, Psychologism, and the Normative Story   146
9   The Possibility of Philosophy of Action   155

Part Two Meta-Ethics

10 Moral Realism   181
11 Does the Evaluative Supervene on the Natural?   208
12 Objectivity and Moral Realism: On the Significance
    of the Phenomenology of Moral Experience   234
13 In Defence of *The Moral Problem*: A Reply to Brink,
    Copp, and Sayre-McCord   259

14 Exploring the Implications of the Dispositional Theory
    of Value   297
15 Internalism's Wheel   318
16 Evaluation, Uncertainty, and Motivation   343
17 Ethics and the A Priori: A Modern Parable   359

Index   381

Preface

The essays reprinted in this collection were written over a fifteen-year period (1987–2002). During this time I had the great privilege and pleasure of working in the Department of Philosophy at Princeton University, the Department of Philosophy at Monash University, and the Philosophy Program at the Research School of Social Sciences, Australian National University. I have also had the good fortune to spend time as a visitor at the University of Arizona at Tucson, Bristol University, the University of Michigan at Ann Arbor, the University of North Carolina at Chapel Hill, the University of Otago, Princeton University, Uppsala University, and Victoria University Wellington. I would like to thank the faculty and students of these institutions for their generous input when my ideas were given their first trial in a colloquium or graduate class or reading group, or over a cup of coffee or a drink down at the local pub.

Though I have corrected the occasional typographical error and put the references in uniform style, I decided that I would not substantially revise any of the essays for this reprinting. Since many of the essays have been responded to in print, it seemed best to reprint them warts and all. Having said that, however, let me immediately admit that there are places where I definitely regret having said what I said; but no matter how much I would like to, I see no real point in pretending that I didn't say what I said in the first place. There is, as a result, a good deal of repetition in the essays. This originally came about because I have been so keen on enabling readers to understand my work without having to have knowledge of anything else I have written. One good upshot of this is that the essays reprinted here can (hopefully) be read and understood in isolation from each other, and, indeed, in isolation from everything else I have written.

Since each essay contains a footnote thanking those who gave me comments, I will not repeat my words of thanks to those who helped give my thoughts their specific shape. Special thanks are, however, due to Jennie Louise, who did a splendid job of preparing the index; to Jeanette Kennett for allowing me to reprint two of our jointly authored papers; and to Frank Jackson and Philip Pettit, not just for their input into my work, but also for their encouragement and support and friendship over the years. I still cannot believe that I had good luck to meet Frank and Philip when I did, or to become their colleague at RSSS. Finally, I am grateful to Ernie Sosa for inviting me to contribute a collection of essays to the Cambridge Studies in Philosophy series.

Sources

The original publication details of these essays are as follows. I am very grateful to the publishers for giving their permission for this reprinting.

1. "Internal Reasons" in *Philosophy and Phenomenological Research*, 55 (1995), 109–31.
2. "The Incoherence Argument: Reply to Schafer-Landau" in *Analysis*, 61 (2001), 254–66.
3. "Philosophy and Commonsense: The Case of Weakness of Will" in Michaelis Michael and John O'Leary-Hawthorne, eds., *Philosophy in Mind: The Place of Philosophy in the Study of Mind* (Dordrecht: Kluwer Academic Publishers, 1994), pp. 141–57 (co-authored with Jeanette Kennett).
4. "Frog and Toad Lose Control" in *Analysis*, 56 (1996), 63–73 (co-authored with Jeanette Kennett).
5. "A Theory of Freedom and Responsibility" in Garrett Cullity and Berys Gaut, eds., *Ethics and Practical Reason* (Oxford: Oxford University Press, 1997), pp. 293–319.
6. "Rational Capacities" in Christine Tappolet and Sarah Stroud, eds, *Weakness of Will and Varieties of Practical Irrationality* (Oxford: Oxford University Press, 2003), pp. 17–38.
7. "On Humeans, Anti-Humeans and Motivation: A Reply to Pettit" in *Mind*, 97 (1988), pp. 589–95.
8. "Humeanism, Psychologism, and the Normative Story" in *Philosophy and Phenomenological Research*, 67 (2003), pp. 460–7.
9. "The Possibility of Philosophy of Action," in Jan Bransen and Stefaan Cuypers, eds., *Human Action, Deliberation and Causation* (Dordrecht: Kluwer Academic Publishers, 1998), pp. 17–41.
10. "Moral Realism," in Hugh LaFollette, ed., *Blackwell Guide to Ethical Theory* (Oxford: Blackwell, 2000), pp. 15–37.

11. "Does the Evaluative Supervene on the Natural?" in Roger Crisp and Brad Hooker, eds., *Well-Being and Morality: Essays in Honour of James Griffin* (Oxford: Oxford University Press, 2000), pp. 91–114.

12. "Objectivity and Moral Realism: On the Significance of the Phenomenology of Moral Experience," in John Haldane and Crispin Wright, eds., *Reality, Representation and Projection* (Oxford: Oxford University Press, 1993), pp. 235–55.

13. "In Defence of *The Moral Problem*: A Reply to Brink, Copp and Sayre-McCord," *Ethics*, 108 (1997), pp. 84–119.

14. "Exploring the Implications of the Dispositional Theory of Value," *Philosophical Issues: Realism and Relativism*, 12 (2002), pp. 329–47.

15. "Internalism's Wheel" in *Ratio*, 8 (1995), pp. 277–302.

16. "Evaluation, Uncertainty, and Motivation," in *Ethical Theory and Moral Practice*, 5 (2002), pp. 305–20.

17. "Ethics and the A Priori: A Modern Parable," in *Philosophical Studies*, 92 (1998), pp. 149–74.

Introduction

When we act, we act for reasons. It is easy to hear this as a truism or platitude. "Surely," it might be said, "what makes an action an *action* is the fact that it is something that someone does for a reason!" (Davidson 1963).

But in fact the claim that when we act, we act for reasons, is ambiguous. When interpreted in one way it is indeed a truism – all actions are things that people, or more generally animals, do for reasons – but, when interpreted in the other, it is no truism at all. Though some acts are done for reasons in this alternative sense, it isn't the case that all acts are done for reasons. Some people act because there is reason *not* to do what they do (Stocker 1979).

The claim that the term "reason" is ambiguous is, of course, familiar in the philosophical literature (Woods 1972; Smith 1987). On the one hand, talk of reasons is much the same as talk of causes. When we talk of reasons for action we thus sometimes have in mind the psychological states that teleologically and causally explain behaviour. This is the use of the word "reason" that is in play when I say that my reason for (say) tapping away on the keys of my laptop is that I want to write an introduction to my collection of essays and believe that something I can do – namely, tap away on the keys to my laptop – will lead to that outcome. It is also the use that is in play when we say that the cat's reason for meowing at the door in the morning is that she's hungry and wants some food. In earlier work I have called these "motivating reasons." Motivating reasons are psychological states that teleologically, and perhaps causally, explain behaviour: they are constituted (or so I say) by pairs of desires and means-end beliefs. On the other hand, however, when we talk of reasons for action we sometimes have in mind something completely different:

1

considerations that (allegedly) justify. This is the use of the word "reason" that is in play when I say that my reason for tapping away on the keys to my laptop is that collections of essays require an introduction. A cat simply isn't sophisticated enough to have reasons in this sense. In earlier work I have called these "normative reasons." Normative reasons are propositions whose truth would justify acting in a certain way: they are (roughly speaking) facts about the desirability of so acting (or so I say).

If a distinction of this kind is along the right lines then the ambiguity in the claim that, when we act, we act for reasons, becomes readily intelligible. For what makes an action an action is the fact that there are certain motivating reasons that teleologically, and perhaps causally, explain an agent's doing something: actions are actions in virtue of their distinctive psychological pedigree. In this sense, the claim that when we act, we act for reasons, is indeed a truism. But it is a substantive truth about any particular action – an achievement on behalf of the agent of that action, an achievement that requires not just conceptual sophistication but also, perhaps, the possibility of conscious control – that there are normative reasons for doing what is done. For it is an achievement to act on a consideration that does, in fact, justify what is done. In this sense, the claim that when we act, we act for reasons, is no truism at all. It is a compliment that at most some of us deserve some of the time. Some of us are even so perverse as to be motivated to act in ways that we believe to be dysjustified, to use Michael Stocker's term (Stocker 2004).

The fact that there are sometimes, but not always, normative reasons for doing what we do, but always motivating reasons, raises several important questions about the nature of motivating and normative reasons and about the relationship between them. The task of the essays in the first part of this collection is to raise and answer some of these important questions.

Part One Moral Psychology

The first question is what, exactly, makes it the case that there is a normative reason to act in one way as opposed to another. In other words, what is the truth-maker of the claim that a certain consideration provides a justification for what an agent does?

This question is taken up in Chapter 1, "Internal Reasons." In Bernard Williams's famous paper "Internal and External Reasons," he argues, in effect, that what makes it the case that there is a normative reason to act in a certain way is the fact that so acting accords with certain of the agent's idealised desires, where the idealisation in question is a matter of the agent's desires conforming to certain principles of reason, and where the agent in question has the capacity to grasp this fact (Williams 1980; see also Pettit and Smith forthcoming). Though this is an intuitively attractive account of normative reasons – it explains, for example, why cats aren't capable of having or acting on normative reasons – once we remember that such idealised desires are supposed to make it the case that we have normative reason to act in a certain way in circumstances that may well be less-than-ideal, we see that there are two very different models of such idealised desires. Moreover we also see that these models aren't on a par in terms of plausibility.

Put colloquially, the first of these models amounts to the idea that what we have normative reason to do is to follow the *advice* of our idealised selves. Thus, according to the advice model, what I have normative reason to do in my less-than-ideal circumstances is a matter of what my idealised self, in his idealised circumstances, would desire me to do in my less-than-ideal circumstances. The second model amounts to the quite different idea that what we have normative reason to do is to follow the *example* set by our idealised selves. Thus, according to the example model, what I have normative reason to do in my less-than-ideal circumstances is a matter of what my idealised self wants himself to do in his ideal circumstances. One of the main aims of "Internal Reasons" is to show how implausible the example model is, and to show how its implausibility points us in the direction of the advice model.

A good deal of time is also spent revisiting Williams's own account of what he calls "internal" reasons. I ask whether his account of internal reasons provides us with a sound basis for an advice model of normative reasons. I argue that, duly amended and supplemented, it does. One main way in which it requires amendment is in the assumptions it makes about the transformative powers of the idealisation process. According to Williams, the desires any particular subject ends up having after we idealise her desires need not be the same as the desires other subjects end up with after we idealise their desires. But I argue that, in order to suppose that the objects of our idealised desires are capable of providing justifications, we cannot go along with Williams on this score. We must assume that subjects would all converge in the desires they have when we idealise, otherwise facts about the objects of our idealised desires would not be facts of the right kind to provide justifications. They would be too arbitrary. (Note that it is consistent with what I've just said that though this is how we *conceive* of normative reasons, there may well be no normative reasons, as there may be no objects of desire upon which subjects would converge if we were to idealise their desires. This issue is taken up again in various of the remaining essays, but especially in Chapter 12 and Chapter 14.)

Towards the end of "Internal Reasons" I argue that, when Williams's internal conception of reasons – that is, his conception of normative reasons in terms of idealised desires – is augmented and supplemented in the way I suggest, then we come to see one of its great attractions. For, I argue, this account enables us to see how and why our beliefs about our normative reasons are capable of both causing and rationalising our having corresponding desires, that is, our having corresponding motivating reasons. However when I wrote "Internal Reasons" I was still unclear in my own mind how *exactly* the account of normative reasons in terms of idealised desires enables us to do this. (I now think that the explanation offered in the paragraph that ends with footnote 9 is completely wrong, for example.) In subsequent work I revisited this explanation. I finally settled on a formulation in terms of coherence.

An idealised set of desires is, as I said above, a set of desires that conforms to all of the principles of reason that govern them. Let's say that when we have such a desire set that desire set is, *inter alia*, maximally coherent. In these terms, what allows us to explain the connection between our beliefs about our normative reasons, on the one hand, and our motivating reasons, on the other, is that coherence itself would seem to require that, if we believe that we would want that we ϕ in certain circumstances C if we had a maximally coherent desire set, then we desire that we ϕ in C. In other words, the coherence of our psychology is itself enhanced when we have desires that accord with our beliefs about what we would desire if we had a maximally coherent desire set. What explains the transition from the belief to the desire is thus none other than the capacity we have, as rational creatures, to have a coherent psychology. In a phrase, our being rational does all of the explaining.

This claim, which is a crucial premise in many of the arguments provided in the essays in this collection – indeed, as will become clear, both the claim and the argument for it (such as it is) is repeated over and over in many of the essays – has received a good deal of attention in its own right. I explicitly respond to two of these discussions in this collection. Chapter 2, "The Incoherence Argument," is an attempt to respond to Russ Schafer-Landau's criticisms of the argument (Schafer-Landau 1999). Since many people object to the Incoherence Argument because they have an interpretation much like Schafer-Landau's, and since such objections turn on a misinterpretation of my intentions, my hope is that this paper will help

4

clarify what is, and what is not, being asserted in the premises of the In-coherence Argument. (The other explicit discussion of the Incoherence Argument appears in Chapter 13, "In Defence of the Moral Problem: A Reply to Brink, Copp, and Sayre-McCord," in which I discuss Geoff Sayre-McCord's criticisms [Sayre-McCord 1997].)

The real significance of the fact that we can explain the transition from having beliefs about our normative reasons to having motivating reasons in terms of the exercise of our rational capacities emerges when we see how this enables us to explain both the nature of various forms of practical irrationality and our ability to respond to the fact that we are practically irrational in these various ways. Chapter 3, "Philosophy and Commonsense: The Case of Weakness of Will" (co-authored with Jeanette Kennett) argues for the superiority of the resultant account of weakness of will by comparing it to Donald Davidson's famous account. Our preferred account of weakness of will is in terms of a subject's having, but failing to exercise, her capacity to have motivating reasons that accord with her beliefs about what she has normative reason to do: in other words, it amounts to her having, but failing to exercise, her capacity to have coherent pairings of belief and desire. We suggest that this gives us the required contrast between weakness and compulsion.

Chapter 4, "Frog and Toad Lose Control" (also co-authored with Jeanette Kennett), argues for the superiority of the resultant account of self-control. The very idea of self-control looks, after all, to be quite puzzling. If all action is motivated by desire, then when we act in a non-self-controlled way we must be acting on a desire, a desire that, in some sense, we shouldn't be acting on. But what exactly does this "should" mean? Furthermore, if all action is motivated by desire, and if an exercise of self-control is needed, then how is that exercise of self-control so much as possible? Wouldn't the exercise of self-control require the presence of a desire that, by hypothesis, we do not have? In "Frog and Toad Lose Control," Kennett and I offer a unified solution to these two puzzles.

The solution turns on two distinctions. First, Kennett and I distin-guish between the exercise of synchronic, as opposed to diachronic, self-control. As we show, the puzzle only arises in cases of the exercise of synchronic self-control: exercises of diachronic self-control are unprob-lematic. Second, we distinguish between the distinct causal roles played, in the genesis of action, by desire, on the one hand, and by beliefs about our normative reasons, on the other. Exercises of synchronic self-control are required because rationality demands that our desires align themselves with our beliefs about what we have normative reason to do: the "should" mentioned above is thus the "should" of rational coherence. However, though our desires should so align themselves, they may fail to do so. It is in such cases that exercises of synchronic self-control are needed. But what makes such exercises possible is that the fact that they are one and all non–actional: that is to say, what causes the realignment of our desires with our beliefs about our reasons is our havings of various thoughts, our engaging in various imaginative exercises, and the like, where these are all in turn explained by the fact that it is rational for us to think such thoughts, to engage in such imaginings, and the like. The relevant causal factor is thus the tendency or capacity we have to move from an incoherent overall psychological state into a more coherent overall psychological state, not a desire and means–end belief pair.

Chapter 5, "A Theory of Freedom and Responsibility," uses the accounts of self-control and a capacity to do otherwise developed in Essays Three and Four to build a comprehensive theory of freedom and responsibility. Here, it seems to me, we see the real pay-off of asking the sorts of questions we asked in the previous essays: in order to build a comprehensive theory of freedom and responsibility we have no choice but to build on the foundation laid by a plausible theory of both normative and motivating reasons and the relations between them. In many respects, the theory of freedom developed here is similar to David Lewis's theory of freedom (Lewis 1981). There are, however, some striking dissimilarities. In particular, the theory offered here assumes that the capacity to act freely consists in two quite distinct capacities: the capacity to match our desires with our beliefs about what we have reason to do, and the capacity to match our beliefs about what we have reason to do with the facts about what we have reason to do. The latter is a crucial component. It explains why freedom is not a power of arbitrary significance. For this reason I argue that the theory of freedom and responsibility developed here brings out the crucial flaw that lies at the core of Harry Frankfurt's account of freedom of the will (Frankfurt 1971).

In the three papers just discussed – "Philosophy and Commonsense," "Frog and Toad Lose Control," and "A Theory of Freedom and Responsibility" – free use is made of the idea that we may have a capacity to make our psychology more coherent and yet fail to exercise this capacity. However, as Gary Watson pointed out some years ago in his seminal essay "Skepticism about Weakness of Will," the idea of an unexercised capacity is much more difficult to make sense of than it might initially appear (Watson 1977). Chapter 6, "Rational Capacities," attempts to provide the needed explication of this idea. I should perhaps say that the problem addressed in this paper − articulating the sense of "could" required for freedom of the will − seems to me to be the most difficult discussed in the essays in this collection. Though I would be amazed if the proposal is entirely successful − if it is then the problem of free will and determinism is solved! − my firm conviction is that a solution to this difficult problem must be found in some such proposal. My hope is that the proposal will stimulate profitable discussion and development of related proposals.

In the final three papers in the first part I return to the issue of motivating reasons. Chapter 7, "Humeans, Anti-Humeans, and Motivation," is a response to Philip Pettit's published reply to "The Humean Theory of Motivation" (Smith 1987; Pettit 1987; note that Smith 1987 is not reprinted in this collection). The aim is to make it clear why two lines of response to my view that motivating reasons are constituted by desires and means-end beliefs are not to the point. According to the first, I overlook the possibility that though motivating states are one and all constituted by desires, since the desires in question *are* beliefs − they are evaluative beliefs − it follows that our motivating states are one and all constituted by such beliefs as well. I point out that this is merely terminologically different from an objection I consider and rebut in "The Humean Theory of Motivation," which is that motivation requires the presence of a kind of psychological state that is both belief-like and desire-like but identical with neither. The second line of response is that I fail to answer the crucial question whether the desires that motivate actions, though distinct from beliefs, are none the less caused and rationalised by beliefs. But though this is a crucial question − indeed, it is the question that animates the essays that appear earlier in this collection − it is distinct from the question about the nature of our motivating states. One issue is whether we should accept a Humean theory of motivation. The argument in favour of this is that an explanation in terms of motivating reasons is a teleological explanation, from which it follows that motivating states must be constituted by desires and means-end beliefs, where belief and desire are distinct existences. Another quite distinct issue is whether we should accept Hume's own account of the rational status of desire. I argue that though we should accept a Humean theory of motivation, it is moot whether we should accept Hume's own account of the rational status of desire. (As the earlier essays make clear, I think we should in fact reject Hume's own account of the rational status of desire.)

In Chapter 8, "Humeanism, Psychologism, and the Normative Story," I respond to Jonathan Dancy's views about the nature of motivating reasons

(Dancy 2000). If we must think that psychological states figure in the explanation of action then, according to Dancy, we should suppose that these psychological states are beliefs rather than desire-belief pairs. But in fact he thinks that we have no business supposing that psychological states typically figure in the explanation of action at all. For though it is indeed a truism that actions are explained by reasons, he argues that psychological states are only rarely, if ever, reasons. He thus prefers what he calls the "normative story," a story which contents itself with explaining actions by laying out the considerations in the light of which the agent acted as he did. But while I find myself agreeing with Dancy's premises, I do not find his conclusion convincing. I explain why.

Chapter 9, "The Possibility of Philosophy of Action," was conceived as a sequel to "The Humean Theory of Motivation." The paper addresses various challenges to the standard account of the explanation of intentional action in terms of desire and means-end belief, challenges that didn't occur to me when I wrote "The Humean Theory of Motivation." I begin by suggesting that the attraction of the standard account lies in the way in which it allows us to unify a vast array of otherwise diverse types of action explanation. I illustrate this with an explanation of action by ignorance. When we explain an action by ignorance, I say, we do not displace, but rather presuppose the availability of an explanation in terms of desire and means-end belief. With this illustration in mind I go on to consider a range of other challenges to the standard account of the explanation of action: Rosalind Hursthouse's challenge based on the possibility of what she calls "arational" actions (Hursthouse 1991); Michael Stocker's challenge based on the idea that some explanations of action are non-teleological (Stocker 1981); Mark Platts's challenge based on the idea that our evaluative beliefs can sometimes explain our actions all by themselves (Platts 1981); a voluntarist challenge based on the possibility of explaining actions by the exercise of self-control; and a challenge from Jonathan Dancy based on the idea that reasons can themselves sometimes explain actions all by themselves (Dancy 1994).

Part Two Meta-Ethics

In the second part of the collection the focus turns from general issues concerning the explanation of action to more specific issues in meta-ethics. As becomes clear, however, these more specific issues in meta-ethics seem to me to be continuous with those that arise regarding action-explanation.

In the essays described previously I defend the view that facts about what agents have reason to do are best understood as facts about what they would ideally want themselves to do. But, as even a casual glance at the meta-ethical literature makes clear, we find a very similar idea in meta-ethics. Indeed, Roderick Firth goes so far as to suggest that something like this idea is defended by all of the classic moralists (Firth 1952). According to the dispositional theory of moral value, for example, facts about moral values are facts about idealised desires. But if this is right then perhaps we can simply collapse the two stories into one: facts about what we have reason to do are simply facts about what it would be good or desirable for us to do where these, in turn, are facts about what we ideally desire ourselves to do. Moral values are a sub-class of the values: facts about what we morally ought to do are a sub-class of the facts about what we have reason to do. The essays in part two defend this conception of moral facts and, as well, locate that defence in the context of broader issues in meta-ethics.

Chapter 10, "Moral Realism," is an extended statement and defence of the version of moral realism that I myself favour. According to this version of moral realism, moral facts reduce to idealised psychological facts, facts which in turn constitute reasons for action. My aim in writing "Moral Realism" was to write something reasonably accessible to those not familiar with the various moves that are standardly made in the vast meta-ethical literature. A wide range of material is therefore covered, including an explanation of the difference between moral realism, nihilism, and expressivism; an explanation of why moral realism becomes truistic on certain minimalist conceptions of truth; an account of the problem that moral realism, so construed, faces; an account of what a moral realist who is a naturalist would say about moral facts; an account of the various standard objections to this kind of naturalistic moral realism; an account of what a non-naturalist would say about the nature of moral facts; an account of the various objections to this non-naturalistic kind of moral realism; two replies that a naturalistic moral realist might give to the objections made earlier, one of which commits the realist to internalism – that is, to the idea that there is an internal or necessary connection between moral judgement and the will – and the other of which commits the realist to externalism; a reason for preferring the version of moral realism that commits the realist to internalism (this is the version that reduces moral facts to a certain sort of idealised psychological fact); a discussion of the relativistic and non-relativistic versions of this kind of moral realism (this is related to my objections to William's view at the end of Chapter 1); and, finally, an argument in favour of the non–relativistic version.

Chapter 11, "Does the Evaluative Supervene on the Natural?," is a discussion of an important challenge to an orthodoxy in meta–ethics. Virtually everyone writing in meta–ethics takes if for granted that evaluative facts supervene on natural facts: no two worlds can be naturalistic duplicates and yet differ in evaluative terms. One notable exception to this orthodoxy is James Griffin (Griffin 1992). I begin the essay by clarifying the claim that the evaluative supervenes on the natural. This proves to be a much more difficult task than we might have thought it would be. I then consider, and ultimately reject, Griffin's various reasons for being skeptical about the supervenience thesis. I trace the attraction of the supervenience thesis to a fact about ordinary moral discourse, namely, the fact that it is always appropriate to ask what makes a moral claim true and that what we require by way of a response is an answer in terms of certain natural features.

Chapter 12, "Objectivity and Moral Realism: On the Significance of the Phenomenology of Moral Experience," is about a well-known exchange between John Mackie and John McDowell. Mackie famously argued for an error theory: in his view, though we have moral beliefs, these beliefs are one and all mistaken (Mackie 1977). John McDowell's reply to Mackie's argument is that it merely underscores the fact that Mackie has a mistaken conception of moral qualities (McDowell 1985). To be sure, McDowell insists, if moral qualities had to be like primary qualities – like being round, being extended, and the like – then, just as Mackie says, it would be impossible to make sense of the internal connection between moral judgement and the will. However, according to McDowell, this simply shows that we should conceive of moral qualities as being more like secondary qualities, rather than primary qualities: more like being red than being round. Once we adopt the secondary quality conception of moral qualities, a conception that he thinks is well supported by the phenomenology of moral experience, McDowell claims that Mackie's error theory becomes a non-starter: moral qualities, so conceived, are both out there in objects and internally connected to the wills of moral agents.

In "Objectivity and Moral Realism," I consider McDowell's argument at some length. I argue that even if we do adopt a secondary quality model of moral qualities, the error theory still looms large. For even if moral qualities are just dispositions to elicit appropriate desires in us under suitable conditions, if, as Mackie seems to think, these conditions would have to be conditions in which, in virtue of our perfect rationality, we all come to have the same desires in response to the same facts – here we once again appeal to the conception of facts about what we morally ought to do as facts about our normative reasons for action, as these are analysed in the essays in the first part of the collection – then skepticism about the possibility of this kind of rationally underwritten convergence in our desires would still provide us with grounds for skepticism about the existence of such dispositions. In other words, to the extent that the phenomenology of moral experience provides us with support for a certain kind of rationalism, which it does indeed seem to do, Mackie's error theory remains an option that needs to be ruled out. McDowell's objection thus misses its mark.

Chapter 13, "In Defence of *The Moral Problem*: A Reply to Brink, Copp, and Sayre-McCord," was written as part of a symposium on my book *The Moral Problem* (Smith 1994; see also Brink 1997; Copp 1997; Sayre-McCord 1997). Because the critical papers in the symposium dealt with so many points of detail I thought that, in some places at least, they together obscured, rather than illuminated, the overall line of argument in the book. This seemed to me to be a pity because, notwithstanding the various telling criticisms, the overall line of argument of the book appeared to me to survive pretty much intact. I therefore took the opportunity to write my own contribution to this symposium as a self-standing paper. I reiterate the main line of argument of *The Moral Problem* and, in the process of so doing, state the critics' objections in my own words. I give various replies to their objections. The overall result is, I think, a paper that not only summarises the overall argument of the book, but which also corrects what I have come to be persuaded is wrong, and explains what is really at issue in those cases in which I think my critics have missed the point.

Chapter 14, "Exploring the Implications of the Dispositional Theory of Value," takes up some further questions about the dispositional theory. Many people assume that the dispositional theory of moral value commits us to cognitivism (the view that moral judgements are expressions of beliefs); relativism (the view that the truth conditions of agents' moral judgements vary depending on their actual desires); and realism (the view that there are moral facts). But, notwithstanding the understandable temptation to think that all of this is so, I argue that the implications of the dispositional theory are either different or, at the very least, much less clear. Though the dispositional theory does give us grounds on which to make a case for cognitivism, I argue that making that case requires that we appeal to certain controversial supplementary premises. As regards relativism, I argue that the dispositional theory of value has no such implication. Indeed, if anything, the dispositional theory seems to commit us to non-relativism rather than relativism, something that becomes plain when we think about the way in which the dispositional theory requires us to distinguish between neutral and relative values. And as regards realism, I argue that the dispositional theory leaves it very much an open question whether realism or irrealism is true. That debate, too, turns on the truth of certain supplementary, and controversial, premises. (Here I echo the conclusion of Chapter 12.)

Chapter 15, "Internalism's Wheel," puts the spotlight on the internalist claim that there is an internal or necessary connection between moral judgement and the will. Internalism has traditionally been thought to function as a high-level conceptual constraint on moral judgement, accounts of which are supposed to be assessed, *inter alia*, by the extent to which they can explain and capture its truth. But the argument of this paper is that this doesn't amount to much in the way of a constraint. There are many different theories about the nature and content of moral judgement that aspire to explain and capture the truth embodied in internalism, and these theories share little in common beyond that aspiration. Worse still, as I demonstrate, these theories may well be best thought of as lying around the perimeter of a wheel, much like Fortune's Wheel, with each theory that lies further on along the perimeter representing itself as motivated by difficulties that beset the theory that precedes it. The mere existence of Internalism's Wheel need not pose a problem for internalists, of course. For they may believe that the truth about ethics lies wherever Internalism's Wheel stops spinning. But a problem evidently does arise if Internalism's Wheel is in perpetual motion, for then the truth about ethics presumably lies nowhere at all on Internalism's Wheel. The main aim of this paper is to consider the sceptical hypothesis that Internalism's Wheel is indeed in perpetual motion: that internalism is false, and externalism true.

In Chapter 16, "Evaluation, Uncertainty, and Motivation," we turn to consider the merits of non-cognitivism. Cognitivists and non-cognitivists agree that evaluative judgements have both belief-like and desire-like features. But whereas cognitivists tend to suppose that they can easily explain the belief-like features, and that they have trouble explaining the desire-like features, non-cognitivists tend to think the reverse: they think that they can easily explain the desire-like features, and that they have trouble explaining the belief-like features. However, as I show, the belief-like features of evaluative judgement are quite complex, and these complexities crucially affect the way in which an agent's values explain her actions. In other words, the belief-like features of evaluative judgements have an impact on the desire-like features. I argue that while at least one form of cognitivism can accommodate all of these complexities – the version of cognitivism I myself prefer: that which holds that evaluative facts are facts about our idealised desires – non-cognitivism cannot. The upshot is that at least one form of cognitivism can explain both the belief-like and the desire-like features of evaluative judgements, and that non-cognitivism can explain neither. The upshot is that we should reject non-cognitivism.

The final essay in the collection, Chapter 17, "Ethics and the A Priori: A Modern Parable," is a further attack on non-cognitivism. Non-cognitivists characteristically defend their view by appeal to the Open Question Argument. Though I've argued in print that such appeals are illicit because they depend on holding bad views about the nature of conceptual analysis (Smith 1994, Ch. 2), I must confess that I secretly feel the sting of the Open Question Argument whenever it is used against me. I have therefore always wondered whether there was a better response. At a certain point it occurred to me that there must be, because non-cognitivism is itself vulnerable to a version of the Open Question Argument. If I am right about this right then we are left having to adjudicate some rather difficult questions about who does and who doesn't have the upper hand in the resultant dialectical situation, the cognitivist or the non-cognitivist. I argue that the cognitivist has the upper hand.

"Ethics and the A Priori: A Modern Parable" is written as a dialogue between two philosophers, Cog and Noncog, both of whom passionately defend their views. It is perhaps fitting that this collection should close with an essay that attempts to put the all-too-human element back into the arguments given for and against the abstract theses that are at stake in its constituent essays. In recognition of the methodology pursued throughout, the essay also gives the book its title.

REFERENCES

Brink, David 1997: "Moral Motivation," in *Ethics* 108, 4–32.
Copp, David 1997: "Belief, Reason and Motivation: Michael Smith's *The Moral Problem*," in *Ethics* 108, 33–54.
Dancy, Jonathan 1994: "Why There Is Really No Such Thing as the Theory of Motivation," *Proceedings of the Aristotelian Society*, 95, 1–18.
_____ 2000: *Practical Reality* (Oxford: Oxford University Press).
Davidson, Donald 1963: "Actions, Reasons and Causes," reprinted in his *Essays on Actions and Events* (Oxford: Oxford University Press, 1980), 3–20.

Firth, Roderick 1952: "Ethical Absolutism and the Ideal Observer," in *Philosophy and Phenomenological Research*, 12, 317–45.

Frankfurt, Harry 1971: "Freedom of the Will and the Concept of a Person," reprinted in Gary Watson, ed., *Free Will* (Oxford: Oxford University Press, 1982), 81–95.

Griffin, James 1992: "Values: Reduction, Supervenience, and Explanation by Ascent," in David Charles and Kathleen Lennon, eds., *Reduction, Explanation and Realism* (Oxford: Oxford University Press), 297–321.

Hursthouse, Rosalind 1991: "Arational Actions," *Journal of Philosophy*, 88, 57–68.

Lewis, David 1981: "Are We Free to Break the Laws?," reprinted in his *Philosophical Papers Volume II* (Oxford: Oxford University Press, 1986).

Mackie, J. L. 1977: *Ethics: Inventing Right and Wrong* (Harmondsworth: Penguin).

McDowell, John 1985: "Values and Secondary Qualities," in Ted Honderich, ed, *Morality and Objectivity* (London: Routledge and Kegan Paul), 110–29.

Pettit, Philip 1987: "Humeans, Anti-Humeans and Motivation," *Mind*, 96, 530–33.

———— and Michael Smith forthcoming: "External Reasons," in Cynthia Macdonald and Graham Macdonald, eds., *McDowell and His Critics* (Oxford: Blackwell).

Platts, Mark 1981: "Moral Reality and the End of Desire," in Mark Platts, ed., *Reference, Truth and Reality* (London: Routledge and Kegan Paul). 69–82.

Sayre-McCord, Geoffrey 1997: "The Meta-Ethical Problem: A discussion of Michael Smith's *The Moral Problem*" in *Ethics*, 108, 55–83.

Schafer-Landau, Russ 1999: "Moral Judgement and Normative Reasons," *Analysis*, 59, 33–40.

Smith, Michael 1987: "The Humean Theory of Motivation," in *Mind* 96, 36–61. A slightly revised version of this paper appears as Chapter 4 of Smith 1994.

———— 1994: *The Moral Problem* (Oxford: Blackwell).

Stocker, Michael 1979: "Desiring the Bad: An Essay in Moral Psychology," *Journal of Philosophy*, 76, 738–53.

———— 1981: "Values and Purposes: The Limits of Teleology and the Ends of Friendship," *Journal of Philosophy*, 78, 747–65.

———— 2004: "Raz on the Intelligibility of Bad Acts," in R. Jay Wallace, Philip Pettit, Samuel Scheffler, and Michael Smith, eds., *Reason and Value: Themes from the Moral Philosophy of Joseph Raz* (Oxford: Oxford University Press). 303–32.

Watson, Gary 1977: "Skepticism about Weakness of Will," in *The Philosophical Review*, 86, 316–39.

Williams, Bernard 1980: "Internal and External Reasons," reprinted in his *Moral Luck* (Cambridge: Cambridge University Press, 1981).

Woods, Michael 1972: "Reasons for Action and Desire," *Proceedings of the Aristotelian Society* Supplementary Volume, 48, 189–201.

Part One

Moral Psychology

1

Internal Reasons

INTRODUCTION

According to one popular version of the dispositional theory of value, the version I favour, there is an analytic connection between the desirability of an agent's acting in a certain way in certain circumstances and her having a desire to act in that way in those circumstances if she were fully rational (Rawls 1971: Chapter 7; Brandt 1979: Chapter 1; Smith 1989, 1992, 1994).[1] If claims about what we have reason to do are equivalent to, or are in some way entailed by, claims about what it is desirable for us to do – if our reasons follow in the wake of our values – then it follows that there is a plausible analytic connection between what we have reason to do in certain circumstances and what we would desire to do in those circumstances if we were fully rational.

The idea that there is such an analytic connection will hardly come as news. It amounts to no more and no less than an endorsement of the claim that all reasons are "internal," as opposed to "external," to use Bernard Williams's terms (Williams 1980). Or, to put things in the way Christine Korsgaard favours, it amounts to an endorsement of the "internalism requirement" on reasons (Korsgaard 1986). But how exactly is the in-ternalism requirement to be understood? What does it tell us about the nature of reasons? And wherein lies its appeal? My aim in this paper is to answer these questions.

The paper divides into three main sections. In the first I distinguish be-tween two different models of the internalism requirement – the "advice" model and the "example" model – and I say why the requirement should be understood in terms of the advice model. In the second and longest sec-tion I spell out the requirement in some detail and I explain why, contrary to Bernard Williams, it is not especially allied to a relativistic conception of reasons – indeed I say why those of us who embrace the requirement should endorse a non-relative conception. And in the third section I use the advice model, understood in the way explained in the second section, to explain the appeal of the internalism requirement. As we will see, the internalism requirement helps us solve an otherwise troubling problem about the effectiveness of deliberation.

1. THE ADVICE MODEL VERSUS THE EXAMPLE MODEL

The internalism requirement tells us that the desirability of an agent's φ-ing in certain circumstances C depends on whether she would desire that she φs in C if she were fully rational. This idea can be made more precise as follows.

We are to imagine two possible worlds: the *evaluated* world in which we find the agent in the circumstances she faces, and the *evaluating* world in which we find the agent's fully rational self. In these terms, the internalism requirement tells us that the desirability of the agent's φ-ing in the evaluated world depends on whether her fully rational self in the evaluating world would desire that she φs in the evaluated world. Note what I have just said, for the precise formulation is important. The idea is that we are to imagine the agent's fully rational self in the evaluating world looking across at herself in the evaluated world (so to speak) and forming a desire about what her less than fully rational self is to do in the circumstances she faces in that evaluated world. We might imagine that the self in the evaluating world is giving the self in the evaluated world advice about what to do. Accordingly, this is what I call the "advice" model of the requirement.

The advice model of the requirement contrasts with the example model. On this alternative way of thinking about the requirement, the idea is that the desirability of an agent's φ-ing in the evaluated world depends on whether her fully rational self in the evaluating world would desire to φ *in the evaluating world*. We are not to suppose that the agent's fully rational self is giving advice to herself in the evaluated world, but rather that the agent's fully rational self is setting up her own behaviour in her own world, the evaluating world, as an example to be followed by the self in the evaluated world. The issue of interpretation, then, turns on whether the internalism requirement tells us that in acting on reasons we follow the *advice*, or the *example*, of our fully rational selves.

I said that the details of the formulation are important, and the reason why is because the details are something about which those who

18

accept the requirement may yet disagree. Consider, for example, Christine Korsgaard's own official formulation of the requirement. According to Korsgaard the internalism requirement is the claim that the considerations that constitute reasons must "succeed in *motivating* us insofar as we are rational" (1986: 15, emphasis is mine). But on the plausible assumption that a fully rational agent's desires will only succeed in motivating *her* if they are desires that concern the circumstances in which *she* finds *herself*, the idea, in our terms, must be that a consideration constitutes a reason in the evaluated world just in case, in the evaluating world, the agent's fully rational self would desire that she acts on that consideration *in the evaluating world*. Korsgaard thus seems to have in mind the example model of the internalism requirement, not the advice model.[2]

But the example model is plainly wrong. In order to see why consider the following case, a variation on an example of Gary Watson's (1975). Suppose I have just been defeated in a game of squash. The defeat has been so humiliating that, out of anger and frustration, I am consumed with a desire to smash my opponent in the face with my racket. But if I were fully rational, we will suppose, I wouldn't have any such desire at all. My desire to smash him in the face is wholly and solely the product of anger and frustration, something we can rightly imagine away when we imagine me in my cool and calm fully rational state. The consideration that would motivate me if I were fully rational is rather that I could show good sportsmanship by striding right over and shaking my opponent by the hand. In that case, does it follow that what I have reason to do *in my uncalm and uncool state* is stride right over and shake him by the hand?

In essence, this is what Korsgaard's formulation of the internalism requirement tells us, for she supposes that a consideration constitutes a reason just in case it would motivate the fully rational person, and this is what my fully rational self would be motivated to do. And yet this is surely quite wrong. Striding right over and shaking my opponent by the hand might be the last thing I have reason to do, especially if being in such close proximity to him, given my anger and frustration, is the sort of thing that would cause me to smash him in the face. Rather, we might plausibly suppose, what I have reason to do in my uncalm and uncool state is to smile politely and leave the scene as soon as possible. For this is something that I can get myself to do and it will allow me to control my feelings. Moreover – and importantly for the advice model – *this is exactly what my fully rational self would want my less than fully rational self to do in the circumstances that my less than fully rational self finds himself*. But, to repeat, it is not something I would be motivated to do if I were fully rational because it is not something that I would have any *need* to be motivated to do if I were fully rational.

The example model of the internalism requirement thus gives us the wrong answer in cases in which what we have reason to do is in part determined by the fact that we are irrational. For what an agent's fully rational self is motivated to do will depend on the circumstances in which she finds herself, and, by definition, these circumstances will never include her own irrationality. It therefore seems to me that we should reject the example model of the internalism requirement in favour of the advice model. What we have reason to do in the circumstances in which we find ourselves is fixed by the advice our fully rational selves would give us about what to do in these circumstances that we face.

2. THE INTERNALISM REQUIREMENT AND THE IDEA OF BEING FULLY RATIONAL

The internalism requirement tells us that it is desirable for an agent to ϕ in certain circumstances C, and so she has a reason to ϕ in C, if and only if, if she were fully rational, she would desire that she ϕs in C. The content of our reasons is thus fixed by the advice we would give ourselves if we were fully rational. However, note that I haven't yet said anything about what being "fully rational" means, and that we must do so if we are to understand what the internalism requirement tells us, substantively, about the reasons we have.

In his own similar analysis of internal reasons Bernard Williams suggests, in effect, that to be fully rational in the practical sphere an agent must satisfy the following three conditions:

  i. the agent must have no false beliefs
 ii. the agent must have all relevant true beliefs
iii. the agent must deliberate correctly

His reason for insisting on the first two conditions is straightforward enough.

If our desire to do something is wholly dependent on false beliefs, then we ordinarily suppose that it isn't really desirable to do that thing. Suppose, for example, I desire to drink from a particular glass, but that my desire to do so depends on my belief that the glass contains gin and tonic when in fact it contains gin and petrol. Then we would ordinarily say that though I might think that it is desirable to drink from the glass, it isn't really desirable to do so. Why not? Because I would not desire that

20

I do so if I were fully rational: that is, if, *inter alia*, I had no false beliefs – thus condition (i).

Similarly, in the case of condition (ii), if we fail to desire something, and if our failure to do so is wholly dependent on our failure to believe something that is true, then we ordinarily suppose that that thing may yet be desirable. Suppose, for example, that I do not desire to drink from a particular glass, but that my failure to do so is to be explained by the fact that I am ignorant of the contents of the glass. In fact it contains the most delicious drink imagineable. Then we would ordinarily say that despite the fact that I do not desire to drink from the glass, doing so may yet be desirable. Why? Because I may well desire that I do so if I were fully rational: that is, if, *inter alia*, I had all relevant true beliefs.

But what about condition (iii)? Williams's idea here is that even if we fail to desire that we φ, φ-ing may still be desirable because we would desire that we φ if our other beliefs and desires interacted in the ways appropriate for the generation of new desires: that is, if we deliberated and did so correctly. For example, the means to an end is desirable, but we will in fact desire the means to our ends only if we reason in accordance with the means-ends principle, for only so does a desire for an end turn into a desire for the means.

Moreover, as Williams points out, means-ends reasoning is only one mode of rational deliberation among many. Another example is

> ...practical reasoning...leading to the conclusion that one has reason to φ because φ-ing would be the most convenient, economical, pleasant etc. way of satisfying some element in...[one's set of desires]...and this of course is controlled by other elements in...[one's set of desires]...if not necessarily in a very clear or determinate way....[And]...there are much wider possibilities for deliberation, such as: thinking how the satisfaction of elements in...[one's set of desires]...can be combined: e.g. by time-ordering; where there is some irresoluble conflict among the elements of...[one's set of desires]...considering which one attaches most weight to...; or, again, finding constitutive solutions, such as deciding what would make for an entertaining evening, granted that one wants entertainment. (1980: 104)

And he thinks that there are other, more radical, possibilities for deliberation as well.

> More subtly,...[an agent]...may think he has reason to promote some development because he has not exercised his imagination enough about what it would be like if it came about. In his unaided deliberative reason, or encouraged by the persuasions of others, he may come to have some more concrete sense of what

would be involved, and lose his desire for it, just as positively, the imagination can create new possibilities and new desires. (1980: 104–5)

Thus, according to Williams, we must include the operation of the imagination in an account of what is involved in deliberating correctly as well.

Williams's conditions (i) through (iii) seem to me to constitute a fairly accurate spelling out of our idea of what it means to be practically rational. An agent who has defective beliefs or who deliberates badly is indeed the sort of agent we tend to think of as being practically irrational in some way. It seems to me that Williams's conditions do require supplementation and amendment, however. For one thing, I see no way in which the effects of anger and frustration could be precluded by conditions (i) through (iii) – unless some such constraint is supposed to be presupposed by condition (iii), the condition of correct deliberation. Yet, as we have seen, emotions can cause us to desire to do what we have no reason to do (remember the effects of that humiliating defeat I suffered in squash). Here, then, there is need for supplementation. And for another – and this is the point on which I wish to focus – it seems to me that Williams omits from his discussion of condition (iii) an account of perhaps the most important form of deliberation. The omission is serious as it leads him to overstate the role of the imagination in deliberation. Here, then, as we will see, there is need for both supplementation and amendment.

Williams admits that deliberation can produce new and destroy old underived desires. As he puts it, an agent "may think he has reason to promote some development because he has not exercised his imagination enough about what it would be like if it came about," just as, more "positively, the imagination can create new possibilities and new desires." When the imagination does create and destroy desires in these ways Williams tells us that we take its operations to be sanctioned by reason.

Williams is right, I think, that deliberation can both produce new and destroy old underived desires. But he is wrong that the only, or even the most important, way in which this happens is via the exercise of the imagination. By far the most important way in which we create new and destroy old underived desires when we deliberate is by trying to find out whether our desires are, as a whole, *systematically justifiable*. And, if this is right, then that in turn requires a significant qualification of Williams's claim that reason sanctions the operation of the imagination.

What do I mean when I say that we sometimes deliberate by trying to find out whether our desires, as a whole, are systematically justifiable? I mean just that we can try to decide whether or not some particular underived desire that we have or might have is a desire to do something that is itself non-derivatively desirable, and that we do this in a certain characteristic way: namely, by trying to integrate the object of that desire into a more *coherent* and *unified* desiderative profile and evaluative outlook. Rawls describes the basics of this procedure of systematic justification in his discussion of how we attempt to find a "reflective equilibrium" among our specific and general evaluative beliefs (Rawls 1951; Daniels 1979). I will restrict myself to saying a little about the way in which achieving reflective equilibrium may also be a goal in the formation of underived desires.

Suppose we take a whole host of desires we have for specific and general things, desires which are not in fact derived from any desire we have for something more general. We can ask ourselves whether we wouldn't get a more systematically justifiable set of desires by adding to this whole host of specific and general desires another general desire, or a more general desire still, a desire that, in turn, justifies and explains the more specific desires that we have. And the answer might be that we would. If the new set of desires – the set we imagine ourselves having if we add a more general desire to the more specific desires we in fact have – exhibits more in the way of coherence and unity, then we may properly think that the new imaginary set of desires is rationally preferable to the old. For the coherence and unity of a set of desires is a virtue, a virtue that in turn makes for the rationality of the set as a whole. This is because exhibiting coherence and unity is partially constitutive of having a systematically justified, and so rationally preferable, set of desires, just as exhibiting coherence and unity is partially constitutive of having a systematically justified, and so rationally preferable, set of beliefs.

The idea here is straightforwardly analogous to what Rawls has to say about the conditions under which we might come to think that we should acquire a new belief in a general principle given our stock of rather specific evaluative beliefs. The thought there is that we might find that our specific value judgements would be more satisfyingly justified and explained by seeing them as all falling under a more general principle. The imaginary set of beliefs we get by adding the belief in the more general principle may exhibit more in the way of coherence and unity than our current stock of beliefs. Likewise, the idea here is that our imaginary set of desires may exhibit more in the way of coherence and unity than our current set of desires.

If we do come to believe that our more specific desires are better justified, and so explained, in this way, then note that that belief may itself cause us to have a new, underived, desire for that more general thing.

23

And, if it does, then it seems entirely right and proper to suppose that this new desire has been arrived at by a rational method. Indeed, the acquisition of the new more general desire will seem rationally required in exactly the same way that the acquisition of the new belief that the object of the desire is desirable will seem rationally required. In fact, if the internalism requirement is right, the acquisition of a new evaluative belief will be the cognitive counterpart of the acquisition of the new desire. For, according to the requirement, an evaluative belief is simply a belief about what would be desired if we were fully rational, and the new desire is acquired precisely because it is believed to be required for us to be more rational.

Moreover, if this is agreed, then note that we can not only explain how we might come to have new underived desires as the result of such reflection, but that we can also explain how we might come to lose old underived desires as well. For, given the goal of having a systematically justifiable set of desires, it may well turn out that, as the attempt at systematic justification proceeds, certain desires that seemed otherwise unassailable have to be given up. Perhaps because we can see no way of integrating those desires into the set as a whole they will come to seem *ad hoc* and so unjustifiable to us. Our belief that such desires are *ad hoc* may then cause us to lose them. And, if so, then it will seem sensible to describe this as a loss that is itself mandated by reason; as again straightforwardly analogous to the loss of an unjustifiable, because *ad hoc*, belief.

As this procedure of systematic justification continues we can therefore well imagine wholesale shifts in our desiderative profile. Systematic reasoning creates new underived desires and destroys old. Since each such change seems rationally required, the new desiderative profile will seem not just different from the old, but better; more rational. Indeed, it will seem better and more rational in exactly the same way, and for the same reasons, that our new corresponding evaluative beliefs will seem better and more rational than our old ones.

To a first approximation, then, this is what I mean by saying that we can create new and destroy old underived desires by trying to come up with a set of desires that is systematically justifiable. But even this first approximation is enough to see why Williams's claims about the role of the imagination in deliberation requires significant qualification. For true though it is that the imagination can produce new and destroy old underived desires via vivid presentations of the facts, its operations are not guaranteed to produce and destroy desires that would themselves be sanctioned in an attempt at systematic justification of the kind just described.

In fact quite the opposite is the case. For the imagination is liable to all sort of distorting influences, influences that it is the role of systematic reasoning to sort out. Consider an example. Vividly imagining what it would be like to kill someone, I might find myself thoroughly averse to the prospect no matter what the imagined outcome. But, for all that, I might well find that the desire to kill someone, given certain outcomes, is one element in a systematically justifiable set of desires. Merely imagining a killing, no matter what the imagined circumstances, may cause in me a thoroughgoing aversion, but it will not justify such an aversion if considerations of overall coherence and unity demand that I have a desire to kill in certain sorts of circumstances, and such considerations may themselves override the effects of the imagination and cause me to have the desire I am justified in having.[3] The role played by attempts at systematic justification is thus what is crucially required for an understanding of how deliberation creates new and destroys old underived desires, not the role played by the imagination.

Let's recap. According to the internalism requirement, the desirability of an agent's φ-ing in certain circumstances C is fixed by whether or not she would desire that she φs in C if she were fully rational. The aim in this section is to spell out the idea of being fully rational. Taking our lead from Bernard Williams the suggestion so far is that an agent is fully rational just in case she has no false beliefs and all relevant true beliefs, and just in case she deliberates correctly in the light of these beliefs, and an agent is in turn understood to have deliberated correctly just in case her underived desires are systematically justifiable: that is, to a first approximation, just in case her underived desires form a maximally coherent and unified desire set. Do we need to say more? Indeed we do, something we see clearly once we focus on a consequence Williams wants us to draw from his own similar analysis of reasons.

According to Williams, the internalism requirement supports a *relative* conception of reasons. He puts the point this way.

[T]he truth of the sentence . . . ["A has a reason to φ"] . . . implies, very roughly, that A has some motive which will be served or furthered by his φ-ing, and if this turns out not to be so the sentence is false: there is a condition relating to the agent's aims, and if this is not satisfied it is not true to say . . . that he has a reason to φ. (1980: 101)

And again later:

Basically, and by definition, . . . [an analysis of reasons] . . . must display a relativity of . . . [a] . . . reason statement to the agent's *subjective motivational set*. (1980: 102)

Now in fact it is initially quite difficult to see why Williams says any of this at all. For, as we have seen, what the internalism requirement suggests is that claims about an agent's reasons are claims about her *hypothetical* desires, not claims about her *actual* desires. The truth of the sentence "A has a reason to ɸ" thus does not imply, not even "very roughly," that A *has* some motive which will be served by his ɸ-ing; indeed A's *motives* are beside the point – that was the difference between the advice model and the example model. What the internalism requirement implies is rather that A has a reason to ɸ in certain circumstances C just in case he *would* desire that he ɸs in those circumstances if he were fully rational.

Williams might concede this. But, he might say, it doesn't show that he is wrong when he says that the requirement supports the relativity of an agent's reasons to her actual desires, it simply shows that the relativity of reasons requires more careful formulation. The crucial point, he might insist, is that the desires an agent would have if she were fully rational are themselves simply functions from her actual desires, where the relevant functions are those described in conditions (i) through (iii). An agent's reasons are thus relative to her actual desires, he might say, because under conditions of full rationality agents would all have different desires about what is to be done in the various circumstances they might face. Even if it is rational for each of us to change our actual desires by trying to come up with a set of desires that can be systematically justified, in the manner captured by conditions (i) through (iii), such changes will always fall short of making us have the same desires as our fellows; they will always reflect the antecedent fact that we have the actual desires that we have. The content of the maximally coherent and unified desire set any particular agent could have will always reflect the content of that agent's actual desires.

As I see it, this is what Williams has in mind when he says that our reasons are all relative.[4] It explains why he rightly insists that he is defending a "Humean" conception of reasons (1980: 102). For his conception of reasons, like Hume's own, is predicated on skepticism about the scope for reasoned change in our desires (Korsgaard 1986); predicated on denying that, through a process of rational deliberation – through attempting to give a systematic justification of our desires, for example – we could ever come to discover reasons that we all share. For what we have reason to do is given by the content of the desires we would have if we were fully rational, and these may differ in content from agent to agent.

Williams claims to derive this relative conception of reasons from the internalism requirement. But as a *derivation* this is hardly compelling. It goes through only if we assume that it is no part of our task, in trying to come up with a systematically justifiable set of desires, to come up with the same set of desires as our fellow rational creatures would come up with if they set themselves the same task. And this suggests, in turn, that there are therefore two quite distinct conceptions of *internal* reasons. There is a relativistic, Humean, conception of internal reasons – the conception embraced by Williams – and there is also a non-relativistic, anti-Humean or Kantian conception according to which, if we were to engage in a process of systematically justifying our desires we would all eventually reason ourselves towards the same conclusions as regards what is to be done. That is, according to the opposing conception, all possible rational creatures would desire alike as regards what is to be done in the various circumstances they might face because this is, *inter alia*, what defines them to be "rational." Part of the task of coming up with a maximally coherent and unified set of desires is coming up with a set that would be converged upon by other rational creatures who too are trying to come up with a maximally coherent and unified set of desires; each rational creature is to keep an eye out to her fellows, and to treat as an aberration to be explained, any divergence between the sets of desires they come up with through the process of systematic justification.[5,6]

The final question to ask, then, in spelling out our idea of "full rationality," is whether Williams is right that our ordinary concept of a reason is Humean or anti-Humean. Does our ordinary concept of a reason presuppose skepticism about the scope for reasoned change in our desires? In other words, does it presuppose that there will, or alternatively that there will not, be a convergence in the desires that we would have under conditions of full rationality? If it presupposes that there will not be such a convergence then our concept of a reason is indeed relative, just as Williams says. If it presupposes instead that there will be such a convergence then our concept of a reason is, by contrast, non-relative.

Let me emphasise that we are asking a conceptual question, not a substantive question. We are asking what we mean when we talk of people being fully rational; whether it is part of what we mean by "rational" that fully rational people converge in their desires, or whether this is no part of what we mean by "rational." And note as well that no matter how we answer this question, we do not thereby beg any substantive questions. For example, even if our concept of a reason is itself non-relative – even if our concept optimistically presupposes that we would all converge on the same desires under conditions of full rationality – the world might disappoint us. Entrenched and apparently rationally inexplicable differences in what we desire might make it impossible to believe, substantively, that there are any such non-relative reasons (Smith 1991, 1993, 1994).

Let's, then, confront the conceptual question head on. Is our ordinary concept of a reason relative or non-relative? The relativity of a claim should manifest itself in the way we talk. Consider, for example, the schematic claim "It is desirable that p in circumstances C." On the non-relative conception of internal reasons – at least if we abstract away from some complications to be dealt with presently – this claim has a straightforward truth condition: it is desirable that p in C just in case we would all desire that p in C if we were fully rational. There is, then, a sense in which we can talk about rational justification or desirability *simpliciter*. When you and I talk about the reasons that there are for acting, we are therefore talking about the same thing. We are talking about reasons *period*; about the common set of reasons that are appreciable by each of us.

On the relative conception, however, matters are quite different. For in order to give the truth condition of the schematic claim "It is desirable that p in C" we need first to know from whose perspective the truth of the claim is to be assessed. For while "It is desirable that p in C" as assessed from A's perspective is true if and only if A would desire that p in C if A were fully rational, "It is desirable that p in C" as assessed from B's perspective is true if and only if B would desire that p in C if B were fully rational, and so on and so forth. There is thus no such thing as desirability or the considerations that rationally justify *simpliciter*, but only desirability$_A$, desirability$_B$, ... ; considerations that rationally-justify-from-A's-perspective, rationally-justify-from-B's-perspective, ... and so on. If I say to you "There is a reason for φ-ing," and you deny this, we are therefore potentially talking about quite different things: reasons$_{me}$ and reasons$_{you}$. The question to ask is therefore whether the way in which we talk about reasons for action and the considerations that rationally justify our actions reflects a relative or a non-relative conception of the truth conditions of reason claims.

One reason for thinking that it reflects the non-relative conception comes from the broader context in which the question is being asked. For it is important to remember that we have a whole range of normative concepts: truth, meaning, support, entailment, desirability, and so on. Between them these concepts allow us to ask all sorts of normative questions, questions about what we should and should not believe, say and do. But how many of these other normative concepts are plausibly thought to give rise to claims having relativised truth conditions? As I understand it, none of them do.

Consider our concept of support, by way of example. It seems quite implausible to suppose that the truth of claims about which propositions support which others is implicitly relative to the individual; that when A says "p supports q" and B says "p does not support q" they are potentially talking about quite different things: that A is talking about what supports$_A$ q and B is talking about what supports$_B$ q, for instance. For if this were the case then we should expect to find that we are sometimes able to dissolve apparent disagreements by finding that both parties are speaking truly. It should be permissable for B to say "A said 'p supports q' and what she said is true, but p does not support q." However it is a striking feature of our talk about which propositions support which others that we *never* dissolve apparent disagreements in this way. Propositions have normative force *simpliciter*, not just normative-force-relative-to-this-individual or -relative-to-that. When one individual says "p supports q" and the other says "p does not support q" they thus express their disagreement about whether p supports q in a *non-relative* sense.

If our concept of desirability were implicitly relativised, then, it seems that this would mark a significant difference between this concept and our other normative concepts. We should expect to find that with claims about what is desirable, unlike claims about which propositions support which, we *are* able to dissolve apparent disagreements in the way just described. But do we find this?

It might be thought that we do. After all, aren't there all sorts of familiar cases in which we say things like "That may be a reason for you, but it isn't for me," "Desirable for you maybe, but not desirable for me," and the like? But though there are indeed such cases, it is important to note that the sort of relativity we signal when we say such things is quite different from the kind just described; quite different from the kind of relativity Williams has in mind. For, in the familiar cases, "That may be a reason for you, but it isn't for me" signals the fact that there is a relativity built in to the *considerations* that we use to rationally justify our choices. It does not signal the fact that *our concept of a reason* is itself relative to the individual; that there is no such thing as which considerations, relative or not, rationally justify our choices, but only which considerations rationally-justify-relative-to-this-person or rationally-justify-relative-to-that-person. Here, then, we come to the complications abstracted away from earlier.

Sometimes what we have in mind when we say "That may be a reason for you, but it isn't for me" is that the considerations that rationally justify our choices are, to use Parfit's terms, *agent-relative*, rather than *agent-neutral* (Parfit 1984). Suppose you are standing on a beach. Two people are drowning to your left and one is drowning to your right. You can either swim left and save two, in which case the one on the right will drown, or you can swim right and save one, in which case the two on the left will drown. You decide to swim right and save the one and you justify your choice by saying "The one on the right is my child, whereas the two on the left are perfect strangers to me."

In one sense, of course, I may well say "That may be a reason for you, but it isn't for me." For if the three people drowning are all perfect strangers to me then, had I been standing on the beach instead of you, I would not have been able to justify the choice of swimming right and saving the one. But in another sense it seems that what is a reason for you may indeed be a reason for me. For if I had been standing on the beach instead of you, and if the one on the right had been my child – that is, if my circumstances had been in all crucial respects *the same* as yours – then surely I too would have been able to justify the choice of swimming right and saving the one by saying "The one on the right is my child." Indeed, if we think that a parent who fails to save her child in such circumstances fails to act on a reason available to her – as it seems to me that we do – then we are in fact obliged to say this; obliged to assume the non-relative conception of internal reasons.

What this sort of example shows is therefore that, even if reasons are non-relative in the crucial sense at issue here, among the considerations that may rationally justify our choices are both considerations that are properly given a *de dicto* formulation and considerations that are properly given a *de se* formulation (see also Lewis 1989). That is there are both *de dicto* and *de se* internal reasons. We can each express the content of the *de dicto* reason relevant in this case by using the words "There is a reason to save people quite generally." And we can each express the content of the *de se* reason by using the words "There is a reason to save my child in particular." In these terms what is a reason for you, in this case, is not a reason for me in the sense that, if it had been me standing on the beach rather than you, and if the same people had been drowning, then the only consideration that would have been relevant to my choice is the *de dicto* reason. The *de se* reason would not have been relevant to my choice because the people who are in fact drowning are all perfect strangers to me. But in another sense what is a reason for you is indeed a reason for me. For if I had been standing on the beach and the one person on the right had been my child, as the one on the right is your child, then both the *de se* and the *de dicto* reason would have been relevant to my choice in just the way they are both relevant to yours.

I said that this sort of relativity is entirely different from the kind that Williams has in mind and it should now be plain why this is so. For, in terms of the analysis, even if some of the considerations that rationally justify our choices are relative because *de se*, the existence of such *de se* reasons may still require a convergence in the desires that we would all have if we were fully rational. That is, the existence of reasons with *de se* contents may still require that, under conditions of full rationality, we would each have desires whose contents we would express by using words like "to help my children," "to promote my welfare," and the like. The mere existence of *de se* reasons is thus quite different from the relativity Williams has in mind. For his claim is that reasons are relative in the sense of requiring no such convergence; that the fact that my act helps my child may constitute a reason$_{me}$ even though the fact that your act helps your child does not constitute a reason$_{you}$.

There is another familiar sort of relativity in our claims about the reasons we have as well, a sort that derives from the fact that what we have reason to do is relative to our circumstances, where our circumstances may include aspects of our own psychology. Suppose, for example, that you and I differ in our preferences for wine over beer. Preferring wine, as you do, you may tell me that there is a reason to go to the local wine bar after work for a drink, for they sell very good wine. But then, preferring beer, as I do, I may quite rightly reply "That may be a reason for you to go to the wine bar, but it is not a reason for me."

Now while this might initially look like the claim that our reasons are relative to our desires in something like the sense Williams has in mind, it again isn't really. For the crucial point in this case is that a relevant feature of your circumstances is your preference for wine, whereas a relevant feature of my circumstances is my preference for beer. That this is a relevant feature of our circumstances is manifest from the fact that I can quite happily agree with you that if I were in your circumstances – if I preferred wine to beer – then the fact that the local wine bar sells very good wine would constitute a reason for me to go there as well, just as it constitutes a reason for you.

This sort of relativity is thus completely different from the kind that Williams has in mind as well. For, in terms of the analysis, even if an agent's preferences may enter into a specification of the circumstances that she faces it might still be the case that whether or not she is rationally justified in taking her own preferences into account, and the way in which she is justified in taking them into account, if she is, depends on whether fully rational agents would all converge on a desire which makes the preferences she in fact has relevant in that way to her choice. In this case, for example, it may be crucial that, under conditions of full rationality we would all converge on a desire to satisfy whatever preferences we might have (perhaps within limits) in deciding where to go for a drink after work.[7] The fact that in rationally justifying our choices our preferences may sometimes be a relevant feature of our circumstances thus does nothing to support Williams's view that our reasons are relative; does nothing to support the view that really there are only the considerations that rationally-justify-relative-to-this-person or rationally-justify-relative-to-that.

In order to find support for the sort of relativity Williams has in mind, we therefore need to look for cases in which it is permissible to make much more radically relativised claims about what there is reason to do. But in fact, as far as I can tell, we find no such claims. Suppose someone tells me that she has a reason to take a holiday and that I think I would have no reason to take a holiday in the circumstances she faces. Provided we have taken proper account of the *de se* considerations that might be relevant to her choice, and provided we have taken proper account of the way in which her preferences may constitute a relevant feature of her circumstances, it seems that I straightforwardly disagree with her about the rational justifiability of her taking a holiday in the circumstances she faces, a disagreement I can express by saying "She thinks that there is a reason to take a holiday in her circumstances, but there is no such reason." If she cites a consideration in support of her taking a holiday that I think fails to justify, then I do not conclude that it may justify-relative-to-her, though not justify-relative-to-me, I conclude that it fails to justify *simpliciter*.

The point is important, for it suggests that when we talk about reasons for action we quite generally take ourselves to be talking about a common subject matter: reasons *period*. We are thus potentially in agreement or disagreement with each other about what constitutes a reason and what doesn't. This is why, when we find ourselves in disagreement – as for example in the case of disagreement about whether or not there is a reason to take a holiday in certain circumstances – we always have the option of engaging in argument in the attempt to find out who is right and who is wrong. Other people's opinions about the reasons that there are thus constitute potential challenges to my own opinions. I have something to learn about myself and my own assessment of the reasons that there are by finding out about others and their assessment. This is why books and films are so engaging. All of this is flat out inconsistent with the claim that our concept of a reason for action is quite generally relative to the

32

individual; that it typically means reason$_{me}$ out of my mouth, reason$_{you}$ out of yours, reason$_{her}$ out of hers, and so on. It suggests rather that our concept of a reason is stubbornly non-relative.

Indeed, it seems to me that we have no choice but to think this. For if reasons were indeed relative then mere reflection on that fact would itself suffice to undermine their normative significance. In order to see why, remember that on the relative conception it turns out that, for example, the desirability$_{me}$ of some consideration, p, is entirely dependent on the fact that *my* actual desires are such that, if *I* were to engage in a process of systematically justifying *my* desires, weeding out those that aren't justified and acquiring those that are, a desire that p would be one of the desires *I* would end up having. But what my actual desires are to begin with is, on this relative conception of internal reasons, an entirely *arbitrary* matter, one without any normative significance of its own. I might have had any old set of desires to begin with, even a set that delivered up the desire that not p after a process of systematic justification! The desirability$_{me}$ of the fact that p thus turns out to be an entirely arbitrary fact about p. But this is surely a *reductio*, as *arbitrariness* is precisely a feature of a consideration that tends to undermine any normative significance it might initially appear to have. Internal reasons on the relative conception are thus without normative significance (Darwall 1983: 218–39; Smith 1989; Darwall, Gibbard and Railton 1992). And if this is right then it follows that *relative* internal reasons are not *reasons* at all.

On the non-relative conception, by contrast, reflection on our concept of desirability reveals no such arbitrariness. For on that conception everyone is supposed able to reason themselves towards the same desires if they engage in a process of systematic justification of their desires, and they are supposed able to do so precisely because the task of systematic justification is *inter alia* a matter of finding desires that can be shared by their fellow rational creatures. Which desires *I* would end up with, after engaging in such a process, thus in no way depends on what *my* actual desires are to begin with, because reason itself determines the content of our fully rational desires, not the arbitrary fact that we have the actual desires that we have. On the non-relative conception, reflection on the concept of desirability thus leaves the normative significance of facts about what is desirable and undesirable perfectly intact.

This, then, is the final element in our account of what it means when the internalism requirement tells us that the desirability of an agent's ϕ-ing in certain circumstances C depends on whether or not she would desire that she ϕs in C if she were "fully rational." Fully rational agents *converge* in their desires about what is to be done in the various circumstances they might face. Of course, the mere fact that a convergence in the hypothetical desires of fully rational creatures is required for the truth of internal reason claims does nothing to guarantee that such a convergence is forthcoming. In defending the non-relative *conception* of internal reasons we have said nothing to suggest that, *substantively*, there are any such reasons. But what we have said does suggest that, in order to discover whether there are any such reasons, and if so what they are, we have no alternative but to give the arguments and see where they lead. Substantive convergence is always assumed available, in so far as we converse and argue about the reasons that we have. But whether or not this assumption is true is always *sub judice*; something to be discovered by the outcome of those very conversations and arguments; something that will emerge when we see where our attempts to systematically justify our desires lead us.

3. THE ADVICE MODEL AND THE APPEAL OF THE INTERNALISM REQUIREMENT

So far I have argued that the internalism requirement on reasons is best understood in terms of the "advice" model, rather than the "example" model, and I have argued that reasons, understood in terms of the "advice" model, are best thought of as being non-relative, rather than relative. The two points are related, of course. For I have argued that it is only if we think of reasons on the "advice" model, and it is only if we think of reasons as being non-relative, that we can properly account for the normative significance of reason claims. However the most important question about the internalism requirement remains yet to be answered. Why exactly should we accept the internalism requirement in the first place? Why shouldn't we think, instead, that reasons have nothing to do, constitutively, with the desires of fully rational agents, as I have defined the idea of "full rationality"? The answer is that the internalism requirement on reasons enables us to solve an otherwise disturbing puzzle about the role of deliberation in the production of action. Let me begin by explaining the puzzle.

Hume taught us that desires and means-end beliefs each play an essential role in the explanation of action (Smith 1987). Suppose, for example, that all we know about someone is that she believes that if she flicks a particular switch the light will go on and that if she refrains the light will stay off. Then, so far, we have no more reason to suppose that she will flick the switch than refrain. Whether she will flick or refrain must therefore

34

depend on something else about her beyond her beliefs about the way the world is. And indeed it does. It depends on what she happens to desire. Does she desire the causal upshot of flicking the switch, the light's being on, or the causal upshot of refraining from doing so, the light's being off? If the former, then she will flick the switch; if the latter, then she will refrain. Desires are thus essential for the explanation of action. But so are beliefs as well. For if all we know about someone is that she desires the light to be on then, again, so far we have no more reason to suppose that she will flick the switch than that she will refrain. For whether she will flick the switch or refrain depends on whether she believes the light's being on is the causal upshot of flicking or refraining. To sum up: beliefs alone are unable to motivate action, for beliefs can only motivate action in conjunction with a separate desire; but desires alone are also unable to motivate action, for desires can only motivate action in conjunction with a separate means–end belief.

Compelling though this Humean story of how we explain action is, it presents us with a disturbing puzzle about the role of deliberation in the production of action. For it seems undeniable that we sometimes deliberate in order to find out what we are rationally justified in doing: that is, we sometimes deliberate in order to form beliefs about what it is desirable to do. And it also seems undeniable that we sometimes act upon the outcome of those very deliberations: that is, we sometimes do what we do because we believe that doing so is desirable. But the Humean story about how we explain action seems to leave no room for these undeniable facts. For the belief that it is desirable to act in a certain way is not itself a desire, it is a belief, and so whether or not we happen to act in accordance with this belief, given the Humean story about how we explain actions, must depend entirely on whether we just so happen to have a desire to act in that way, or just so happen to have some other desire which can combine with this belief to yield a desire to act in that way.[8] On Hume's account of the matter it thus appears to be a massive fluke, an inexplicable miracle of nature, that our desires match our beliefs about what it is desirable to do to the extent that they do. For there is nothing in the nature of our evaluative beliefs to explain why this should be the case. What is needed is an extra desire, an extra desire we are not rationally required to have.

Here we see the real appeal of the internalism requirement. For it promises to explain how it can be that our beliefs about what we are rationally justified in doing play a proper causal role in the genesis of our actions, and it promises to do so while leaving Hume's story about the way in which actions are explained largely intact. In order to see why, consider again what the requirement tells us about the content of our evaluative beliefs, at least on the advice model.

When I believe that it would be desirable to φ in certain circumstances C, the internalism requirement tells us that my belief has the following content: that I would desire that I φ in C if I were fully rational. But now, if indeed I do believe this, and if I believe that I am in circumstances C, then surely the only rational thing for me to desire is to φ. For a psychology that includes both the belief that I would desire that I φ in C if I were fully rational – that is, the belief that I would have that desire if my desires formed a maximally coherent and unified set – *and* the desire that I φ in C is itself a more coherent and unified psychology than one that includes the belief that I would desire to φ in C if I were fully rational and yet *lacks* the desire to φ in C. Coherence and unity are thus on the side of a *match* between the content of our evaluative beliefs and our desires.

Here is another way of putting the same point. What would an agent's fully rational self want her less than fully rational self to desire in circumstances in which her less than fully rational self believes that she would desire to φ in C if she were fully rational? On the plausible assumption that the agent's fully rational self desires that the psychology of her less than fully rational self is as coherent as possible she will want her less than fully rational self to desire that she φs in C. It thus follows that it is desirable for an agent to desire that she φs in C in circumstances in which she believes that it is desirable that she φs in C. Agents thus quite generally have a reason to desire in accordance with their evaluative beliefs.[9]

But if this is right then it follows that in *rational* creatures at least – that is, in those who do not manifest the form of unreasonableness or irrationality just described, those who are sensitive to the apparent facts about what they have reason to do – we would therefore expect there to be a causal connection between believing that it is desirable to act in a certain way and desiring to act in that way. That is, given the internalist account of the content of our evaluative beliefs, we would expect a rational deliberator's evaluative beliefs to cause her to have matching desires in much the same way, and for much the same reason, as the rational thinker's beliefs that p and that p → q cause her to believe that q. For the psychological states of rational deliberators and thinkers connect with each other in just the way that they rationally should. In this way, then, the internalism requirement can thus underwrite not just the rationality of desiring in accordance with our evaluative beliefs, but also the effectiveness of our evaluative beliefs in bringing about these desires in those who are rational.[10]

Note that the explanation just given is simply unavailable if we reject the internalism requirement. For on an externalist conception of reasons, the reasons we have are not themselves defined in terms of what we would desire if our psychology exhibited maximal coherence and unity. Without inquiring further into what exactly the content of a reason claim on such a conception is we can therefore already see that there is no reason to expect that a psychology which pairs a belief that there is reason to φ in circumstances C with a desire to do something other than φ in C will exhibit less in the way of coherence and unity than a psychology that pairs that belief with the desire to φ in C. It thus appears that externalists will be unable to explain why it is rational to desire in accordance with our beliefs about the reasons that we have.

Note also that the explanation just given presupposes not just the internalism requirement, but the internalism requirement understood in terms of the advice model. For if we interpret the internalism requirement in terms of the example model, the argument just given simply fails to go through at the crucial point. Suppose, for instance, that you believe your fully rational self would desire to φ in the circumstances she faces; that this is the example she would set for you in her own world. Why should this have any effect at all on what you desire to do in the circumstances you face? If your circumstances are quite unlike hers, then you can quite rationally acknowledge her example, and be impressed by it, while still being left entirely unmoved. Coherence and unity do not argue in favour of acquiring a desire like hers because her example – marvelous though it is in the circumstances in which *she* finds *herself* – doesn't engage with the circumstances in which *you* find *yourself*. This is not the case if instead we interpret the requirement in terms of the advice model. For then what you have to believe is that your fully rational self would want your less than fully rational self to φ in the circumstances your less than fully rational self actually faces. Your fully rational self's advice engages with your predicament because it is precisely tailored to it. You may still say "So what?," of course, but if you do you simply reveal that you are unable to accept good advice; you reveal the extent to which your psychology fails in terms of norms of coherence and unity that define a systematically justified psychology. You thus simply betray your own irrationality.

Here, then, we see the real appeal of the internalism requirement. It offers us an explanation of how and why our evaluative beliefs come to play a proper causal role in the production of our desires, an explanation that leaves the Humean's claim that intentional actions are themselves the product of desires and means-end beliefs perfectly intact. The crucial idea, to repeat, is that given the content of an agent's evaluative beliefs – that is, given the internalism requirement – the desires that the Humean rightly supposes play a causal role in the genesis of intentional actions will themselves be caused by the agent's evaluative beliefs to the extent that she is a rational deliberator. The Humean's account has thus been supplemented, not replaced.

CONCLUSION

My aim in this paper has been to answer three questions. How exactly is the internalism requirement on reasons to be understood? What does it tell us about the nature of reasons? And wherein lies its appeal?

As regards the first question, I have argued that the content of the internalism requirement is best captured by what I have called the "advice" model rather than the "example" model. According to the advice model, the desirability of an agent's φ-ing in certain circumstances C is fixed by whether or not her fully rational self would advise her less than fully rational self to φ in the circumstances that she, the less than fully rational self, faces: that is, in circumstances C. The idea is not that the desirability of an agent's φ-ing in C is fixed by the example her fully rational self would set for her less than fully rational self by her own behaviour in her own world. Thus, even though the requirement is concerned with the *desires* of a fully rational agent, it is crucially not concerned with the *motivations* of a fully rational agent.

As regards the second question, I have argued that the substantive content of the internalism requirement depends on the way in which we understand the key idea of having certain desires under conditions of "full rationality." My claim has been that it is part of our concept of "full rationality" that fully rational agents are those who have a systematically justifiable set of desires, where this idea is to be cashed out in terms of having a psychology that is maximally coherent and unified, and where it is presupposed that the maximally coherent and unified set of desires any one particular fully rational agent would come up with is exactly the same as the maximally coherent and unified set of desires any other rational agent would come up with. The internalism reqirement is thus best understood as offering us a non-relativistic, rather than a relativistic, conception of reasons.

Finally, as regards the third question, I have argued that, given our answers to the earlier two questions, the appeal of the internalism re-quirement is easy to understand. For it allows us to see that though the

Humean is right that all *actions* are caused by desires, in rational deliberators at least, the *desires* that cause an agent's actions may themselves be caused by her evaluative beliefs. The internalism requirement thus enables us to assign a proper causal role to an agent's beliefs about the rational justifiability of her actions when she deliberates.

For all I have said it of course remains an open possibility that there are no internal reasons – and hence that there are no reasons for action at all. After all, the mere fact that our concept of a reason presupposes that fully rational creatures would converge in their desires does nothing to show that such a convergence is forthcoming. But that is no objection to what has been said here. For my aim has not been to argue that there are any reasons, it has rather been to articulate the conceptual framework in which debates about what our reasons are, if there are any, can sensibly take place.[11]

REFERENCES

Brandt, Richard 1979: *A Theory of the Good and the Right*. Oxford: Oxford University Press.

Daniels, Norman 1979: "Wide Reflective Equilibrium and Theory Acceptance in Ethics," *Journal of Philosophy*. 256–82.

Darwall, Stephen 1983: *Impartial Reason*. Ithaca, NY: Cornell University Press.

———, Allan Gibbard, and Peter Railton 1992: "Toward *Fin de siecle* Ethics: Some Trends," *Philosophical Review*. 115–89.

Korsgaard, Christine 1986: "Skepticism about Practical Reason," *Journal of Philosophy*. 5–25.

Lewis, David 1989: "Dispositional Theories of Value," *Proceedings of the Aristotelian Society* Supplementary Volume. 113–37.

Johnston, Mark 1989: "Dispositional Theories of Value," *Proceedings of the Aristotelian Society* Supplementary Volume. 139–74.

Parfit, Derek 1984: *Reasons and Persons*. Oxford: Oxford University Press.

Pettit, Philip 1993: *The Common Mind*. New York: Oxford University Press.

——— and Michael Smith 1990: "Backgrounding Desire," *The Philosophical Review*. 565–92.

——— and Michael Smith 1993: "Brandt on Self-Control," in Brad Hooker, ed., *Rationality, Rules and Utility*. Boulder, CO: Westview Press.

——— and Michael Smith 1997: "Parfit's P," in Jonathan Dancy, ed., *Parfit and his Critics 2: Reasons*. Oxford: Blackwell. 71–95.

Railton, Peter 1986: "Moral Realism," *The Philosophical Review*. 163–207.

Rawls, John 1951: "Outline of a Decision Procedure for Ethics," *Philosophical Review*. 177–97.

——— 1971: *A Theory of Justice*. Cambridge, MA: Harvard University Press.

Shope, Robert K. 1978: "Rawls, Brandt, and the Definition of Rational Desires," *Canadian Journal of Philosophy*. 329–40.

Smith, Michael 1987: "The Humean Theory of Motivation," *Mind*. 36–61.

———— 1989: "Dispositional Theories of Value," *Proceedings of the Aristotelian Society* Supplementary Volume. 89–111.

———— 1991: "Realism," in Peter Singer, ed., *A Companion to Ethics*. Oxford: Basil Blackwell. 399–410.

———— 1992: "Valuing: Desiring or Believing?," in David Charles and Kathleen Lennon, eds., *Reduction, Explanation, Realism*. Oxford: Oxford University Press. 323–60.

———— 1993: "Objectivity and Moral Realism: On the Phenomenology of Moral Experience," in John Haldane and Crispin Wright, eds., *Reality, Representation and Projection*. Oxford: Oxford University Press. 235–36.

———— 1994: *The Moral Problem*. Oxford: Basil Blackwell.

Watson, Gary 1975: "Free Agency," reprinted in Gary Watson, ed., *Free Will*. Oxford: Oxford University Press. 1982. 96–110.

Bernard Williams 1980: "Internal and External Reasons," reprinted in his *Moral Luck*. Cambridge: Cambridge University Press. 1981.

NOTES

1. Adherents of other versions of the dispositional theory may agree that desirability is a feature that elicits an appropriate response in subjects under conditions of full rationality, but disagree about whether that response is desire (Johnston 1989 appears to take this view), or they may instead agree that desirability is a feature that elicits desire in agents under the appropriate conditions, but disagree about whether those are conditions of full rationality (Lewis 1989 appears to take this view).

2. Rawls (1971) and Brandt (1979) seem to have had in mind the example model of the internalism requirement as well. Contrast Peter Railton's account of a person's own good (1986) which is formulated in terms of the advice model precisely to avoid problems like those I go on to describe in the text. For criticisms of Rawls's and Brandt's "example" versions of the internalism requirement, see Shope (1978) and Pettit and Smith (1993). (Here I am grateful to Stephen Darwall.)

3. Mark Johnston (1989) pursues a similar line in his criticism of David Lewis's account of the role of imaginative acquaintance in valuing (1989).

4. See especially Williams's discussion of the Owen Wingrave example (1980: 106–11).

5. Compare Philip Pettit on rule-following (1993: esp. 96–97).

6. The claim is not that on the non-relative conception of reasons the existence of reasons-in-the-actual-world presupposes a convergence in the desires of fully rational creatures in the actual world. For this is itself a relative conception of reasons: reasons are *world*-relative. The non-relative conception really is *non*-relative. It claims that there is a convergence in the desires that all possible creatures would have, so long as those creatures are fully rational, whether those creatures exist in the actual world or not. Angels, ourselves in other possible worlds, the inhabitants of Mars – on the non-relative conception we are all of us supposed to desire the very same thing for the various circumstances we might face, at least insofar as we are rational.

7. Note that the preferences we have are not always a relevant feature of our circumstances. If I just so happen to prefer kicking the cat to leaving it sleep in peace, my fully rational self might want that I do not kick the cat despite my preference. For relevant discussion of this point, and the relevance of actual desires to the desirability or justifiability of our actions generally, see Pettit and Smith 1990, 1993, 1997.

8. For example, it might be supposed that when we deliberate we *de facto* have a desire to do what we believe it is desirable to do. I will have more to say about this in footnote 10. The point here is simply that the Humean must regard it a happy accident that we all just so happen to have such a desire. For the Humean cannot agree that such a desire is itself required by reason.

9. It is, of course, consistent to claim both that: (i) it is desirable that an agent desires to φ in C *in circumstances in which she believes that it is desirable to φ in C*, and (ii) it is not desirable that an agent desires to φ *in circumstances C*. For whereas (i) tells us what an agent's fully rational self would want her less than fully rational self to desire in one set of circumstances, (ii) tells us what her fully rational self would want her less than fully rational self to desire in another, quite different, set of circumstances. The point is important, as it serves to explain why certain theories of reasons for action are properly thought to be *self-effacing* (Smith 1994: Chapter 5, footnote 2).

10. Note that the externalist who tries to explain the effectiveness of deliberation by positing an extra desire to do what we believe desirable (see footnote 8) has an explanation that is inferior to the internalist's explanation just given in two respects. First, since the externalist claims that the extra desire to do what we believe desirable is itself rationally optional, he is committed not just to the view that it is a miracle of nature, a massive fluke, that so many of us just so happen to have such a desire, but also to the view that if someone just so happened to lack such a desire, that would not itself suffice to show that that person was irrational. By contrast the internalist has a principled reason for insisting that someone who lacks a desire to φ while believing that φ-ing is desirable is *as such* irrational. Second, the externalist who posits a quite general desire to do what is desirable must think that if we end up desiring to, say, φ in C, as a result of coming to believe that it is desirable to φ in C, then the desire to φ in C must itself, of necessity, be an *instrumental* desire. The externalist must therefore hold that deliberation never produces a non-instrumental desire to do what we believe desirable, where this is read *de re* rather than *de dicto*. The only thing we desire to do non-instrumentally, when we deliberate, is what it is desirable to do, where this is read *de dicto* rather than *de re*. This seems to me to be an extremely implausible claim. Indeed, as I have argued elsewhere, it seems to constitute a *reductio* of externalism (1994: Chapter 3). The internalist, by contrast, has an explanation of how the belief that it is desirable to φ in C generates a desire to φ in C that is perfectly consistent with the claim that the resulting desire to φ in C is *non-instrumental* in character.

11. An earlier version of this paper was presented at "Internal and External Reasons," a symposium held at the Pacific Division APA meetings in Los Angeles, April 1994. I would like to thank Stephen Darwall for the many useful suggestions and observations he made as commentator on that occasion, suggestions and

observations that have helped me greatly improve the paper. I also received useful advice from John Broome, David Copp, Frank Jackson, Douglas Maclean, Kevin Mulligan, Philip Pettit, Denis Robinson, Holly Smith, Galen Strawson, Anita Superson, Sigrun Svavarsdottir, David Velleman, and Susan Wolf. The second section of the paper draws on material that appears in Chapter 5 of *The Moral Problem* (Oxford: Basil Blackwell, 1994).

2

The Incoherence Argument: Reply to Schafer-Landau

Russ Schafer-Landau's "Moral Judgement and Normative Reasons" is admirably clear and to the point (Schafer-Landau 1999). He presents his own version of the argument for the practicality requirement on moral judgement – that is, for the claim that those who have moral beliefs are either motivated or practically irrational – that I gave in *The Moral Problem* (Smith 1994), and he then proceeds to identify several crucial problems. In what follows I begin by making some comments about his presentation of the argument. I then confront the problems.

1. DOES SCHAFER-LANDAU ADEQUATELY REPRESENT THE ARGUMENT?

Shafer-Landau represents my argument, which he usefully labels "the incoherence argument," as comprising four premises (Schafer-Landau 1999: 34–35).

The first

(1) If S believes that an action is right, then S believes that S has a normative reason to do it

is a premise that I accept, provided the normative reasons mentioned are understood to be *pro tanto* normative reasons. Since, as I point out (Smith 1994: 183), moral reasons have to be weighed against other sorts of reasons, (1) would be implausible if the normative reasons it mentions were understood to be all things considered normative reasons.

The second premise

(2) S has a normative reason to do *x* in C if and only if, and because, S's fully rational counterpart (i.e., S if possessed of all true beliefs, no false ones, and a maximally coherent set of desires) would advise S to do *x* in C

is misleading. The problem is not that (2) is false. As we will see, there is an interpretation under which it comes out true. The problem is rather that, when given that interpretation, (2) is not a premise that matches up with the content of (1). It is therefore not a premise that can play any role in the incoherence argument.

The premise that plays a role in the incoherence argument is instead the official analysis of normative reasons that appears in *The Moral Problem*: S has a normative reason to do *x* in C if and only if, if S had a maximally informed and coherent and unified desire set, he would desire himself to do *x* in C (Smith 1994: 151ff.). In this premise, S's normative reasons are analysed in terms of the *desires* of his fully rational counterpart, not in terms of his *advice*.

The main reason this figures as a premise, and not the premise about advice, is that S's fully rational counterpart may, and presumably will, often have conflicting desires about what S is to do in C. If we analyse normative reasons in terms of such desires then the reasons thus analysed will themselves have to be reasons that can conflict with, and so be weighed against, each other. In other words, they will correspond to our commonsense idea of *pro tanto* normative reasons (Smith 1996: 167). But S's fully rational counterpart will presumably not give S conflicting advice about what he is to do in C – not, at any rate, unless circumstances C are circumstances that provide S with an irresolvable dilemma. The advice that S's fully rational counterpart gives to S will be advice he gives having already weighed the competing *pro tanto* normative reasons against each other. At best, that advice will therefore constitute S's all things considered normative reasons.

An example might help make the reason for making this distinction clear. Imagine a situation in which, by doing *x* in C, S will make his father happy and his mother miserable. Now suppose that S's fully rational counterpart has two conflicting desires about S's conduct in C: he desires that he does whatever will make his father happy, but he also desires that he doesn't do anything to make his mother miserable. We can then suppose that there are two conflicting *pro tanto* normative reasons that apply to S's conduct in C, normative reasons that must be weighed against each other. S has a normative reason to do *x* in C (grounded in his fully rational counterpart's desire that he does what makes his father happy), and S has a competing normative reason not to do *x* in C (grounded in his fully rational counterpart's desire that he not do what will make his mother miserable). These are *pro tanto* normative reasons because they are reasons that retain their force even when outweighed.

If the desire of S's fully rational counterpart not to make his mother miserable is stronger than his desire to make his father happy, and these are all the desires that are in play, then S's fully rational counterpart will presumably advise S not to do x in C: this is what S will have all things considered normative reason to do. But the outweighed normative reason to do x in C will still retain its force. There will be something for S's fully rational counterpart to regret about S's not doing x in C, notwithstanding the fact that this is what he advises him to do. He will regret the fact that S has to act in circumstances in which, if he is not to make his mother miserable, he is unable to make his father happy. These are regrettable circumstances in the relatively straightforward sense that S's fully rational counterpart would desire S not to be in them. More of his desires would be satisfied if S were in circumstances that allowed him to make his father happy without making his mother miserable.

To sum up, since the second premise of the incoherence argument has to match up with the content of (1), the notion of a normative reason in play must be that of a *pro tanto* normative reason, as in (1), not that of an all things considered normative reason. The second premise of the incoherence argument proper is therefore not Shafer-Landau's (2), but rather:

(2*) S has a normative reason to do x in C if and only if, and because, S's fully rational counterpart (i.e. S if possessed of all true beliefs, no false ones, and a maximally coherent set of desires) would desire S to do x in C.

(2)'s talk of advice is replaced in (2*) by talk of desire, where desires are understood to be states that can conflict with, and so weigh against, each other. In (2*) the normative reasons thus analysed are *pro tanto* normative reasons, the same sort of reasons mentioned in (1).

For the same reasons, parallel modifications must be made to

(3) Therefore if S believes that x is right then S believes that S's fully rational self would advise S to do x

and

(4) Failing to desire to do x, while believing that one's ideal self would advise one to do x, is a form of incoherence that signals practical irrationality.

The premises that play a role in the incoherence argument are rather:

(3*) Therefore if S believes that doing x in C is right then S believes that S's fully rational self would desire that S does x in C

45

and

(4*) Failing to desire to do x in C, while believing that one's ideal self would desire that one do x in C, is a form of incoherence that signals practical irrationality.

Talk of advice in both of these premises must be replaced by talk of desire.

Once these modifications are made, it seems to me that the practicality requirement on moral judgement

(5) Therefore either one is motivated to do what one judges right or one is practically irrational

does indeed follow. Importantly, however, not that (5) must be understood as saying that, on pain of practical irrationality, someone who believes that there is a *pro tanto* normative reason to do x in C (a normative reason that may be outweighed by other normative reasons) must have some desire to do x in C (a desire that may be overridden by other desires).[1] As we will see, this is rather different from the conclusion Shafer-Landau has in mind.

2. IS PREMISE (2) FALSE?

According to Shafer-Landau, premise (2) of the incoherence argument is false (Shafer-Landau 1999: 37–39). We are already in a position to see why his objection is both mistaken and beside the point.

(2) states that S has a normative reason to do x in C if and only if S's fully rational counterpart would advise S to do x in C. Shafer-Landau's objection to (2) is that it is refuted by two main kinds of counter-example.

In the first class are cases in which one possesses a normative reason that is overridden by other normative reasons of the same kind. I may have a moral reason to keep our lunch date, but my ideal self would advise against it, as keeping the date prevents me from attending to an even greater moral concern that's just unexpectedly arisen. In the second class of cases, a normative reason is overridden by normative reasons of a different category. One may possess legal reasons to perform or refrain from certain actions, even though one's fully rational self would advise against compliance with the law, perhaps because in a given case the law would require conduct so immoral or imprudent as to outweigh the force of the relevant overridden (*not* extinguished) legal reason. (Schafer-Landau 1999: 37–38)

According to Schafer-Landau, cases of these two kinds show that we can have normative reasons to do things that fully rational agents would find inadvisable.

The first problem with Schafer-Landau's objection is that it depends on an unnatural interpretation of (2). Though my fully rational counterpart may well advise me to act contrary to a normative reason when it is outweighed by a more important normative reason, that itself suggests a more natural interpretation of (2), an interpretation according to which the normative reasons mentioned are all things considered normative reasons, not *pro tanto* normative reasons. So interpreted, Schafer-Landau's claim that (2) is false is, I think, simply mistaken. (2) is true. The objection to (2) is not that it is false, but that its content doesn't match the content of (1). (1) is about *pro tanto* normative reasons, whereas (2) is (naturally interpreted as being) about all things considered normative reasons.

However, as this makes plain, there is a second and more fundamental problem with Schafer-Landau's (2) as well. Since the content of (2) does not match the content of (1), it is irrelevant whether (2) is true or false. (2) is not a premise that has any role to play in the incoherence argument. The premise that plays a role is rather a modified version of (2), (2*), a premise that replaces (2)'s talk of "advice" by talk of "desire," where desires are understood to be states that can conflict with each other. Only so does the second premise match up with the content of (1). But once that modification is made it is plain that the premise is not in conflict with the cases to which Schafer-Landau appeals. Even if my fully rational counterpart advises against my keeping a lunch date in the circumstances he describes, this doesn't undermine the claim that my fully rational counterpart has a(n overridden) desire that I keep that lunch date. Schafer-Landau's objection to (2) is therefore beside the point.

3. IS PREMISE (4) UNSUPPORTED?

Schafer-Landau argues that premise (4) lacks support (Schafer-Landau 1999: 35–37). His argument, if successful, would equally show that (4*), the modified version of (4) which in fact plays a role in the incoherence argument − the premise that S's failing to desire to do x in C while believing that his fully rational counterpart would desire him to do x in C is a form of incoherence that signals practical irrationality − lacks support as well. His misgivings must therefore be assessed on their merits.

Suppose S's belief that his fully rational counterpart would desire him to do x in C is false. It then follows, given (2*), that there is no normative reason for S to do x in C. Because his belief is false, we can easily imagine that S's fully rational counterpart would not desire him to desire to do x in C either. But if S's fully rational counterpart wouldn't desire him to

47

desire to do x in C it follows, again from the modified version of (2), that, in these circumstances, he has no normative reason to desire to do x in C. But in that case how can it be plausible to suppose, as I do, that S's failure to desire to do x in C when he believes that his fully rational counterpart would desire him to desire to do x in C suffices for his irrationality? If he has no normative reason to have the desire, how can he be irrational for failing to have it? (Schafer-Landau 1999: 36.)

These are good questions. Moreover, as Schafer-Landau notes, they are questions that I have been asked, and attempted to answer, before (Dreier 1996; Smith 1996: 162, n. 1; Sayre-McCord 1997: 61–76; Smith 1997: 92–97). My answer, in short, is that there is irrationality because the pair of psychological states that comprises S's belief (true or false) that if he had a maximally informed and coherent and unified desire set he would want himself to do x in C, together with his *desire* to do x in C, is a more coherent pairing of psychological states than either of the following pairings: the pairing that comprises S's belief (true or false) that if he had a maximally informed and coherent and unified desire set he would want himself to do x in C, together with his *indifference* to doing x in C; or the pairing that comprises S's belief (true or false) that if he had a maximally informed and coherent and unified desire set he would want himself to do x in C, together with his *aversion* to doing x in C. S's desiring to do x in C when he has the belief, true or false, that if he had a maximally informed and coherent and unified desire set he would want himself to do x in C, *makes sense* in a way in which his indifference or aversion to doing x in C simply doesn't.[2]

Schafer-Landau doesn't comment on this answer at all. What he comments on instead is my suggestion that there is a parallel with belief (Schafer-Landau 1999: 37). There is, I think, a parallel between the case just described and the following case in which we compare triples of belief. Abstract away from S's other beliefs and consider the triple that comprises his belief that p, his belief that the minimally extended but maximally coherent belief set that comprises the belief that p will also comprise the belief that q, and the belief that q, and compare this triple with two other triples: the triple that comprises S's belief that p, S's belief that the minimally extended but maximally coherent belief set that comprises the belief that p will also comprise the belief that q, and S's *lack of belief* as regards q; and the triple that comprises S's belief that p, S's belief that the minimally extended but maximally coherent belief set that comprises the belief that p will also comprise the belief that q, and *disbelief* on S's behalf that q. Now ask which triple is more coherent.

The answer seems to me to be plain enough. The first triple is much more coherent than the other two. S's believing that q, when he believes that p and also believes that the minimally extended but maximally coherent belief set that comprises the belief that p will also comprise the belief that q *makes sense* in a way in which his lack of belief as regards q, or his disbelief in q, simply doesn't. Abstracting away from other beliefs that S might have, it thus seems that there is, in this situation, a kind of irrationality involved in S's failing to believe that q. Moreover, as in the earlier case, it seems that this is so quite independently of whether S's beliefs are true or false.

Schafer-Landau's response is, in effect, to deny this last claim (Schafer-Landau 1999: 37). If it is *false* that the minimally extended but maximally coherent belief set that comprises the belief that p will also comprise the belief that q, then, he says, my claim that the triple that comprises the belief that p, the belief that a minimally extended but maximally coherent belief set that comprises the belief that p will also comprise the belief that q, and the belief that q, is a more coherent belief set than the alternatives, must be false as well. But this is a non sequitur.

Even if it is false that the minimally extended but maximally coherent belief set that comprises the belief that p will also comprise the belief that q, it may yet be true that the minimally extended but maximally coherent belief set that comprises *both* the belief that p *and* the belief that the minimally extended but maximally coherent belief set that comprises the belief that p will also comprise the belief that q, will also comprise the belief that q. The former is a claim about a pair of beliefs, whereas the latter is about a triple, of which that pair is a subset. Schafer-Landau's objection to the parallel with belief in effect turns on forgetting the fact that the coherence of a belief set depends on the relations between *all* its members, not just the relations between a *subset* of its members.

4. DO CASES OF INDIRECTION CONSTITUTE A *REDUCTIO* OF THE INCOHERENCE ARGUMENT?

Schafer-Landau argues that cases of indirection provide a *reductio* of the conjunction of premises (2) and (4) of the incoherence argument (Schafer-Landau 1999: 35–36). Once again his arguments, if successful, would constitute a *reductio* of the conjunction of even the modified versions of (2) and (4) that I accept, (2*) and (4*). We must therefore consider these arguments on their merits as well.

Assume, for *reductio*, that (2*) and (4*) are true, and suppose that (say) S has a normative reason to maximize happiness and minimize suffering in C. It follows from (2*) that S's fully rational counterpart desires S to maximize happiness and minimize suffering in C. However, because the only plausible version of utilitarianism is an indirect version – that is, because S's desiring to maximize happiness and minimize suffering in C will not maximize happiness and minimize suffering in C – we must also suppose that S has a normative reason not to desire to maximize happiness and minimize suffering. It thus follows, again from (2*), that S's fully rational counterpart will desire S not to desire to maximize happiness and minimize suffering in C as well.

Schafer-Landau claims, in effect, that when we combine this conclusion with premise (4*) of the incoherence argument we thereby commit ourselves to the implausible conclusion that simply by coming to believe himself to have a normative reason to maximize happiness and minimize suffering in C, a belief we may assume to be both true and well-supported by all the available evidence, S inevitably becomes irrational.

If S believes that she has a normative reason to do *x*, she either lacks or possesses a desire to do *x*. If the former, she is irrational, according to the practicality requirement. If the latter, she is also irrational, because a fully rational agent would not advise possession of such a desire. (Schafer-Landau 1999: 36)

If he fails to desire to maximize happiness and minimize suffering in C then, from (4*), it follows that his psychology suffers from incoherence, and hence he is irrational. But if he desires to maximize happiness and minimize suffering in C he is irrational as well because his fully rational counterpart would desire that he not have this desire. In other words he is irrational because, given (2*), he has a desire that he has a normative reason not to have.

Schafer-Landau is so convinced of the implausibility of supposing that someone can become irrational simply by acquiring a true belief that he thinks we should rather conclude that one or another of (2*) and (4*) is false. But is it really so implausible to suppose that someone can become irrational simply by acquiring a true belief? I do not think that it is in the least implausible. Schafer-Landau supports the idea that it is as follows:

the idea that possession of a true belief alone is sometimes sufficient to trigger irrationality . . . is . . . problematic, especially since the true belief that one is faced with in an indirection case needn't conflict with one's existing beliefs, and it may be well-supported by available evidence. (Schafer-Landau 1999: 36)

But it is hard to see the relevance of this remark. It would indeed be strange if we were committed to attributing *theoretical* irrationality to S when he so evidently doesn't suffer from any recognizable form of theoretical irrationality. But, of course, the suggestion is not that S's possession of a true belief alone is sufficient to trigger his being *theoretically* irrational, but rather that it is sufficient to trigger his being *practically* irrational.[3]

In any case, the real problem with Schafer-Landau's attempt at a *reductio* is that it overlooks the fact that cases of indirection already undermine so many of our ordinary assumptions about the relationship between morality and rationality, on the one hand, and deliberation, on the other (Parfit 1984). True enough, if (2*) and (4*) are correct, then cases of indirection undermine yet another of our ordinary assumptions: the assumption that someone cannot become practically irrational simply by acquiring a belief that is both true and well-supported. That is a somewhat surprising conclusion, I must admit, but in the context of the other surprising conclusions we have been forced to accept in the light of cases of indirection, it is not so surprising as to constitute a *reductio* of the premises that entail it.[4]

5. IS THE ARGUMENT INVALID?

According to Shafter-Landau the incoherence argument is invalid: (3) does not follow from (1) and (2) (Schafer-Landau 1999: 35). His reasons for thinking that this move is invalid would, if correct, equally undermine the validity of the move from (1) and (2*) to (3*). We must therefore once again judge his objection on its merits.

Even if we can analyse rightness in terms of the desires of fully rational agents, Schafer-Landau suggests that it simply doesn't follow that someone who has beliefs about right actions has beliefs about the desires that fully rational agents have about those actions. In explaining why this doesn't follow he appeals to a premise that I myself accept. I claim that sentences expressing conceptual truths can be true without people who are competent with the words that make up those sentences knowing that they are true. A competent English speaker may therefore believe that an act is right but not believe that the sentence "My act is one that my fully rational counterpart would desire me to perform" expresses a truth. Schafer-Landau supposes that the mere fact that this is so suffices to undermine the validity of the move from (1) and (2*) to (3*).

I cannot see why Schafer-Landau should suppose any such thing. The reason I think that speakers who are competent with the word "right" may believe that doing x in C is right, and hence believe that their fully rational counterpart would desire them to do x in C, and yet not believe that the sentence "My fully rational counterpart would desire me to do x in C" expresses a truth, is because I think that competent speakers can have *false* beliefs about the meanings of the words with which they are competent. Competence is primarily a measure of people's ability to use the words that they use correctly, not a measure of their ability to have true beliefs about their own pattern of word usage. In my view it is these *false* beliefs about the meaning of the word "right" that stops competent English speakers who believe that doing x in C is right believing that the sentence "My fully rational counterpart would desire me to do x in C" expresses a truth even though it does express a truth. As I see things, the upshot is therefore that we should resist drawing any conclusion at all about the content of S's belief that his doing x in C is right from the fact that he does not believe that the sentence "My fully rational counterpart would desire me to do x in C" expresses a truth. In particular, we should resist drawing the conclusion that Schafer-Landau draws: the conclusion that the belief does not have, as its content, that S's fully rational counterpart would desire S to do x in C.

This is all well and good, but what can be said in support of the move from (1) and (2*) to (3*)? As I see things, that transition is valid because of the very tight connection between the account we give of the pattern of word usage of a speaker who is competent with the word "right," and the account we give of what someone believes, when they believe that doing x in C is right. The pattern of word usage of a speaker who is competent with the word "right" – by contrast with their beliefs about that pattern – charts the analytic connections between the feature they pick out by "right," as so picked out, and other features of acts, agents, and the environment, analytic connections that in turn correspond to conceptual discriminations that competent speakers can make. These discriminations constitute conceptual structure that is reflected in the competent speaker's beliefs about right acts. My reason for thinking that (1) and (2*) are true is thus that, as I see things, the conceptual structure of the belief that doing x in C is right is best captured by supposing that what someone who has this belief believes is that their fully rational counterpart would desire them to do x in C. Thus the transition to (3*).

As Schafer-Landau himself points out, however, the issues involved in adjudicating the plausibility of this argument, and hence the general question of the validity of the transition from (1) and (2*) to (3*), are all very difficult and controversial. I am not surprised if people are unconvinced by the considerations that convince me. But the difficulties and controversies involved are, I think, independently regrettable. They are regrettable because they have caused some commentators to overlook the real power of the incoherence argument – for example, Copp (1997) and Sayre-McCord (1997).

What that argument purports to provide, after all, is an explanation of something that has so far eluded explanation entirely: an explanation, in more or less commonsensical terms, of the mechanism involved when a belief, unaided by a desire, causes and rationalizes a desire. Now, as it happens, I think that the incoherence argument establishes something even stronger than this. I think it provides an explanation of the mechanism involved when a moral belief, unaided by a desire, causes and rationalizes a desire. The explanation is that since anyone who believes that doing x in C is right either desires to do x in C or is practically irrational, in the sense of being in an incoherent psychological state, it follows that all we need to posit, in order to explain the transition from the belief that doing x in C is right to desiring to do x in C, is the tendency a rational creature has towards having a coherent psychology.[5]

The important point to realize, however, is that the real power of this argument remains intact even if it doesn't establish the stronger conclusion. Even if the transition from (1) and (2*) to (3*) were invalid, the incoherence argument would still succeed in providing an explanation, in more or less commonsensical terms, of the mechanism involved when a belief, unaided by a desire, causes and rationalizes a desire. The explanation is that if (1) is true and the analysis of normative reasons is correct – that is, if (1) and (2*) is true – then anyone who believes that their doing x in C is right will acquire the desire that they do x in C provided they appreciate the truth of (1) and the analysis – that is, provided they believe (1) and (2*), both of which are a priori accessible – and provided they have sufficient logical acumen to draw the relevant conclusion. No desire is required to explain why S makes the transition from believing that his doing x in C is right to the belief that his fully rational counterpart would desire that he does x in C, and no desire is required to explain why S makes the transition from believing that his fully rational counterpart would desire that he does x in C to desiring to do x in C either.

The incoherence argument thus still entails the weaker, but still remarkable, conclusion that all we need posit in order to explain the transition from the belief that doing x in C is right to desiring to do x in C is the appreciation of two a priori truths, logical acumen, and the tendency a rational creature has towards having a coherent psychology. I am therefore doubly unhappy with Schafer-Landau's suggestion that the incoherence argument is invalid. The reason he gives for thinking that it is invalid seems to me not to support its invalidity. Moreover, even if it were invalid for the reasons he suggests, he fails to notice that the real power of the argument would remain intact.

REFERENCES

Copp, D. 1997: "Belief, Reason and Motivation: Michael Smith's *The Moral Problem*," *Ethics* 108: 33–54.

Dreier, J. 1996: "Review of *The Moral Problem*," *Mind* 105: 363–67.

Kennett, J., and M. Smith 1994: "Philosophy and Common Sense: The Case of Weakness of Will," in M. Michael and J. O'Leary Hawthorne, eds., *Philosophy in Mind*. Dordrecht: Kluwer Press. 141–57.

Parfit, D. 1984: *Reasons and Persons*. Oxford: Clarendon Press.

Pettit, P., and M. Smith 1993: "Practical Unreason," *Mind* 102: 53–79.

Sayre-McCord, G. 1997: "The Metaethical Problem," *Ethics* 108: 55–83.

Schafer-Landau, R. 1999: "Moral Judgement and Normative Reasons," *Analysis* 59: 33–40.

Smith M. 1994: *The Moral Problem*. Oxford: Blackwell.

Smith M. 1995: "Reply to Ingmar Persson's Critical Notice of *The Moral Problem*," *Theoria* 61: 159–81.

Smith, M. 1996: "Normative Reasons and Full Rationality: Reply to Swanton," *Analysis* 56: 160–68.

Smith, M. 1997 "In Defence of *The Moral Problem*," *Ethics* 108: 84–119.

Smith, M. 1999. "The Definition of 'Moral.'" In D. Jamieson, ed., *Singer and His Critics*, Oxford: Blackwell.

NOTES

1. Indeed, as we will see (n. 2 below), (5) is true because the incoherence argument entails a slightly more fine-grained conclusion.

2. It seems to me that we can draw the even more fine-grained conclusion that S's having a desire *of a certain strength* to do x in C, when he has the belief, true or false, that if he had a maximally informed and coherent and unified desire set then he would have a desire *of that strength* that he does x in C, makes sense in a way in which his having a desire *of some alternative strength* to do x in C simply doesn't (Pettit and Smith 1993; Kennett and Smith 1994).

3. Philip Pettit suggested to me that Newcomb's Problem commits even the instrumentalist's theory of normative reasons to the conclusion that someone can become practically irrational simply by acquiring true and well-supported beliefs. An agent who believes himself to confront a Newcomb choice is practically irrational because, no matter which course of action he chooses, he will fail to choose the option that best satisfies his desires.

4. Ironically, when I wrote *The Moral Problem* I thought that cases of indirection provided support for my analysis of normative reasons. The reason I gave is that my

analysis can explain why indirect theories tend so often to be self-effacing (Smith 1994: 212–13, n. 2).

5. Note that the tendency towards coherence is not itself well thought of as a desire to be coherent (Smith 1995: 168; Smith 1999, §6). The role of the tendency towards coherence is, after all, to explain how psychological states with the potential to link up rationally with each other so as to generate further psychological states do in fact link up with each other. Suppose the tendency towards coherence were a desire to be coherent. It could then only have effects when combined with means-end beliefs about the ways in which coherence can be achieved. But in that case we would need some mechanism to explain how the link-up is effected. We would need to postulate a mechanism much like the original tendency towards coherence. For this reason we should deny that the tendency towards coherence is a desire to be coherent.

3

Philosophy and Commonsense: The Case of Weakness of Will

Here is a little story. As he has done a hundred times before, John heads off to the local shop to buy some chocolate bars. He knows that eating so much chocolate isn't good for him. Being over forty and doing no exercise, a passion for chocolate simply adds to an already significant weight problem. But thoughts like this do not move him. Each day, fully cognizant of the effects of eating chocolate upon his health, John heads off to the local shop, arrives, buys several chocolate bars, unwraps one, and then proceeds to eat it, unwraps another, and then proceeds to eat it, and so on and so on and so on.

Now here is a bit of commonsense. In certain crucial respects the story we have just told is underdescribed. For as Gary Watson points out, a story like this can be filled out in at least three different ways, ways that in turn reflect our commonsense understandings of recklessness, weakness of will, and compulsion (Watson 1977). Moreover, whether we fill out the story in one or another of these ways is of great practical significance. For the allocation of moral responsibility is in large part determined by whether we think of John, in the story, as being either reckless, or weak, or compelled.

Consider recklessness first. To fill out the story in this way it is sufficient to imagine John being fully in control of what he does, eating chocolate because he judges it better to do so than to refrain and so regain his health, but making his judgement as a result of some sort of culpable mistake or error of reasoning. John is reckless if, knowing full well that it will harm him if he eats chocolate, he none the less freely acts upon his judgement that it is best to eat chocolate, where this judgement is not necessarily wrong, but is at least wrong by his own lights; a judgement he himself would not have made if only he had taken more care. Commonsense tells us that, when the case is filled out in this way, John is fully responsible for what happens to him. For responsibility attaches to the known consequences of what we freely choose to do and John freely chooses to eat chocolate bars while knowing the consequences.

Next consider compulsion. This time it is sufficient to imagine John judging the benefits of eating chocolate to be less than the benefits of refraining, but then eating the chocolate anyway, despite his judgement, because his desire for chocolate is simply irresistible. For John is compelled when he is literally out of control, and an irresistible desire is precisely a desire that an agent cannot control. Commonsense tells us that, in this case, John is not responsible for what he does. For, again, responsibility attaches to the known consequences of what we freely choose to do and, in this case, John does not freely choose to eat chocolate bars.

Finally, there is weakness of will. When we fill out the story in this way we imagine a case interim between the two just described. It is like the case in which we imagine John being compelled in that we suppose he eats chocolate despite judging it more desirable to refrain. But it is also like the case in which he is reckless in that we imagine him having the capacity to control what he does. When John is weak, his problem is not that he is out of control, but rather that, despite having the capacity to control himself, he simply gives in to the temptation of the chocolate bars. He eats another chocolate bar despite his judgement that it would be better to refrain, and despite his ability to resist his desire. In this case, commonsense thus once again tell us that John is responsible. For, again, responsibility attaches to the known consequences of what we freely choose to do, and, since his actions are under his control, John evidently freely chooses to eat chocolate bars.

Now here is some philosophy. Though commonsense delivers up these distinctions between recklessness, weakness and compulsion, the distinctions should be accepted only if they can be vindicated philosophically. For commonsense, unlike philosophy, has no final authority of its own. The question is therefore whether these distinctions mark *real* differences, differences that can be articulated in any systematic way.

The problematic category is, of course, weakness of will. Being interim between recklessness and compulsion it occupies a potentially unstable middle ground. The instability emerges when we attempt to spell out the connections between better judgement, desire, and free and intentional action. For, as Donald Davidson points out (1980), the idea that someone may act freely and intentionally contrary to her better judgement is difficult to square with two apparently plausible principles connecting, on the one hand, desire with action:

P1. If an agent wants to do x more than she wants to do y and believes herself free to do either x or y, then she will intentionally do x if she does either x or y intentionally

and, on the other, better judgement with desire:

P2. If an agent judges that it would be better to do x than to do y, then she wants to do x more than she wants to do y

For, given P2, if an agent judges it best to do x, then she most wants to do x. And then, given P1, since she most wants to do x, x is what she will freely and intentionally do if she does anything freely and intentionally. So P1 and P2 together entail that an agent will never act freely and intentionally contrary to her *better* judgement. How, after all, can an agent judge it best to do x and yet *better* to do y?[1]

If this is right, then a question naturally arises about the status of the commonsense distinctions between recklessness, weakness and compulsion. For if the middle-ground between recklessness and compulsion disappears then we will have to decide whether to assimilate cases of what were thought to be weakness to recklessness, or rather to compulsion. But which way should we go?

If we assimilate weakness to recklessness, then though we hold on to the idea that the weak-willed are responsible, we do so at the price of thinking that they do not really judge to be best the actions that they say they deem best. We must conclude that, in addition to acting badly, they think it best to act in this way, contrary to their insincere reports about what they value in the way of action. And if we assimilate weakness to compulsion, then though we hold on to the idea that the weak really do judge it better to act in one way, despite acting in another, we do so at the price of thinking that they are not really responsible for what they do. Either way, a dissolution of the commonsense distinctions between recklessness, weakness and compulsion promises to bring with it a significant revision of our ordinary moral practices.

For the record, we doubt very much whether philosophy could ever force us to give up on commonsense distinctions like those between recklessness, weakness and compulsion, and we therefore doubt whether it could ever force us to revise our ordinary moral practices in the ways just described. However, and unfortunately, we do not know how to argue for these conclusions in full generality. Rather it seems to us that the arguments for such conclusions have to be given piecemeal. In this particular case, the arguments in favour of commonsense are, we think, relatively easy to provide. For the reasons so far given for thinking that there is no such thing as weakness of will are crucially flawed. Our task in this paper is thus to present our own solution to Davidson's problem, a solution that, in our view, constitutes one small but important part of an ongoing defence of commonsense in moral psychology (see also Pettit and Smith 1990, 1993a, 1993b; Smith 1992; Kennett 1991, 1993; Kennett and Smith 1996).

The remainder of the paper divides into four main sections. In the first we introduce a distinction between two sorts of reasons and argue that this distinction shows P2 to be false for more or less commonsense reasons. In the second section we argue that whatever plausibility attaches to P2 attaches to it because a closely related principle, P2*, is indeed true. However, as we show, P2*, together with P1, leaves room for all sorts of divergences between better judgement and desire. In the third section we show how P2*, together with P1, suggests a story about the nature and operation of self-control that allows us to distinguish an agent's having a capacity for self-control which she fails to exercise from her having no capacity for self-control at all. And in the fourth and final section we show how our account underwrites the commonsense distinctions between recklessness, weakness of will and compulsion.

1. NORMATIVE REASONS VERSUS MOTIVATING REASONS

In "Reasons for Action and Desire," Michael Woods observes that "the concept of a reason for action stands at the point of intersection, so to speak, between the theory of the explanation of actions and the theory of their justification" (1972: 189). This suggests a more or less commonsense distinction between kinds of reasons depending on whether we use the concept in a way more at home in the theory of the explanation of action or more at home in the theory of their justification. When we say of someone that she has a reason to ϕ, we might mean that she is in a state that is potentially explanatory of her ϕ-ing, whether or not she would be justified in ϕ-ing. Or we might mean that she is justified in ϕ-ing whether or not she is in a state potentially explanatory of her ϕ-ing.

As we said, we think that this is a more or less commonsense distinction. Here is an example of Gary Watson's to prove the point (1982). Imagine a mother with a screaming baby. At her tether's end, she finds herself desiring to drown her screaming baby in the bathwater. To remove unnecessary complications, suppose that the desire is non-instrumental in character. The mother's anger and frustration produce the desire directly, much as anger can directly produce a desire to smash a glass or punch a hole in a wall (Hursthouse 1991).

What are we to say about such a woman? Suppose she succeeds in acting on her desire. It seems that we should then certainly say that she drowns her baby intentionally. But it also seems that we may do so without supposing that she acts with rational justification. In other words, we may suppose that she has a reason of the explanatory kind but entirely lacks a reason of the justificatory kind. Or consider the claim that what she would be rationally justified in doing, in her distraught state, is taking her baby out of the bathwater, drying it, dressing it, and then putting it out of harm's way while she goes into another room to calm down. It seems to us that this claim may well be true, and that this may accordingly be what she has a reason of the justificatory kind to do. But even if it is, it seems that we need not suppose that she has a reason of the explanatory kind to act in this way. For we may suppose not just that her anger and frustration produces aberrant desires, like the desire to drown her baby, but also that it destroys any desire whatsoever to care for her baby.

This ambiguity in our concept of a reason is, as we have said, more or less commonsensical. Let's therefore introduce a distinction to keep track of the ambiguities. Let's call reasons of the explanatory kind "motivating" reasons, and reasons of the justificatory kind "normative" reasons (Smith 1987). The question naturally arises whether we can give a more precise and systematic account of the distinction between motivating and normative reasons.

In virtue of their explanatory role, motivating reasons are best thought of as being psychological states, states with the potential for explaining, teleologically, and perhaps causally, our doing what we do. In our view, the best account of such states is therefore Humean in character. A motivating reason to ϕ is constituted by a desire for an outcome of a certain kind and a belief to the effect that ϕ-ing will produce an outcome of that kind (Smith 1987, 1988).

Normative reasons, by contrast, have the role of justifying actions. In our view they are therefore best thought of not as psychological states at all – for psychological states do not justify anything (Pettit and Smith 1990) – but rather as propositions to the effect that this or that course of action is to some extent worth doing; propositions whose truth would justify, to a corresponding extent, acting in this way or that. In our view, the best account of such propositions is given by a dispositional theory of value (Johnston 1989; Lewis 1989; Smith 1989). Normative reasons are propositions concerning the desirability of acting in certain ways, where facts about desirability are in turn simply facts about our idealised desires. To say that we have a normative reason to φ in circumstances C, then, is simply to say that, under conditions of increasing information and rational reflection, we would come stably to desire that we φ in C. Or, for short, it is simply to say that, if we were fully rational, we would desire that we φ in C.[2]

This more systematic way of making out the distinction between motivating reasons and normative reasons allows us to make good sense of our examples. On the one hand, according to this account the angry and frustrated mother has a motivating reason to drown her baby just in case she has a desire to drown her baby combined with a suitable means–end belief. And of course this she does have. But it does not follow that she has a normative reason to drown her baby, because this would require that, under conditions of full rationality, she would desire that she drowns her baby in circumstances like those she currently faces. And on the plausible assumption that under conditions of full rationality she would no longer be angry and frustrated, there is no reason to suppose this to be so. For, recall, we are supposing that her desire to drown her baby is produced by her anger and frustration.

On the other hand, according to this account, the mother has a normative reason to take her baby out the bathwater, dry it, dress it, and then put it out of harm's way while she goes into another room to calm down, just in case, under conditions of full rationality, she would desire that this is what she does in her distraught state. And, again, we may well suppose this to be so. For, recall, though we are assuming that her anger and frustration destroys her desire to care for her baby, were her anger and frustration to go, as it would under conditions of full rationality, her desire to care for her baby would plausibly return. Our analysis thus suggests that she may indeed have normative reason to act in this way towards her baby, though she needn't have any desire at all to act in this way in her distraught state.

With this distinction between motivating and normative reasons in place we are finally in a position to give our argument against P2. P2 purports to be a principle connecting better judgement with desire. To the extent that P2 maps on to distinctions delivered up by common sense, it should therefore be equivalent to a principle connecting an agent's beliefs about her normative reasons with her motivating reasons. In other words, P2 should be equivalent to the principle:

If an agent believes that she has more normative reason to do x than to do y, then her motivating reason to do x is stronger than her motivating reason to do y.

But this principle is evidently implausible, as we can see by considering once again our example.

The mother with the screaming baby may well believe that she would desire to take her baby out the bathwater, dry it, dress it, put it out of harm's way, and then go into another room to calm down, if she were forming a desire about what to do in her distraught state under conditions of full rationality: that is, while not in a distraught state. Accordingly, this may be what she believes she has normative reason to do. But, not being fully rational, being rather in a distraught state, she may have no motivating reason, no actual desire, to act in this way at all. P2 is thus false.

(Just for the record, note that the converse principle is false as well. Though the mother does in fact desire to drown her screaming baby in the bathwater in her distraught state, it does not follow that she believes that she would desire herself to do this in her distraught state if she were in conditions of full rationality. For she may well, and indeed typically would, know that her desire is one which is entirely the result of the anger and frustration of the moment.)

P2 is, then, quite evidently false, false for more or less commonsense reasons. For once we distinguish normative from motivating reasons, we see that an agent's beliefs about her normative reasons may come apart from her motivating reasons in a quite systematic way. And in that case it follows that better judgement may come apart from desire in a quite systematic way as well.[3]

2. NORMATIVE REASONS AND THE EFFECTIVENESS OF DELIBERATION

Though P2 is false, we think that it is an attempt to articulate an important insight about the connection between our beliefs about our normative reasons and our motivating reasons. The insight emerges when we ask about the ways in which normative and motivating reasons relate to deliberation.

It is plausible to assume that action is the product of reasons that we discover through deliberation. But, if this is right, then we must ask how this is possible. For when we deliberate, we don't just try to find out what we actually want, we try to find out whether what we actually want is worth wanting. In other words, we attempt to find out whether what we actually want is desirable; something that we would come stably to want under conditions of ever increasing information and rational reflection. And so, in our view, when we deliberate we attempt to discover normative reasons.

But if this is right, if we are concerned to discover normative reasons rather than motivating reasons when we deliberate, then it follows immediately that deliberation is only *contingently* practical in its issue. For, as the distinction between motivating and normative reasons together with P1 makes plain, what we do is a matter not of the normative reasons we believe ourselves to have, but is instead a matter of the motivating reasons we actually have. A piece of deliberation favouring φ-ing issues in an attempt to φ just in case, contingently, the deliberator's actual desires *match* the desires she believes she would have if she were fully rational.

Is this contingency objectionable? It might well be thought that it is. For, it might be said, if deliberation is only contingently effective, then the connection between deliberation and action is altogether *fortuitous*. We have no right to think, as we ordinarily do, that action is the product of the reasons that we discover through deliberation. Rather, our beliefs about our normative reasons are mere epiphenomena, causally irrelevant in the production of action.

In our view it is this line of thought that leads theorists to embrace P2. For one striking feature of P2 is that it guarantees the effectiveness of deliberation. If better judgement entails desire, then there is no gap between discovering that an action is worth performing, and desiring to act accordingly. However, and unfortunately, as we have seen, better judgement does not entail desire. It is thus wrong to suppose that we can plausibly capture the insight that the connection between deliberation and action is not altogether fortuitous by embracing P2. And so we must ask whether we can capture that insight in some other way.

We believe that the insight can be captured by a weaker principle than P2. Specifically, it is captured by the principle we get by adding a "*ceteris paribus*" clause to P2. According to this modified principle, the claim that deliberation is effective is equivalent to the idea that *ceteris paribus* action is one product of the reasons that we discover through deliberation. But is this weakened principle itself any more plausible than P2? What does the "*ceteris paribus*" clause amount to?

In our view, it amounts to the assumption that the deliberating agent whose deliberations are effective is a *rational* deliberator. And nor should this be surprising. For the agent who believes that it is desirable to φ and yet does not desire to φ *is* irrational (Smith 1992; Pettit and Smith 1993a, 1993b). In order to see this, suppose an agent believes that she would desire to φ in circumstances C if she were fully rational, but that she does not desire to φ in it. What can we say about this agent? The clearest thing to say is surely that she is *irrational by her own lights*. For she fails to have a desire that she believes she would have if she were more rational. And, so long as irrationality by one's own lights is a species of irrationality – an extension of the requirement of coherence, perhaps – it follows immediately that this agent is irrational *tout court*.

If this is right, then it would seem to follow that rationality demands of us that we desire to act in ways that we believe we have normative reason to act. Indeed, it would seem that rationality demands of us something even stronger. It demands of us not just that we desire to act in ways that we believe ourselves to have normative reason to act, but also that the relative strength of our desires *matches* the relative importance of these normative reasons. For suppose we believe ourselves to have a normative reason to φ in circumstances C: that is, we believe that amongst the desires we would have if we were fully rational is a desire that we φ in C. Importantly, this may well be only one of the desires we imagine ourselves having, for it is perfectly possible for us to believe that we would have other different, and perhaps even conflicting, desires concerning what to do in C if we were fully rational. Now suppose that we do. Then we presumably believe that our desire to φ would have a certain *strength* vis-à-vis these other desires we imagine ourselves having. This, the relative strength of our imagined desire to φ in C, fixes something important about the normative reason we believe ourselves to have for φ-ing in C. Specifically, it fixes the *relative importance* of that normative reason. Or so we claim.

Thus, if our imagined desire to φ in C is the strongest of our imagined desires concerning what to do in C, then it follows that this is the normative reason to which we attach most importance. If we imagine it to be a relatively weak desire – suppose we believe that we would also have a much stronger desire to ψ in C if we were fully rational – then, though we take ourselves to have some normative reason to φ in C, we judge ourselves to have more normative reason to ψ in C. And so we could go on.

If this is right, if the connection between the normative reasons we believe ourselves to have after we have deliberated and our motivating reasons is a *rational*, albeit *contingent*, connection, then that suggests that we should accept the following principle connecting the normative reasons we believe ourselves to have with desire:

If an agent believes that she has more normative reason to do x than to do y, then she *should* want to do x more than she wants to do y

or, equivalently,

P2*. If an agent judges that it would be better to do x than to do y, then she *should* want to do x more than she wants to do y

For according to P2*, rationality demands of us that we have desires that match in both *content and strength* the desires we believe we would have if we were fully rational.

In our view, P2* suffices to capture the insight that the connection between deliberation and action is not altogether fortuitous. But, if this is right, then it follows that there are all sorts of ways in which better judgement and desire may fail to coincide, even when we do desire in the way we judge best.

Suppose, for example, that we believe that we have a normative reason to φ and that we do desire to φ, just as we should. Given P2*, our desire to φ may still be rationally criticizable. For, on the one hand, our desire to φ may be *stronger* than it should be. The strength of our desire to φ may be such that we are disposed to φ instead of ψ even when we take ourselves to have more normative reason to ψ than φ; disposed to φ instead of κ even when we take ourselves to have more normative reason to κ than φ; and so on. (The limiting case of this, of course, would be desiring to φ when we believe ourselves to have no normative reason to φ.) Or, alternatively, our desire to φ may be *weaker* than it should be. For the strength of our desire to φ may be such that we are disposed to ψ instead of φ even when we take ourselves to have more normative reason to φ than ψ; we are disposed to κ instead of φ even when we take ourselves to have more normative reason to φ than κ; and so on. (The limiting case of this, of course, would be our having no desire at all to φ, despite the fact that we judge ourselves to have some normative reason to φ.)

To sum up: the reasons we discover through deliberation reliably lead to action just in case we are rational in the sense captured by P2*. And, accordingly, whatever plausibility attaches to P2 derives from the plausibility of P2*. Rationality demands of us not just that we actually desire to act in the ways we believe we have normative reason to act, but also that the strength of our actual desires be isomorphic with the importance of our believed reasons. And what this means is that a space may open up between the normative reasons an irrational agent believes herself to have, and the desires she actually has.

3. SELF-CONTROL

It should now be clear what sorts of circumstances call for the exercise of self-control, in our view. When an agent deliberates, and decides which course of action she has most normative reason to pursue, she all too often finds that she is motivated to do something else instead. In such situations, she will in fact act otherwise if she does not take appropriate steps. This is when self-control is called for.

Consider again the example of John described at the outset. When we imagine John being weak or compelled we suppose that, though he judges it most desirable to refrain from eating chocolates, his desires are out of line with his judgement. Perhaps we imagine his desire to experience the taste of chocolate being much stronger than it should be, or his desire to be healthy being much weaker than it should be, so that he ends up desiring to eat chocolate more than he desires to regain his health, despite judging it far less desirable to experience the taste of chocolate than to regain his health. Without the exercise of self-control John will knowingly fail to do what he takes himself to have most reason to do. When we imagine John being weak, we imagine such an exercise of self-control to be possible. When we imagine him being compelled, we imagine him incapable of such an exercise of self-control.

But what does it mean to say that John can or cannot exercise self-control? Talk of exercising self-control sounds like talk of action, and, as we have seen, action is motivated by an antecedent desire. But in that case, doesn't a regress threaten? If the exercise of self-control is itself to be explained by the presence of desires that may themselves be either too weak or too strong, then won't an agent's exercise of self-control itself need to be under her control?

According to some, questions like these suggest a paradox in the very idea of self-control (Mele 1988). But in our view they suggest something rather different. When we talk of an agent exercising self-control we may seem to be supposing that every exercise of self-control is itself an action. But, if we do, that supposition is false. Some exercises of self-control must themselves be, not actions, but rather manifestations of our cognitive dispositions. In order to see how they can be manifestations of our cognitive dispositions, we need to consider in some detail how John might exercise self-control in the case described.

Let's suppose that John believes that it is most desirable to refrain from eating chocolate because he believes that it is more desirable to be healthy than to get pleasure, and because he believes that, though it will also lead to less in the way of pleasure, refraining from eating chocolate will cause him to be healthy. And let's suppose further that he doesn't have any actual desire to be healthy at all, despite his judgement. He believes that it is desirable to be healthy because he believes that, under conditions of full rationality, he would desire to be healthy. But, not being in conditions of full rationality in fact, he does not have any actual desire to be healthy.

In order to make the case as simple and uncontroversial as possible, let's assume further that conditions of full rationality may simply be understood as conditions of full information. In the past, whenever John has thought long and hard about what health is and involves, he has found that he ends up desiring very strongly to be healthy. But he has also found that this desire is difficult to keep. When thoughts about what health is and involves are not before his mind, he finds that his desire to be healthy simply lapses. This is why John believes that he would desire very strongly to be healthy, if he were fully rational, though he does not in fact desire to be healthy.

If this is John's situation, what might happen when he exercises self-control? One obvious answer suggests itself. Before he is about to enter the shop and buy some chocolate John might simply think about what health is and involves. For if John has these thoughts, and if his having these thoughts causes him to desire to be healthy, and if the desire it causes in him is strong enough, then he will find himself with a desire to be healthy strong enough to resist the temptation of the chocolate bars (Pettit and Smith 1993b; Kennett and Smith 1996).

Importantly, note that this answer does not suggest any sort of regress. For John's having certain thoughts about the nature of health need not itself be thought of as an action, and so we need not suppose that John has any antecedent desires which explain why they are had. His having certain thoughts may rather be just what they seem to be: thoroughly cognitive matters to be explained in terms of his cognitive dispositions, not actions that require explanation in terms of antecedent desires that might themselves be either weaker or stronger than they should be, and which themselves must therefore be capable of being brought under his control.

And note that talk of cognitive dispositions is important here, for having thus distanced ourselves from the idea that an exercise of self-control is it-self an action, we don't want to commit ourselves to the suggestion that an agent's having certain thoughts is all there is to the exercise of self-control.

After all, to return to John's case, if his having the thoughts about health that cause him to desire health is simply a matter of luck, then this could hardly constitute his exercise of self-control. For his having these thoughts would then reflect no credit upon him, whereas his exercise of self-control does.

The answer lies in the idea that John's exercise of self-control is the manifestation of a cognitive disposition. In other words, John's having thoughts that cause him to desire health is no mere accident, and in turn reflects credit upon him, if his having those thoughts is itself a manifestation of a disposition he has to have such thoughts when he is otherwise disposed to act on his desires and contrary to his better judgement. For, as we have already seen, it is rational for an agent to do what she believes she has most normative reason to do. And, since this is so, her being disposed to have such thoughts is simply a way of shoring up her tendency to act rationally. What reflects credit upon an agent, when she exercises self-control, is thus the rationality of her having the thoughts she has in her difficult circumstances. John does well when he has thoughts that cause him to desire health because that it is a rational thing for him to think in circumstances where having such thoughts will cause him to have the desire that will in turn cause him to act in the way he believes he has most normative reason to act.

There is a problem looming here, however. For, as we have seen, the capacity for self-control is supposed to be one that an agent *may or may not* exercise. This, you will recall, is the crux of the distinction between weakness and compulsion: the weak agent is supposed to have a capacity for self-control that she fails to exercise whereas the compulsive agent is supposed not to have the capacity for self-control at all. But if the capacity for self-control is simply a disposition to have the right thoughts at the right times, then what is the difference between failing to exercise self-control and having no capacity for self-control at all? An agent who fails to exercise self-control fails to have the right thoughts at the right times. And an agent who has no capacity for self-control at all also fails to have the right thoughts at the right times. The agent who fails to exercise self-control and the agent who fails to have the capacity for self-control would therefore seem to be one and the same. We have lost the distinction between weakness and compulsion. Or so it might seem.

The problem here is more apparent than real. We have said that an agent who has the capacity for self-control has a disposition to have those thoughts that will cause her to act in accordance with her beliefs about what she has most normative reason to do, when she is otherwise disposed to act on her desires and contrary to her beliefs. But for this to be so it is not necessary for her to have the right thoughts on each and every occasion that she is disposed otherwise to lose control. It is enough that, in circumstances where she will act contrary to her better judgement, she could have had such thoughts.

Thus, consider two agents who fail to exercise self-control, one of whom we we would ordinarily describe as weak, the other as compelled. We just do ordinarily distinguish a sense of "could" in which we can truly say of one that she *could* have had thoughts that would cause her to act in accordance with her beliefs about what she has most normative reason to do, whereas the other *could not* have had such thoughts. The truth of the claim that an agent could have had such thoughts, in this ordinary sense of "could," is thus to be determined in a largely *pragmatic* fashion. We might, for example, appeal to her past behaviour. If an agent has, in the past, had similar thoughts in similar situations then, for ordinary purposes, this might be enough to show that she could have had such thoughts in the situation she in fact faces here and now. The pragmatic character of the "could" is evident once we notice that it is our interests in an agent and her predicament that fix the standards of similarity.

For example, if in the past John has had thoughts about the nature of health when, say, he went into yet other shops to buy chocolate, and his having these thoughts then caused him to desire health with sufficient strength to resist the temptation of the chocolates, then we might take this to be sufficient to show that he could have had such thoughts in the situation that he in fact faces here and now. Or perhaps it is sufficient that he had similar thoughts when he went into yet other shops in the past to buy cake, something else he has a passion for, and on those occasions his thoughts led him to desire health strongly enough to overcome the temptation of the cakes. Which similarity counts depends on which similarity is salient for us, given our interest in John and the way we think about his current predicament. A full account of these similarities would constitute a significant part of our understanding of rational agency. Ideally, an analysis of self-control would need to spell out these details. But the general idea should be plain enough.

Armed with this sense of "could," we see that we can indeed distinguish between an agent who possesses the capacity for self-control, but fails to exercise it, and an agent who has no capacity for self-control at all. In short, an agent has a capacity for self-control that she fails to exercise when there is a nearby possible world in which she has the thoughts that cause her to have the desire that causes her to act in accordance with her better judgement, whereas an agent has no capacity for self-control at all when there is no nearby possible world in which she has the thoughts that cause her to have the desire that causes her to act in accordance with her better judgement. And whether or not this is so is in turn a function of our ordinary, pragmatically determined, standards of similarity, standards that in turn fix which possible worlds are to be deemed "nearby."

4. HOW TO DISTINGUISH RECKLESSNESS, WEAKNESS, AND COMPULSION

Let's return to the beginning. Commonsense tells us that we can distinguish between recklessness, weakness, and compulsion. Our own account of the distinction between normative and motivating reasons, and our story about the nature and operation of self-control, allows us to make these distinctions in a more or less commonsense way.

An agent acts recklessly when, in forming her beliefs about what she has most normative reason to do – that is, in deciding what she would most want to do in the circumstances she faces if she were fully rational – she takes insufficient care, making a judgement she would not have made if only she had taken her time and thought about matters more carefully. But, having made her judgement, her desires match her beliefs perfectly. When an agent is reckless, her capacity for self-control is thus not at issue. She acts freely and intentionally in accordance with her sloppily formed beliefs about what she has most normative reason to do.

By contrast, when agents are weak or compelled, their capacity for self-control is precisely what is at issue. An agent acts weakly when she acts on her desires, and contrary to her beliefs about what she has most normative reason to do, but it is still the case that she could have had thoughts which would have led her to act in accordance with her beliefs, despite her desires. She has the capacity for self-control, but she fails to exercise it. And an agent acts compulsively when she acts on her desires, and contrary to her beliefs about what she has most normative reason to do, and it is not the case that she could have had thoughts which would have led her to act in accordance with her beliefs despite her desires. She lacks the capacity for self-control altogether. Thus, just as commonsense tells us, the weak agent gives in to her desires, whereas the compulsive agent is overcome by them.

Indeed, our own account of the distinctions between recklessness, weakness and compulsion suggests that there is a rich diversity of ways in which agents may be reckless, or weak, or compelled. Consider the case of compulsion, just by way of illustration. In addition to being compelled by their desires, as for instance we can imagine John being compelled by his desire to eat chocolate, our account suggests that agents may also be compelled by their own decision-making processes. Imagine an agent who is brain-washed and is therefore incapable of assessing evidence in forming her judgement about what it is desirable to do; someone who would have ended up deciding that a certain course of action is desirable no matter what evidence came before her. Our own account suggests that this agent may be just as compelled, and so just as lacking in responsibility for what she does when she acts on her judgement, as John is, even though, unlike John, she may have and exercise the capacity for self-control when she acts: that is, even though she may have the capacity to have the right thoughts at the right times so as to ensure that she acts in accordance with her compulsive judgement should she find that she has desires that are out of line with her judgement.

In our view this is a desirable consequence of our view. For the idea that recklessness, weakness of will and compulsion are richly diverse in their nature, richly diverse in just the ways that our own account predicts, is, after all, just more good commonsense.[4]

REFERENCES

Davidson, D. 1970: "How is Weakness of the Will Possible?," in his *Essays on Actions and Events*. Oxford: Oxford University Press. 1980.

Hurley, S. L. 1985: "Conflict, Akrasia and Cognitivism," *Proceedings of the Aristotelian Society*: 23–49.

Hursthouse, R. 1991: "Arational Actions," *Journal of Philosophy*: 57–68.

Johnston, M. 1989: "Dispositional Theories of Value," *Proceedings of the Aristotelian Society*, Supplementary Volume: 139–74.

Kennett, J. 1991: "Decision Theory and Weakness of Will," *Pacific Philosophical Quarterly*: 113–30.

Kennett, J. 1993: "Mixed Motives," *Australasian Journal of Philosophy*: 256–69.

Kennett, J., and Smith, M. 1996: "Frog and Toad Lose Control," *Analysis* 56: 63–73.

Lewis, D. 1989: "Dispositional Theories of Value," *Proceedings of the Aristotelian Society*, Supplementary Volume: 113–37.

Mele, A. 1988: "*Irrationality*: A Precis," *Philosophical Psychology*: 173–7.

Peacocke, C. 1985: "Intention and Action," in Bruce Vermazen and Merrill B. Hintikka, eds., *Essays on Davidson: Actions and Events* (Oxford: Oxford University Press).

Pettit, P., and Smith, M. 1990: "Backgrounding Desire," *Philosophical Review*: 565–92.

Pettit, P., and Smith, M. 1993a: "Practical Unreason," *Mind*: 53–79.

Pettit, P., and Smith, M. 1993b: "Brandt on Self-Control," in Brad Hooker, ed., *Rules, Utility and Rationality* (Boulder, CO: Westview Press). 33–50.

Smith, M. 1987: "The Humean Theory of Motivation," *Mind*: 36–61.

Smith, M. 1988: "On Humeans, Anti-Humeans and Motivation: A Reply to Pettit," *Mind*: 589–95.

Smith, M. 1989: "Dispositional Theories of Value," *Proceedings of the Aristotelian Society*, Supplementary Volume: 89–111.

Smith, M. 1992: "Valuing: Desiring or Believing?," in D. Charles and K. Lennon, eds., *Reduction, Explanation and Realism*. Oxford: Oxford University Press.

Watson, G. 1977: "Skepticism about Weakness of Will," *Philosophical Review*: 316–39.

Watson, G. 1982: "Free Agency," in Gary Watson, ed., *Free Will*. Oxford: Oxford University Press.

Woods, M. 1972: "Reasons for Action and Desire," *Proceedings of the Aristotelian Society*, Supplementary Volume: 189–201.

NOTES

This paper was coauthored with Jeanette Kennett.

1. Davidson's own solution to this problem, which turns on his distinction between a conditional and an unconditional version of better judgement, has been criticized by others (Watson 1977; Peacocke 1985; Hurley 1985). We think that these criticisms decisively refute Davidson's own solution. Since they are familiar enough, we will not repeat them here.

2. For an exploration of some of the complications of this formulation, see Pettit and Smith (1993b).

3. In essence our own view is like that developed by Gary Watson (1977, 1982). Watson insists that we distinguish between an agent's *valuational* system and her *motivational* system, and this is much like our distinction between an agent's beliefs about her normative reasons and her motivating reasons. However Watson thinks that in embracing this distinction we are forced to accept a Platonic, rather than a Humean, conception of beliefs and desires, a conception according to which beliefs about what is desirable *are* desires. But for the reasons given in the text, we think that such a conception is implausible. Since an agent may have beliefs about what is desirable without having corresponding desires at all, beliefs about what is desirable cannot themselves be desires. See also Smith 1987, 1988, 1992; and, especially, Pettit and Smith 1993a.

4. Earlier versions of this paper were read at the University of Auckland, the University of Melbourne, and a conference on *Philosophy in Mind* held at the University of New South Wales. We are grateful to all of those who participated in useful discussions on these occasions, and to Gerald Dworkin and Philip Pettit who subsequently gave us very helpful comments.

4

Frog and Toad Lose Control

"You know, Toad," said Frog with his mouth full, "I think we should stop eating. We will soon be sick." . . .

"Frog," said Toad, "let us eat one very last cookie, and then we will stop." Frog and Toad ate one very last cookie.

"We must stop eating!" cried Toad as he ate another.

"Yes," said Frog, reaching for a cookie, "we need will power."

"What is will power?" asked Toad.

"Will power is trying hard *not* to do something that you really want to do," said Frog.

(Arnold Lobel, *Frog and Toad Together*, 32–35)

Frog's final remark is more than just a little puzzling. It seems to be a truism that whenever we do something – and so, given the omnipresence of trying (Hornsby 1980), whenever we try to do something – we want to do that thing more than we want to do anything else we can do (Davidson 1970). However, according to Frog, when we have will power we are able to try not to do something that we "really want to do." In context the idea is clearly meant to be that what we really want to do and what we most want to do are one and the same. But how is this meant to be so much as possible? It seems to require that our desire not to do what we most want to do is both our strongest desire and not our strongest desire. And that is a blatant contradiction. This is the so-called paradox of self-control (Mele 1987).

The aim of our paper is to explain how to make sense of the story of Frog and Toad. The paper divides into four main sections. In the first we explain, in relatively uncontroversial terms, why Frog and Toad might need to exercise self-control. The explanation is a failure of instrumental rationality: the capacity to satisfy our desires given our beliefs (see also

Brandt 1988; Pettit and Smith 1993b). In the second section we give a slightly more controversial explanation of why Frog and Toad might need to exercise self-control. The explanation is a failure of "orthonomy," where orthonomy is the capacity to act in accordance with our normative reasons, a kind of rationality which, as we explain, is distinct from mere instrumental rationality (Pettit and Smith 1990, 1993a, 1993b; Kennett and Smith 1994). In the third section we outline two ways in which Frog and Toad might try to exercise self-control, whether in the service of instrumental rationality or orthonomy: they might exercise self-control diachronically or synchronically. We therefore have the following combinations.

Self-Control	Diachronic	Synchronic
Instrumental	1	2
Orthonomous	3	4

As will become clear, combinations 2 and 4 are the cases in which we need to be careful not to contradict ourselves when we explain how Frog and Toad are able to control themselves. In the fourth and final section we tell how Frog and Toad fare at the end of the story, as Arnold Lobel tells it, and we use our distinctions to give an interpretation of Lobel's ending.

1. LOSING CONTROL AS INSTRUMENTAL IRRATIONALITY

Let's assume, to begin at any rate, that Frog and Toad both have two intrinsic desires: a desire to be healthy and a weaker desire to have immediate pleasure. If they are instrumentally rational then they will have extra extrinsic desires as well. Because they intrinsically desire to have immediate pleasure and believe that eating cookies will produce it, they will extrinsically desire to eat more cookies; and because they intrinsically desire to be healthy and believe that eating cookies will make them sick, they will also extrinsically desire not to eat any more cookies. Let's now ask what Frog and Toad should do.

If we interpret this as asking what they would do if they were fully instrumentally rational then the answer is clear: Frog and Toad should not eat any more cookies. Their intrinsic desire to be healthy is, after all, stronger than their intrinsic desire to have immediate pleasure, and so the strengths of their extrinsic desires to eat more cookies and not to eat more cookies should simply follow suit. But, of course, it doesn't follow that their desire not to eat more cookies is stronger than their desire to eat more cookies, because it does not follow that they are fully instrumentally rational.

Here, then, we find one natural interpretation of the Frog and Toad story. When Frog says that they should stop eating cookies he is reporting the fact that they would have and act upon an extrinsic desire not to eat cookies if they were fully instrumentally rational. However, because they are not fully instrumentally rational, they have no such extrinsic desire.

When he goes on to say that they really want to eat more cookies, rather than not, he is therefore reporting on the relative strengths of their actual extrinsic desires; reporting on the fact that while they do in fact have an extrinsic desire to eat cookies, and a strong one at that, they do not have any extrinsic desire at all not to do so. This is because, even though they are not fully instrumentally rational, they are sufficiently instrumentally rational for their intrinsic desire to have immediate pleasure to have transmitted its force across the means-end relation.

This interpretation of the story is natural because failures of instrumental rationality, though perhaps unusual, are not so unusual as to be incomprehensible. We all know what it is like when the smell and taste of cookies makes the immediate pleasure of eating them especially vivid and salient, at least when compared with the pallid and inert nature of our knowledge that refraining will lead to good health. In such situations we would ordinarily say of ourselves, much as Frog says, that if only we had sufficient will power we would be able to control ourselves: that is, we would be able to try hard not to do what we really want to do. We will see how our account of why Frog and Toad are out of control allows us to make sense of this part of the story presently.

2. LOSING CONTROL AS A LACK OF ORTHONOMY

So far we have assumed that Frog and Toad have two intrinsic desires, a desire to be healthy and a weaker desire to have immediate pleasure, and that they lose control because they are instrumentally irrational. Let's now drop that assumption and suppose instead that Frog and Toad have just one intrinsic desire, a desire to have immediate pleasure, and that they are fully instrumentally rational.

We have so far interpreted Frog's saying that they must stop eating cookies because they will soon be sick to mean that, given their intrinsic desire for health, their strongest extrinsic desire would be to stop eating cookies if they were fully instrumentally rational. But clearly we cannot give Frog's claim this interpretation any longer. If their strongest intrinsic desire is for immediate pleasure then, though being sick is clearly no fun, the lack of pleasure it brings lies in the future with the sickness itself. Immediate pleasure is therefore to be gained by eating more cookies, not by stopping.

On this new interpretation of the story we suggest that when Frog says that they must stop eating cookies because they will soon be sick he means that they have a compelling normative reason to stop eating cookies, where an agent has a compelling normative reason to act in a certain way in certain circumstances just in case she would, if she were fully rational *tout court* – not merely fully instrumentally rational – desire most strongly that she acts in that way in those circumstances (Smith 1992, 1994, 1995). So as not to be too controversial we will assume that being fully rational requires only one thing in addition to being fully instrumentally rational: knowledge of all the relevant facts. When Frog says that they must stop eating cookies in the circumstances in which they in fact find themselves, then, in circumstances in which all they intrinsically desire is immediate pleasure, we will therefore interpret him to be saying that if they were fully rational – that is, if they had knowledge of all the relevant facts and they were fully instrumentally rational – then they would have an overriding extrinsic desire that they not eat any more cookies in just these circumstances. But is it plausible to suppose that Frog and Toad have a compelling normative reason to stop eating cookies in these circumstances? We think it is.

Suppose that though they do not in fact have an intrinsic desire to be healthy, both Frog and Toad used to have this desire in the past. They first acquired the desire as a by-product of engaging in a fitness program which they enrolled in out of curiosity. But as they became more and more healthy, and gained a vivid sense of what constitutes good health – the level of energy you have, the body image, the openness to new possibilities, and so on and so forth – they found themselves wanting, intrinsically, very much to be healthy. Indeed, it was their strongest intrinsic desire, so much so that they became fitness fanatics. However let's suppose that, for some reason or other, they were unable to attend the fitness program for a month, and when the month was over and they were able to return, they found that they didn't want to. They no longer had a vivid sense of what constitutes good health – they had more or less forgotten – and they found that, without the constant reflection on what constitutes good health, their intrinsic desire to be healthy simply vanished. Given this background, let's now ask what Frog and Toad should do in the circumstances they face.

If we interpret this as asking what they would most want themselves to do, in their present circumstances, if they were fully rational – that is, if they had knowledge of all the relevant facts and were fully instrumentally rational – then the answer is clear. They should not eat any more cookies. For if they once again had a vivid sense of what constitutes good health they would regain their intrinsic desire that they be healthy, and then, knowing that eating more cookies will make them sick, they would extrinsically desire themselves not to eat any more cookies. This would be their strongest desire. Moreover, Frog and Toad know that this is what they would desire. For though they no longer have a vivid sense of what constitutes good health, they remember what it was like when they did.

Here, then, we find yet another natural interpretation of the Frog and Toad story. When Frog says that they must stop eating cookies he is reporting the fact that they would most want themselves to do so if they were fully rational: that is, if they had knowledge of all the relevant facts and were fully instrumentally rational. However, because they do not have knowledge of all the relevant facts – because they no longer have a vivid sense of what constitutes good health – they have no such desire. When he goes on to say that they really want to eat more cookies, rather than not, he is therefore reporting on the relative strengths of their actual desires; reporting on the fact that while they do have a very strong extrinsic desire to eat cookies, they have no actual desire whatsoever not to do so, and no actual intrinsic desire from which such an extrinsic desire might be derived.

If Frog and Toad eat more cookies in this situation they will not manifest any failure of instrumental rationality. They will, however, manifest a failure of rationality of another kind, a failure of what we call "orthonomy." Orthonomy is a matter of being under the rule of the *right* as opposed to the *wrong*; a matter of having the desires we *rationally should* have rather than those we *rationally shouldn't*. An agent is therefore orthonomous when her desires are in line with the normative reasons she has: that is, when her desires match in content and strength the desires she would have if she were fully rational. Orthonomy thus has two parts. First, the orthonomous agent has true beliefs about the normative reasons she has, and second, she desires to do what she (truly) believes she has normative reason to do. Frog and Toad manifest a failure of orthonomy because, as they know, their strongest intrinsic desire should be a desire to be healthy, not a desire for immediate pleasure, and their strongest extrinsic desire should therefore be a desire not to eat more cookies, not a desire to do so.

We said that this interpretation of the Frog and Toad story is natural. It is natural because we are all familiar with situations in which we have no desire at all to act in the way we judge ourselves to have a compelling normative reason to act: failures of memory, figments of our imaginations, and other more non-cognitive personality disorders like depression can all cause us to lose desires that we would have, and believe we would have, in a more fully rational state. In such situations we would ordinarily say of ourselves, much as Frog says, that if only we had will power we would be able to control ourselves: that is, we would be able to try hard not to do what we really want to do. Let's now see whether we can explain how Frog and Toad might do so.

3. HOW TO EXERCISE SELF-CONTROL

Note, to begin, that there are at least two ways in which we can control ourselves, whether our loss of control is a failure of instrumental rationality or a failure of orthonomy. Suppose we envisage, at time t_1, that we will be out of control at time t_2, at least absent an exercise of self-control. The two ways in which we might exercise self-control reflect the fact that t_1 and t_2 might be the *same* time, or *different* times.

Suppose that t_1 and t_2 are different times. We are then in a position to ask ourselves what we most want to do at t_1, and the answer might well be that we most want to ensure that at t_2 we do not lose control. Here, then, is one completely straightforward way in which we can exercise control over our own actions, especially if we are not out of control at t_1: we can exercise control diachronically, at an earlier time, by so arranging the circumstances of action at the later time as to remove the possibility of our then losing control.

Thus, for example, if at an earlier time when he was fully instrumentally rational (or fully rational *tout court*: that is, orthonomous), Frog had foreseen that he and Toad would no longer be instrumentally rational (or no longer be orthonomous) when in the presence of so many cookies, he could, if he had most wanted to do so, have made sure that they were unable to act in an irrational way later by, say, ensuring that the only option available to them then is the one that they would have chosen if they had been instrumentally rational (or orthonomous). For example, he could have made sure that there were only enough cookies for them to eat one each; that eating cookies until they became sick simply wasn't an option.

In this way he could have ensured that, despite their potential to act in an instrumentally irrational way (or a non-orthonomous way) at the later time, that potential was never realised.

In general, then, though in cases of diachronic self-control our trying not to do what we really want to do does indeed require that our strongest desire is not to act on our strongest desire, there is no contradiction once we see that these desires are had at different times. When we exercise diachronic self-control at t_1 our strongest desire at t_1 is not to act on what, absent this very exercise of diachronic self-control, would have been our strongest desire at t_2.

But what if t_1 and t_2 are the same time? At the very moment that they desire most strongly to eat more cookies, are Frog and Toad able not to act on this, their strongest, desire? In other words, can Frog and Toad exercise self-control not just diachronically, but also synchronically? Certainly Frog and Toad cannot, at one and the same time, both want most to eat cookies and want even more to prevent themselves from eating cookies. That is a contradiction. However it does not follow that there is nothing that they can do to control themselves at the moment of vulnerability, at least not if we adopt a more relaxed, commonsensical, attitude to what we can properly be said to "do."

In order to see that this is so consider, to begin, the case in which Frog and Toad have the potential to lose control because they are instrumentally irrational. Imagine that, despite the fact that the smell and taste of the cookies makes the immediate pleasure of eating them especially vivid and salient, at least when compared with the pallid and inert nature of their knowledge that refraining will lead to good health, Frog and Toad are – at precisely this time and for this very reason – disposed to have certain sorts of thoughts. When they look at the cookies, imagine that they find themselves thinking of them not as causes of pleasure, but rather as lumps of fat, and that when they think about eating them, they imagine the fat curdling in their stomachs. Furthermore, let's suppose that the effect of having these thoughts is that Frog and Toad find themselves desiring, extrinsically, not to eat any more cookies; that when they have these thoughts their intrinsic desire for health combines with their belief that if they eat more cookies then they will be sick to produce an extrinsic desire not to eat more cookies, whereas before they had these thoughts it did not. Having these thoughts enables their intrinsic desire for health to transmit its force across the means–end relation. (We will say a little about the empirical plausibility of this supposition presently). Under such circumstances we think that it would be natural to say that

Frog and Toad exercise self-control at the very moment at which they were vulnerable to a loss of control, and that they do so by having these thoughts.

Now this may come as a surprise, for we are perhaps initially inclined to think of the exercise of self-control as an action, and our suggestion is precisely that, in this case, the exercise of self-control is not an action, but is rather simply a matter of Frog's and Toad's having certain sorts of thoughts. But the inclination to think of the exercise of self-control as an action is, we think, an over-generalization. We begin by observing, correctly, that exercising self-control is something that we do, but then we over-generalize: since all doings are actions, exercising self-control is an action. But this is an over-generalization because not all doings are actions. If someone asks "What are you doing?" it is legitimate to reply "I am thinking." But thinking need not be an action, because the having of thoughts need not be a causal consequence of a desire to achieve something and a belief that that can be achieved by having those very thoughts (Davidson 1963, 1971).

Frog's and Toad's having the thoughts that they have is a case in point. Their having the thoughts that enable the transmission of their otherwise disabled intrinsic desire to be healthy across the means–end relation need not be supposed to be a consequence of a desire and means–end belief they possess: a desire to exercise self-control, say, and a belief that they can do so if they have certain thoughts. Indeed, it had better not be given that their having these thoughts is supposed to restore their disposition to desire extrinsically in the way that they should, given their intrinsic desires and their means–end beliefs: that is, restore their capacity for instrumental rationality! It may rather be just what it seems to be: a manifestation of a reliable cognitive disposition they possess to have such thoughts at such times.

How plausible is the supposition that Frog and Toad enable the trans-mission of their intrinsic desire for health across the means–end relation by having the thought that cookies are just lumps of fat? We think that it is quite plausible, though we would immediately add that its effectiveness is at best a contingent fact about Frog and Toad. We are not predicting that the same thoughts would have the same effect on every single person who over-indulges in cookies, though it may well have the same effect on some. Feelings of shame, the thought that one is stupid, a certain inward focus of attention, any of these may have the requisite effect, and folk wisdom tells us that one or another of these, or something similar, will have the requisite effect upon most of us. But people differ, and so do the things that cause them to regain their instrumental rationality when they are being instrumentally irrational. When people learn self-control what they learn is what works for them.

Our suggestion, then, is that a disposition to have certain thoughts – thoughts which are such that, by having them, otherwise disabled intrinsic desires are enabled to transmit their force across the means-end relation – provides us with a back-up mechanism whereby we can get ourselves to be instrumentally rational when we might otherwise fail even at the very moment of our potential failure. Having this disposition therefore partially constitutes the capacity for synchronic self-control in the service of instrumental rationality. We say it only "partially" constitutes our capacity because it is also partially constituted by our dispositions to feel stupid and ashamed and the like. Moreover, our suggestion is that if Frog and Toad possess this capacity then they may indeed, at a certain time, try hard not to do what they most want to do at that time. There is no contradiction because their attempt need not itself be an action explained by a desire. It may rather be a matter of their having certain thoughts about cookies, thoughts the having of which is explained by their disposition to have such thoughts at such times.

With our explanation of the way in which Frog and Toad may exercise synchronic self-control in the service instrumental rationality in place, it is easy to see how they might exercise synchronic self-control in the service of orthonomy. For example, if Frog and Toad were disposed to have vivid thoughts about what constitutes good health at the moment at which they were disposed to over-indulge in cookies then, by hypothesis, their having these thoughts would suffice to rekindle an overriding intrinsic desire to be healthy, a desire which, once rekindled, would lead them to stop eating cookies in the normal way. The disposition to have such thoughts at the right times, thoughts that would cause us to have desires which match in content and strength the desires we would have if we were fully rational, thus provides us with a back-up mechanism whereby we can get ourselves to be orthonomous when we might otherwise fail, even at the very moment of our potential failure. It therefore partially constitutes our capacity for synchronic self-control in the service of orthonomy.

4. INTERPRETING THE END OF THE STORY

Lobel does not tell us whether Frog and Toad are in need of will power because they are instrumentally irrational or lacking in orthonomy.

81

However the ending of his story is still of some interest, given our distinctions.

Frog put the cookies in a box.
"There," he said. "Now we will not eat any more cookies."
"But we can open the box," said Toad.
"That is true," said Frog.
Frog tied some string around the box. "There," he said. "Now we will not eat any more cookies."
"But we can cut the string and open the box," said Toad.
"That is true," said Frog.
Frog got a ladder. He put the box up on a high shelf. "There," he said. "Now we will not eat any more cookies."
"But we can climb the ladder and take down the box from the shelf and cut the string and open the box," said Toad.
"That is true," said Frog.
Frog climbed the ladder and took the box down from the shelf.
He cut the string and opened the box. Frog took the box outside.
He shouted in a loud voice, "HEY BIRDS, HERE ARE COOKIES!"
Birds came from everywhere. They picked up the cookies in their beaks and flew away.
"Now we have no more cookies to eat," said Toad sadly. "Not even one."
"Yes," said Frog, "but we have lots and lots of will power."
"You may keep it all, Frog," said Toad. "I am going home now to bake a cake."

(*Frog and Toad Together*, 36–41)

Because Frog is able, at the very moment of vulnerability, to stop himself eating more cookies, we may conclude that he has the capacity for synchronic self-control. However he clearly doubts his ability to stay in control in the future. This is why he is unhappy about the idea of simply putting the cookies in a box, or in a box tied up with string, or in a box tied up with string on a high shelf. What he is looking for, as he exercises synchronic self-control, is therefore a way of simultaneously exercising diachronic self-control. And the strategy he comes up with seems to be as good as any. Once he feeds all of the cookies to the birds he and Toad no longer have any cookies to eat, neither now nor in the future. They cannot lose control – or so he thinks.

Enter Toad. Lacking the capacity for both synchronic and diachronic self-control, and lacking the opportunity to indulge himself once Frog feeds the rest of the cookies to the birds, he heads off home to bake a cake. He thus remains as out of control at the end of the story as he was at the beginning. Worse still, by baking a cake Toad undermines Frog's attempt at diachronic self-control. Later on they will no doubt find themselves simply eating cake rather than cookies. That is the unstated joke at the end of Lobel's story. However in real life the joke is no joke at all. Our own efforts at self-control are always potentially undermined by opportunities for action that we would prefer not to have, and that are only made available to us because those who are out of control make them so. Success in the project of self-control is always going to be more likely when those around us are not themselves out of control.

REFERENCES

Brandt, R. B. 1988: "The structure of virtue," in P. A. French et al., eds., *Midwest Studies in Philosophy Volume XIII*. Notre Dame: University of Notre Dame Press.

Davidson, D. 1963: "Actions, Reasons and Causes," reprinted in his *Essays on Actions and Events*. Oxford: Oxford University Press. 1980.

Davidson, D. 1970: "How Is Weakness of the Will Possible?," reprinted in his *Essays on Actions and Events*. Oxford: Oxford University Press. 1980.

Davidson, D. 1971: "Agency," reprinted in his *Essays on Actions and Events*. Oxford: Oxford University Press. 1980.

Hornsby, J. 1980: *Actions*. London: Routledge and Kegan Paul.

Kennett, J., and M. Smith 1994: "Philosophy and Commonsense: The Case of Weakness of Will," in M. Michael and J. O'Leary-Hawthorne, eds., *Philosophy in Mind*. Dordrecht: Kluwer Press.

Lobel, A. 1971: *Frog and Toad Together*. New York: Scholastic.

Mele, A. 1987: *Irrationality: An Essay on "Akrasia," Self-Deception, and Self-Control*. New York: Oxford University Press.

Pettit, P., and M. Smith 1990: "Backgrounding Desire," *Philosophical Review* 99: 565–92.

Pettit, P., and M. Smith 1993a: "Practical Unreason," *Mind* 102: 53–79.

Pettit, P., and M. Smith 1993b: "Brandt on self-control," in Brad Hooker, ed., *Rationality, Rules and Utility*. Boulder, CO: Westview Press.

Smith, M. 1992: "Valuing: Desiring or Believing?," in D. Charles and K. Lennon, eds., *Reduction, Explanation, Realism*. Oxford: Oxford University Press.

Smith, M. 1994: *The Moral Problem*. Oxford: Basil Blackwell.

Smith, M. 1995: "Internal Reasons," *Philosophy and Phenomenological Research* 55: 109–31.

NOTE

This paper was coauthored with Jeanette Kennett.

5

A Theory of Freedom and Responsibility

Once we equip ourselves with a suitable version of the dispositional theory of value we can solve the various metaphysical, epistemological, and motivational puzzles that standardly arise in meta-ethics. So, at any rate, I have argued.[1]

Even if I am right about this, however, it might be thought that another set of problems in meta-ethics remains, problems which the dispositional theory of value goes no way towards solving. These are problems about the nature of freedom and the conditions of moral responsibility. A solution to these problems, it might be said, requires some super-added theory about the nature of the moral agent, something about which the dispositional theory of value remains silent. My task in the present essay is to address this concern and to show that it is unfounded. The dispositional theory delivers an intuitive and compelling conception of freedom. It delivers, more or less in and of itself, a plausible conception of the responsible moral agent.

I begin by drawing out some assumptions we make about the belief-forming capacities of those we are prepared to engage in conversation about what is the case: people whose beliefs we are willing to use as a reality check on our own. Since it seems undeniable that at least some people do have these belief-forming capacities, and that we are therefore right to make them answer for their beliefs, it is irresistible to ask whether these sorts of capacities, and the responsibility for our beliefs that they engender, could serve as the basis for an account of freedom and responsibility in the arena of action. The answer argued for in the remainder of the essay is that they can, and that the dispositional theory of value is what enables them to.

The essay divides into four main sections. In the first I outline the assumptions we make about people's belief-forming capacities when we take them to be answerable for their beliefs. In the second section I briefly rehearse the main features of the version of the dispositional theory of value I favour – the theory is non-relativist, rationalist, cognitivist, and internalist – and I explain why, because the theory has these features, it enables us to conceive of agents as responsible for their desires and actions in much the same way as they are responsible for their beliefs. Moreover, I explain why the capacities we take agents to enjoy, in so far as we take them to be responsible – capacities to form evaluative beliefs and desire accordingly – amount to nothing less than a capacity to be free in the arena of action. In the third section I consider some standard puzzle cases in the free-will literature, and I explain how the conceptions of freedom and responsibility that emerged in the previous section enable us to handle them. And then in the fourth and final section I compare the conception of freedom and responsibility that we get from the dispositional theory of value with its main competitor, the theory defended by Harry Frankfurt.[2]

1. RESPONSIBILITY FOR BELIEF[3]

When we engage people in conversation about some matter of fact we oftentimes find ourselves in disagreement with them. Such disagreements can sometimes be resolved. Perhaps those with opposing views can learn from us, as we are better placed to have knowledge of the relevant part of reality than they are, something about which we can convince them, or we can learn from them, as they are better placed to have knowledge of the relevant part of reality than we are, something about which they can convince us. The picture we have, then, is of conversation as an arena in which people can talk through their reasons for and against their beliefs with others who may or may not have taken such reasons into account in forming their own contrary beliefs, thereby attempting to come to a resolution of their differences. Through conversation they work their way towards a common view as to how things are.

Conversations of this sort seem to involve some rather specific assumptions about the norms to which the believers who are our conversational partners are subject, and about the capacities which they enjoy.[4] First, we assume that there are various norms governing what people ought to believe and ought not to believe – these "ought's" are, of course, all merely prima-facie – norms that we assume to be inescapable. Thus, for example, if we are discussing whether Mt. Kosciuszko is the tallest mountain in Australia then we assume that we should have this belief just in case Mt. Kosciuszko is the tallest mountain in Australia, and that we should not have the belief just in case it is not. If we take the geographical maps of Australia that are found in atlases to be one possible source of evidence as to whether Mt. Kosciuszko is the tallest mountain in Australia, then we assume that we should have the belief that Mt. Kosciuszko is the tallest mountain in Australia just in case the maps show it to be, and that we should not have the belief just in case they do not. And if we take it that we already have beliefs which bear on whether Mt. Kosciuszko is the tallest mountain in Australia – as we might if, for instance, we already have beliefs both about where, in Australia, the tallest mountain is to be found, and what the tallest mountain in that region of Australia is – then we assume that we should have the belief that Mt. Kosciuszko is the tallest mountain in Australia just in case that is implied by what we already believe – provided, of course, we aren't prepared to revise our antecedent beliefs instead (I will omit this qualification from here on) – and that we should not believe that it is the tallest mountain in Australia just in case it is not. And so on and so forth.

I said we assume that these norms are inescapable. What I meant is that we assume that such norms apply to us simply in virtue of the fact that we are believers: they do not apply to us only because we are believers with a certain cultural background, say, or because we are believers with certain tastes or preferences. Thus, for example, the norm "You ought to believe p just in case p" is not one that applies to us just in case we happen to come from a Western culture, or an analytic philosophy department, or a certain socio-economic background, or just in case we happen to have a taste for the true rather than the false. No psychological state could so much as count as a belief if it did not have representing things to be the way that they are as part of its proper function. It is in this sense that the norm is inescapable. The same goes for the other norms governing our beliefs.

This is not to say that our present views about the norms that govern belief are infallible. Indeed, quite the opposite is the case. Our beliefs about the norms that govern beliefs – our views about the nature of logic, say, or about the nature of evidence – can themselves vary from person to person, and so are as subject to the norm "You ought to believe that p just in case p" as any other belief. The norms that govern our beliefs may therefore become the topic of a conversation whose aim is to figure out what the norms really are. The point is simply that – notwithstanding their contestable status – the norms that govern belief enter directly into the definition of the concept of belief itself by defining its proper function, and so enter directly into the definition of the concept of a believer as well. It therefore follows that we cannot separate out our views about which norms govern beliefs from our views about who the class of believers is. To think of someone as a believer at all is to think of them as falling under the norms that we think govern beliefs.

A second assumption we make concerns the capacities of believers. We assume not just that there are norms that govern belief, but that believers are capable of recognizing these norms. Thus, for example, if we have a disagreement with someone about which is the tallest mountain in Australia then we assume that they are capable of recognizing norms like "You ought to believe that Mt. Kosciuszko is the tallest mountain in Australia just in case it is the tallest mountain in Australia," and "You ought to believe that Mt. Kosciuszko is the tallest mountain in Australia if that is implied by other things you believe." Someone who didn't have the capacity to recognize such norms – someone who, say, refused to believe that Mt. Kosciuszko is the tallest mountain in Australia but who didn't acknowledge that they ought to believe that it is, given that that is implied by other things they believe – would not be someone with whom you could even begin to engage in a conversation as to whether or not Mt. Kosciuszko is the tallest mountain in Australia. Their beliefs would not constitute a challenge of any sort to your contrary belief.

A third assumption we make also concerns the capacities of believers. We assume not just that they are capable of recognizing the norms that govern their beliefs, but that they are capable of responding appropriately to their recognition of such norms. Thus, to stick with our example, if we have a disagreement with someone over which is the tallest mountain in Australia – let's suppose that we believe it to be Mt. Kosciuszko whereas they disbelieve this – then we assume not just that they are capable of recognizing that they ought to believe that it is Mt. Kosciuszko, if their other beliefs imply that it is, but also that they are capable of responding appropriately. We assume, that is, that they are capable of actually coming to believe that Mt. Kosciuszko is the tallest mountain in Australia because of their recognition of the reasons available to them for so believing. Someone who didn't have the capacity to respond would, once again, not be someone with whom you could even begin to engage in a conversation as to whether or not Mt. Kosciuszko is the tallest mountain in Australia. Their beliefs would not constitute a challenge of any sort to your contrary belief.

The talk of capacities here is important because people can retain their capacity to recognize and respond to the norms that govern their beliefs even when they fail to recognize and respond to those norms on some particular occasion. Thus, for example, though there is a norm telling people to believe what is implied by the rest of their beliefs, they can still have beliefs that are inconsistent with the rest of their beliefs from time to time, despite retaining their capacity to recognize and respond to this norm. Indeed, the fact that they can retain their capacity even while failing to exercise it is what makes conversation about matters of fact appropriate. Through conversation we try to get people, ourselves included, to believe in the ways that they should, something that would hardly be appropriate if they were unable to do so.

Suppose someone fails to believe that Mt. Kosciuszko is the tallest mountain in Australia, and yet believes both that the tallest mountain in Australia is near Canberra, and that the tallest mountain near Canberra is Mt. Kosciuszko. If we did not think that this person had the capacity to recognize the gap in his beliefs, and then to respond appropriately by, say, acquiring the belief that Mt. Kosciuszko is the tallest mountain in Australia, then we would not bother conversing with him. Note, more-over, that the capacity that we imagine him to have is entirely *his*. Our role in raising the gap in his beliefs with him in conversation is not essential. He has the capacity to recognize the gap not just when it is pointed out to him by someone else, but when he scrutinizes his own beliefs and updates them, something we assume to be a more or less permanent possibility in a believer.

Of course, there are various conditions believers can be in that remove – whether temporarily or permanently, locally, or globally – their capacity either to recognize the norms that govern their beliefs, or their capacity to adjust their beliefs in response to their recognition of such norms, or both. Unconsciousness, illness, stubbornness, arrogance, self-deception, and drunkenness are some among them. We all know what it is like to talk with someone who has a belief which they cannot support in any way, but which they none the less find themselves totally committed to, just as we all know what it is like to talk with people who are not like this. It is in people of the latter sort that belief revision is assumed to be a more or less permanent possibility. Think again of some relatively normal person who believes both that the tallest mountain in Australia is near Canberra, and that the tallest mountain near Canberra is Mt. Kosciuszko. He should indeed believe that Mt. Kosciuszko is the tallest mountain in

Australia because he could, right here and now, recognize the gap in his beliefs and respond appropriately. Or so we assume.

So far I have described only interpersonal conversations. But, of course, thinking itself is a kind of intrapersonal conversation. Suppose I find myself believing that Mt. Kosciuszko is the tallest mountain in Australia when I remember that my earlier self believed otherwise. I then have to engage in a kind of conversation with my past self. I have to make sure that my reasons for now believing that Mt. Kosciuszko is the tallest mountain in Australia are sufficient, in the light of my earlier self's reasons for having a contrary belief. I have to be able to tell myself a story either about why my earlier self made a mistake or error, or, failing that, why I have made a mistake or error now. In engaging in this sort of intrapersonal conversation I thus make various assumptions about the capacities of my present self and my earlier self to recognize and respond to the norms that govern my beliefs, assumptions which are exactly the same as those we make about each other in the context of interpersonal conversations.

This means that the conversational assumptions – the assumptions we make about the existence of norms and the capacities of believers to recognize and respond to their recognition of such norms – form the backdrop not just of all conversations we have with other people about what is the case, but of all our own thoughts about what is the case as well. To call into question the propriety of making these assumptions is thus to call into question the propriety not just of conversing with others, but of all thought. Even so, the fact that we enjoy these sorts of capacity can be made to seem more problematic than it ordinarily appears. An argument of Peter van Inwagen's has just this effect.[5]

Consider a philosophical discussion in which you reply in a certain way to a question, but realize later that another response would have been much better. There are at least two ways of fleshing out this case. You might think that the response you gave at the time was the best you could have given. Perhaps the later response only occurs to you after a good deal of subsequent discussion and further thought, or only after you read even more books and articles. Or, alternatively, you might think that the response you gave at the time isn't the best you could have given. You reprimand yourself for having failed to think of a better response at the time, a response you are convinced you could have thought of. Perhaps it was the obvious thing to say, and you'd even thought of working it into your answer before you began to speak, but it slipped from your mind as you went on.

Enter van Inwagen. Suppose that the actual world is deterministic, and consider the total state of the actual world at some time prior to you birth. That state of the world in conjunction with the laws of nature entail that, during the time of the discussion, you were not going to think of that response while you spoke. In order to have thought of that response you would therefore either have to have changed the past or violated a law of nature. But you have the ability to do neither of these things. In a perfectly straightforward sense, then, you did not have the ability to think of the better response, and so you could not have given the better response because you could not have thought of it. If the actual world is deterministic, then van Inwagen's argument shows that the second possibility collapses into the first. Or does it?

Suppose you were able to think of the better response, and that if you had thought of it, then you would have given the better response. In fact, however, you did not think of it. Since all counterfactuals purport to tell us what would have happened had things been otherwise in some respect, in order to give an interpretation of this counterfactual we need to say where in the space of possibilities we are to find the possible worlds that differ from the actual world in history only in so far as you think of that better response. And since, if the actual world is deterministic, the actual history together with the actual laws of nature entail that you did not think of the better response, it follows that the possible worlds at issue will have to differ from the actual world in either or both history and laws. So much is clear.[6] But even though the possible worlds at issue must differ from the actual world in history or laws, it doesn't follow that we have to suppose ourselves to have the ability to change history or violate laws.

David Lewis points out that the possible worlds in which we are interested are those which, despite their differences, are yet maximally similar to the actual world – this is because similarity relations between possible worlds, relative to some interest we have, give us our fix on what could and could not have happened – and this in turn means that the possible worlds in which we are interested are those whose history and laws differ minimally from the history and laws of the actual world.[7] Lewis suggests that the smallest difference is one in which a local miracle occurs just prior to the time at which we suppose that you could have thought of the better response, a miracle which in turn causes you to think of that better response. This is because it is a very important fact about the actual world, in gauging its similarity to other worlds, that it has the history it actually has. And Lewis also suggests that the miracle should only be a miracle relative to the actual world, because possible worlds which have ever so slightly different laws to the laws of the actual world – laws whose differences suffice to ensure that the local miracle, relative to the actual world, is not a miracle at all relative to the laws of those worlds – are more similar to the actual world than are those possible worlds in which there are violations of their own laws. This is because it is a very important fact about the actual world, in gauging similarities, that there are no violations of law.

When we interpret the counterfactual in Lewis's way, it thus emerges that, in the possible world in which you exercise your ability to think of the better response, we do not have to suppose that you exercise an ability to change history or violate a law at all. The local miracle that we have to imagine, in order to fix on the possible worlds which are maximally similar to the actual world in history, save for the fact that you think of the better response, is the cause of your action, not vice versa. Since you do not even cause the miraculous event, in the possible worlds we imagine, it follows that we do not have to suppose you to have the ability to cause it. Thus, though in giving an interpretation of the counterfactuals – as with any counterfactuals – we have to imagine possible worlds in which there is an ever so slightly different history, and ever so slightly different laws, we do not have to imagine that you have the ability to make the history or laws different. The van Inwagen style argument that if the world is deterministic then you do not have commonsense abilities – abilities like the ability to think of a better response to an argument than the one you in fact thought of – thus collapses.

This is all well and good. But what exactly does it mean to say that you were able to think of a better response to an argument than the one you in fact thought of? Does your possession of that ability require anything weird or transcendental of you? No it does not. Indeed, the discussion of Lewis shows that we can spell out the meaning of this claim in terms of possible worlds. To say that you were able to think of a better response to an argument than the one that you in fact thought of means, *inter alia*, that the possible worlds in which you think of the better response are nearby, or very similar to, the actual world in which you don't. More commonsensically, the crucial point is that we do not need to imagine a massive transformation of your nature in order to imagine you thinking of a better response. We need simply to imagine you, pretty much as you actually are, but giving a better response. This will, of course, be the obvious thing for us to imagine if your failure to think of a better response to the argument on that occasion is atypical. If it is what happens in the actual world that we find hard to comprehend, not what we imagine happening in the possible world in which you give the better response instead, it will hardly be difficult to imagine the possibility in which you give the better response without imagining a massive transformation of your nature!

By contrast, when we say that you thought of the very best response that you could, and so weren't able to think of a better response, what we mean is *inter alia* that the possible worlds in which you think of a better response are remote from, or rather dissimilar to, the actual world. That is, in more commonsense terms, we do need to imagine a massive transformation of your nature in order to imagine you thinking of a better response because we first of all need to imagine you having read more books, or having had more discussions that impact on your background knowledge, or whatever. This will, of course, be the obvious thing for us to imagine if you typically fail to give better responses to arguments, and if those who manage to give better responses differ from you in so far as they have read more books, or had more discussions.

Let me sum up the argument of this section. When we engage each other in conversation about what is the case – and, indeed, when we think about what is the case – we make various assumptions about both the norms that govern our beliefs and the capacities we possess as believers. We assume that there are norms governing what people ought to believe, and we assume that at least some people have the capacity to recognize these norms and respond to their recognition of them. These assumptions we make about people's capacities are in no way called into question by the possibility of determinism. Possession of such abilities requires nothing weird or transcendental of believers. Our reasons for believing that people have such abilities are more or less commonsensical.

2. RESPONSIBILITY FOR EVALUATIVE BELIEFS AND DESIRES

What does all of this have to do with giving an account of freedom in the arena of action and moral responsibility? As I see things, it has everything to do with it.[8]

The assumptions we make about the norms governing our beliefs, and about the capacities of believers, give us a picture of what it is to be a responsible believer, where responsibility presupposes certain abilities, abilities much like those traditionally associated with freedom. People ought to have certain beliefs, and because they have the capacity to recognize this fact and respond accordingly, we rightly hold them responsible for what they believe. We demand that such people believe what they should, and so rightly think well of them and praise them when they succeed – they might have failed, but to their credit they did not – and think less well of them and blame them when they fail – they could and should have believed otherwise: namely, rightly. If you accept the version of the dispositional theory of value I favour, then this story about responsibility for our beliefs is easily parlayed into a story about responsibility for our desires and actions as well.

According to the version of the dispositional theory I favour, facts about desirability are facts about the desires of our fully rational selves. More precisely, there is an analytic connection between the desirability of an agent's acting in a certain way in certain circumstances, and her desiring that she acts in that way in those circumstances if she were fully rational: that is, if she had the set of desires all agents would converge upon if, under the impact of increasing information, they came up with a maximally coherent and unified desire set. This theory has several important features.

First, the theory is non-relativist and rationalist. It is non-relativist and rationalist because facts about the desirability of our actions are facts about the reasons or justifications we have for performing them, where these reasons or justifications are reasons or justifications for all. The desirability of Bloggs's keeping his promise in certain circumstances C, for example, is a function of the fact that Bloggs would desire that he keeps his promise in C if he had the set of desires we would all converge upon if, under the impact of increasing information, we each came up with a maximally coherent and unified desire set. But if we would all converge upon the same set of desires, then the desirability of Bloggs's keeping his promise in C is not simply a fact about the desirability of his doing so relative to him. We too would desire that we keep our promise in circumstances C, so keeping our promise in C is the desirable thing for us to do in C as well. Reasons for one are thus reasons for all.

Note that the dispositional theory does not tell us anything yet about the content of our reasons. Thus it is so far consistent with the dispositional theory that if we had the set of desires we would all converge upon if we attempted to come up with a maximally coherent and unified desire set under the impact of increasing information, then we would all want ourselves to act on the same agent-neutral principles in all possible circumstances: maximize happiness and minimize suffering, say. But it is also consistent with the dispositional theory that we would all want ourselves to act on the same agent-relative principles: perhaps each of us would want ourselves to maximize our own happiness and minimize our own suffering, or, more radically and more implausibly, perhaps each of us would want ourselves to act on whichever beliefs and desires we happen to have in the circumstances of action that we face.[9] The substance of our reasons is thus a matter of discovery, according to the dispositional theory, a matter of finding out what we would all want if we had the set of . . .

A second important feature of the dispositional theory follows on as a consequence. If facts about desirability are facts about the desires of our fully rational selves then, since there are *facts* about desirability, evaluative claims turn out to be truth-assessable – that is, they purport to represent these facts – and so a proper object of belief. Thus, an agent who, say, believes that her ϕ-ing in certain circumstances C is desirable has a belief which is true just in case she would desire that she ϕs in C if she had the set of desires all agents would converge upon if, under the impact of increasing information, they came up with a maximally coherent and unified desire set, and which is false otherwise.

This is not, of course, to say that any of our evaluative beliefs are true. Perhaps there is some argument which decisively demonstrates that there are no desires that all agents would converge upon under conditions of full rationality, and so all such claims are false. I will return to this possibility towards the end. But that is neither here nor there with regard to the present point, which is that since evaluative claims are the proper object of belief, we therefore know what would be required for our evaluative beliefs to be true if any of them were true. The theory is thus a form of cognitivism.

A third feature of the theory is a consequence of the fact that it is cognitivist, non-relativist, and rationalist. The dispositional theory is internalist. Since so many people deny that this is so, and since it is so important to establish that it is so in order to see how the dispositional theory enables us to conceive of agents as both responsible and free in the arena of action, the point is worth dwelling on.

In "The Normativity of Instrumental Reason," Christine Korsgaard considers the idea that facts about the desirability of our actions are facts about the desires of our fully rational selves, but rejects it on the grounds that it violates the internalism requirement.[10] She argues that, properly interpreted, it amounts to the idea that the desirable actions, those we ought to perform, are the actions that our fully rational selves would perform. "The model suggests that the normativity of the *ought* expresses a demand that we should emulate more perfect rational beings (possibly including our own noumenal selves)."[11] She then goes on to argue, convincingly, that evaluative beliefs, so interpreted, do not satisfy the internalism requirement. "The model ... seems to invite the question: but suppose I don't care about being rational? What then?" However, the question is invited only because Korsgaard gives the idea that desirability is a matter of what our fully rational selves would want such an implausible interpretation. Let me first say why that interpretation is so implausible, and then say how the idea should be interpreted instead.

Suppose I suffer from an irrational fear of spiders, but there is a spider on the wall of my eight-year-old son's bedroom, a spider he is desperate for me to remove. I am frozen solid, utterly averse to the prospect of removing it. My feelings for him simply do not translate into a desire to do what he is desperate for me to do. Perhaps my fear causes me to be means-end irrational.[12] Now imagine I am told that my fully rational self, who doesn't suffer from an irrational fear of spiders at all and is thoroughly means-end rational, would simply pick up the spider in a tissue and remove it. Korsgaard's point – the point behind the question "But suppose I don't care about being rational? What then?" – is that this information might well quite rightly leave me completely cold. Though there are no grounds for faulting my fully rational self's desire about what he is to do in his circumstances – he is, after all, fully rational, and so perfectly placed to form desires that are beyond reproach – there is a real question as to the relevance of what he would do in his circumstances for what I am to do in mine. I am in circumstances in which I have to deal with my completely irrational fear. I have to deal with a breakdown of my means-end rationality. Aren't these relevant considerations in deciding what I should do? If so, then the actions of my fully rational self are irrelevant.

For this reason I agree with Korsgaard that we go wrong if we interpret the idea that facts about desirability are facts about the desires of our fully rational selves in the way that she suggests. There is an alternative and more plausible interpretation of the idea, however. On this more plausible interpretation the desirable thing for me to do in my circumstances is whatever my fully rational self would desire, not himself to do in his circumstances, but me to do in my actual circumstances. As I have put it elsewhere, the model is not one in which we are supposed to emulate the behaviour of our fully rational selves, or to treat their behaviour as an example we are to follow, but rather one in which we are supposed to think of our fully rational selves as perched above us, in a superior position to give us advice about what we are to do in our less than fully rational circumstances.[13]

This interpretation of the idea that facts about desirability are facts about the desires of our fully rational selves – the advice model rather than the example model – seems to me to be the natural one given the processes in which we engage when we try to figure out what we have a rational justification for doing. Imagine me wondering what I should do. I have a dread fear of spiders, but there I see my son, hysterical, and anxiously waiting for me to remove the cause of his panic. He is relying on me. I am being put to the test. What am I to do?

If an answer to this question doesn't spring to mind immediately then one thing that might well is an image of myself reflecting on this situation on some later occasion, an occasion on which I am able to get some distance from my fear and to reflect, in a cool, calm state of mind, on all that happened. What will I then wish myself to have done here and now? This kind of thought has at least prima-facie normative force. The idea behind the dispositional theory, interpreted in the way I have suggested, is simply to extend this standard way of answering the question "What should I do?" into a full-blown analysis. I should ask myself what I would want myself to do, here and now, with all my fears and foibles, not just on some later occasion on which I am able to get some distance from my fear, but in the possible world in which I have a maximally informed and coherent and unified set of desires. Presumably the answer will be that I would want myself to get the spider away from my son by one of the means available to me. Perhaps I should call for help, or if I am alone then perhaps I should just remove my son from the room and then try to chase the spider away, or perhaps I should do something else along these lines.[14]

Much as with the earlier interpretation, because the person whose desires I imagine is beyond rational reproach – he knows everything that is relevant, his desires have been arrived at by integrating mine into a systematic whole, and so on – I cannot fault his desires about what I am to do here and now in my actual circumstances. But because his desires concern my actual circumstances, and not his circumstances, I cannot rationally ignore his desires either.

In order to see this, compare two psychologies. One pairs the belief that acting in a certain way is what I would want myself to do in certain circumstances, if I had a maximally informed and coherent and unified set of desires, with a desire to act in that way. The other pairs that belief with indifference to acting in that way, or perhaps with an aversion to doing so. The former psychology seems clearly to exhibit more in the way of coherence or equilibrium than the latter. In the latter situation, my indifference or aversion indicates a failure to have a desire that is clearly rationally better, in my own terms, than the desire I have, and this failure constitutes, in and of itself, a sort of disequilibrium or incoherence in my psychology.

This means, in turn, that we can explain why rational people acquire desires that match those they believe their fully rational selves would have in terms of their disposition towards coherence. They do not just so happen to care about being coherent – something an equally rational creature may just so happen not to care about – rather, being rational is, *inter alia*, a matter of being disposed to restore coherence: the disposition towards coherence is partially constitutive of being rational, like the disposition to infer according to modus ponens.

The upshot is thus that when we interpret the idea that facts about desirability are facts about what our fully rational selves would want in the most natural way – that is, in terms of an advice model rather than an example model – evaluative beliefs do indeed satisfy the internalism requirement. Someone who believes that she would want that she φs in C if she had the desires all agents would converge upon if they had a maximally informed and coherent and unified set of desires either desires that she φs in C or else suffers from a sort of disequilibrium or incoherence in her psychology: agents thus desire what they believe desirable, in so far as they are rational.

We are now in a position to see how the dispositional theory enables us to conceive of agents as both free and responsible. Because the theory is cognitivist it follows that those with the capacity to recognize and respond to the norms that govern their evaluative beliefs are rightly thought well of for having evaluative beliefs that conform to these norms – they might have failed to have such beliefs but, to their credit, they succeeded – and they are rightly thought badly of for having beliefs that do not conform to these norms – they could and should have had beliefs that did. Moreover because the dispositional theory is rationalist and non-relativist, and because, as a result, it is also internalist, it follows that those with the capacity to restore and retain coherence in their overall psychology when they recognize the potential for incoherence or disequilibrium, even if perhaps only via stratagems of self-control, are rightly thought well of for desiring and acting in accordance with their evaluative beliefs – they could have failed but, to their credit, they succeeded – and they are rightly thought badly of for failing to desire and act in this way – they could and should have had such desires, and so performed such actions.[15]

It follows that people who satisfy two conditions are free and responsible in the arena of action. First, they must have the capacity to have the evaluative beliefs that they should have: that is, they must have the capacity to recognize and respond to the norms that govern evaluative beliefs, which are beliefs about the reasons or justifications that there are for acting. And second, they must have the capacity to have the desires that they should have: that is, they must have the capacity to restore and retain coherence in their overall psychology by acquiring desires that match their evaluative beliefs – that is, their beliefs about these reasons or justifications – when they notice the potential for disequilibrium or incoherence. Those whose actions are the product of these dual rational capacities act freely because it is up to them whether the beliefs and desires that cause their actions are the right beliefs and the right desires, and they are responsible for their actions because, equipped as they are with these dual capacities, they can therefore rightly be made to answer for their successes and for their failures.

3. SOME PUZZLE CASES

Equipped with this conception of freedom and responsibility we are in a position to make plausible judgements about freedom and responsibility in various otherwise puzzling cases. In order to illustrate this fact consider four such cases, all of them familiar from the free-will literature.

(i) *Brainwashed*

Brainwashed has been kidnapped by a group of political activists who brainwash her into believing that the most desirable thing she could do is kill the president. She emerges from the brainwashing procedure utterly convinced, but squeamish. Because she possesses incredible powers of self-control, however, she manages to acquire a desire to kill the president, and subsequently acts. Intuitively, it seems that we would not think that Brainwashed acts freely. We would not hold her responsible. But why not?

Cases of brainwashing provide a problem for those accounts of freedom and responsibility according to which agents act freely, and so are responsible for what they do, if their first-order desires and actions accord with their values, or if their first-order desires and actions accord with their desires about which of their first-order desires are to be effective in action.[16] They provide a problem because we may suppose that Brainwashed's first-order desires and actions do accord with her values, and we may suppose that they also accord with her desires about which of her first-order desires are to be effective in action. The effect of brainwashing is, after all, precisely to change, and render immune from revision, an agent's values; or, alternatively, brainwashing can be thought of as changing an agent's desires about which of her first-order desires are to be effective in action.[17] Cases of brainwashing provide no problem at all for the account of freedom and responsibility made available by the dispositional theory of value, however, because brainwashing evidently diminishes the capacity an agent has rationally to evaluate alternative hypotheses.

When Brainwashed acquires evidence that counts against the truth of the claim that killing the president is the most desirable thing to do, her having been brainwashed either causes her to ignore that evidence or to reinterpret it, or in some other way prevents the evidence from playing its proper cognitive role. We thus rightly deny that Brainwashed is free and responsible because we rightly deny that she could have believed otherwise than that it is most desirable to kill the president. In other words, Brainwashed's defect lies in the first of the two elements of a capacity for rational agency that we were forced to distinguish: her capacity to recognize and respond to the norms that govern belief.

Note that the political activists who kidnapped Brainwashed, and who are therefore like her in that they too believe that the most desirable thing for her to do is to kill the president, might well be quite unlike her in having arrived at their belief via the exercise of the capacity to form evaluative beliefs in the light of the norms that govern them. They might therefore be responsible for believing that the most desirable thing for Brainwashed to do is kill the president, and they might be responsible for the actions they perform because of the fact that they hold this belief. Thus, in kidnapping and brainwashing Brainwashed they might well do something for which they are properly held responsible. But if their belief is false, and if they should have realized this to be so – possessing as they do the capacity to evaluate beliefs in light of the norms that govern them – then they would properly be held responsible for getting their beliefs so badly wrong. We would blame them, and rightly so.

(ii) *Kleptomaniac*

Kleptomaniac has a compulsive desire to steal groceries. Whenever he goes to the supermarket he therefore finds himself concealing items and bringing them home without paying for them. He does not believe that this is in any sense a desirable thing to do. Indeed, he thinks that it is completely irrational behaviour. He believes that the desirable thing for him to do in his circumstances is to avoid the supermarket altogether and get someone else to buy his groceries on his behalf. None the less he regularly finds himself at the supermarket, stealing groceries. Intuitively, we would not think that Kleptomaniac steals groceries freely. We would not hold him responsible. But why not?

Cases of compulsion provide a problem for those accounts of freedom and responsibility according to which agents act freely, and so are responsible for what they do, if they would have done otherwise if they had so chosen or desired.[18] Perhaps Kleptomaniac would not have stolen if he had chosen or desired not to do so. But this is evidently quite irrelevant. The problem with Kleptomaniac is precisely that he could not have chosen or desired to do otherwise.[19] Cases of compulsion provide no problem at all for the account of freedom and responsibility made available by the dispositional theory of value, however.

What is the effect of Kleptomaniac's compulsion? His compulsion ensures that his belief that it is not desirable to steal plays no role at all in the genesis of his actions because it ensures that no technique of self-control available to him enables him to resist his desire. We are thus led to deny that Kleptomaniac could have desired or done otherwise than steal, and so quite properly deny that he is either free or responsible. In other words, Kleptomaniac's defect lies in the second of the two elements of a capacity for rational agency that we were forced to distinguish: his capacity to restore coherence in his overall psychology by acquiring desires that match his evaluative beliefs when he notices the potential for disequilibrium or incoherence. In more everyday terms, Kleptomaniac has no self-control, and so could not have done otherwise.

(iii) Pre-emptive Agent

Black wants Pre-emptive Agent to move his hand, but he doesn't want to interfere unnecessarily.[20] He therefore waits until Pre-emptive Agent is about to decide whether or not to move his hand and then, if he judges that Pre-emptive Agent is going to move his hand – Black is an excellent judge of such things – he does nothing. If he judges that Pre-emptive Agent is not going to move his hand, however, he has things so arranged that Pre-emptive Agent will decide, and do, just that. This is because Black, a mad scientist, has implanted an appropriate device in Pre-emptive Agent's brain, a device that is under his control and which will trigger the required decision in Pre-emptive Agent if needs be. As it happens, Pre-emptive Agent decides to move his hand and does so. Intuitively, we would think that Pre-emptive Agent moves his hand freely. We would hold him responsible for moving his hand. But why?

Cases in which agents act, thereby pre-empting a standby causal process that would have caused them to do just what they did if they hadn't already decided to do so for themselves, provide a problem for all accounts of freedom and responsibility according to which agents act freely, and so are responsible for what they do, just in case they could have done otherwise than what they in fact did.[21] If Black had foreseen that Pre-emptive Agent was going to decide to leave his hand at rest then he would have set in train the causal process that would have caused the device to cause him to decide to move his hand. In a relatively straightforward sense, then, Pre-emptive Agent could not have done otherwise than move his hand.[22] Cases of pre-emptive causation provide no problem at all for the account of freedom and responsibility that emerges if we accept a dispositional theory of value, however.

In order to see why this is so it will help if we first consider a rather different sort of case. Mark Johnston describes a shy but powerfully in-tuitive chameleon.[23] This is a chameleon that is green in the dark but which, when it intuits that it is about to be put into a viewing condition, instantaneously blushes bright red. Though it is green in the dark, if it were to be viewed it would thus look red. Does the case of the shy but powerfully intuitive chameleon show that there is something wrong in principle with the idea that something is a certain colour just in case it has a disposition to look that colour in standard viewing conditions?

The answer is that it does not. Rather, as Johnston points out, it sim-ply shows that a dispositionalist about colour needs to remember two things. First, the dispositions of an object that interest us are constituted dispositions: in each case there is an intrinsic property the objects possess which causes the manifestation of the disposition in the appropriate view-ing condition. And second, because the dispositions that interest us are constituted dispositions, it follows that they may therefore be "masked," as Johnston puts it, either by other properties that the object possesses, or by properties possessed by other objects in its environment.

How can the dispositionalist characterize the dispositions that interest us? The dispositionalist can characterize them in terms of conditionals that abstract away from the effects of masking. He thus needs to distinguish those cases in which an object has no intrinsic property sufficient to underwrite the conditionals that interest us, from those in which it does have such an intrinsic property, but there is also some other property possessed by the object, or by another object in its environment, and

101

this pair of properties underwrites a conditional that doesn't interest us. Because a disposition to look green is constituted by intrinsic properties of the surface of the chameleon, and because its shyness and intuitiveness are not constituted by intrinsic properties of its surface, it follows that we can abstract away from the latter in considering the former. The chameleon is then green because, roughly, it has an intrinsic property, and this intrinsic property is sufficient to underwrite its looking green if viewed, at least in worlds in which it doesn't have the intrinsic properties that underwrite its being shy and intuitive as regards the presence of a viewer.

Let's now return to the case of Pre-emptive Agent. I have suggested that people whose actions are the product of two rational capacities act freely and responsibly. First, their actions must be the product of their capacity to have the evaluative beliefs that they should have – such people must therefore have the capacity to recognize and respond to the norms that govern beliefs – and, second, their actions must be the product of their capacity to have the desires that they should have – such people must therefore have the capacity to restore and retain coherence in their overall psychology by acquiring desires that match their evaluative beliefs when they notice the potential for disequilibrium or incoherence. In determining whether or not people's actions are the product of these dual capacities we will certainly be interested in the various counterfactuals that are true of them. But as the case of the shy but powerfully intuitive chameleon reminds us, in constructing such counterfactuals we must be careful to weed out the effects of masking.

When we weed out the effects of masking it seems quite clear that Pre-emptive Agent's moving his hand is the product of these dual rational capacities. His action is the product of these dual rational capacities because, abstracting away from the presence of Black, he instantiates the right pattern of counterfactuals. Holding fixed his belief that it is desirable to move his arm, he would have exercised self-control if he had desired to act otherwise, and if he had believed it desirable to perform a different act, he would have desired and acted differently. Of course, in evaluating the truth of this last counterfactual we abstract away from the presence of Black, but we are entitled to do so in figuring out whether Pre-emptive Agent's moving his hand is the product of his dual rational capacities. We are entitled to do so because Black's presence does not, as such, undermine Pre-emptive Agent's possession of these capacities. Pre-emptive Agent does not stop being a rational agent in virtue of Black's presence. His intrinsic properties, those that ground his dual rational capacities, are in no way affected by Black's presence. Black's presence simply ensures that if certain actions are not the product of Pre-emptive Agent's dual capacities for rational agency, then they will happen anyway, despite Pre-emptive Agent's possession of these dual rational capacities. In this respect, Black's presence is much like Johnston's chameleon's intuitiveness and shyness. Pre-emptive Agent is thus free and responsible because, abstracting away from Black's presence, he could have done otherwise.

(iv) *Willingly Addicted*

Willingly Addicted has a desire for heroin so strong that no technique of self-control would enable him to resist. Willingly Addicted knows this, but doesn't care less. He has thought things through and decided, quite independently of his addiction, that the most desirable thing for him to do is to inject himself with heroin. Does Willingly Addicted take heroin freely? Is he responsible for what he does?

The answer is that he does take heroin freely and that he is responsible. This is because Willingly Addicted's addiction is just like Black's disposition to interfere with Pre-emptive Agent should he not do what he wants him to.[24] Just as the mere fact of Black's presence, with his disposition to interfere with Pre-emptive Agent, does not cause any relevant change in Pre-emptive Agent's intrinsic nature, and so does nothing to change the fact that in Black's presence – provided, of course, that Black does not cause any change in Pre-emptive Agent's desires – Pre-emptive Agent manifests the same dual rational capacities required for free and responsible action that he manifests in Black's absence, so Willingly Addicted's addiction need not itself be thought of as causing any change in the relevant aspects of Willingly Addicted's intrinsic nature, and so need not be thought of as changing the fact that when addicted – provided the addiction does not cause any change in Willingly Addicted's desires – Willingly Addicted manifests the same dual rational capacities required for free and responsible action that he manifests in the absence of his addiction.

Now this might seem wrong, on the face of it. Willingly Addicted is, after all, *addicted*. While we can go along with the stipulation that his addiction has no effect on his capacity to reflect critically on the relative merits of alternative courses of action, surely we cannot suppose that it has no effect on his capacity to desire what he believes desirable. We cannot seriously suppose that Willingly Addicted retains the same capacity to desire what is desirable that he had in the absence of his addiction, because the fact that he will desire to take heroin no matter what he believes desirable shows that he is out of control, in this respect. But if Willingly Addicted is out of control, then doesn't it follow that he lacks one of the capacities required for free and responsible action: namely, the capacity for self-control?

The answer is that Willingly Addicted needn't be thought of as being out of control because, despite his addiction, his psychology can retain aspects of the tendency towards overall coherence that it had in the absence of his addiction. Suppose, then, that Willingly Addicted acquires the desire to take heroin because, once he acquires the belief that it is desirable to take heroin, the desire to take heroin is produced in him by the tendency of his psychology towards overall coherence. We can then think of his taking heroin as pre-emptively caused by the desire to take heroin that is caused in him by his rational tendency, not by a desire that is caused in him by his addiction. His taking heroin manifests a rational tendency, not an addictive desire.

When we think of Willingly Addicted in this way his addiction looks, for all the world, just like Black's disposition to interfere with Pre-emptive Agent. It is a standby cause, a cause which has no effects of its own in the circumstances. Thus, just as in evaluating whether Pre-emptive Agent possessed the requisite capacity for self-control required for free and responsible agency we need to establish the truth of various counterfactuals which abstracted away from Black's presence, so in evaluating whether Willingly Addicted possesses the requisite capacity for self-control required for free and responsible agency we need to establish the truth of various counterfactuals which abstract away from the fact that he is addicted. We need to ask whether Willingly Addicted would have desired not to take heroin, if he had believed it desirable not to do so, and in evaluating this counterfactual we must abstract away from the fact that Willingly Addicted is addicted. If the answer is "yes," then Willingly Addicted acts freely and responsibly when he takes heroin.

The lesson to draw from our discussion of these four examples is clear enough. The dispositional theory of value makes the possession of the dual capacities to have the right evaluative beliefs and the right desires crucially relevant to the assessment of agents as free and responsible. As our discussion of the four examples makes plain, these dual capacities are indeed crucially relevant to the assessment of agents as free and responsible in just the way the dispositional theory insists they are. The dispositional theory's elegant handling of these otherwise puzzling cases thus provides an indirect argument for the theory.

In this final section, I want to compare the account of freedom and responsibility made available by the dispositional theory of value with perhaps its main competitor, the account of freedom and responsibility developed by Harry Frankfurt.[25] In drawing out the similarities and the differences between the two accounts we will see not just how compelling the account of freedom and responsibility sketched here really is, but also how radical it is as well.

According to Frankfurt, to be capable of willing a creature needs only to be able to act on its first-order desires. All sorts of creatures are therefore capable of willing, including many non-human animals. Willing as such is thus not a phenomenon about which interesting questions of freedom can arise because the first-order desires a creature has may simply be the product of its environment. There may be no further feature such desires have that picks them out as desires which are such that, when a creature acts upon them, it is free in the special sense in which we suppose ourselves to be free.

Because we humans are capable of reflection, however, Frankfurt thinks that some of our first-order desires can have such a feature. We can act on first-order desires that answer, in an important way, to our reflective nature. We can step back and reflect on our wills and ask ourselves whether we have the wills we want, where such reflection is supposed to result in our having higher-order desires about which of our first-order desires are to be effective in action. When the effective first-order desires an agent has are those he wants, at the higher-order level, Frankfurt tells us that the agent identifies with his will, and when an agent acts on the basis of desire with which he identifies, Frankfurt tells us that he can be said to act freely. He acts freely because he acts on the basis of the will he wants. This is the special sense in which we suppose ourselves to be free.

As Frankfurt points out, his theory is a version of compatibilism. It is a version of compatibilism because an agent may have the will he has because of causal forces beyond his control: the effects of his socialization and enculturation, say. But even if he does he may none the less act freely, according to Frankfurt, because he can make that will his own by identifying himself with it. This will be the case if, when he reflects, the agent comes up with a higher-order desire to have just those desires effective in action, and if in addition no further reflection would lead him to revise his higher-order desire. Agents who act freely are therefore responsible for what they do. They are responsible because in making

105

their wills their own, they have made the actions that are the product of their wills their own as well.

There are many similarities between Frankfurt's view of freedom and responsibility in terms of higher-order identification and the idea of freedom and responsibility sketched here. According to both theories, the mere fact that an agent is able to act on the basis of her first-order desires tells us nothing about whether or not she acts freely or is responsible. According to both theories, whether or not an agent is free and responsible when she acts depends on whether her first-order desires answer, in a certain way, to her reflective nature.

There is, however, at least one crucial difference between Frankfurt's view of freedom and responsibility in terms of higher-order identification and the idea of freedom and responsibility sketched here. Whereas Frankfurt thinks that when an agent reflects, what that pattern of reflection causes in her is simply a further, higher-order, desire about which first-order desire is to be effective in the circumstances of action that she faces, according to the view of freedom and responsibility sketched here when an agent reflects what that pattern of reflection causes in her is an evaluative belief: that is, a belief about what she would want herself to do in the circumstances of action she faces if she had the set of desires all agents would converge upon if, under the impact of increasing information, they came to have a maximally coherent and unified desire set.

So much for the similarities and differences. Which theory of freedom and responsibility is more plausible? Popular though it is, it seems to me that Frankfurt's theory faces a formidable problem, and that the problem it faces can only be solved if we reject it and adopt instead the conception of freedom and responsibility made available by the dispositional theory. On the one hand, Frankfurt concedes that an agent who has a first-order desire to ϕ, and who acts on the basis of that desire, may or may not be acting freely. Merely desiring to ϕ, then, and acting on the basis of that desire, is insufficient to make that action the agent's own because the desire on which the agent acts may be one that he was caused to have by forces beyond his control, by the forces of socialization and enculturation or whatever. First-order desires thus stand in need of vindication in order for an agent to act freely when he acts on their basis. But, on the other hand, he then goes on to claim that what does the vindicating is simply another desire, a desire whose special status that equips it for its role as vindicator is that it is *higher order* and *formed on the basis of reflection*. But, as I will now argue, a desire's being higher order is irrelevant, and unless we give reflection the gloss suggested by the dispositional theory of value – a gloss Frankfurt evidently didn't intend – a desire's being formed on the basis of reflection is irrelevant as well. Neither of Frankfurt's conditions, neither severally nor jointly, is sufficient to equip a desire for its role as a vindicator of our first-order desires.

Consider a desire's being higher order first. Might it be this feature of a desire that enables it to vindicate a lower-order desire? Gary Watson points out that merely being higher order doesn't confer any special status on a desire that would make it an appropriate vehicle of vindication.[26] An agent who desires to ϕ, and who also desires not to desire to ϕ, is indeed someone who has at least one desire from which she will be alienated in some way. However it isn't obvious why the desire from which she should be alienated is the first-order rather than the second-order. It therefore isn't obvious why the second-order desire is the appropriate vehicle of vindication. Merely being higher order, then, is nothing special about a desire.

In that case, might it be the fact that a desire, even a first-order desire, has been formed on the basis of reflection that confers its special status upon it? Reflection can confer a special status on a desire only if the desire so formed is special relative to that reflective process. But the only way in which desires could be special relative to a reflective process is if, on the basis of such reflection, agents would all converge on the very same desires, or so it seems to me. Reflection thus confers a special status on desires only if "reflection" is given a rationalistic gloss, a gloss Frankfurt evidently did not intend.

In order to see that being formed on the basis of reflection confers a special status on a desire only if "reflection" is given a rationalistic gloss, suppose for a moment that we don't give "reflection" this gloss. We will then need to invoke something other than reflection in order to explain why agents end up with the different desires they end up with when they reflect. If we are anti-rationalists, what we will invoke is, of course, our non-rational nature.[27] According to anti-rationalists, the desires agents end up with after reflection are a function of the desires they actually have to begin with, the desires they were caused to have by the forces of socialization and enculturation that made them what they are. Once we see that this is so, however, the difficulty involved in supposing that the desires we form on the basis of reflection could vindicate our first-order desires becomes manifest.

First-order desires stand in need of vindication, you will recall, because they may simply be caused in us by forces that are beyond our control. We are thus trying to find a special feature of our first-order desires, a feature *other than* having been caused by forces beyond our control, that will vindicate them. But on the anti-rationalist's picture the desires we form on the basis of reflection themselves contain traces of just these sorts of causal forces. The desires one agent ends up with after reflection differ from those another agent ends up with because of the different causal forces to which they were subject in their pre–reflective state, the differences in their socialization and enculturation. If we give "reflection" an anti-rationalistic gloss, then, having been formed on the basis of reflection is not a special feature of our desires, because it is not a feature that picks out desires that are *different enough* from those that have been caused in us by forces beyond our control.

Not so if we give "reflection" a rationalistic gloss, however. The idea is then that reflection would lead us all to converge on the very same desires – or at any rate, that is what we suppose – because when we reflect we try to form beliefs about which acts it is desirable to perform in various circumstances, and what we believe when we believe that it is desirable to perform a certain act in certain circumstances is that we would all converge upon a desire that we act in that way in those circumstances if we attempted to come up with a maximally coherent and unified desire set under the impact of increasing information, and, when we form such a belief, provided we are rational, the belief we form will cause in us a corresponding desire.

It is therefore possible for the desires we form on the basis of reflection to be maximally different from those formed in us by the forces of socialization and enculturation because nothing but our natures as rational creatures is required to explain why we have them. At the limit, rational agents, provided they form their evaluative beliefs in the light of their capacity to have the beliefs they should have, and provided they form desires in the light of their capacity to have the desires they should have, will all end up with the same desires, provided they face the very same circumstances. It is irrelevant which desires we were caused to have by the forces of socialization and enculturation because these are transcended by our powers of rational reflection. Or so we suppose.

The failure of Frankfurt's theory of freedom thus leads us naturally to embrace the view of freedom and responsibility sketched here, the theory that emerges naturally once we accept a version of the dispositional theory of value that is non–relativist, rationalist, cognitivist, and internalist. Importantly, however, note that though the theory tells us that desires that are formed by the forces of socialization and enculturation are inappropriate vehicles of vindication, it may well be the case that, if we attempted to come up with a maximally coherent and unified desire set under the impact of increasing information, we would all converge upon a desire that we act in accordance with the desires that have been formed in us by the cultural or social practices in whose midst we find ourselves. The rationalistic conception of the self forced upon us by the dispositional theory is consistent with the idea that these culturally and socially formed desires do have rational significance.[28] It simply insists that what makes them have such significance is the fact that we would all converge upon a desire that we act in accordance with them if we were to . . .

5. CONCLUSION

If what I have said here is along the right lines then it seems to me that there needs to be a crucial shift in our thinking about freedom and responsibility. Let me conclude by saying a little about this shift.

The standard view, following Kant, has been that freedom is a kind of *autonomy*: that is, in Kant's words, freedom is "the property which will has of being a law to itself."[29] But, if I am right, freedom is not a matter of autonomy, not a matter of being a law unto oneself, but rather of *orthonomy*, a matter of having the capacity to be ruled by the right as opposed to the wrong.[30] This is because we are free and responsible to the extent that our actions are the product of our capacity for rational agency, and that in turn requires first, that we are able to have the right as opposed to the wrong beliefs about what it is desirable to do, and second, that we are able to have the right as opposed to the wrong desires.

This shift in our thinking about freedom and responsibility should be welcomed, I think, because it forces us to face up to the difficult questions we ought to be facing up to in deciding questions of moral responsibility. If people act in ways we deem wrong because they have very different evaluative beliefs from those that we have then we have to ask whether they could reasonably have been expected to believe otherwise, and if people act in ways we deem wrong because, despite the fact that they share our evaluative beliefs, they have desires that fail to match these evaluative beliefs, then we have to ask whether they could reasonably have been expected to exercise the requisite powers of rational self-control. In many cases it will be difficult to answer these questions.[31] But, if I am right, it is only by answering these questions that we will know whether or not the people involved are really free and responsible.

It should be noted, however, that this shift in our thinking about freedom and moral responsibility comes at a price. For though I have argued that our concept of freedom presupposes a rationalistic conception of ourselves, I have not argued that that self-conception will survive critical scrutiny in the light of the empirical facts. Thus, for example, for all I have said here it may well be the case that if normative ethics progresses but without making any significant impact on the deep-seated disagreements that exist in the community on evaluative matters, then we will, for good reasons, come to lose our conviction that we would all converge on a single set of desires if we attempted to come up with a maximally coherent and unified desire set under the impact of increasing information. If what I have said here is right, then coming to this conclusion may be tantamount to coming to believe that there are no values, and coming to that conclusion would be tantamount to coming to believe that we have no capacity to form the right evaluative beliefs. It would be tantamount to coming to believe that freedom and responsibility are an *illusion*.

Having said that I should add that I do not myself believe that we should draw this conclusion, but I well recognize that nothing I have said here tells against doing so.[32] Nor should this be thought a flaw in my argument, for my interests in this essay have been wholly conceptual. I have been concerned to spell out what our concepts of freedom and responsibility are. Whether or not we are in fact free and responsible, and the extent to which we are free and responsible if we are, is another question, one which needs to be addressed in its own terms. As these final remarks perhaps make clear, however, it seems to me that the answer to this question will be decided by engaging in substantive debate on normative matters and seeing whether such debates leave our commitment to non-relative evaluative facts, and the rationalistic conception of the self with its dual rational capacities, intact. Whether our concepts of freedom, responsibility, and value stand or fall, they do so together.[33]

NOTES

1. See Michael Smith, "Dispositional Theories of Value," *Proceedings of the Aristotelian Society*, suppl. 63 (1989), 89–111; "Realism," in Peter Singer (ed.), *A Companion to Ethics* (Oxford: Blackwell, 1991), 399–410; "Valuing, Desiring or Believing?," in David Charles and Kathleen Lennon, eds., *Reduction, Explanation, Realism* (Oxford: Oxford University Press, 1992), 323–60; *The Moral Problem* (Oxford: Blackwell, 1994); "Internal Reasons," *Philosophy and Phenomenological Research*, 55 (1995), 109–31; "Internalism's Wheel," *Ratio*, 8 (1995), 277–302.
2. See Harry Frankfurt, "Freedom of the Will and the Concept of a Person," repr. in Gary Watson, ed., *Free Will* (Oxford: Oxford University Press, 1982), 81–95, and "Identification and Wholeheartedness," repr. in Frankfurt, *The Importance of What We Care About: Philosophical Essays* (Cambridge: Cambridge University Press, 1988), 159–76.

3. In this section I repeat a line of argument that first appeared in the second section of Philip Pettit and Michael Smith, "Freedom in Belief and Desire," *Journal of Philosophy*, 93 (1996), 429–49.

4. See also Philip Pettit, *The Common Mind* (Oxford: Oxford University Press, 1993).

5. Peter van Inwagen, "The Incompatibility of Free Will and Determinism," repr. in Watson, ed., *Free Will*, 46–58.

6. See esp. David Lewis, "Counterfactual Dependence and Time's Arrow," repr. in his *Philosophical Papers*, ii (Oxford: Oxford University Press, 1986), 32–52.

7. David Lewis, "Are We Free to Break the Laws?," repr. in his *Philosophical Papers*, ii, 291–8.

8. Pettit and Smith, "Freedom in Belief and Desire," 440–9.

9. Why do I say that this is implausible? Because if I were caused by a drug pusher to desire heroin, or by an evil scientist to desire to eat dirt, or by someone else to perform some other activity that I deem utterly worthless and as having no rational justification at all, then, according to the suggestion just made in the text, the very fact that I come to have such a desire makes it desirable to act upon it. The acquisition of the desire provides the rational justification. I cannot imagine why anyone would believe this to be so. The mere fact that I have a desire, particularly one caused in the manner described, does not seem to me to have any normative significance at all. The important point, however, is that its being so is not ruled out, so far, by the dispositional theory of value. The dispositional theory tells us that whether it is or isn't so depends on whether, if we were fully rational, we would want ourselves to act on whatever beliefs and desires we happen to have. This is a matter that can be decided in a decisive way only after critical reflection and argument.

10. Christine M. Karsgaard, "The Normativity of Instrumental Reason," in Garrett Cullity and Berys Gaut, eds., *Ethics and Practical Reason* (Oxford: Oxford University Press, 1997) 239–46.

11. Ibid. 240.

12. For an explanation and discussion of this idea see Philip Pettit and Michael Smith, "Brandt on Self-Control," in Brad Hooker, ed., *Rationality, Rules and Utility* (Boulder, CO: Westview Press, 1993), 33–50; Jeanette Kennett and Michael Smith, "Frog and Toad Lose Control," *Analysis*, 56 (1996), 63–73.

13. See also Smith, "Internal Reasons," sect. 1; "Normative Reasons and Full Rationality, Reply to Swanton," *Analysis*, 56 (1996), 160–8. A similar distinction is made by Peter Railton when he attempts to analyse the concept of an individual's good in his "Moral Realism," *Philosophical Review*, 95 (1986), 163–207.

14. Now we can see why my fully rational self's actions are irrelevant as regards what I should do in my circumstances. Whereas I am in circumstances in which the options that are available to me are determined by my irrationality, my fully rational self is evidently never in such circumstances. For further discussion of this point, see Pettit and Smith, "Brandt on Self-Control."

15. Various techniques of self-control are discussed in Philip Pettit and Michael Smith, "Practical Unreason," *Mind*, 102 (1993), 53–79; Pettit and Smith, "Brandt on Self-Control"; and Kennett and Smith, "Frog and Toad Lose Control."

16. Gary Watson makes a suggestion of the first kind in "Free Agency," repr. in Watson, ed., *Free Will*, 96–110; Harry Frankfurt makes a suggestion of the second kind in "Freedom of the Will and the Concept of a Person."

17. Gary Watson, "Introduction," in Watson, ed., *Free Will*, 7 n. 9; Susan Wolf, *Freedom Within Reason* (Oxford: Oxford University Press, 1990), 23–45.

18. A. J. Ayer, "Freedom and Necessity," repr. in Watson, ed., *Free Will*, 15–23; Bruce Aune, "Hypotheticals and 'Can,' Another Look," repr. in Watson, ed., *Free Will*, 36–41.

19. Roderick Chisholm, "Human Freedom and the Self," repr. in Watson, ed., *Free Will*, 24–35; Keith Lehrer, "Cans Without Ifs," repr. in Watson (ed.), *Free Will*, 41–5.

20. This example comes from Frankfurt, "Alternate Possibilities and Moral Responsibility," repr. in Frankfurt, *The Importance of What We Care About, Philosophical Essays*, 1–10.

21. G. E. Moore, *Ethics* (Oxford: Oxford, University Press, 1966); Ayer, "Freedom and Necessity"; van Inwagen, "The Incompatibility of Free Will and Determinism."

22. This is the main point Frankfurt makes in "Alternate Possibilities and Moral Responsibility." My aim here is, *inter alia*, to say why Frankfurt is wrong.

23. Mark Johnston, "Objectivity Refigured, Pragmatism Without Verificationism," in John Haldane and Crispin Wright, eds., *Reality, Representation and Projection* (Oxford: Oxford University Press, 1994), 85–130.

24. See e.g. Frankfurt, "Freedom of the Will and the Concept of a Person." I am grateful to Jay Wallace and David Aman for conversations about the argument in this section.

25. "Freedom of the Will and the Concept of a Person" and "Identification and Wholeheartedness."

26. Watson, "Free Agency," 107–9.

27. This seems to be Bernard William's view in "Internal and External Reasons," repr. in Williams, *Moral Luck* (Cambridge: Cambridge University Press, 1981), 101–13. Contrast this with the view in Smith, *The Moral Problem*, 164–74.

28. Here I echo the point I made in note 9. Much as I said then, note that it would be implausible to suppose that we would all converge upon a desire to act in accordance with whatever desires happened to be caused in us by whatever cultural and social practices in the midst of which we find ourselves. It is easy enough to imagine cultural and social practices that cause us to desire to do things which are utterly worthless, so having no redeeming features whatsoever. Though consistent with assigning rational significance to the desires formed in us by social and cultural practices, the rationalistic conception of the self thus offers a critical perspective on the products of these practices as well.

29. H. J. Paton, *The Moral Law* (London: Hutchinson, 1948), 101.

30. The idea of orthonomy was first introduced in Philip Pettit and Michael Smith, "Backgrounding Desire," *Philosophical Review*, 99 (1990), 565–92. The idea is elaborated in Pettit and Smith, "Practical Unreason" and "Freedom in Belief and Desire."

31. See, e.g., Gary Watson's illuminating discussion of thrill-killer Robert Harris in his "Responsibility and the Limits of Evil," in Ferdinand Schoeman, ed.,

Responsibility, Character and the Emotions: New Essays in Moral Psychology (Cambridge: Cambridge University Press, 1987), 256–86. An insightful discussion of various allocations of moral responsibility along lines similar to those suggested here can be found in Jeanette Kennett's *Agency and Responsibility: A Commonsense Moral Psychology* (Oxford: Oxford University Press, 2001).

32. But see Smith, *The Moral Problem*, 187–9; "Internalism's Wheel," 299–302.

33. An earlier version of this chapter was read under the title, "Freedom, Reason and the Analysis of Value," at a conference on Ethics and Practical Reason held at The University, St. Andrews, in 1995. I would like to thank Garrett Cullity, my commentator on that occasion, for his helpful response. It was also read to audiences at the Australian National University and Monash University. Robert Audi, David Braddon-Mitchell, Richard Holton, Brad Hooker, Lloyd Humberstone, Frank Jackson, Jeanette Kennett, Christine Korsgaard, Rae Langton, John O'Leary-Hawthorne, Philip Pettit, Peter Railton, John Skorupski, David Velleman, Jay Wallace, and Susan Wolf all gave me very useful comments. Finally, thanks to Garrett Cullity and Berys Gaut for a separate set of comments which they made as editors of the volume in which it was originally published.

6

Rational Capacities, or: How to Distinguish Recklessness, Weakness, and Compulsion

In "Skepticism about Weakness of Will," Gary Watson invites us to consider the distinction between recklessness, weakness, and compulsion.

> Suppose that a particular woman intentionally takes a drink. To provide an evaluative context, suppose she ought not to have another because she will then be unfit to fulfill some of her obligations. Preanalytically, most of us would insist on the possibility and significance of the following three descriptions of the case. (1) the reckless or self-indulgent case; (2) the weak case; and (3) the compulsive case. In (1), the woman knows what she is doing but accepts the consequences. Her choice is to get drunk or risk getting drunk. She acts in accordance with her judgement. In (2) the woman knowingly takes the drink contrary to her (conscious) better judgement; the explanation for this lack of self-control is that she is weak-willed. In (3), she knowingly takes the drink contrary to her better judgement, but she is the victim of a compulsive (irresistible) desire to drink. (Watson 1977: 324)

These three different ways of filling out the case are in turn important, Watson tells us, because they purport to legitimize the very different moral reactions that we have to the three cases.

We blame the woman who is reckless or self-indulgent, and what we blame her for is having the wrong belief about what she should do in the circumstances of action that she faces. She believes that the value associated with having another drink makes it worthwhile for her to risk being unable to fulfill some of her obligations, whereas we disagree. Though Watson doesn't say this, it is thus important that we blame her just to the extent that she could have believed otherwise than that she should have another drink in the light of that evidence. It would be totally inappropriate if she lacked the capacity to evaluate such evidence, or if, though she possesses this capacity, her belief was the product of (say) self-hatred which she could neither acknowledge nor get rid of. When we blame the woman who is weak, by contrast, we blame her not for her belief – she has the belief that she should have, after all – but rather for her failure to act on that belief. Blaming her is appropriate to the extent that she could instead have exercised self-control and desired otherwise. It would be totally inappropriate if she was unable to exercise self-control. This is why we don't blame the woman who is compelled. Given that she has the belief that she should have, she succeeds to the extent that she can. Being compelled, she could not have exercised self-control and desired otherwise, and so blame for that is inappropriate.

The important point on which I wish to focus in what follows is the point that has just emerged. In giving our accounts of the nature of recklessness, weakness, and compulsion, and the way in which each of these in turn legitimizes our different moral reactions, we have had to assume the truth of various "could" claims. We suppose that the reckless woman *could* have had the right belief about what she should do, the belief that she shouldn't have another drink; we suppose that the weak woman *could* have acted in accordance with her belief that she shouldn't have another drink; and we suppose that the compulsive woman *could not* have acted in accordance with her belief that she shouldn't have another drink. But what do these various "could" claims mean? This question turns out to be exceedingly difficult to answer. My suggestion will be that the "could" claims that we assume to be true (or false) when we describe someone as reckless, or weak, or compelled, all mean much the same thing. Specifically, they all signify the presence (or absence) of a rational capacity which we take to explain the relevant behaviour. The difficult task is to say what, precisely, makes it the case that someone has (or lacks) such a rational capacity.

To anticipate, the account I go on to offer of rational capacities is in much the same ballpark as earlier accounts (see, for example, Wolf 1990; Wallace 1994; Kennett and Smith 1994, 1996; Pettit and Smith 1996; Smith 1997a; Fischer and Ravizza 1998). The novelty of the present account lies in part in the explicit suggestion that the "could" required for responsibility in such cases can be elucidated in terms of the possibility of exercising such a rational capacity. Here there is a striking contrast with, say, Wallace's (1994) account of the capacity for reflective self-control, and Fischer and Ravizza's (1998) account of reasons responsiveness. For, under the influence of Harry Frankfurt (1969), these theorists have denied that the relevant notion of "could" can be elucidated in such terms (see

Watson 2001 for an expression of skepticism about this). The novelty also lies in part in the fact that I explicitly connect the difficulty involved in giving such an elucidation of the notion of "could" with the issue in metaphysics about finkish dispositions (Martin 1994; Lewis 1997).

The paper divides into two main sections. In the first I focus on the case of recklessness. In this section I give an account of what it means to say that someone has the capacity to have beliefs other than those she has, and how her failure to exercise that capacity might explain her having the beliefs she has. In the second section the focus shifts to the cases of weakness and compulsion. In this section I give an account of what it means to say that someone has the capacity to have desires other than those she has, and how her failure to exercise that capacity, if she has it, or her lack of that capacity, if she lacks it, might explain her having the desires that she has.

1. RATIONAL CAPACITIES AND BELIEF

Let's begin by considering a purely cognitive case. Let's suppose that John is in the middle of a complicated philosophical argument with someone when she asks him a crucial question to which he doesn't have an answer. Let's assume that there is an answer, one which supports the line of argument that John has been defending. He thinks the question through carefully, but he doesn't think of the answer at the time. However, later on that night he comes to realize what the answer to the question is. As with Watson's example of the woman who takes a drink, it seems that we can fill out this story in various different ways. Let me focus on just two for the moment.

In the first, what John does when he gets home is read some papers about the topic he had been discussing. Perhaps he hasn't read these papers before, but he has good reason to believe that they will address the question he was asked by his interlocutor. While reading through these papers he learns what the answer to the question he was asked is. The answer is complicated, but he comes to appreciate it by reading the article. He has the "Now I see!" experience. He feels relief that what he was saying was defensible, albeit, as he now admits, that he wasn't able to see how it was to be defended at the time.

When we fill out the story in this way it seems that, in one perfectly ordinary sense of "could," we do not suppose that John could have thought of the answer to the question he was asked at the time he was asked. Rather we admit that making moves in philosophical discussions requires that you have a relevant base of knowledge to begin with, and, by hypothesis, we acknowledge that John did not have the relevant base of knowledge at the time at which he was asked the question. He was simply ignorant.

Now consider a second way of filling out the story. Suppose that John doesn't need to read any further material in order to figure out what the answer to the question is. The answer occurs to him while he is driving home, or while he is cooking dinner, or during an ad break when he is watching TV, or while he is taking a shower. Moreover, when it occurs to him he is overwhelmed not by the "Now I see!" experience, but rather by the "Oh dear! Of course!" experience. He doesn't feel relieved, but rather embarrassed at his failure to think of the answer on the spot. Perhaps it is an argumentative move similar to one that he has made elsewhere, or perhaps it is just, as we might say, "so obvious."

When we fill out the story in this way it seems that, again in one perfectly ordinary sense of "could," we almost certainly would suppose that John could have thought of the relevant response when he was having his conversation, and that this is crucial in explaining the way he feels about himself. Embarrassment is the right reaction because he let himself down. He could have thought of the right response, the response he should have thought of, but he didn't. He just blanked.

In order to distinguish between these two ways of filling out the story let's call the first the story of Ignorant John and the second the story of Blanking John. Indeed, for ease of exposition in what follows let's imagine that there were in fact duplicate conversations going on in different places, one between an interlocutor and Ignorant John and the other between an interlocutor and Blanking John. The question on which I wish to focus is what exactly it means to say, in this perfectly ordinary sense of "could," that Blanking John could have thought of the right answer to the question at the time, whereas Ignorant John could not. Plainly it is to make a modal claim, but what modal claim?

A first suggestion is in the spirit of the usual elucidation of the "could" at issue in the free will debate (van Inwagen 1983). To say that Blanking John could have thought of the right answer to the question at the time is to say that there is a possible world which is identical in history and laws to the actual world in which he fails to think of the right answer to the question, but in which he instead thinks of the right answer to the question. The trouble with this first suggestion, however, is that, at least for the purposes of the present argument, we should suppose that there is no such possible world.

The problem is that if causal determinism is true in the actual world, a possibility that it seems best not to rule out for present purposes, then the history of the actual world up to the point at which Blanking John failed to think of the right answer to the question he was asked, plus a statement of the causal laws that hold in the actual world, entails that Blanking John fails to think of the right answer to the question he was asked. There is therefore no possible world identical in history and laws in which Blanking John thinks of the right answer. If this is right then, in yet another perfectly ordinary sense of the word "could," it follows that Blanking John could no more have thought of the right answer than Ignorant John.

Libertarians might object to the suggestion that, for present purposes, we should not rule out the possibility that causal determinism is true. They might insist that the falsity of causal determinism is precisely what is required for the truth of the various "could" claims in which we are interested. But even if they were right about this – which, for the record, it seems to me they are not – I would see no need to take a stand on this issue just yet. For if the libertarians were right then we would expect that to emerge in what follows. It would emerge because we would be unable to give any alternative compatibilist account of what the various "could" claims mean. I therefore propose to put the libertarian objection to one side for the time being.

So far we have seen one thing that we cannot mean when we say that Blanking John could have thought of the right answer at the time. Is there something else that we might mean instead? A familiar weakening of the constraints on possible worlds that we deem to be alternatives to the actual world, a weakening suggested by the literature on counterfactual reasoning, suggests that there is. According to the weakening I have in mind to say that there is a possible world in which Blanking John thinks of the right answer to the question he was asked at the time is simply to say that there is a possible world which is similar to the actual world in terms of history and laws – similar, but not identical, of course – but which contains a small difference, the smallest difference which allows Blanking John to think of the right answer to the question he was asked at the time. This would be a "divergence miracle," in Lewis's terms (1979, 1981). The suggestion is thus that Blanking John could have thought of the right answer to the question he was asked at the time because there is such a possible world.

The trouble with this suggestion, however, is that it doesn't allow us to divide the cases in the right way. There is, after all, a possible world which is similar in terms of history and laws to the actual world in which Ignorant John thinks of the right answer to the question at the time as well. This sense of "could" is thus very weak indeed. It is therefore not a sense of "could" which is going to help us explain why Blanking John could, whereas Ignorant John could not, have thought of the right answer to the question at the time at which he was asked.

Perhaps, though, we are on the right track. Perhaps we should say that Blanking John could, whereas Ignorant John could not, have thought of the right response at the time because the possible world in which Ignorant John thinks of the right response is much more dissimilar to the way the world actually is than is the possible world in which Blanking John thinks of the right response. The idea behind this suggestion is that the problem with the earlier proposal is that it fails to discriminate between possible worlds that are, as we might say, only remote possibilities – these are the possible worlds that are very dissimilar to the actual world in terms of history and laws – and those possible worlds that are real live possibilities – these are the possible worlds that are very similar indeed to the actual world in terms of history and laws.

Though an improvement, however, it seems to me that this account of what makes it true that Blanking John could have thought of the right response, whereas Ignorant John could not, cannot be right either. It cannot be right because it leaves various inappropriate hostages to empirical fortune. For all we know, the actual world is such that the possible world in which Blanking John thinks of the correct answer to the question is far less similar to the actual world in terms of history and laws than is the possible world in which Ignorant John thinks of the correct answer to the question.

An initial case that shows why this is so is a variation on an example of Harry Frankfurt's (1969). Let's suppose that there is an evil scientist, Black, who wants Blanking John not to think of the right answer to the question that he was asked at the time. As it happens, Blanking John would have blanked of his own accord, but Black preemptively stops him having that thought. (Note that this is the relevant difference between this case and Frankfurt's original example.) Black is, however, totally indifferent to whether or not Ignorant John thinks of the right answer to the question that he was asked at the time.

With these assumptions in place it seems to me quite plausible to suppose that the possible world in which Ignorant John thinks of the correct answer to the question at the time it is asked is much more similar to the actual world than is the possible world in which Blanking John thinks of the correct response. It is quite plausible because we may have to imagine many more changes to the way things actually are in order to imagine Blanking John thinking of the correct response than we have to imagine in order to imagine Ignorant John thinking of the correct response. We have to imagine away not just whatever it is that made Blanking John blank, but Black and all of his devilish plans as well, whereas we only have to imagine away Ignorant John's ignorance.

What has gone wrong? At this point it seems to me important to remember that we are trying to figure out what makes it true that Blanking John could have thought of the answer to the question at the time in the sense of having a capacity to do so, albeit a capacity that he didn't exercise at that time. The problem, in these terms, is that the proposal we are currently considering doesn't zero in on what makes it true that Blanking John has that capacity. Instead, it zeroes in on, if anything, what makes it true that the entire possible world that Blanking John inhabits – a possible world that, in our variation on the Frankfurt example, includes Black with all of his devilish plans – has the capacity to manifest the thought of the correct answer to the question in Blanking John at the time at which he was asked the question. And what it tells us, unsurprisingly given Black's devilish plans, is that it doesn't. What we thus need to do is to zero in in a more fine-grained way on Blanking John and his capacities.

Some might be doubtful that this is the proper diagnosis of what has gone wrong. In order to see that it is, it might be helpful to consider an analogous case, a case of what has come to be called a "finkish" disposition (Martin 1994; Lewis 1997). Mark Johnston describes a shy but powerfully intuitive chameleon (Johnston 1993). This is a chameleon that is green but which, when it intuits that it is about to be put into a viewing condition, instantaneously blushes bright red. Does the shy but powerfully intuitive chameleon lack the disposition that greenness is, that is, the disposition to look green in standard viewing conditions, when it is put into a viewing condition? (The point of asking the question about this analogous case is, I hope, plain, but in case it isn't let me make the point of analogy explicit. The question is whether the chameleon's being shy and intuitive falsifies the claim that it has the disposition to look green in standard viewing conditions, and this, I am suggesting, is analogous to asking whether the presence of Black, with all of his devilish plans, falsifies the claim that Blanking John has the capacity to think of the correct answer to the question at the time it was asked.)

The answer, Johnston suggests, is that the mere fact that the chameleon is shy but powerfully intuitive does nothing to make it lack the disposition that greenness is, that is, the disposition to look green in standard viewing conditions. It simply reminds us how much care we need to take in assessing whether or not an object has such a disposition. We need to take such care because dispositions to look a certain way in standard viewing conditions are constituted dispositions. That is to say, there are intrinsic properties that objects with such dispositions possess, properties of their surfaces, which cause the manifestation of the disposition they have to look a certain way in standard viewing conditions. But since these are constituted dispositions, and since what they are constituted by are properties of their surfaces, it follows that the effects of these constituting properties can be "masked," or "mimicked," as Johnston puts it, by other properties that the object possesses or by properties possessed by other objects in the object's environment.

Johnston's suggestion is thus that, when we assess whether or not objects have such constituted dispositions we must abstract away from all but the relevant intrinsic properties of the object itself, in this case, all but the properties of the surface of the chameleon that constitute its disposition to look certain ways. The reason we can say that the shy but powerfully intuitive chameleon has the disposition to look green in standard viewing conditions, notwithstanding the fact that it is shy and intuitive, is thus (roughly speaking) that in the nearby possible worlds in which it doesn't have intrinsic properties that underwrite its being shy and intuitive as regards the presence of a viewer, but retains the intrinsic properties of its surface, it does indeed look green when viewed.

Let's now return to the case of Blanking John and apply the lesson we have just learned. What we have been trying to figure out is what makes it true that Blanking John could have answered the question at the time, in the sense of having the capacity to think of the correct answer to the question he was asked at the time at which it was asked, whereas Ignorant John couldn't, in the sense of lacking that capacity. The proposal we have been considering is that Blanking John has this capacity, and Ignorant John lacks it, because the possible world in which Ignorant John thinks of the right response is much more dissimilar to the way the actual world is than is the possible world in which Blanking John thinks of the right response. The objection to this proposal, recall, is that it leaves an inappropriate hostage to empirical fortune. If, as a matter of empirical fact, Black has set things up so as to guarantee that Blanking John will fail to think of the correct answer to the question, but is indifferent to whether or not Ignorant John thinks of the correct response, then the possible world in which Blanking John thinks of the correct response may be far more dissimilar to the actual world than is the possible world in which Ignorant John thinks of the correct response to the question. However the discussion of the shy but intuitive chameleon suggests a principled response to this objection.

Note, to begin, that the reason the objection gets going in the first place is that Blanking John's capacity to think of the correct answer to the question when asked is a constituted capacity. That is to say, there is some intrinsic feature possessed by those who have this sort of capacity and it is their possession of this intrinsic feature that causes the thought of the answer to the philosophical question in appropriate circumstances. The capacity is presumably constituted by whatever it is that underwrites psychological states in general, which, for the sake of argument, we can assume to be some state of the brain. The reason the objection gets going in the first place is thus, in Johnston's terms, that the effects of this intrinsic property can be masked and mimicked by other causal factors, in this case, by Black with his devilish plans.

Accordingly, in testing whether or not Blanking John has the capacity to think of the correct answer to the question at the time we should narrow the possible worlds in which we consider whether he thinks of the correct response when asked in a way analogous to the way in which Johnston suggests that we should narrow the possible worlds in which to test for the presence of the disposition to look green in standard viewing conditions. The revised suggestion is thus that Blanking John could, whereas Ignorant John could not, have thought of the right response at the time he was asked because he differs from Ignorant John in the following respect. Abstracting away from all those properties that could have an effect on what either of them think except the relevant properties of Blanking John's and Ignorant John's brains, the possible world in which Ignorant John thinks of the right response is much more dissimilar to the way the actual world is than is the possible world in which Blanking John thinks of the right response.

Now, though a vast improvement on the previous suggestion, it seems to me that this suggestion is still deeply flawed. The problem is that it still fails to capture the fact that we are trying to find out what makes it true that Blanking John could have thought of the correct answer to the question when asked in the sense of having a capacity to answer that question. In order to see that that is so it suffices to note that the current suggestion still leaves an inappropriate hostage to empirical fortune. It would, after all, seem to be at least possible that, even after abstracting away from the presence of Black with his devilish plans, Ignorant John's brain only needs to be different in a tiny way – perhaps only one neuron needs to fire instead of failing to fire – for the thought of the right response to the question that he was asked to occur to him, whereas a larger change in Blanking John's brain is required for the thought of the right response to the question he was asked to occur to him.

Indeed, this suggests a further variation on the story we have been considering thus far. In this variation, the answer occurs to John while he is driving home, or while he is cooking dinner, or during an ad break when he is watching TV, or while he is taking a shower – so far this is like the story of Blanking John – but when it occurs to him he is not overwhelmed by the "Oh dear! Of course!" experience, or by the "Now I see!" experience, but rather by the "Why on earth did that occur to me!" experience. He doesn't feel relieved, and nor does he feel embarrassed at his failure to think of the answer on the spot. He has no qualms admitting that he could not have thought of the answer on the spot. Rather, he feels utter amazement that the right answer should have popped into his head as it did. In this variation on the case it seems that we do not think of John as having manifested a capacity to answer the question he was asked at all, notwithstanding the fact that his thinking of the correct answer entails that he could have. Rather, we think of him as having had a completely fluky flash.

What has gone wrong this time? Let's call this the case of Fluky John. What this case shows – and, for that matter, what the case of Ignorant John we just imagined shows as well (the case in which only a tiny change in his brain state is required for him to think of the correct answer) – is a problem with all of the suggestions considered so far. They are all far too focussed on single possibilities when, to repeat, what we are trying to establish is what makes it true that Blanking John could have thought of the right answer to the question when asked in the sense of having had a capacity to think of the right answer. Fluky John might even have had that fluky thought at the very moment he was asked the question. But the mere fact that he has the fluky thought does nothing to show that he could have thought of the correct answer at the time in the sense of having had the capacity to think of it.

What we need to add to the suggestions considered thus far is therefore some recognition of the fact that capacities are essentially general or multi-track in nature, and that they therefore manifest themselves not in single possibilities, but rather in whole rafts of possibilities. If Blanking John really could have thought of the correct answer to the question at the time he was asked, in the sense of having had the capacity to think of that answer, then (the idea is) he must likewise have had the capacity to think of the answer to a whole host of slight variations on the question that he was asked, variations in the manner in which the question was asked, and perhaps in the exact content of the questions, and in the exact timing of the question, and so on. It is difficult to spell out exactly what these variations are in any precise way, but I take it that the basic idea is clear enough. (Think of how many philosophical conversations you need to have with students before you get a sense of their philosophical capacities, and of how often you are initially impressed by students, but then reconsider after becoming convinced that the good points that they made aren't evidence of an underlying capacity but are, rather, just flukes.)

Once we see the need to recognize the multi-track nature of capacities, a quite different explanation of why the possible world in which Blanking John thinks of the correct answer to the question is closer to actuality than are the possible worlds in which Ignorant John and Fluky John think of the correct answer suggests itself. The crucial point is that this whole host of similar counterfactuals is true of Blanking John, but false of Ignorant John and Fluky John. In other words, we engage in a triangulation exercise. Begin from the fact that, abstracting away from all of those properties that could have an effect on what any of them thinks except the relevant properties of their brains, in those nearby possible worlds in which Blanking John is asked a whole host of similar questions he has the right thought in response to the similar questions when asked, whereas in the nearby possible worlds in which both Ignorant John and Fluky John are asked that whole host of similar questions, they systematically fail to have the right thought in response. From this we draw the conclusion that, in that same nearby region of logical space, Blanking John is, whereas both Ignorant John and Fluky John are not, having the right thought in response to the question he was in fact asked at the time at which it was asked. This, accordingly, is why the possible world in which Blanking John has the right thought in response to the question when asked is nearer to actuality than is the possible world in which Ignorant John and Fluky John have the right thought in response to the question when asked. It is why Blanking John could, whereas Ignorant John and Fluky John could not, have thought of the right response to the question when asked.

Note that this suggestion, unlike the previous suggestion, is not vulnerable to the same sorts of empirical counterexample. Whether or not, as a matter of empirical fact, someone like Black with his devilish plans is present is irrelevant because we abstract away from everything that underwrites the truth of the relevant counterfactuals apart from the relevant properties of Blanking John's, Ignorant John's and Fluky John's brains. And whether or not, as a matter of empirical fact, Blanking John's actual brain is more or less similar to his brain in those nearby possible worlds in which he is thinking the correct thought in response to the question when asked, than are the actual brains of Ignorant John and Fluky John to their brains in the nearby worlds in which they are thinking the correct thought in response to the question when asked, is likewise irrelevant. It is irrelevant because the crucial question is whether the whole host of relevantly similar counterfactuals is true of Blanking John, Ignorant John and Fluky John.

This provides us with a response to a more general worry that has in fact been in the background all along. For even if that whole host of counterfactuals described were true of Blanking John, we would surely still think that he lacked the capacity to think of the right answer to the question we asked him at the time if we discovered that there was no common structure to what underwrites the truth of that whole host of counterfactuals. For example, suppose that Blanking John was much like Ned Block's famous Blockhead (1981), and each individual answer he gave to a question he was asked was the result of some aspect of his internal condition that was dedicated to giving exactly that answer in response to exactly that formulation of the question, an aspect that has nothing in common with any other aspect of his internal condition. In that case, even if Blanking John's internal nature was so complex that it could underwrite the truth of that whole host of similar counterfactuals, we would surely deny that he was intelligent at all. In other words, we would plainly resist the triangulation suggested, and so deny that he has any rational capacities at all.

As with the case of Blockhead, it seems to me that the right response to this more general worry is to insist that, if indeed Blanking John does have rational capacities, then there must be relevant structure in what underlies the truth of the various counterfactuals that we take to be true of him. After all, when Blanking John is asked the answer to a whole range of slightly different philosophical questions, he must exploit the very same capacities in order to answer many of those questions. The assumption must therefore be that what underwrites the truth of the counterfactuals that we take to be true of him is similarly structured. Spelling out what precisely this structure amounts to would be a mammoth task, one which goes way beyond the scope of the present essay. However I take it that the general idea should be plain enough, at least in the light of other similar responses to the Blockhead example itself (see, especially,

Braddon-Mitchell and Jackson 1996). It is this structure in what underlies the truth of the various counterfactuals that are true of Blanking John that licenses our triangulation to the existence of a nearby possible world in which he doesn't blank. This, at any rate, is my conjecture.

Doubtless further refinements would be necessary for the present suggestion to be made completely convincing. However, even without these further refinements, it seems to me that it has already become plain, via the various responses we have been able to give to the counterexamples offered, that an analysis along the present lines is on the right track. The time has therefore come to see how the general idea can be applied to the reckless woman Watson describes.

As I said, what we blame the reckless woman for is having the wrong belief about what she should do in the circumstances of action that she faces. She believes that the value associated with having another drink makes it worthwhile risking being unable to fulfill some of her obligations. We disagree that that belief is supported by the evidence she considers. Blaming her is thus, as I said, appropriate just to the extent that she could have believed otherwise than that she should have another drink in the light of that evidence. It would be totally inappropriate if she lacked the capacity to evaluate such evidence, or if, though she possesses this capacity, her belief was the product of (say) self-hatred which she could neither acknowledge nor get rid of. We can now explain what the difference is between these various possibilities.

To begin, we must determine whether or not a particular woman who fails to form the belief that is supported by the evidence she considers has the capacity to form the belief supported by that evidence. We must therefore abstract away from all those properties that could have an effect on what she believes except the relevant properties of her brain, and we must then ask whether a whole raft of counterfactuals are true of her. Would she have formed a whole host of similar beliefs in response to similar evidence? If she would have then, the suggestion is, assuming that there is relevant structure in what underlies the truth of those counterfactuals, we can triangulate to the conclusion that, in that same nearby region of logical space, that same woman forms the right belief in response to the evidence she in fact considers. If all this is so then it follows that she has the capacity to form the right belief in response to the evidence she in fact considers.

Next we must determine whether her failure to form the correct belief is appropriately explained by her failure to exercise her capacity to form the correct belief in response to the evidence available to her. Is her failure to exercise her capacity the relevant explanation, or was her belief the product of (say) self-hatred which she could neither acknowledge nor get rid of? In order to answer this question we must ask whether the woman had the capacity to form the correct belief in response to the evidence available to her, but now instead of abstracting away from her various emotions, we take her emotions into account. If, for example, she does suffer from self-hatred, does her self-hatred undermine the truth of the relevant counterfactuals? If so then we conclude that her self-hatred was the explanation, rather than her failure to exercise her capacity. If not then we conclude that, since she had the capacity to form the correct belief notwithstanding her self-hatred, her failure to exercise her capacity was the relevant explanation.

So far so good. But now suppose someone asks us *why* the reckless woman failed to exercise her capacity to form the correct belief in response to the evidence available to her. Can we give an answer to this question? It seems to me that we might be able to give an answer, but that we might not. The important point I wish to emphasize here, however, is that the mere fact that we might not be able to give an answer to the question is of no real concern. Let me explain why.

Suppose that the reckless woman would have formed the correct belief about what she should do if she had first thought of something else that she didn't in fact think of. Perhaps she had made similar comparisons of the significance of alternatives in the past, and in those cases she had always come up with the correct answer about the relative significance of the value of drinking and failing to fulfill her obligations. Perhaps if she had only thought of those past decisions on this occasion, then she would have formed the correct belief this time as well. If all of this is the case, and if we suppose that she could have thought of those past decisions on this occasion, then, it seems to me, we do indeed have available an explanation of her failure to exercise her capacity to form the correct belief on this occasion. For we can explain her failure by citing the fact that she failed to think of the similar case that she had considered in the past.

But, of course, as is perhaps already plain, perfectly good though this explanation is, it is an explanation of why the woman failed to exercise her capacity to form the correct belief which simply takes it for granted that she had the capacity, on this occasion, to think of those decisions that she made in the past. Perhaps we can explain why she failed to exercise this capacity as well. But perhaps we can't. In any case, at some point we will have to admit that our explanations simply come to an end. In other words, at some point we will have to rest content with explaining the reckless woman's failure to exercise her capacity to have a thought, or whatever, by saying that she simply blanked, and for that we will be unable to give anything by way of an explanation – not, at any rate, without retreating to brain science.

Importantly, however, this will give us no reason whatsoever to suppose that we cannot hold the reckless woman responsible for failing to think of whatever it is, and hence for blanking. For so long as we are right to assume that her failure of thought, or her blanking, occurs in a suitable context of nearby possible worlds in which she does have that thought, it thereby follows, analytically, both that she could have had that thought, or could have not blanked, in the sense of having had a capacity to have the thought, or not to have blanked, and that her failure to exercise her capacity is the relevant explanation of her failure to have the thought, or of her blanking. And this, in turn, is what legitimizes our holding her responsible. The fact that our explanations run out is neither here nor there.

2. RATIONAL CAPACITIES AND DESIRE

We now have an account of what makes the "could" claims true that we have to suppose to be true for it to be appropriate to hold the reckless woman responsible for her failure to have the right belief. The question is whether we can extend this to give an account of what makes the "could" claims true that we have to suppose to be true for it to be appropriate to hold the weak woman responsible for her failure to have the right desire, and that we have to suppose to be false for it to be appropriate not to hold the compulsive woman responsible for her failure to have the right desire. At this point, however, a familiar problem arises.

The problem is, in essence, that whereas it is easy to see how the reckless woman's beliefs should and could have been the product of a rational capacity, it is difficult to see how the weak woman's desires should and could have been the product of a rational capacity. Since belief is a psychological state whose very nature is, *inter alia*, to be sensitive to evidence, so it comes as no surprise that we are able to think of someone with beliefs as someone who possesses a capacity to revise her beliefs in a rational manner. But Hume, for one, thought that desires were, by contrast, "original existences", and the point of his so labeling them was precisely to suggest that they were, by their very nature, a psychological state that is not sensitive to rational considerations of any sort (Hume 1740). However it seems to me that this Humean account of desire is radically mistaken (Smith 2004). Let me therefore briefly sketch a picture of evaluative belief which makes it clear how and why desires both should and could be the product of a rational capacity. Since I have spelled out the story in detail elsewhere (Smith 1994, 1997b, 2001), I will be brief.

What exactly is it that an agent believes when she believes some action to be desirable? It seems to me helpful, in answering this question, to begin from the more or less common sense assumption that for an agent to believe it desirable to act in a certain way in certain circumstances is for her to believe that so acting is advisable: that is – and this is meant to be strictly equivalent – a matter of her believing that she would advise herself to perform that act in those circumstances if she were herself in circumstances in which she was best placed to give herself advice. If this is right, however, then two questions naturally spring to mind. First, what are these circumstances in which agents are best placed to give themselves advice, and second, what fixes the content of the advice that the agents in those circumstances would give themselves?

The answer to the first question is, I suggest, that agents are best placed to give themselves advice when their psychologies have been purged of all cognitive limitations and rational failings, and the answer to the second question, the question about the content of the advice that agents would give to themselves, is that the content of such advice is fixed by the contents of the desires that they would have, were their psychologies thus purged, about what they are to do in the circumstances of action about which they are seeking advice. In other words, when I believe that my performance of a certain action is desirable that amounts to my believing that my performance of that act is advisable, where that, in turn, amounts to my believing that I would want myself so to act if I had a desire set that was purged of all cognitive limitations and rational failings.

If something like this is along the right lines then all we need to do in order to get a full-blown analysis of desirability is to give an account of the conditions that need to be met by a desire set which is devoid of cognitive limitations and rational failings. My suggestion in this regard is basically a development of an idea of Bernard Williams's (1980). For a desire set to be devoid of cognitive limitations and rational failings is, I suggest, for it to be one which is maximally informed and coherent and unified. What it is desirable for an agent to do in certain circumstances is thus a matter of what she would want herself to do in those circumstances if she had a set of desires that was maximally informed and coherent and unified. The suggestion can be formulated more precisely as follows. Let's call the possible world in which the agent has the desires that she actually has in the circumstances of action she faces the "evaluated" world, and the possible world in which she has that set of desires that is maximally informed and coherent and unified the "evaluating" world. In these terms the suggestion is that what it is desirable for an agent to do in the evaluated world is fixed not by what, in the evaluated world she wants herself to do in the evaluated world, and not by what, in the evaluating world, she wants herself to do in the evaluating world, but rather by what, in the evaluating world, she wants herself to do in the evaluated world. This, accordingly, is the property that an agent must believe her act to have when she values the performance of that act.

Once this is agreed it seems to me that there is no difficulty at all in seeing why the desires of the weak woman should and could be the product of a rational capacity. In order to see why, imagine a case in which, on reflection, a woman comes to believe that (say) she would desire that she abstains from drinking in the circumstances of action that she presently faces if she had a maximally informed and coherent and unified set of desires, but imagine further that she doesn't have any desire at all to abstain. She desires to drink instead. Now consider the pair of psychological states that comprises her belief that she would desire that she abstains from drinking in the circumstances of action that she presently faces if she had a maximally informed and coherent and unified set of desires, and which also comprises the desire that she abstains from drinking, and compare this pair of psychological states with the pair that comprises her belief that she would desire that she abstains from drinking in the circumstances of action that she presently faces if she had a maximally informed and coherent and unified set of desires, but which also comprises instead a desire to drink. Which of these pairs of psychological states is more coherent?

The answer would seem to me to be plain enough. The first pair is much more coherent than the second. There is disequilibrium or dissonance or failure of fit involved in believing that she would desire herself to act in a certain way in certain circumstances if she had a maximally informed and coherent and unified desire set, and yet not desiring to act in that way. The failure to desire to act in that way is, after all, something that she disowns. From her perspective it makes no sense, given the rest of her desires. By her lights it is a state that she would not be in if she were in various ways better than she actually is: more informed, more coherent, more unified in her desiderative outlook. There would therefore seem to be more than a passing family resemblance between the relation that holds between the first pair of psychological states and more familiar examples of coherence relations that hold between psychological states. Coherence would thus seem to be on the side of the pair that comprises both the woman's belief that she would desire that she abstains from drinking in the circumstances of action that she presently faces and the desire that she abstains from drinking.

If this is right, however, then it follows immediately that if the woman is rational, in the relatively mundane sense of having a capacity to have the psychological states that coherence demands of her then, at least when that capacity is exercised, she will end up having a desire that matches her belief about what she would want herself to do if she had a maximally informed and coherent and unified desire set. In other words, in the particular case under discussion, she will end up losing her desire to drink and acquiring a desire to abstain from drinking instead. The belief that she would desire that she act in a certain way if she had a set of desires that was maximally informed and coherent and unified would thus seem able to cause her to acquire a corresponding desire when it operates in conjunction with the capacity to have coherent psychological states. Put another way, it would thus seem to be in the nature of desires that they are psychological states that are sensitive to our beliefs about what we would desire that we do if we had a set of desires that was maximally informed and coherent and unified, sensitive in the sense of being psychological states that we would acquire in the light of such beliefs given that we have a capacity to have the psychological states that coherence demands of us.

We are now in a position to put this account of how desires can appropriately be seen as the product of a rational capacity together with the lessons that we learned earlier about what it means to say that someone has a rational capacity governing her beliefs, and thereby to tell a story about the difference between the weak woman and the compulsive woman. The suggestion is that both the weak woman and the compulsive woman are best interpreted as believing that they would want themselves to refrain from having another drink if they had a maximally informed and coherent and unified desire set. Both of them are therefore subject to coherence's demand that they desire to abstain from drinking. Both of them none the less desire to have another drink. The difference between them, however, lies in the fact that the weak woman could have desired to refrain from having another drink, notwithstanding her desire to drink, in the sense of having a capacity to have that desire, given that coherence demands that desire of her, and her failure to exercise that capacity is the explanation of her drinking. The compulsive woman, by contrast, given that she has a desire to drink, could not have desired to refrain from having another drink in the sense of lacking the capacity to have that desire, notwithstanding the fact that coherence demands that desire of her.

More precisely, we can explain the difference between them in the following terms. (Here we simply apply the account given in the cognitive case.) We begin by abstracting away from all those properties that could have an effect on what the weak woman and the compulsive woman desire except the relevant properties of their brains. We then note that the weak woman would, whereas the compulsive woman would not, have a whole host of counterfactuals true of her. She would desire to refrain from similar drinks, and the like – drinks of ever so slightly different kinds, in ever so slightly different circumstances, and so on – in those nearby possible worlds in which she believes that she would want herself so to act if she had a maximally informed and coherent and unified desire set. Assuming that there is relevant structure in what underwrites the truth of these counterfactuals, we then triangulate much as before. That is, we conclude that in that same nearby region of logical space the weak woman does, whereas the compulsive woman does not, have a desire to refrain from having the very drink that she has in response to the very belief she has that she would want herself to refrain from having this drink if she had a maximally informed and coherent and unified desire set. This is what it means to say that the weak woman could, whereas the compulsive woman could not, have resisted her desire to drink.

If this is right then note that though we can acknowledge both that the weak woman failed to exercise her capacity to desire in accordance with her belief, and that her failure explained her drinking, we must once again be careful not to suppose that we will always be able to give an explanation of why she failed. Of course, on certain occasions we might be able to give such an explanation (Pettit and Smith 1993; Kennett and Smith 1996). For example, if there is a routine that she regularly goes through when she desires a drink – perhaps she imagines her children looking at her pick up the drink and put it to her lips, and then homes in on the look of utter disappointment in their eyes – and if this routine has in the past reliably firmed her in her resolve to abstain from drinking, then, if we in addition suppose that she could have gone through that process of the imagination on this occasion, then we may well have available an explanation of her failure to desire to refrain on this occasion. For we could then explain her failure to desire to refrain from drinking by citing the fact that she failed to go through the routine of imagining the look on her children's faces when she was about to take a drink. However this explanation, like the earlier explanation in the cognitive case, simply takes for granted that she has another capacity that she failed to exercise at the relevant time – namely, the capacity to imagine the look on her children's faces when she was about to take a drink – and for this we have given no explanation at all. As in the cognitive case, it thus seems that at some point we will have to rest content with fact that we cannot give an explanation of the weak woman's failure to exercise her capacity to desire to refrain from drinking – not, at any rate, without retreating to brain science.

Importantly, however, note that this gives us no reason whatsoever to suppose that we cannot hold the weak woman responsible for failing to desire to refrain from drinking. For so long as we are right to assume that that failure to desire to refrain from drinking occurs in a suitable context of nearby possible worlds in which she does desire to refrain, it thereby follows, analytically, both that she could have had that desire, notwithstanding the fact that she failed to have that desire in fact, in the sense of having a rational capacity to have the desire, and that her failure to exercise her capacity is the relevant explanation of her failure to desire to refrain from drinking. And this, in turn, is what legitimizes our holding her responsible. The fact that our explanations run out is neither here nor there.

CONCLUSION

I said at the outset that the "could" claims we assume to be true (or false) when we describe someone as reckless, weak, or compelled, all mean much the same thing: specifically, they all signify the presence (or absence) of a relevant rational capacity. We can now see why that is so.

In the case of the reckless woman we assume that, notwithstanding the fact that she has the incorrect belief about the relative value of drinking and risking failing to fulfill her obligations, she could have had the correct belief in the sense of having a capacity to have that belief. As we have seen, this in turn means, *inter alia*, that she exists in a suitable context of nearby possible worlds in which, because she is suitably responsive to the evidence, she has not just this correct belief, but a whole host of similarly correct beliefs. In the case of the weak woman we assume that, notwithstanding the fact that she desires, incorrectly, to have another drink, she could have had the right desire in the sense of having a capacity to have that desire: that is, the desire to refrain. As we have seen, this in turn means, *inter alia*, that she exists in a suitable context of nearby possible worlds in which, because her desires fit coherently together with her beliefs about what she would want herself to do if she had a maximally informed and coherent and unified desire set, she has not just this right desire, but a whole host of similarly right desires. The compelled woman could not desire otherwise in the sense of lacking this capacity.

In the case of both the reckless woman and the weak woman we have seen that this provides us with a plausible account of what it means to say that the women have capacities that they failed to exercise. The reckless woman has the capacity to believe correctly, but she failed to exercise that capacity. The weak woman has the capacity to desire otherwise, but she failed to exercise that capacity. Moreover, we have seen that though we might be able to explain their failure to exercise this capacity, we might not be able to explain it. Importantly, however, we have also seen that even if we are unable to explain their failure, that would give us no reason to be skeptical about the truth of such claims. For the truth of the claim that someone has a capacity to believe or desire correctly that they failed to exercise might simply be constituted by their failure of belief or desire in the context of a suitable raft of nearby possible worlds of the kind described.

REFERENCES

Block, Ned 1981: "Psychologism and Behaviourism," *Philosophical Review*, 90: 5–43.
Braddon-Mitchell, David, and Frank Jackson 1996: *Philosophy of Mind and Cognition*. Oxford: Blackwell.
Frankfurt, Harry 1969: "Alternate Possibilities and Moral Responsibility," reprinted in Frankfurt 1988.
————— 1988: *The Importance of What We Care About*. Cambridge: Cambridge University Press.
Fischer, John Martin, and Mark Ravizza 1998: *Responsibility and Control: A Theory of Moral Responsibility*. Cambridge: Cambridge University Press.
Hume, David 1740: *A Treatise of Human Nature*. Oxford: Clarendon Press. 1968.
Johnston, Mark 1993: "Objectivity Refigured: Pragmatism Without Verificationism," in John Haldane and Crispin Wright, eds., *Reality, Representation and Projection*. Oxford: Oxford University Press. 85–130.
Kennett, Jeanette, and Michael Smith 1994: "Philosophy and Commonsense: The Case of Weakness of Will," in Michaelis Michael and John O'Leary-Hawthorne, eds., *Philosophy in Mind: The Place of Philosophy in the Study of Mind*. Dordrecht: Kluwer Academic. 141–157.
————— 1996: "Frog and Toad Lose Control," in *Analysis*. 56: 63–73.
Lewis, David 1979: "Counterfactual Dependence and Time's Arrow," reprinted in Lewis 1986.
Lewis, David 1981: "Are We Free to Break the Laws?," reprinted in Lewis 1986.
Lewis, David 1986: *Philosophical Papers Volume II*. Oxford: Oxford University Press.
Lewis, David 1997: "Finkish Dispositions," *Philosophical Quarterly*. 47: 143–58.

Martin, C. B. 1994: "Dispositions and Conditionals," *Philosophical Quarterly*. 44: 1–8.

Pettit, Philip, and Michael Smith 1993: "Practical Unreason," in *Mind*. 102: 53–79.

Pettit, Philip, and Michael Smith 1996: "Freedom in Belief and Desire," in *Journal of Philosophy*. 93: 429–49.

Smith, Michael 1994: *The Moral Problem*. Oxford: Blackwell.

———— 1997a: "A Theory of Freedom and Responsibility," in Garrett Cullity and Berys Gaut, eds., *Ethics and Practical Reason*. Oxford: Oxford University Press. 293–319.

Smith, Michael 1997b: "In Defence of *The Moral Problem*: A Reply to Brink, Copp and Sayre-McCord," in *Ethics*. 108: 84–119.

Smith, Michael 2001: "The Incoherence Argument: Reply to Schafer-Landau," in *Analysis*. 61: 254–66.

Smith, Michael 2004: "Humean Rationality," in Alfred Mele and Piers Rawling, eds., *Handbook of Rationality*. Oxford: Oxford University Press. 75–92.

van Inwagen, Peter 1983: *An Essay on Free Will*. Oxford: Clarendon Press.

Wallace, R. Jay 1994: *Responsibility and the Moral Sentiments*. Cambridge, MA: Harvard University Press.

Watson, Gary 1977: "Skepticism about Weakness of Will," in *The Philosophical Review*. 86: 316–39.

———— 2001: "Reasons and Responsibility," *Ethics*. 111: 374–94.

Bernard Williams 1980: "Internal and External Reasons," reprinted in Williams 1981. 101–13.

Williams, Bernard 1981: *Moral Luck*. Cambridge: Cambridge University Press.

Wolf, Susan 1990: *Freedom Within Reason*. New York: Oxford University Press.

NOTE

An earlier version of this paper was read at a conference on weakness of will organized by Fabienne Pironet, Sarah Stroud and Christine Tappolet at the University of Montreal in 2001. Subsequent versions were presented at the Australian National University, Keio University, the Ethics Group in North Carolina, the University of North Carolina at Chapel Hill, Oriel College in Oxford, Stanford University, and the University of St. Andrews. I would like to thank all those who participated in these seminars. Special thanks are due to the editors, to two anonymous readers for Oxford University Press, and to Michael Bratman, Bill Brewer, Sarah Broadie, Richard Holton, Lloyd Humberstone, Thomas Hurka, Philip Pettit, Geoffrey Sayre-McCord, Laura Schroeter, John Skorupski, Timothy Williamson, and the students and faculty who attended the graduate seminar on philosophy of action I gave at the University of Arizona in 2001.

7

On Humeans, Anti-Humeans, and Motivation: A Reply to Pettit

1. In "The Humean Theory of Motivation" (hereafter HTM) I argued for the thesis that R at t is a motivating reason of an agent A to φ if and only if there is some ψ such that R at t consists of a desire of A to ψ and a belief that were he to φ he would ψ.[1] I called this "P1." I claimed, further, that P1 is definitive of the Humean theory of motivation.

The argument I gave for P1 was relatively simple (HTM: 50–8). It is a commonplace that when an agent has a motivating reason to φ his reason is partially constituted by a state that embodies his having φ-ing as a goal. But how does this map on to talk of beliefs and desires? Well, what belief and desire are may uncontroversially be characterized using the metaphor of directions of fit.[2] Beliefs are states that aim to fit the world, whereas desires are states that aim to have the world fit them. This metaphor can be rendered non-metaphorical in terms of a functional analysis. Thus, very roughly, the belief that p is a state that tends to go out of existence in the presence of a perception that not-p, whereas the desire that p is a state that tends to endure in the presence of a perception that not-p, disposing the subject to bring it about that p. Now having φ-ing as a goal is also a state that aims to have the world fit it. It too must therefore be a disposition to realize φ-ing. But in that case we can say that, since the desire to φ is a disposition to realize φ-ing, and since we have no good reason to think that any other state is such a disposition (in particular, since we have good reason to believe that no belief is a disposition to φ), so only desires (and certainly no belief) can constitute an agent's having φ-ing as a goal. Thus P1. Call this the "direction of fit" argument.

In "Humeans, Anti-Humeans, and Motivation" (hereafter HAM) Philip Pettit makes two claims against me.[3] He insists that, first, I do not "highlight the really central issue between Humeans and anti-Humeans," and that, second, I do not "provide arguments which would settle that issue in the Humean's favour" (p. 530). I will consider these claims in turn.

2. In HTM I say that the issue dividing Humeans from non-Humeans is P1. Pettit says he disagrees. His reason for disagreeing is that, in his view, the non-Humeans can accept P1, the claim that motivating reasons are constituted, *inter alia*, by desires, for what they disagree with is rather the Humean's claim that the desires that constitute motivating reasons are themselves non-cognitive states, "states which reason on its own is incapable of producing" (HAM: 531). In Pettit's view P1 is relevant to that issue "only because it is assumed that desires are non-cognitive states of this kind" (HAM: 531). But this cannot be assumed (he continues) as there is at least one plausible way of denying it.[4]

Suppose that some of the desires which figure in motivating reasons are such that their presence is entailed by the presence of certain beliefs. In particular, suppose that an agent's desire that p is entailed in this way by a belief – a desiderative belief, we might call it – that it is good or appropriate or useful that p . . . It will be a state, or so it appears, which reason alone is capable of producing. In order for the Humean to establish his point of view he needs to be able to resist at least the possibility that desires can inherit cognitive status in this way. (HAM: 531)

In Pettit's view we therefore need to distinguish between two kinds of desire in order to state clearly the Humean's view: desires whose presence is entailed by the presence of beliefs (call these "desires = beliefs") and desires whose presence is not entailed by the presence of beliefs (call these "desires $\neq$ beliefs").[5] The Humean's view is then that R at t is a motivating reason of agent A to ϕ if and only if there is some ψ such that R at t consists of a desire $\neq$ belief of A to ψ and a belief that were he to ϕ he would ψ. Call this "P-Pettit". In Pettit's view, non-Humeans deny P-Pettit, not P1. Indeed the most plausible form of non-Humean theory denies P-Pettit by arguing for the existence of desires = beliefs, and hence by accepting P1.

Does this suffice to show that I do not highlight the really central issue between Humeans and non-Humeans? I do not think so. Pettit's way of characterizing that issue differs from my own only if P1 and P-Pettit are different principles. But they are not. P1 and P-Pettit are the same principle.

P1 and P-Pettit are the same principle just in case "desire" in P1 means the same as "desire $\neq$ belief" in P-Pettit. Of course, I did not use the word "desire ≠ belief" in P1. But I would have thought that in HTM I said enough about the relationship between beliefs and desires to indicate that, in the terminology of HTM, what Pettit calls a "desire = belief" would not deserve the name "desire" or "belief," but ought rather to be called a "quasi-belief," and hence that what Pettit calls a "desire ≠ belief" would rather be called a "desire" pure and simple. Here is what I said:

> The [non-Humean] might insist that we recognize that [belief-desire psychology] cannot explain all the phenomena; that there are certain goings on that we can explain only if we enrich our psychological theory with the concept of a state that has, in a more relaxed sense, both directions of fit. He might cite the example of a moral "quasi-belief" that x is good ("quasi-belief" because, as we shall see, it is no ordinary belief). For, he might point out, since a subject who has such a quasi-belief tends to go out of this state when presented with a perception that x is not good, this makes it appropriate to describe a moral quasi-belief as being such that it must fit the world. But since a subject's having the moral quasi-belief that x is good disposes him to promote x, this makes it appropriate to describe such a quasi-belief as being, in a more relaxed sense, such that the world must fit with it. Indeed, he might go on to insist that since the factor that determines the kinds of concept our psychological theories can make use of is the evidence that needs to be explained by our theories, so the example just given shows that we positively have reason to enrich our austere [belief-desire] psychological theories with the concept of a quasi-belief: *a state that is both belief-like and desire-like though identical with neither.* For the evidence – our moral practices – can only be explained by the richer theory. (HTM: 56 – emphasis added)

The crucial feature of a quasi-belief is thus that it has, in the loose sense I define, both directions of fit. That is, it has the functional properties of a belief with respect to one content ("x is good") and a desire with respect to another ("I promote x"). I resisted calling this state both a "belief" and a "desire" because, as I said in HTM, I supposed an objector might insist that desires (and beliefs) have only one direction of fit (p. 56). Indeed, I said that that was an assumption of the original argument (p. 55). But, of course, if we relax this assumption, then what in the jargon of HTM is a quasi-belief will be a desire = belief, and then what in the jargon of HTM is a desire, will be a desire ≠ belief. But then, since P1 is written within the set of assumptions about how to use the terms "belief," "desire," and "quasi-belief" I proposed in HTM, it turns out that P1 is P-Pettit.

Pettit and I therefore agree about the issue dividing Humean from non-Humean theorists of motivation. Pettit chooses to describe final resistance to the Humean's view in terms of a commitment to the existence of desires = beliefs, I choose to describe such resistance in terms of a commitment to the existence of quasi-beliefs. But this does not signal a disagreement about what the issue *is*, it merely signals a disagreement about how to use the terms "desire" and "belief" in *describing* that issue.

3. Though Pettit and I agree about what the issue is that divides Humean from non-Humean theorists of motivation, I think that confusion would result if we were to take too literally his initial quite general formulation of that issue (I am not saying that Pettit is himself confused about this). He tells us that, "by all accounts," what divides Humeans from non-Humeans is "a difference of view about the potency of reason in motivating behaviour," and that they therefore disagree about whether motivating reasons "always involve the presence of non-cognitive states, states which reason on its own is incapable of producing" (HAM: 531). But what exactly does it mean to say that reason can (or cannot) produce a motive? Does it mean the same as saying that having certain beliefs entails (or does not entail) having certain desires?

The claim that reason can produce a motive is generally made in the course of describing the disagreement between Hume and Kant over whether reason "is, and ought only to be the slave of the passions."[6] In context, this is a disagreement about whether the norms of morality reduce to the norms of reason. The rationalists (following Kant) insist that they do, and the anti-rationalists (following Hume) insist that they do not. The disagreement thus very quickly becomes a disagreement about the precise content of the norms of reason. Rationalists and anti-rationalists can of course agree about quite a lot. They can agree that there are norms of theoretical reason telling us that, for example, if a subject believes both that p and that p $\rightarrow$ q, then he prima facie ought to believe that q. But rationalists think, in addition, that there are norms of practical reason, in particular, that there are norms telling us that if an agent has certain beliefs – for example, the belief that someone is in pain and that he (the believer) can relieve his pain by φ-ing – then he (the believer) prima facie ought to have certain motives – for example, the motive to φ.[7] The rationalist's view is then that, just as in the theoretical case fully rational creatures will believe that q when they believe that p and that p $\rightarrow$ q, for the beliefs that p and that p $\rightarrow$ q will produce the belief that q in such creatures (something with which anti-rationalists will presumably agree), so in the practical case fully rational creatures will be motivated to φ when they believe that someone is in pain and that they can relieve his pain by φ-ing, for the relevant beliefs will produce this motive. For his part, the anti-rationalist denies that there are such principles of practical reason.

139

It should now be clear that this issue is quite different from the issue that Pettit and I agree divides Humean from non-Humean theorists of motivation. After all, do the rationalists think that the presence of the relevant beliefs entails the presence of these motives? No. They think that the relevant beliefs only entail the presence of these motives in fully rational creatures. Creatures who are less than fully rational may well have the beliefs without the motives, much as (the suggestion goes) creatures who are less than fully rational may fail to believe that q when they believe that p and that p → q.[8]

Moreover, and more importantly, it should also be evident that even if reason does produce a motive in this sense, that will be neither here nor there as regards the debate in the theory of motivation. For to say that beliefs may produce motivating reasons in this sense is not to tell us about the nature of motives, it is rather to tell us about their rational genesis. True, if the rationalists win this debate then certain motives are, in a sense of that term, cognitive states: they will be fit subjects of a certain kind of rational criticism. But, in another perfectly good sense of that term, their cognitive status will be left indeterminate. For you could think that the rationalists win this debate and yet still be baffled about what motives are, or consist in. That is, the question "Are motives desires or beliefs or states of some other kind?" might still remain open, a real question. And answering this question seems the proper task of a theory of motivation. Indeed, it was precisely because I wanted to keep these different sorts of issue separate that I insisted, in HTM, that "the tasks of constructing a theory of motivating reasons and a theory of the normative reasons of rationality are just different tasks" (HTM: 42–3). So though I think that Humean and non-Humean theorists of rationality disagree about whether reason can produce a motive in this sense, and thus whether motives are in this sense cognitive, I think that we would be wrong to suppose that this is the issue that divides Humean from non-Humean theorists of motivation.[9]

4. Let me now return to Pettit's second criticism of HTM. The criticism is that we do not find there "arguments that would settle [the] issue in favour of the Humean side" (HAM: 530). But why does Pettit find the argument I gave so unconvincing?

Pettit and I agree that the direction of fit argument provides a compelling argument against the view that motivating reasons might be constituted by a belief whose presence does not entail the presence of a desire, what in HTM I called a "belief*." What we disagree about is whether the direction of fit argument provides an argument against the view that motivating reasons might be constituted by desires = beliefs, what in HTM I called a "quasi-belief" (from now on I will omit the translations and simply adopt Pettit's terminology).[10] As I understand it, this turns on whether the non-Humean can provide us with good reason to believe that there are any desires = beliefs. And, as the extended quotation from HTM above indicates, it seems to me that his best shot at convincing us that there are desires = beliefs is to focus on examples of what appear to be practical beliefs. He should therefore focus our attention on moral practice. For in moral practice it may certainly appear that having a belief about what is of value entails being motivated to promote what we believe to be of value. But does moral practice provide the kind of evidence we would need to believe that there are desires = beliefs? In HTM the suggestion is that it does not. For, I argued, if we think of values as (roughly) properties that elicit certain desires in us under certain conditions, then we can explain both why agents do have beliefs about what is of value, and why agents tend to desire to promote what they believe to be valuable, without supposing that their having beliefs about what is of value entails their having desires to promote what they believe valuable; that is, without postulating the existence of desires = beliefs.[11] This is what Pettit finds unconvincing:

But it is not enough for Smith to show that this accommodation is possible. What he has to show is not that it is an available account, but that it is the best account on offer: in particular, that it is a better account of desiderative beliefs than that which the anti-Humean provides. Smith may think that he has ground for ignoring this demonstrative task. He casts the Humean theory as "an 'austere' psychological theory" and he may think that its austerity makes it preferable to any anti-Humean story, just so long as it can account, however awkwardly, for the data cited by the anti-Humean (pp. 56–7). This thought ought not to move him however, for he acknowledges . . . that the enterprise about which Humean and anti-Humean quarrel is one of "formulating a philosophical conception of folk psychological states" (p. 48); it is not one of constructing a psychological theory from scratch but of analysing the theory with which we all already operate. The debate between the Humeans and anti-Humeans remains open. (HAM: 532)

I take Pettit's point. But it seems to me that he ignores an important part of what I said in HTM. To be sure, this strategy will be successful only if moral practice seems better explained by a theory that thus weakens the connection between evaluative beliefs and motivation – a tendency is not the necessary connection postulated by the non-Humean. No mere "awkward" accommodation of the data will do. But in HTM I do in fact cite some examples of Michael Stocker's that count against the stronger connection but not the weaker (HTM: 57, n. 44). For, as I point out, Stocker reminds us that in certain fits of depression, or self-deception, or in certain conditions of physical tiredness, we sometimes believe that a certain course of action is good and yet seem totally indifferent to it; not motivated at all to do what we believe good.[12] Such examples are an embarrassment to the non-Humean who thinks that the evidence provided by moral practice supports the view that there are desires = beliefs. But they are no embarrassment to the Humean who follows the strategy I offer him. For he will think that such examples merely help to give content to the "certain conditions" in which alone values that we recognize in fact elicit desires in us. If this argument is successful – and Pettit says nothing to make us think that it is not – then, far from the issue between the Humean and the non-Humean remaining open, in HTM that issue was adjudicated in the Humean's favour.

5. Unimpressed by my own efforts, Pettit closes HAM by outlining three ways in which the Humean might try to argue for his view. He tells us that these "turn around three claims which would individually undermine the possibility of desiderative beliefs to which the anti-Humean clings" (HAM: 532). Pettit does not himself comment on the relative merits of these three argumentative strategies. But it seems to me fairly plain that only two are really worth considering, and that only one shows any sensitivity to the strength of the non-Humean's case. Let's consider them in turn.

The first claim that the Humean might try to defend is a psychological one: the proposition that there are no such states as desiderative beliefs. The argument, familiar from subjective theories of decision, will be that the only evidence for the existence of desiderative beliefs is the occurrence of desiderative assertions and that the occurrence of such assertions is better explained as the expression of desires. (HAM: 532)

But this is unconvincing. It is as if the Humean has to be blind to part of the evidence provided by moral practice; as if all he can see in need of explanation is why we make moral assertions. For many urge that an important part of what needs explaining about moral practice is its distinctive phenomenology.[13] The experience of moral value, they say (supposedly platitudinously), presents itself to us as the experience of a property possessed by the thing that is of value, not as the experience of your own inner state – a desire or whatever – and the best explanation of this is that moral experience is the experience of moral value. Of course, the evidence is merely prima facie. But it does suggest that there is no knock-down argument against the existence of desiderative beliefs; that there is no alternative to considering head-on what it would be for there to be desiderative facts.

The second claim that the Humean might seek to support is a metaphysical one: the thesis that even if there are belief-like states of a desiderative kind, there are no desiderative facts, and therefore no desiderative perceptions for them to be sensitive to. That will mean that contrary to appearances the desiderative beliefs, and the desires associated with them, will not be cognitive or discursive. (HAM: 532)

But this seems to me plainly wrong. After all, in the spirit of certain recent discussions along these lines, it might be said that if there are no desiderative facts then that means just that all of our desiderative beliefs are false.[14] That would certainly undermine the claim that we have any veridical experience of desiderative facts. But it does not seem to undermine the claim that we have such experience and such beliefs now, prior to the discovery of the metaphysical truth, at all. Indeed, it seems to presuppose that. Thus, for all that the Humean who defends this claim tells us, motivating reasons may actually be constituted by desires = beliefs now, though these are none of them true. This brings us to Pettit's final suggestion.

Finally, the Humean might try to defend a common analytical thesis to the effect that whatever of the psychological and metaphysical matters involved, the only sort of belief which could get close to entailing the presence of desires is a belief which bears on the existence of precisely those appetitive states. The accommodation of desiderative beliefs for which Smith looks would be supported on the grounds of being the only satisfactory account available. (HAM: 532–3)

And so I have been trying to argue.[15]

NOTES

1. See my "The Humean Theory of Motivation," *Mind*, 1987, pp. 36–61.
2. See G. E. M. Anscombe's *Intention* (Oxford, Basil Blackwell, 1957), section 2.
3. See his "Humeans, Anti-Humeans, and Motivation," *Mind*, 1987, pp. 530–3.
4. Pettit actually mentions two, but he only thinks that one is plausible. I omit discussion of the conception of desire that Pettit thinks is implausible, although it seems to me that what I go on to say in the text is relevant by way of a response there as well.

5. If having certain beliefs entails having certain desires then, as Pettit puts it, "it would seem natural to say that the desires are constituted by the beliefs, that the beliefs are themselves desires" (HAM: 531, n. 5). This is why I refer to them as "desires = beliefs."

6. See David Hume's *Treatise of Human Nature*, ed. Selby-Bigge (Oxford: Clarendon Press, 1958), p. 415.

7. As the example indicates, I am taking Tom Nagel as my candidate rationalist (see his *The Possibility of Altruism* [Princeton, NJ: Princeton University Press, 1970]).

8. Tom Nagel is quite explicit about this in *The Possibility of Altruism*, pp. 63–7, as is Christine Korsgaard in her "Skepticism About Practical Reason," *Journal of Philosophy*, 1986, pp. 13–15.

9. I further discuss the issue dividing rationalists from anti-rationalists in my "Reason and Desire," *Proceedings of the Aristotelian Society*, 1987–8.

10. Pettit's terminology may indeed be preferable. For, as Pettit has pointed out to me, the choice of the term "quasi-belief" to describe the states in question may carry the undesired implication that these states have a content that is not really truth-assessable. That is certainly not what I had in mind, as the quotation from HTM above indicates. Perhaps James Altham's term "besire" would be even better (see his "The Legacy of Emotivism," in Graham Macdonald and Crispin Wright, eds., *Fact, Science and Morality: Esssays on A. J. Ayer's Language, Truth and Logic* [Oxford: Basil Blackwell, 1986]).

11. Actually, in HTM the argument is more guarded still. For, as I said there, I am not sure that the concept of a desire = belief is really coherent (HTM: 56–7). In HTM I argued rather that, even if the concept of a desire = belief is coherent, the non-Humean offers us no good reason to believe that there are any desires = beliefs. Note, however, that David Lewis and John Collins have recently made the somewhat stronger logical objection that the non-Humean's claim that there are desires = beliefs collides with decision theory (see Lewis's "Desire as Belief" and Collins's "Belief, Desire and Revision," both in *Mind*, 1988).

12. See Michael Stocker's "Desiring the Bad: An Essay in Moral Psychology," *Journal of Philosophy* (1979).

13. This seems to be a common theme running through the writings of David Wiggins and John McDowell (see, for example, Wiggins's "Truth, Invention and the Meaning of Life" and "A Sensible Subjectivism?," both in his *Needs, Values, Truth* [Oxford: Basil Blackwell, 1987], and McDowell's "Values and Secondary Qualities," in Ted Honderich, ed., *Morality and Objectivity* [London and New York: Routledge & Kegan Paul, 1985]). But, perhaps more importantly in the present connection, many of those who reject the conception of value Wiggins and McDowell argue for actually accept the point about phenomenology (see, for example, John Mackie's *Ethics: Inventing Right and Wrong* [Harmondsworth: Penguin, 1977], Chapter 1, and Colin McGinn's *The Subjective View* [Oxford: Clarendon Press, 1983], pp. 145–58). I discuss the phenomenological issues further in my "Objectivity and Moral Realism: On the Significance of the Phenomenology of Moral Experience," in *Realism and Reason*, ed. Crispin Wright and John Haldane (Oxford: Oxford University Press,1993), pp. 235–55.

14. I have in mind John Mackie's discussion in Chapter 1 of his *Ethics: Inventing Right and Wrong*.
15. I have had the benefit of useful comments from and conversations with Simon Blackburn, James Dreier, Gideon Rosen, Jay Wallace, and, especially, Philip Pettit. The final version of this paper was written while I was a Visiting Fellow at the Department of Philosophy, Research School of Social Sciences, Australian National University.

8

Humeanism, Psychologism, and the Normative Story

What explains an agent's actions? Many different answers can be given to this question. But the mark of the answers in which philosophers have principally been interested is that they purport to be constitutive answers, that is, answers of a kind whose absence would mean that the event under consideration isn't an action at all. *Humeanism* – the claim that actions are to be explained by an agent's wanting some outcome and his believing that what he is doing is something that he can just do that will bring that wanted outcome about – purports to be such an answer. If we have an event for which such a belief-desire explanation cannot be given then, according to Humeanism, we do not have an action at all but, rather, something that merely happened.

Humeanism is intimately related to the truism that whenever an agent acts there is some description of what he does under which he does what he does intentionally, or, equivalently, for a reason (Davidson 1963). I take it that the link between Humeanism and this truism is supposed to run thus. It is constitutive of an agent's actions that, under some description, they are done for reasons. But since an action is motivated behaviour, these reasons must be the motivating reasons the agent has for doing what he did. So the question naturally arises as to the nature of these motivating reasons, and the obvious answer to give is that suggested by Humeanism. Motivating reasons are desire-belief pairs.

Jonathan Dancy's *Practical Reality* is, I think, best understood as an attempt to undermine our allegiance to these two purported constitutive claims about action. If we must think that psychological states figure in the explanation of action then, according to Dancy, we should suppose that those psychological states are beliefs rather than desire-belief pairs. Dancy thus prefers *pure cognitivism* to Humeanism. But in fact he thinks that we have no business accepting any form of *psychologism* in the first place; no business accepting a theory that explains an agent's actions by reference to that agent's psychological states. For though it is indeed a truism that actions are explained by reasons, Dancy argues that psychological states are only rarely, if ever, reasons. He thus prefers the unadorned *normative story*, a story which contents itself with explaining actions by laying out the considerations in the light of which the agent acted as he did, to any form of psychologism. I will consider Dancy's arguments for these claims in turn.

1. HUMEANISM

Dancy agrees that desire and belief are states with different directions of fit; he agrees that states with these different directions of fit are distinct existences; and he agrees that, at least if we must suppose that psychological states figure in the explanation of action (from here on I will omit this qualification), then we should suppose that desires – that is, states with the desire direction of fit – are essential to that explanation (Dancy 2000: 13, 90). Dancy thus concedes that wherever we have a case of action, we find a desire figuring in its explanation – a desire, note, not a besire, that is, not a state that is desire-like with respect to one content and belief-like with respect to another (contrast McDowell 1979) – and that sounds for all the world like the Humean's constitutive claim. However there remains a residual and significant disagreement.

On my view, a desire is never a necessary part of what motivates. So we have two beliefs which together motivate. One of these is a belief about how things are, and the other is about how things would be if the action were successfully performed. I called this "pure cognitivism." . . . Pure cognitivism accepts . . . the asymmetry of belief and desire, i.e. the fact that belief and desire play quite different roles in motivation. . . . Pure cognitivism accepts that what belief does desire cannot do, and vice versa. But it rejects the characteristic Humean stress on the dominance of desire in the generation of motivation. . . . Desires occur, and . . . [t]heir occurrence is required for motivation, but this is not surprising, since to desire is just to be motivated. (Dancy 2000: 13–14)

In other words, the belief that (say) something is desirable together with a belief about how to bring that desirable thing about can be what explains my acting, but, when they do, they may do so by explaining, *inter alia*, my desiring so to act. This is because desiring is just being motivated. Thus, according to Dancy, the two beliefs in question motivate both the desire and the action; the desire motivates nothing.

At this point, however, it seems to me important that we distinguish the two halves of Dancy's claim. Though Hume denied that either desires or actions could be explained by beliefs, and so in this sense denied that beliefs could be "leading" or "dominant," it has to be said that a Humean theory of motivating states requires no such commitment, at least not strictly speaking. For suppose that beliefs could rationally explain desires but that, when they do, they do not motivate them. That would leave the Humean's theory of *motivating states* intact. For desires may none the less be what motivates subsequent actions.

Once we see that this is so, however – and note that this is the kind of Humean theory I have defended myself (Smith 1988) – it becomes quite striking that Dancy gives no independent argument for the claim that beliefs that rationally explain desires, supposing that some do, motivate those desires. Yet an independent argument is surely needed, as we see when we consider the similarities and differences between the following two cases of the rational explanation of belief.

Case 1: A believes that p, and A believes that p supports q, so A comes to believe that q.
Case 2: A desires that he believes that q, so A comes to believe that q.

Though in both cases 1 and 2 the belief that q is rationally explained by psychological states – beliefs in case 1, desire in case 2 – we only say that the belief that q is *motivated* in situations like case 2, not in situations like case 1. Moreover we say this for good reason.

Rationalizing explanations of belief divide into two kinds. There are those which explain because of the presence of a motive for the belief, that is, a desire that is served by the having of the belief (this is what we have in case 2), and there are those that explain because of the presence of a belief whose content purports to provide the explained belief with some sort of evidential support (this is what we have in case 1). Motivated beliefs thus *contrast*, quite generally, with putatively evidentially well-supported beliefs.

With this lesson in mind as regards the rational explanation of belief, let's consider how we should classify the following two cases of the rational explanation of desire.

Case 3: A believes that it is desirable that he Φs, so A comes to desire that he Φs.
Case 4: A desires that the Φs, and A believes that he can Φ by Ψ-ing, so A comes to desire that he Ψs.

Parity of reasoning forces us to say that, just as motivated beliefs are beliefs that are explained by desires a subject has, so motivated desires must be desires that are explained by desires a subject has. Case 4 must therefore be assimilated to case 2. When a desire is not just explained by another psychological state, but motivated by it, that psychological state must itself be a desire. But then, by this same line of reasoning, we must resist saying that the belief that explains the desire in case 3 motivates that desire. The explanation in case 3 must rather, and I think unsurprisingly, be seen as having much more in common with the explanation in case 1.

The upshot is that even if we suppose, with Dancy, that there are cases of desire rationalization like that described in case 3, we must suppose that the belief in such cases explains the desire in a way that is much like putative evidential support, and nothing like motivation. This, then, is the first problem with Dancy's argument for rejecting the Humean's theory of motivating states. But there is also a second problem as well.

Suppose what I have just said is wrong and beliefs can be motivating states. That would not show that beliefs can do the job of work Humeans insist that their motivating states – that is, desire-belief pairs – can do. For remember, the Humeans' interest in the claim that motivating states are constituted by desire-belief pairs is fuelled by their belief that an event's being suitably explained by such motivating states is constitutive of that event's being an action. The real question, then, is not whether beliefs *can* be motivating states, but rather whether this would show that Humeanism's constitutive claim about action is false or uninteresting.

The suggestion that if beliefs can be motivating states then Humeanism's constitutive claim is false is plainly mistaken. For, as we have already seen, even if beliefs can motivate, since the way in which they explain actions when they do is by way of motivating the desires that Dancy concedes to be essential to the explanation of action, it follows that pure cognitivism *entails* Humeanism's constitutive claim. But nor is it plausible to suppose that if beliefs can motivate then Humeanism's constitutive claim is uninteresting either. To be sure, if beliefs had to explain the desires that explain actions, then Humeanism's constitutive claim would be uninteresting. For its truth would then derive entirely from the truth of a quite different claim about action, namely, that the beliefs that explain those desires are essential to the explanation of action. But this stronger claim is plainly mistaken.

At various points Dancy does flirt with the stronger claim. He tells us, for example, that "the explanation of action . . . can always be achieved by laying out the considerations in the light of which the agent saw the action as desirable, sensible, or required" (Dancy 2000: 136). Assuming that psychological states explain actions, this means that whenever we have an action, and thus whenever we have a desire that explains that action, we have a belief about what is desirable, or sensible, or required that rationally explains that desire. But elsewhere Dancy makes it quite clear that, and why, this cannot be not so.

> Some desires, of course, cannot be explained. But if they cannot be explained, then neither can the action that, in desiring as we do, we are motivated to perform. If we cannot say why we want to do it, the fact that we want to offers nothing by way of explanation for the action. It merely means that we were incomprehensibly motivated to do this incomprehensible thing. (Dancy 2000: 85–6)

Dancy concedes that some desires cannot be explained by the agent's beliefs about what he took to be desirable, sensible, or required (Stocker 1979), and he goes on to draw the conclusion that, in such cases, we cannot explain the agent's action by laying out such considerations either. But it is in this sense, and this sense alone, that he is correct to say that the action cannot be explained *simpliciter*. Since, as he implicitly admits, we do at least have a case of *action* in such cases, and since it is therefore legitimate to ask what makes the actions in such cases actions, as opposed to mere happenings, and since the only answer left for him to give is the Humean's answer that the event is an action because it can still be suitably explained – explained in a different sense, of course – by a desire-belief pair, it looks like Dancy thereby commits himself to the deeper truth of Humeanism. Since he agrees that there are actions that aren't motivated by beliefs, it follows that beliefs could not be motivating states of a kind that can play the role required of a theory of motivating states in a constitutive story about action. The only motivating states capable of playing this sort of role are desire-belief pairs, much as Humeanism insists.

2. MOTIVATING REASONS

So far we have assumed that psychological states figure in the explanation of action. However Dancy's much more radical claim is that this assumption too should be rejected. He agrees with the truism that actions are always explained by reasons. But, he argues, psychological states are only rarely, if ever, reasons.

Dancy's argument for this conclusion is premised on an observation about the nature of reasons for action: reasons are, quite in general, *considerations in the light of which we act* (Dancy 2000: 2). Motivating reasons must therefore be considerations that motivate us when we act. But now, suppose that motivating reasons were belief-desire pairs, as Davidson suggests, or suppose that they were simply beliefs, as pure cognitivism might suggest. It would then follow that the considerations that motivate us would have to be considerations about our beliefs and desires (if Davidson were right), or considerations about our beliefs (if pure cognitivism were right). Yet, as Dancy rightly points out, such claims fly in the face of the facts. The considerations that motivate us are only rarely, if ever, considerations about our own psychology.

To illustrate, imagine I have just bought a new car and someone asks me what considerations motivated me. We would expect an answer such as "The car I bought can comfortably seat the whole family." But the striking fact is that this consideration picks out a feature of the car itself, not a desire or a belief. Of course, as Dancy admits, such a consideration could motivate me only if I had certain psychological states which bear on it. But he insists that we mustn't confuse this claim, which is a claim about psychological states being an *enabling* condition in the explanation of action (Dancy 2000: 127–8), with the crucial claim that those who insist that motivating reasons *are* psychological states need to defend. They need to defend the claim that the consideration that motivates me is a consideration about my own psychological states: that I believe that the make of car I bought can comfortably seat the whole family (say). Yet what the example shows is that this is not normally the case.

Dancy is surely right that it is only in very special sorts of circumstances that the consideration that motivates me is a consideration about some psychological state of mine. We can, for example (Dancy 2000: 124–5), imagine a situation in which the fact that I believe that a cliff is crumbly is sufficient to motivate me to stay away from it, because I know that if I go near it when I believe that it is crumbly, I will get nervous and be more likely to fall off. In these circumstances, Dancy points out, the consideration that motivates me does indeed seem to be *that I believe that the cliff is crumbly*. But, to repeat, this is a very special sort of circumstance indeed. The problem with the Davidsonian theory of motivating reasons thus appears to be that it is committed to the claim that I quite generally face circumstances relevantly similar to those I face in the example of the crumbly cliff. Or, rather, it is committed to this claim *assuming that Dancy's observation about reasons is correct*.

It is here, it seems to me, that we come to the crucial question. Is Dancy right that reasons are, quite in general, *considerations*? He himself notes an ambiguity in the term "reason" (Dancy 2000: 131). Sometimes, as when (say) we ask for the reason why the bridge collapsed, we use the term "reason" to pick out not a *consideration*, but a *state*, specifically, a state that figures in a suitable explanation, generally a causal explanation, of the occurrence in question. An alternative reading of the truism that we always act for reasons would thus be the following: whenever an agent acts there is always some description of what he does under which what he does can be seen to be suitably explained, perhaps causally explained, by a particular kind of state. But if we read the truism in this way then Dancy's argument against the identification of motivating reasons with psychological states collapses. For it is simply irrelevant to this identification that the considerations that motivate us are not considerations about our own psychological states.

Worse still, when we put this conclusion together with the conclusion of the previous section we see that, for reasons Dancy himself concedes, if we use the term "motivating reason" to pick out a state of a kind that explains an event whenever that event is an action, not only is it plausible to suppose that that kind of state is indeed a psychological state, but it is in fact plausible to suppose that that kind of state is a desire-belief pair. This is the upshot of Dancy's concession that some actions cannot be explained by laying out the considerations in the light of which the agent saw the action as desirable, sensible, or required. For desire-belief pairs are the only kind of psychological state that are guaranteed to explain what an agent does whenever he acts.

3. THE NORMATIVE STORY

I said earlier that Dancy's preferred approach to the explanation of action is to give a purely normative story. According to this approach, when we explain an action we content ourselves with laying out "the considerations in the light of which the agent saw the action as desirable, sensible, or required" (Dancy 2000: 136). The agent's psychology is – crumbly cliff cases to one side – irrelevant to the explanation. We have already seen one limitation of this approach. Since agents sometimes act without supposing that there are considerations that show what they are doing to be desirable, sensible, or required, the approach cannot be used to explain all actions. A psychological approach to the explanation of such goings on – a psychological account of what makes them actions – would seem to be the only one in the offing. But the normative story is limited in another way as well. The important question is whether we can fully understand how the considerations in the light of which the agent saw acting in a certain way as desirable, sensible, or required make it rational for an agent to act in that way without, at some point, invoking a more or less independently conceived feature of the relationship between the agent's belief that those considerations obtain and his desiring so to act.

An analogy might help. Hume famously argued that we cannot explain the rationality of inductive reasoning merely by focussing on the evidence that supposedly makes it rational for someone to acquire an inductively supported belief. These days few people follow Hume in drawing the radical conclusion it must therefore not be rational to engage in inductive reasoning. Instead they conclude that an explanation of the rationality of inductive reasoning must proceed by focussing on some more or less independent feature of the relationship between the subject's beliefs that the evidence obtains and the belief that is supposed thereby to be inductively supported (Harman 1986). Psychological considerations are therefore primary. The real question for Dancy's normative story is thus whether the same is true.

My own hunch is that it is (Smith 1994). As I see things, in order to explain why the considerations in the light of which an agent saw acting in a certain way as desirable, sensible, or required make it rational for the agent to act in that way we need to recognize, first, the fact that his believing that acting in that way is desirable is a matter of his believing that he would want himself so to act if he had a desire set that was maximally informed and coherent and unified, and second, that his having a belief with that content coheres better with his desiring to act accordingly than with his being either indifferent or averse to so acting. Dancy rejects an explanation of this kind, prioritising, as it does, features of the agent's psychology. It would be interesting to know what kind of explanation he would give in its place.

REFERENCES

Dancy, Jonathan 2000: *Practical Reality*. Oxford: Oxford University Press.
Davidson, Donald 1963: "Actions, Reasons and Causes," reprinted in his *Essays on Actions and Events*. Oxford: Oxford University Press, 1980. 3–20.
Harman, Gilbert 1986: *Change in View: Principles of Reasoning*. Cambridge, MA: MIT Press.
McDowell, John 1978: "Are Moral Requirements Hypothetical Imperatives?," *Proceedings of the Aristotelian Society* Supplementary Volume: 13–29.

Smith, Michael 1988: "On Humeans, Anti-Humeans and Motivation: A Reply to Pettit," in *Mind*: 589–95.

Smith, Michael 1994: *The Moral Problem*. Oxford: Blackwell.

Smith, Michael 2001: "The Incoherence Argument: Reply to Schafer-Landau," in *Analysis*: 254–66.

Stocker, Michael 1979: "Desiring the Bad: An Essay in Moral Psychology," *Journal of Philosophy*: 738–53.

9

The Possibility of Philosophy
of Action

Fred moves his finger, thereby flicking the switch, turning on the light, illuminating the room and alerting the prowler (Davidson 1963). What explains the action or actions he performs?

Commonsense tells us that we can give many different answers to this question. We might say that Fred moves his finger because he wants to flick the switch, that he flicks the switch because he thinks that doing so will enable the light to go on, that he turns on the light because doing so illuminates the room, that he illuminates the room because he has an obsessive aversion to darkness, that he alerts the prowler because he is ignorant of her presence, and so we might go on. Here, in one and the same situation, we see a rich panoply of commonsense *explanans*: some actions are explained by desires alone, others by beliefs alone, others by non-psychological facts about the world, others by psychological disorders, and still others by ignorance.

Whenever commonsense delivers up this sort of diversity philosophers get nervous. Since these explanations are all given in one and the same situation we clearly assume that they can co-exist. But is it so obvious that this assumption is correct? When we grant one sort of explanation, isn't it possible that we thereby, in effect, preclude others? And, if that isn't so, then why not? How and why is it that diverse explanations of the kind mentioned fit so neatly together? The need for a philosophy of action is upon us. The question we must ask is whether that need can be met: that is, whether a coherent, unifying, story can be told.

If philosophy of action begins when we attempt to state a principle that allows us to unify diverse explanations like those described above then, as I see it, philosophy of action begins with the claim that it is always possible to construct a Humean, belief/desire, explanation of action. The idea

155

is that once we see the central place occupied by Humean belief/desire explanations, we see that all the other explanations we give simply supplement this basic Humean story. So long as the supplementations do not contradict each other, they can quite happily co-exist. The key thus lies in telling a compelling Humean story about the explanation of action, a story which can be supplemented in appropriate ways.

The Humean story has been defended most forcefully and fully by Donald Davidson (1963). The story as he tells it comes in two parts. Consider again the example we began with. In the first, properly Humean, part we identify certain descriptions of what Fred does such that we can raise and answer the question "Why does Fred perform the action so described?" by citing his reasons for so acting, where his reasons are in turn taken to be constituted by belief/desire pairs (more on this use of term "reason" in Section 3). Thus, for example, since we can raise and answer the question "Why does Fred move his finger?" by citing his reasons – he desires to illuminate the room and believes he can do so by moving his finger against the switch – this means that we can cite Fred's reasons – this particular belief/desire pair – by way of explaining why Fred moves his finger: Fred moves his finger *because* he wants to illuminate the room and believes he can do so, in the way described, by moving his finger. The "because" here signals both a teleological and a causal explanation.

In the second part we proceed to show how this basic Humean story can be supplemented. For example we might argue, as Davidson does, that the actions that are not described in ways that can be given a Humean belief/desire explanation of the sort just described are not different events which require their own separate explanation, but are rather redescriptions of the action or actions that we have already explained. So, for example, even though we cannot raise and answer the question "Why does Fred alert the prowler?" by citing his reasons for doing so – for, as we have already said, Fred does not believe that he is alerting the prowler – we have in fact already explained this action because his alerting the prowler is one and the same action as his moving his finger. The explanation is thus given in two stages: Fred's alerting the prowler *is* his moving his finger, and he moves his finger *because* he wants to illuminate the room and believes he can do so, in the way described earlier, by moving his finger.

I said that the first part of Davidson's story is Humean in character. The story is Humean because it sees all actions as explicable, at bottom, by pairs of desires and means–end beliefs, where desires and beliefs are in turn conceived of as states with different, complementary, directions of fit (Smith 1987, 1994a): desires are states that represent how the world is to be, whereas beliefs represent how the world is, and thus how it has to be changed, if it is to be made that way. These states are distinct existences because, for any desire and belief pair we come up with, we can always imagine someone who has the belief but lacks the desire, and vice versa. Desires and beliefs are therefore both essential for the explanation of action. In some contexts it may not be necessary to mention both the desire and the belief. It may be obvious to all concerned that the one or the other is present. Logically speaking, however, it is never completely trivial to mention both a desire and belief in explaining an action because the presence of the one is not entailed by the presence of the other.

I said that the Humean story occupies a central, unifying, place in the philosophy of action. This is because all of the other explanations that we commonsensically give presuppose this basic Humean story. Thus, for example, if in addition to the story we have already told about Fred, the following counterfactual is true:

Had Fred not been ignorant of the prowler's presence then he would not have turned on the light in the first place, and so wouldn't have alerted her,

then it follows that we can cite Fred's ignorance in explaining why he alerts the prowler. The explanation in terms of ignorance thus does not compete with the Humean story, but rather takes it as given and adds a claim about what would have happened if things had been otherwise to it.

This suggests other obvious ways of expanding the sorts of explanations that are available once we accept the basic Humean story. Quite generally, if a desire and belief pair explains an action then it follows that the things that explain the desire and the things that explain the belief explain the action too. Thus, given that we can explain Fred's turning on the light by citing, *inter alia*, his belief that he can illuminate the room by turning on the light, and given that the fact that he can illuminate the room by turning on the light explains his belief, it follows that we can explain Fred's turning on the light by citing, *inter alia*, that very fact: that is, we can say that Fred turns on the light because he can illuminate the room by doing so. Again, when we explain an action by citing a fact it follows that we do not compete with the basic Humean story in terms of desire and belief, but rather presuppose and add to it.

Moreover in such cases there may well be reasons to prefer the new expanded explanation to the original Humean one. If, for example, we explain Fred's turning on the light by citing his desire to illuminate the room and his *belief* that he can do so by turning on the light when we are in a position to give the expanded explanation in terms of his desire and *the fact* that he can illuminate the room by turning on the light, then, for standard Gricean reasons, we thereby conversationally imply that we cannot confirm that Fred in fact illuminates the room when he turns on the light, and this may mislead (Grice 1961). Gricean reasons will therefore always augur in favour of an explanation, like the explanation in terms of a fact rather than a belief, that expands to accommodate the interests of those to whom we are offering our explanations. But in another sense such explanations are, of course, much worse than the Humean's. For while an explanation in terms of a fact presupposes the availability of a Humean belief/desire explanation, the reverse is not true.

The case of explaining actions by citing facts suggests a way in which we might demonstrate the central place occupied by the Humean story. The idea would be to begin by cataloguing as many different commonsense explanations of action as we can, and then to demonstrate the ways in which each of these presupposes a Humean, belief/desire, explanation. Induction would then suggest that Humean explanations must always be available. My aim in this paper is to begin an argument of this kind. The commonsense explanations I consider have all been thought to resist being brought within the Humean fold, and for good reasons. Indeed, as we will see, at least some of them threaten not just the idea that belief/desire explanations of actions are always available, but the idea that any coherent, unifying, story can be told about the explanation of action. My task in what follows, then, is to vindicate not just the Humean's story about the role of beliefs and desires, but the possibility of philosophy of action more generally.

1. ACTIONS EXPLAINED BY EMOTIONS

According to Rosalind Hursthouse, the distinctive feature of the Humean's account of action explanation is that it makes all actions, by their nature, a means by which agents realise their desires given their beliefs (Hursthouse 1991). Humean explanations thus portray all actions as a species of *rational* action, and, as a result, cannot be used to explain what Hursthouse calls "arational" actions. She gives, as examples of arational actions, actions which can be explained by grief:

... tearing one's hair or clothes, caressing, clutching, even rolling in, anything suitable associated with the person that is the object of grief, e.g., pictures, clothes, presents from her ... (Hursthouse 1991: 58)

According to Hursthouse such actions are arational, and so elude explanation in Humean terms, because they are not means by which agents realise their goals given their beliefs.

I maintain . . . that on very many occasions on which such actions were performed it would be true to say . . . : (i) that the action was intentional; (ii) that the agent did not do it for a reason in the sense that there is a true description of action of the form "X did it (in order) to . . ." or "X was trying to . . ." which will reveal the favourable light in which the agent saw what she did and hence involve, or imply, the ascription of a suitable belief; and (iii) that the agent would not have done the action if she had not been in the grip of whatever emotion it was, and the mere fact that she was in its grip explains the action as much as anything else does. (Hursthouse 1991: 59)

Crucially, then, Hursthouse thinks that such actions are not means by which agents realise their goals, given their beliefs, because agents may not have suitable beliefs. But why does she think this?

Focus on the example of someone who rolls around in his dead wife's clothes because he is grieving for her. Because she thinks that this action is appropriately explained by grief, Hursthouse thinks that the very best the Humean can do by way of explaining it is to say that the man rolls around in his dead wife's clothes because he wants to express his grief and believes that he can do so by rolling around in his dead wife's clothes (Hursthouse 1991: 60–62). She therefore objects that in order to give a Humean explanation we have to ascribe to someone who is grieving for his dead wife a desire and belief that he simply need not have. Someone who expresses his grief by rolling around in his dead wife's clothes need not be thought of as having any such self-conscious desire – a desire to express his grief – and nor, therefore, need he be thought of as having a belief about how he might go about satisfying such a self-concious desire.

Hursthouse's mistake, however, lies in thinking that when we give a Humean explanation of an action we should try to capture the fact that it is explicable in terms of grief, even if it is. This is a mistake because, according to the Humean, we begin the task of action explanation by asking why the person involved is doing what he is doing, and, in answering this question, we must look for an appropriate desire and belief pair among those he *actually has*. But once we ask this "Why?" question a rather obvious answer suggests itself. The man is doing what he is doing because he desires to roll around in his dead wife's clothes and believes that he can do so by doing just what he is doing: that is, by rolling around in those particular clothes that he is rolling around in. To be sure, the explanation doesn't mention grief. But it is most certainly an explanation we can give of what the man is doing because it correctly identifies the man's reasons for acting, in the sense of the belief/desire pair that produced his action, relatively bizarre though they may be.

Now in one respect, this is just as it should be. After all, the Humean must not go beyond his brief. If all there is to say about the desires and beliefs of a man who rolls around in his dead wife's clothes out of grief is what we have just said then so be it. But in another respect, the Humean's explanation is distinctly unsatisfying. Though it is not completely trivial – it rules out the possibility that he wants to roll around in his sister's clothing, for example, and mistakenly believes that the clothes he is rolling around in belong to her – it provides us with very little illumination. It simply prompts the question "And why would anyone want to roll around in his dead wife's clothes?" Here is where a supplement to the Humean's explanation is both required and possible.

When we say that the man is rolling around in his dead wife's clothes because he is grieving for her we thereby locate the belief/desire pair that explains his action in a context in which having them makes a certain sort of sense. This is because grief at the loss of a loved one is, by definition, a state in which we are disposed to think, and to desire, and to do, all sorts of things: cry, dwell on memories of the loved one, seek out things that remind us of the loved one and hold them close, and so on and so forth. Given that grief is such a state, it should therefore come as no surprise that we can explain the man's action by citing the fact that he is grieving for his dead wife. Moreover the explanation explains because it takes the fact that there is a Humean explanation available for granted. For it in effect tells us that the man is acting on the basis of some desire that it is typical for people who are grieving to have: in this case, the desire to roll around in his dead wife's clothes.

Nor should it be thought that the point that I am making here requires the assumption that we can reductively characterise grief in terms of a disposition to think, desire and do all sorts of things: that is, the point that I am making goes through even if the "and so on and so forth" clause mentioned above cannot be spelled out without saying something like "and the person is disposed to think, desire and do all sorts of other things as well, things which it is typical for someone who is in a state of grief to think, desire and do." For the essential point is simply that, whenever someone is in a state of grief and she acts intentionally because she is in a state of grief, she must have, *inter alia*, a desire/belief pair that it is typical for someone in a state of grief to have, and that it is this belief/desire pair that explains her action. This remains true even if we concede that grief cannot be reductively characterised.

Of course, the Humean must agree that an explanation of an action in terms of an emotion like grief is, in many ways, a better explanation than a standard Humean explanation. It is better because it provides us with more information, information about why people have the desires they have, and information about what else we might expect from them in the way of behaviour as well. Gricean reasons will therefore always tell in favour of providing an explanation in terms of an emotion if we are in a position to do so. But in another respect such an explanation is, of course, much worse than the Humean's. For while an explanation in terms of an emotion presupposes the availability of a Humean explanation, the reverse is not true. Agents sometimes act on their desires but not on the basis of any emotion.

2. ACTIONS EXPLAINED BY FEELINGS OF FRIENDSHIP

Michael Stocker argues that we must distinguish two quite different kinds of action explanation: the *for the sake of* kind and the *out of* kind (Stocker 1981). Explanations of the *for the sake of* kind are teleological in character. Humean explanations are all of this kind, because an agent's desires specify that for the sake of which he acts. But explanations of the *out of* kind are different, Stocker tells us, and not reducible to explanations of the *for the sake of* kind. If he is right, then it follows that the Humean's is only part of the story of action explanation. It needs to have a story of the *out of* kind super-added to it, a story that does not in turn presuppose the availability of a Humean explanation.

In order to illustrate this difference in kinds of explanation, consider a man who has a friend, and who acts – perhaps he pays him a visit – so increasing his welfare. There are, Stocker tells us, at least two possible explanations we might give of his action. He might have acted *for the sake of the friendship*, or he might have acted *out of friendship*. These explanations are distinct and incompatible because someone who acts for the sake of friendship need not act out of friendship, and someone who acts out of friendship need not act for the sake of friendship. Acting out of friendship presupposes that the agent is disposed to have all sorts of feelings and thoughts and concerns, feelings and thoughts and concerns that mean he is directly concerned with his friend, not with their friendship. These feelings might be utterly lacking when someone acts for the sake of a friendship, however. Indeed, a typical reason why someone acts for the

161

sake of friendship is that the sorts of feelings and concerns that are characteristic of being in a friendship are temporarily lacking. The agent is not concerned for the friend, he is rather concerned, more abstractly, for their friendship. This distinction is certainly plausible. But does it really threaten the Humean's claim that belief/desire explanations – teleological explanations of the *for the sake of* kind – occupy a central unifying place in the explanation of action?

The Humean's obvious reply is to insist that though acting out of friendship does not reduce to acting for the sake of friendship, it does amount, though perhaps only *inter alia*, to acting for the sake of something or other, where acting for the sake of something or other is a matter of acting on the basis of a suitable belief/desire pair (here we recall the previous discussion of Hursthouse). In support of this idea note that the man Stocker describes who acts out of friendship does act for the sake of his friend: or, perhaps better, for the sake of his friend's welfare. He therefore does act on the basis of a belief/desire pair: a desire to promote someone's welfare and a belief that he can do so by paying him a visit.

Stocker in effect admits the possibility of this sort of Humean reply.

My argument so far has been that there are no ends, properly so-called … the seeking of which is, as such, to do a friendly act. This is an argument about the nature of an act's purpose. To that extent, it is consistent with the claim that the character structure out of which friendly acts issue is, itself, somehow constructed out of, analysable in terms of, complex nests of purposes, dispositions to have purposes, hypothetical purposes, and the like. (Stocker 1981: 756)

But he immediately goes on to reject the idea that such a "construction" is possible.

If acting out of friendship is composed of purposes, dispositions to have purposes and the like, where these are purposes properly so-called, and thus not essentially described by the phrase "out of friendship," there seems … no guarantee that a person, even with those collocated purposes, has friendship or acts out of it. For even with all those purposes, there is no guarantee that the person cares about and likes, has friendship for, the "friend." (Stocker 1981: 756–7)

Stocker's claim here is, in effect, that because we cannot give a reductive analysis of acting out of friendship, it follows that we are in no position to insist that whenever an agent acts out of friendship he does something that can be explained in a *for the sake of* way. But even if we concede

162

the truth of the premise, I do not see how it is supposed to support the conclusion (again, recall the previous discussion of Hursthouse).

Let's agree that acting out of friendship amounts only *inter alia* to acting for the sake of something or other, where acting for the sake of something or other is a matter of acting on the basis of a suitable belief/desire pair, and let's agree further that the conditions we need to add in order to spell out the *inter alia* clause cannot be specified without saying something along the lines of "and the two people involved have other sorts of desires and thoughts and feelings as well, the sorts of desires and thoughts and feelings that people have when they are close friends." As far as I can see this concession is irrelevant to the Humean's crucial point. For the Humean's crucial point is simply that, whenever someone does act intentionally out of friendship, she acts on the basis of a belief/desire pair, and that has been *conceded* by Stocker in this reply. The fact that we cannot reductively characterise the circumstances in which someone acts out of friendship is thus neither here nor there. It follows that *out of* explanations do indeed presuppose explanations of the *for the sake of* kind.

The Humean should of course admit, once again, that *out of* explanations are, in some respects, better than *for the sake of* explanations. We learn more when we are told that a man acts out of friendship than when we are told that he acts because he desires to increase someone's welfare. *Out of* explanations give additional information about the cares and concerns and thoughts of the person who acts. If we are in a position to give such an explanation then Gricean reasons will always tell in favour of doing so. But in another sense *out of* explanations remain much worse than Humean *for the sake of*, or belief/desire, explanations. For while *out of* explanations of actions presuppose the availability of Humean *for the sake of*, or belief/desire, explanations, the reverse is not true.

3. ACTIONS EXPLAINED BY BELIEFS ABOUT THE DESIRABILITY OF ACTIONS

Mark Platts has argued that it is not always possible to find a Humean belief/desire explanation of an action because some actions are explained by evaluative beliefs, and not by desires (Platts 1979).

We perform many intentional actions . . . that we apparently do not desire to perform. A better description of such cases appears to be that we perform them because we think them desirable. The difficulty of much of moral life then emerges as a consequence of the apparent fact that desiring something and thinking it desirable are both distinct and independent. The premise . . . [that desires are always part of the explanation of an action] . . . can, of course, be held true by simply claiming that, when acting because we think something desirable, we do indeed desire it. But this is either phenomenologically false, there being nothing in our inner life corresponding to the posited desire, or utterly vacuous, neither content nor motivation being given to the positing of the desire. Nothing but muddle (and boredom) comes from treating desire as a mental catch-all. (Platts 1979: 256)

Platts's objection has the form of a dilemma. On one horn the Humean is supposed to be saying something contrary to commonsense, for we ordinarily do admit that some actions are directly explained by our evaluative beliefs. On the other horn – the horn the Humean launches himself onto if he insists that in such cases there always are accompanying, though perhaps unnoticed, desires – Platts objects that there is nothing there for the Humean's posited desire to be. The desire certainly isn't phenomenologically salient, and what else could the Humean have in mind?

Let's begin with the phenomenological point. Platts assumes, rightly, that the Humean has a coherent position only if there is some determinate content to his ascription of a desire. He also assumes, again rightly (though see Smith 1987), that one way of assigning determinate content would be to conceive of desires in terms of their characteristic affective nature or feel. If the Humean chooses to assign determinate content in this way, however, Platts's objection is that the Humean's view is phenomenologically false, as we need have no feelings of attraction or aversion when we act.

Platts is surely right about the phenomenology. But is the best story the Humean can tell about what we ascribe when we ascribe a desire a phenomenological story? It would seem not. We have already seen that the distinctive feature of desires is not their characteristic feel, but rather their characteristic direction of fit vis-à-vis that of belief. If we cash out these facts about the characteristic directions of fit of belief and desire in functional terms, then it turns out that the Humean can give determinate content to his ascription of desire by insisting, familiarly, that what he thereby ascribes is a state with a certain sort of functional role (Smith 1987).

This conclusion is very important, because it undermines the other horn of Platts's dilemma. Once we agree that phenomenological considerations are irrelevant, and agree also that to have a desire is simply to be in a state with a certain sort of functional role vis-à-vis the production of action, it follows that Platts is quite wrong to deny that desire is at least part of the explanation of every action, *even granting* that we sometimes act because we believe that doing so is desirable. For he can hardly deny that, whenever we so act we are in a psychological state with the functional role that the Humean takes to be constitutive of desiring; and nor can he deny that our being in such a functionally characterised state explains our action: our being in a state with this sort of functional role explains our act as well as dispositions ever do. In so far as there is anything left of Platts's objection to the Humean, the objection can therefore be at best that once the Humean assigns a causal role to the desire, he is precluded from assigning any causal role to the agent's evaluative belief *as well*.

Now it seems to me that there is a profound challenge to the Humean view lurking here, but before I state and confront that challenge head-on I want to make it clear that the challenge exists only if we assume the truth of a contested view in meta-ethics. The contested view in meta-ethics is sometimes called "internalism" or the "practicality requirement on moral judgement": the view that there is some sort of necessary, or internal, connection between believing an act to be desirable and having at least some motivation to perform that act (Smith 1994a: 60–3). The argument requires this assumption because if we do not grant it then the Humean has no problem at all assigning the belief that an act is desirable a proper causal role in the production of action. If there is merely a contingent, or external, connection between believing an act to be desirable and having some motivation to perform it, then the Humean can surely quite rightly insist that the extra contingency, or external fact, that is required to obtain in order for the belief to play that causal role is the presence of a suitable desire, a desire which will combine with the belief to produce a motivation to perform the act in the normal desire and means-end belief way. What is needed is therefore a desire to do what is desirable.

Thus, to consider an example, the Humean could say that the belief that keeping a particular promise is desirable can indeed play a causal role in the production of action, a role coeval with that played by the relevant desire, but only on the contingency that it combines with a desire to do what is desirable. For, in combination, this belief/desire pair can produce a desire to keep that promise, a desire that can in turn combine with yet another suitable means-end belief to produce an act of promise keeping. To have an objection to the Humean at all, then, Platts requires us to assume that an *externalist* account of evaluative motivation of the kind just described is inappropriate.

Now, as it happens, I agree with Platts's *internalist* assumption. To stick with the example, it seems to me wildly implausible to suppose, as we have just supposed, that the belief that keeping a promise is desirable only ever plays a causal role in the production of action in combination with an independent and prior desire *to do what is desirable* (Smith 1994a: 71–6). This is wildly implausible because it is tantamount to the idea that people who are motivated to keep their promises because they believe that doing so is desirable really only care about the keeping of their promises instrumentally – that is, as a means to the end of doing what they believe to be desirable – and that the only thing that such people care about non-instrumentally is doing what is desirable. As I see it the internalist assumption should be accepted precisely because it allows us to deny this wildly implausible claim (Smith 1996). For if the belief that it is desirable to keep a promise is a belief about the non-instrumental value of keeping a promise, rather than a belief about the instrumental value of doing so, then internalism tells us that there is a necessary, or internal, connection between an agent's having this belief and desiring, non-instrumentally, to keep a promise. In other words, it tells us that the belief that keeping a promise is desirable and the desire to keep a promise may both play a causal role in the production of action, but that no such role need be played by the desire to do what is desirable, because agents who act on their evaluative beliefs need have no such desire.

But now the enormity of the problem the Humean faces becomes clear. If there is a necessary, or internal, connection between believing that acting in a certain way is desirable and desiring to act in that way then, on the assumption that there are no necessary connections between distinct existences, it would seem to follow that this belief and desire *are not* distinct existences. There must therefore be at least one pairing of belief and desire such that we *cannot* imagine someone having the belief but lacking the desire: every possible world in which someone believes that, say, keeping promises is desirable is a world in which they also desire to keep promises. The Humean thesis that the beliefs and desires that are part of the explanation of every action are *distinct existences* must therefore be rejected (see also McDowell 1978; Pettit 1987; but contrast Smith 1988).

The anti-Humean's objection here has some force. He has appealed to the commonsense idea that, even when not mediated by a desire to do what is desirable, beliefs about the desirability of our actions can still play a proper causal role in the production of our actions, and he has used this commonsense idea to try to force the conclusion that these beliefs are therefore not distinct psychological states from desires to act accordingly, a conclusion Humeans simply cannot accept. Now it might be thought that the anti-Humean is clearly right, and that we should therefore give up that aspect of the Humean story. It might be thought that it would be no big deal to admit that some of the beliefs that explain our action *are* desires. Unfortunately, however, we cannot simply give up that aspect of the Humean story. There is an equally powerful line of argument pushing in the opposite direction, a line of argument equally based in commonsense.

Consider any occasion on which someone acts on his belief that keeping a promise is desirable, and let's stipulate that his action is not caused by the desire to do what is desirable. Here is the commonsense observation. It is still merely a *contingent* fact that the agent in question does not suffer from weakness of will, for no mere mortal is *necessarily* virtuous (Smith 1994b). But to say that it is merely a contingent fact that the agent in question does not suffer from weakness of will means that there is a possible world in which, *on that very occasion*, though he still believes that it is desirable to keep the promise he doesn't desire to keep it, but rather desires to do something else instead. But now consider the upshot. The mere fact that an agent could have suffered from weakness of will on each and every occasion on which he acts in a virtuous way entails that his beliefs about the desirability of his actions and his desires to act accordingly *are* distinct existences. They are distinct existences because we can always imagine a possible case in which the agent has the evaluative belief without the desire: the possible case in which the agent is weak.

The real problem should now be apparent. If we accept the premises of both these lines of argument, and if both are valid, then it follows that our beliefs about the desirability of our actions both *are* and *are not* distinct from desires to act accordingly, and that is a blatant contradiction. What is called into question by these sorts of arguments is thus not merely the adequacy of a Humean story about the explanation of action, as opposed to an anti-Humean story, but rather the very idea that the diverse explanations of action that we commonsensically give can be brought together in a unified, non-contradictory, way. What is called into question is thus the very possibility of a philosophy of action.

I want now to argue that we do not have to accept this disturbing conclusion, however, as the anti-Humean's line of argument is manifestly invalid. The anti-Humean wrongly assumes that our beliefs about the desirability of our actions can play a proper causal role in action, a role not mediated by the desire to do what is desirable, only if our evaluative beliefs are identical with desires to act accordingly. But this is wrong because there is an alternative explanation of the necessary, or internal, connection between our evaluative beliefs and our desires, an explanation that leaves the assumption that belief and desire are distinct existences intact. The explanation has the great virtue of enabling us to understand what weakness of the will actually consists in.

If it is possible for our evaluative beliefs to causally explain our desires, and so our actions, then they must do so in virtue of their distinctive evaluative content. We therefore need to ask what it means to say that an act is desirable. As I have argued elsewhere, the best analysis of such facts is given by a dispositional theory of value (Johnston 1989; Lewis 1989; Smith 1989, 1992, 1994a). According to the dispositional theory, facts about the desirability of our actions are themselves facts about our idealised desires concerning those actions. The fact that it is desirable to, say, keep a promise in certain circumstances C is equivalent to the fact that, if we had a maximally informed and unified and coherent set of desires – that is, for short, if we were fully rational – we would desire that we keep that promise in C. Equipped with this dispositional theory of value we are in a position to provide an explanation of how and why our beliefs about the desirability of our actions can explain our actions, an explanation consistent with the claim that beliefs and desires are distinct existences.

Imagine someone who *believes* that, if she were fully rational, then she would desire that, when in certain circumstances C, she keeps her promise, and who also *desires* that, when in those circumstances, she keeps that promise, and compare this agent's overall psychological state with that of someone else who also has the belief but *lacks* the desire. What can we say about the relative merits of their psychologies? The obvious thing to say is that the former psychology exhibits more in the way of *coherence* than the latter (Smith 1995). For, quite in general, an agent's desiring that she Φs in circumstances C fits better, or better coheres, with her believing that she would desire that she Φs in circumstances C if she were fully rational, than does her failing to desire to Φ in C.

If this is right, however – that is, if coherence is on the side of psychologies that pair beliefs about the desirability of acting in certain ways in certain circumstances with desires to act in those ways in those circumstances – then it follows that in a rational agent – by which I mean simply an agent whose psychology tends towards coherence, in the sense just described – we will rightly expect her belief that she would desire that she Φs in C if she were fully rational to be accompanied by the desire that she Φs in C, and where it is not accompanied by such a desire, or where such a desire begins to wane, we will rightly expect the desire to

Φ in circumstances C to be produced or sustained in her by her belief. In agents with no such tendency we will not expect to find the belief that she would desire that she Φs in C if she were fully rational to be accompanied by the desire to Φ in C.

Here, then, we have a thoroughly Humean explanation of how and why an agent's believing that, say, keeping his promise in certain circumstances is desirable can cause him to act without any role being played by the desire to do what is desirable. For an agent who has the belief that keeping his promise in certain circumstances is desirable, and whose psychology tends towards coherence in the sense just identified, will, for the reasons just given, have the desire to keep that promise in those circumstances sustained or produced in him by his belief, a desire that can in turn explain his act of promise-keeping in the normal, Humean, way. The belief thus plays a direct causal role in producing the desire that in turn produces action, a causal role that is mediated by the overall tendency of his psychology towards coherence, not by his desiring to do what is desirable.

The explanation just provided is thoroughly Humean because it presupposes, in true Humean spirit, that an agent's believing that keeping a particular promise in certain circumstances is desirable and his desiring to keep that promise are not one and the same psychological state, but are rather distinct existences. They are distinct because we can pull them apart modally. In possible worlds in which the agent's psychology does not exhibit the tendency towards coherence the agent may have no desire at all to keep his promise despite the fact that he believes it desirable to do so. Lacking such a tendency towards coherence is what (one kind of) weakness of will consists in. But when, contingently, his psychology does exhibit the requisite tendency towards coherence – that is, when he is strong-willed or virtuous – that is all that is required for his belief that it is desirable to keep his promise to cause his desiring to keep his promise. A desire to do what is desirable is simply not required. Platts is therefore wrong to suppose that the mere fact that our evaluative beliefs can sometimes play a direct causal role in the production of our actions counts against the Humean claim that a belief/desire pair, where these are conceived of as distinct existences, is part of the explanation of every action.

Of course the Humean must admit that in some respects explanations of actions in terms of evaluative beliefs may be better than Humean, belief/desire, explanations. They may be better because, if we are in a position to provide them and we don't, our failure to do so may be taken to imply, via a conversational implicature, that such explanations are unavailable:

169

that the desires that cause agents to act *have not* been either sustained or produced in them by relevant evaluative beliefs. Gricean reasons will therefore always tell in favour of providing explanations of agents' actions in terms of their beliefs about the desirability of their actions if we are in a position to do so. For all that, however, Humeans should insist that in at least one respect such explanations are still much worse than belief/desire explanations. For while an explanation of an action in terms of a belief about the desirability of acting in a certain way presupposes the availability of a Humean belief/desire explanation, the reverse is not true. As cases of weakness of will remind us, agents sometimes act on the basis of their desires and means-end beliefs but *in spite of* their beliefs about what it is desirable to do.

4. ACTIONS EXPLAINED BY THE EXERCISE OF SELF-CONTROL

We have just seen that an agent may believe that it is desirable to act in a certain way without desiring to act in that way. This possibility gives rise to one of the more profound challenges to the Humean's claim that belief/desire explanations constitute the core of our commonsense modes of action explanation.

Imagine that I have to choose between eating carrot sticks and chocolate. Though I believe it would be pleasurable to eat chocolate, and though I think that pleasure is indeed desirable, suppose I believe both that it is more desirable to eat healthy food, and that carrot sticks are a more healthy source of food. Despite my evaluative belief, however, imagine that I have no desire at all to be healthy, and that I have a very strong desire to experience pleasure. In other words, imagine that I am suffering from weakness of will, or some similar form of practical irrationality. Under such circumstances, unless I exercise self-control, I will act contrary to my evaluative beliefs – that is, contrary to my beliefs about what I would want myself to do if I were fully rational – and choose the chocolate over the carrot sticks. I therefore need to exercise self-control. Moreover commonsense tells us that we can at least sometimes succeed in the exercise of self-control. I am able to resist the chocolate, and to choose the carrot sticks, despite the fact that I have no desire at all to eat the carrot sticks, and a very strong desire to eat the chocolate.

As is perhaps already evident, the very idea that we can both need to exercise self-control in such cases and succeed in doing so presents a huge problem for the Humean. Choosing the carrot sticks is, after all, an *action*.

But how is it supposed to be so much as possible for me to choose the carrot sticks if I have no desire to do so, and no desire from which such a desire could be derived? The idea that we could both need to exercise self-control and then succeed in doing so thus seems to generate what Alfred Mele calls the "paradox of self-control" (Mele 1987). In order to *succeed* in exercising self-control I must have sufficient desire to perform an action, the very same action which in order to *need* to exercise self-control I must at the same time lack sufficient desire to perform.

It might be thought that we can avoid the contradiction by distinguishing two distinct but causally related actions. One action is the exercise of self-control. If I perform this action then what I cause in myself is a desire to eat carrot sticks, a desire which can in turn cause me to perform a distinct action: the choice of carrot sticks over the chocolate. But while the suggestion that what we do, when we exercise self-control, is cause ourselves to have appropriate desires sounds right, I do not think that the suggestion that whenever we exercise self-control there are two distinct actions, related as cause and effect, is in the end going to help. Here is why.

If every exercise of self-control is an action then we can presumably ask two separate questions about each exercise of self-control an agent contemplates. Does the agent believe that it is desirable to exercise self-control? And, if so, does the agent have corresponding desires? Since, for the reasons already given, the answer may be "Yes" to the first question and "No" to the second, it follows that – on the assumption that every exercise of self-control is an action – in order to successfully exercise first-order self-control an agent may have to perform an act of second-order self-control in order to cause herself to have a desire to do so. To explain how the successful exercise of first-order self-control is possible we would therefore need to explain, first, how the successful exercise of second-order self-control is possible. But, once again, we can ask two separate questions about an agent's exercise of second-order self-control. . . .

This way lies a hierarchy of exercises of self-control, a hierarchy in which we have been led to believe by assuming two things: first, that we can both need to exercise self-control and succeed in doing so, and second, that every exercise of self-control is an action. Since the first assumption is commonsensical, the way to escape the hierarchy, in my view, is to rethink the claim that every exercise of self-control is an action. Of course, it is a truism that every time we exercise self-control we do something. I am not suggesting we reject that truism. My suggestion is simply that the leap from this truism to the conclusion that every exercise of self-control is an action is both unjustified and mistaken. In order to see why, consider again the example.

By hypothesis, I believe that I would desire that I choose the carrot sticks over the chocolate if I were fully rational. So as to be as uncontroversial as possible, let's stipulate that conditions of full rationality are simply those in which I have all relevant information and I am fully instrumentally rational, and, given that stipulation, let's suppose that I have this belief for the following reason. Some time ago I received a free subscription to a health club. Though I had no desire to be healthy, I went along, though initially only out of curiosity. As time passed, however, and I became healthier and healthier, I noticed that I was going along not merely out of curiosity, but because I had acquired a desire to be healthy. This is because, through attending the club and becoming healthy, I gained knowledge of what it is like to be healthy – the body image, the clear head, and the like – and this knowledge caused the desire to be healthy in me. However when, for some reason, I was unable go for a month, I found at the end of that month that not only had I lost my vivid sense of what it is like to be healthy, but that I had also lost all my desire to be healthy as well. With this story in mind note that we are now in a position to explain the successful exercise self-control.

Suppose I have a tendency to recollect, or to think of, the sorts of things that will cause me to have the desires that I believe I would have if I were fully rational in circumstances in which I do not have such desires. If I do have such a tendency then, at the very moment that the chocolates tempt me, my tendency may cause me to recollect what it is like to be healthy, and these memories may cause me to desire to be healthy once again. And if all this takes place then, provided my desire to be healthy is strong enough, I will choose the carrot sticks over the chocolate. In such circumstances my recollecting what it is like to be healthy would surely qualify as an exercise of self-control. But – and here is the crucial point – my recollecting what it is like to be healthy is manifestly not an action caused by a desire to engage in a pattern of recollection. It is rather a cognitive occurrence that is properly explained by my tendency to have such thoughts and recollections at such times, a tendency which we might now, and with good reason, label my "capacity" for self-control. This shows that the assumption that every exercise of self-control is an action is simply mistaken.

If this is right then note that the appearance of paradox in the idea that we can both need to exercise self-control and then successfully do so simply disappears. What makes me need to exercise self-control is indeed the fact that, though I believe it most desirable to eat the healthy carrot sticks, I do not desire most to do so, but desire more strongly to eat the chocolate instead. The successful exercise of self-control, if it takes place at all, takes place against this background. But what takes place is not an action, but a certain pattern of recollection and thought: I have certain recollections of what it is like to be healthy, and these cause me to have a desire to be healthy, a desire that in turn causes me to desire to choose the carrot sticks. The appearance of paradox disappears because, properly conceived, the exercise of self-control is not itself an action that needs to be explained by a desire to exercise self-control. It is rather a purely cognitive occurrence caused by my tendency to have the sorts of recollections or thoughts that will cause me to have the desires that I believe I would desire myself to have if I were fully rational when I do not in fact have such desires.

Moreover note that though we are denying that every exercise of self-control is an action, we are not denying that exercising self-control is something that we do. After all, if in ordinary everyday parlance someone asks you "What are you doing?" it is legitimate to reply "I am thinking" (Kennett and Smith 1996). Thinking is therefore ordinarily taken to be something that we do. But thinking is evidently not an action. The suggestion, then, is that though every exercise of self-control may well be a doing, at least some exercises of self-control are doings that are more like thinkings than actions: that is, they are doings that are not actions (see also Pettit and Smith 1993; Kennett and Smith 1994).

I said at the beginning of this section that cases of self-control constitute one of the more profound challenges to the idea that the Humean can provide us with a coherent and unified account of our commonsense modes of action explanation. This is because, given the Humean account of action explanation, the exercise of self-control looks to be quite paradoxical. As I hope to have shown, however, that challenge can be met. Moreover, in meeting the challenge we have kept in place the idea that Humean, belief/desire, explanations occupy a central place in explanations of action. This is because what the exercise of self-control, itself not an action, causes in an agent is precisely the desire that in turn figures in a Humean explanation of his action.

Of course, the Humean should once again admit that an explanation of an action in terms of the exercise of self-control will often be a better explanation than a regular belief/desire explanation. Gricean reasons will always tell in favour of our giving an explanation in terms of the exercise of self-control when one is available because our failure to do so may imply, via a conversational implicature, that as far as we know the agent was able to act without having to exercise self-control. But in another respect the Humean should insist that explanations in terms of the exercise of self-control are much worse than belief/desire explanations. For while an explanation of an action in terms of the exercise of self-control always presupposes the availability of a Humean belief/desire explanation – for, to repeat, the exercise of self-control causes the desire that figures in the Humean explanation – the reverse is not true. Agents can, after all, sometimes act without having to exercise self-control. But no one ever acts without acting on their beliefs and desires.

5. ACTIONS EXPLAINED BY FACTS ABOUT WHAT IT IS DESIRABLE TO DO

The arguments in the previous two sections have in essence required Humeans to assume that the term "reason" is ambiguous. The term "reason" can be used to pick out an agent's *motivating reasons* – that is, those of her psychological states with the potential to explain her actions: belief/desire pairs – or it can be used to pick out her *justifying reasons* – that is, those facts or considerations which would rationally justify actions on her behalf: facts about the desirability of her actions. As we have seen, the payoffs of this assumption are great. Once the Humean embraces this distinction between justifying and motivating reasons, and adopts a certain view about the nature of justifying reasons – the dispositional theory of value – he can tell a rich and plausible story about the way in which our beliefs about our justifying reasons, and our exercises of self-control, can explain our actions.

Ironically, however, Jonathan Dancy has recently objected to the Humean account of action explanation precisely on the ground that Humeans are forced to make some such distinction between motivating and justifying reasons. The problem he sees is that the distinction is inconsistent with the following maxim in the theory of practical reason.

A reason must be something for which someone could have acted, and in any case where someone does act for that reason, the reason contributes to the explanation of her action. This maxim is . . . in conflict with the . . . [Humean] . . . account of the distinction between motivating and justifying reasons. . . . For the maxim appears to say that justifying reasons must be capable of being motivating ones, and this is directly denied by the claim that motivating reasons are beliefs and desires, while justifying reasons are truths. The categorical difference between truth and psychological state means that no one thing could be a reason of both sorts. (Dancy 1994: 4)

Thus, as Dancy sees things, though the maxim is not violated by the Humean's motivating reasons – for motivating reasons are indeed part of the explanation of any action for which they are the agent's motivating reasons – it is most certainly violated by the Humean's justifying reasons. According to Dancy the Humean simply cannot admit that facts about what rationally justifies what can ever explain an action. At best he tells us that the Humean can admit that our *beliefs* about our justifying reasons explain our actions by causing us to have corresponding motivating reasons, along the lines already described. But beliefs about justifying reasons are not themselves justifying reasons.

Dancy has fallen into the trap of thinking that just because the Humean thinks that beliefs and desires have to be part of the explanation of every action, it follows that he cannot think that facts about justifying reasons – which are not themselves beliefs and desires – can be part of the explanation of any action. But for reasons which I hope are by now familiar, this is manifestly false. Because the Humean admits that an agent's beliefs about her justifying reasons can explain her actions, it follows that he admits that facts about her justifying reasons can explain her actions as well. Facts about an agent's justifying reasons explain an agent's actions whenever they explain why she has the (true) beliefs she has about her justifying reasons, beliefs that in turn explain her actions.

Of course, the Humean must once again admit that such an explanation of an action – an explanation in terms of a fact about a justifying reason – may be, in many ways, a better explanation than not just a standard Humean belief/desire explanation, but also better than an explanation in terms of the agent's beliefs about the desirability of her actions. For reasons already given in earlier discussions, Gricean reasons will always tell in favour of providing an explanation in terms of a fact about a justifying reason if we are in a position to do so. But in another respect the Humean should insist that such an explanation is much worse than a belief/desire explanation. For while an explanation in terms of a fact about a justifying reason presupposes the availability of both a Humean belief/desire explanation and an explanation in terms of an evaluative belief, the reverse is doubly untrue. Because evaluative beliefs can be false, and because agents can sometimes act contrary to their beliefs about what it is desirable for them to do, they can act in ways that are not just unjustified in fact, but that are unjustified even by their own lights.

CONCLUSION

The commonsense explanations of action we have considered here have all been said to be inconsistent with Humean, belief/desire, explanations. But, as we have seen, any appearance of inconsistency disappears under careful analysis. Far from being inconsistent with Humean explanations, these commonsense explanations all presuppose the availability of a standard, Humean, belief/desire explanation. We therefore have strong inductive grounds for supposing that the availability of a Humean explanation is indeed what allows us to see the unity in our diverse commonsense explanations of actions. Though it does not end there, the philosophy of action most certainly begins with the Humean's story.

REFERENCES

Dancy, Jonathan 1994: "Why There Is Really No Such Thing as the Theory of Motivation," *Proceedings of the Aristotelian Society*: 1–18.

Davidson, Donald 1963: "Actions, Reasons and Causes," reprinted in his *Essays on Actions and Events*. Oxford: Oxford University Press. 1980.

Grice, H. P. 1961: "The Causal Theory of Perception," *Proceedings of the Aristotelian Society*: 121–52.

Hursthouse, Rosalind 1991: "Arational Actions," *Journal of Philosophy*: 57–68.

Johnston, Mark 1989: "Dispositional Theories of Value," *Proceedings of the Aristotelian Society* Supplementary Volume: 139–74.

Kennett, Jeanette, and Michael Smith 1994: "Philosophy and Commonsense: The Case of Weakness of Will," in Michaelis Michael and John O'Leary Hawthorne, eds., *Philosophy in Mind*. Dordrecht: Kluwer Press. 141–57.

Kennett, Jeanette, and Michael Smith 1996: "Frog and Toad Lose Control," *Analysis*: 63–73.

Lewis, David 1989: "Dispositional Theories of Value," *Proceedings of the Aristotelian Society*. Supplementary Volume: 113–37.

McDowell, John 1978: "Are Moral Requirements Hypothetical Imperatives?," *Proceedings of the Aristotelian Society* Supplementary Volume: 13–29.

Mele, Alfred 1987: *Irrationality: An Essay on Akrasia, Self-Deception and Self-Control*. New York and Oxford: Oxford University Press.

Pettit, Philip 1987: "Humeans, Anti-Humeans and Motivation," *Mind*: 530–33.

Pettit, Philip, and Michael Smith 1993: "Brandt on Self-Control," in Brad Hooker, ed., *Rationality, Rules and Utility*. Boulder, CO: Westview Press. 33–50.

Platts, Mark 1979: *Ways of Meaning*. London: Routledge and Kegan Paul.

Smith, Michael 1987: "The Humean Theory of Motivation," *Mind*: 36–61.

Smith, Michael 1988: "On Humeans, Anti-Humeans and Motivation: A Reply to Pettit," *Mind*: 589–95.

Smith, Michael 1989: "Dispositional Theories of Value," *Proceedings of the Aristotelian Society* Supplementary Volume: 89–111.

Smith, Michael 1992: "Valuing: Desiring or Believing?," in David Charles and Kathleen Lennon, eds., *Reduction, Explanation, Realism*. Oxford: Oxford University Press. 323–60.

Smith, Michael 1994a: *The Moral Problem*. Oxford: Basil Blackwell.

Smith, Michael 1994b: "Minimalism, Truth-Aptitude and Belief," *Analysis*: 21–6.

Smith, Michael 1995: "Internal Reasons," *Philosophy and Phenomenological Research*: 109–31.

Smith, Michael 1996: "The Argument for Internalism: Reply to Miller," *Analysis*: 175–84.

Stocker, Michael 1981: "Values and Purposes: The Limits of Teleology and the Ends of Friendship," *Journal of Philosophy*: 747–65.

NOTE

I would like to thank Anita Avaramides, John Bigelow, Bill Brewer, John Campbell, Bill Child, Henry Fitzgerald, Elizabeth Fricker, Steve Gardner, Frank Jackson, Dale Jamieson, Jakob Hohwy, Richard Holton, Jeanette Kennett, Daniel Nolan, Philip Pettit, and Daniel Stoljar for their very helpful comments on a draft.

Part Two

Meta-Ethics

10

Moral Realism

In the past twenty years or so the debate over moral realism has become a major focus of philosophical activity. Unfortunately, however, as a glance at the enormous literature the debate has generated makes clear, there is still no consensus as to what, precisely, it would take to be a moral realist (Sayre-McCord 1988a). My aims in this essay are thus twofold: first, to clarify what is at stake in the debate over realism, and, second, to explain why, as it seems to me, the realist's stance is so much more plausible than the alternatives.

MORAL REALISM VERSUS NIHILISM VERSUS EXPRESSIVISM

What do moral realists believe? The standard answer is that they believe two things. First, they believe that the sentences we use when we make moral claims – sentences like "Torturing babies is wrong" and "Keeping promises is right" – are capable of being either true or false, and, second, they believe that some such sentences really are true. Moral realism thus contrasts with two quite distinct kinds of view.

The first view shares realism's first commitment, but rejects the second. According to this first alternative, when we make claims about acts being right and wrong we intend thereby to make claims about the way the world is – we intend to say something capable of being either true or false – but none of these sentences really are true. When we engage in moral talk we presuppose that rightness and wrongness are features that acts could possess, but we are in error. There are no such features for acts to possess. This view generally goes under the name of Nihilism or the Error Theory (Nietzsche 1887; Mackie 1977).

181

The second more radical view shares neither commitment. According to this view, the sentences we use when we make moral claims are not used with the intention of saying something that is capable of being either true or false. We do not use them in an attempt to make claims about the way the world is. By contrast with Nihilism, we therefore do not presuppose that rightness and wrongness are features that acts could possess. Rather we use moral sentences to express our feelings about acts, people, states of the world, and the like. When we say "Torturing babies is wrong" it is as if we were saying "Boo for torturing babies!" This view generally goes under the name of Expressivism or Non-Cognitivism (Hare 1952; Gibbard 1990; Blackburn 1994).

Expressivism and Nihilism share a conception of the world as value-free and so devoid of any moral nature. However they differ in a crucial respect as well. Because Nihilism insists that moral thought and talk presupposes that rightness and wrongness are features of acts, it sees the value-free nature of the world as something that demands a reform of moral practice: we can hardly sincerely continue to assert falsehoods once we know them to be falsehoods. Moral thought and talk thus has the same status as religious thought and talk once we become convinced atheists. By contrast expressivism holds that the value-free nature of the world has no such consequence. It holds that moral thought and talk can proceed perfectly happily in the knowledge that the world is value-free because, in making moral claims, we never presupposed otherwise.

The upshot is that there are therefore two fundamental – if rather abstract and general – questions that need to be answered to resolve the moral realism debate. The first is whether sentences that ascribe rightness and wrongness to actions are capable of being true or false: if we answer "yes" to this question then we thereby refute Expressivism. And the second question, which presupposes an affirmative answer to the first, is whether any sentences ascribing rightness and wrongness to actions really are true: if we answer "yes" to this second question then we thereby eliminate the Nihilist option as well. We thereby commit ourselves to the truth of moral realism.

AN INITIAL DIFFICULTY

So described, moral realism looks to be a very demanding doctrine. It can go wrong in two distinct ways: perhaps it wrongly supposes that sentences ascribing rightness and wrongness to actions are capable of truth and falsehood; or, granting that it is right about that, perhaps it wrongly supposes that some of these sentences really are true. However, as we will see, the real danger is that moral realism, so understood, is insufficiently demanding.

The distinctive feature of the two abstract and general questions just asked is that they each involve semantic ascent: that is, they each speak of a feature that must be possessed by the sentences we use when we make moral claims, or a relation that must obtain between these sentences and the world. But the fact that they each involve semantic ascent poses an initial difficulty. If a commitment to the truth of moral realism comes by answering "yes" to these two abstract and general questions, then it looks like such commitment might come cheaply, at least to competent speakers of English who have any moral commitments at all. Let me illustrate the difficulty.

Like most people reading this essay, I have various moral commitments. For example, I am quite confident that torturing babies is wrong. As a competent speaker of English, I am therefore willing to say so by using the English sentence "Torturing babies is wrong." Imagine me saying this out loud:

Torturing babies is wrong.

Moreover, as a competent speaker of English, I am also willing to say so by not just *using* this sentence of English, but also by *mentioning* it. Imagine me saying this out loud:

"Torturing babies is wrong" is true.

or even

"Torturing babies is wrong" is really true.

This is because, in common parlance, mentioning this sentence, and saying of it that it is true, is simply an alternative way of saying what I could have said by using the sentence.

"'Torturing babies is wrong' is true" and "'Torturing babies is wrong' is really true" are simply long-winded ways of saying that torturing babies is wrong, ways that involve semantic ascent.

Given the initial characterization of what it takes to be a moral realist, it therefore seems to follow that I am a moral realist. After all, since I willingly assert the truth of "Torturing babies is wrong" it follows that I think that the sentences I use when I make moral claims – sentences like "Torturing babies is wrong" – are both capable of being true or false and that some of these sentences really are true. . . . Something has clearly gone wrong. Perhaps a commitment to moral realism follows from the mere fact that I have moral commitments, together with the fact that I am a competent speaker of English, but it seems very unlikely. But what exactly has gone wrong?

An obvious suggestion is that the surface grammar of moral sentences is potentially misleading, masking some deeper metaphysical fact. Though we *say* that these sentences are true and false, this is loose talk. What moral realists really believe, the suggestion might be, is that the sentences we use when we make moral claims are capable of being true or false *strictly speaking*, rather than merely *loosely speaking*. Everything thus turns on what it is to speak strictly, as opposed to loosely, when we say of sentences that they are true or false.

MINIMALISM

What do the words "true" and "false" mean, strictly speaking? One very popular view nowadays is *minimalism about truth* (Horwich 1990; Wright 1992). According to this view, the role of the words "true" and "false" in our language is simply to enable us to register our agreement and disagreement with what people say without going to the trouble of using all the words that they used to say it.

For example, suppose A says "Snow is white, and grass is green, and roses are red, and violets are blue," and that B wants to register his agreement. If the word "true" wasn't a part of our language then, in order to do so, B would have to quote what A said and then disquote. He would have to say "A said 'Snow is white' and snow is white, and A said 'Grass is green' and grass is green, and A said 'Roses are red' and roses are red, and A said 'Violets are blue' and violets are blue." But that requires B to use more than twice the number of words that A used. The role of the word "true," according to minimalism, is simply to allow B to register his agreement more efficiently. Because we have the word "true" in our language, B can quantify over all of the things that A said and then say, all at once, "Everything B said is true."

The upshot, according to minimalism, is that all there is to say about the meaning of the words "true" and "false" strictly speaking is precisely what we said when we noted the initial difficulty. All there is to know about the meaning of the word "true" is that, when "s" is a meaningful sentence of English, and when "'s' is true" is also a meaningful sentence of English, someone who says "'s' is true" could just as well have disquoted and said instead "s." When you mention or quote an English sentence, and meaningfully append "is true" to it, that is just another way of saying what could have been said by using or disquoting that English sentence. Minimalism about truth thus suggests that when I say "'Torturing babies is wrong' is true," rather than "Torturing babies is wrong," I *am* speaking strictly, for I thereby register the appropriateness of disquotation.

Accordingly, it seems to me that we should therefore put a very first realist option on the table. *Minimal Moral Realists* believe three things. First, they believe that the sentences we use when we say that actions are right and wrong are true or false strictly speaking, rather than merely loosely speaking; second, they believe that some of these sentences really are true; and third, they believe that, strictly speaking, the meanings of the words "true" and "false" are fully explained by the minimalist's story.

Minimal Moral Realism is a very cheap doctrine indeed: if you accept the minimalist's story about truth then, if you have any moral commitments at all, you are a moral realist – or, at any rate, you are a Minimal Moral Realist. Nihilism and Expressivism are eliminated in one fell swoop. The obvious question to ask is thus whether we should all be Minimal Moral Realists. The answer depends on something orthogonal to the moral realism debate itself: the plausibility of the minimalist's story about truth. As I will now argue, however, the minimalist's story is seriously inadequate.

THE MAIN PROBLEM WITH MINIMALISM

Minimalists about truth tell us that all there is to know about the meaning of the word "true" is that, when "s" is a meaningful sentence of English, and when "'s' is true" is also a meaningful sentence of English, someone who say "'s' is true" could just as well have disquoted and said instead "s." But this story – at least in the form in which it has just been told – buries an extra, crucially important, piece of information about truth, for it fails to tell us the conditions that need to be satisfied by "s" in order for "'s' is true" to be a meaningful sentence of English. In other words, it fails to tell us what it is about a sentence that is capable of truth and falsehood that *makes* it capable of truth and falsehood. Let me spell out this problem in greater detail (Jackson, Oppy, and Smith 1994).

Everyone agrees that "Snow is white" and "'Snow is white' is true" are both meaningful sentences of English. Moreover, everyone also agrees that though "Hooray for the Chicago Bulls!" is a meaningful sentence of English, "'Hooray for the Chicago Bulls!' is true" is not. But why is there this difference between the two sentences? What do the meaningful strings of English words that are truth-apt have in common, that they don't have in common with those strings of English words that are non-truth-apt? What feature of the truth-apt sentences of English makes them truth-apt? Minimalism about truth, as so far characterized, does not provide us with an answer. Yet surely an answer to this question is part of what we need to know, when we know all there is to know about the meaning of the word "true."

Minimalists about truth typically insist that they can provide a suitably minimal answer to this question (Wright 1992; Horwich 1992). Consider three strings of English words: "Snow is white," "Torturing babies is wrong," and "Hooray for the Chicago Bulls!" The standard minimalist suggestion is that the first two strings of English words are truth-apt, and the third isn't, because of a purely *syntactic* feature that they possess and the third lacks. The first two strings of English words, they suggest, are of an appropriate grammatical type to figure in a whole array of contexts: the antecedents of conditionals (for example, "If snow is white, then it is the same color as writing paper" and "If torturing babies is wrong then I will support the existence of a law against it" are both well-formed sentences), propositional attitude contexts ("John believes that snow is white" and "John believes that torturing babies is wrong" are both well-formed sentences), and so on and so forth. But the third, by contrast, is not of the appropriate grammatical type to figure in these contexts (neither "If hooray for the Chicago Bulls then I will get tickets to see them play next season" nor "John believes that hooray for the Chicago Bulls" are well-formed sentences). It is this syntactic feature of the first two sentences that, according to the minimalists, makes it appropriate for them to figure in "'_____' is true" contexts, and it is the fact that the third lacks this feature that makes it incapable of figuring in such contexts. So, at any rate, minimalists typically argue.

However, for reasons Lewis Carroll made plain in his wonderful poem *Jabberwocky*, this minimalist account of truth-aptitude is unsatisfactory (1872). "'Twas brillig, and the slithy toves did gyre and gimble in the wabe" looks like a conjunction of sentences which, syntactically, are of the appropriate grammatical type to figure in the antecedents of conditionals (thus, for example, "If the toves are gyring and gimbling in the wabe then I will watch them" looks for all the world to be a well-formed sentence), to be embedded in propositional attitude contexts ("I believe that the toves are gyring and gimbling" looks to be a well-formed sentence), and so on. Indeed, it looks like these sentences can have "true" predicated of them ("'The toves are gyring and gimbling in the wabe' is true" looks to be a well-formed sentence). But it doesn't follow that these sentences are truth-apt. Indeed, we know that they aren't truth-apt because, notwithstanding their syntax, they are nonsense sentences, sentences without any meaning whatsoever. They are therefore incapable of being either true or false. The idea that mere syntax is sufficient to establish truth-aptitude is thus absurd.

We must therefore ask what a sentence with the right syntax must have added to it in order to make it truth-apt. For example, what feature would Carroll's sentence "The slithy toves did gyre and gimble in the wabe" have to have added to it, in order to make it truth-apt? The answer is both straightforward and commonsensical: the sentence would have to be meaningful, rather than nonsense, and for this to be the case the constituent words in the sentence – words like "tove," "gyre," "gimble," and "wabe" – would have to be associated with patterns of usage which make it plain what information about the world people who use the words in those ways intend to convey when they use them.

But if this is right then it seems to follow immediately that truth-aptitude cannot be a minimal matter. If sentences which are truth-apt have to be sentences that could, in principle at least, be used to convey information, then they must be sentences that could, in principle, be used to give the content of people's beliefs (or, in order to avoid Moorean problems with meaningful sentences like "I have no beliefs," they must be sentences that are suitably related by some grammatical transformation to sentences that could, in principle, be used to give the contents of people's beliefs [I will ignore this complication in what follows]). But no minimalist story could be told about the sentences that are suited to play this role. It is a substantive fact about a sentence that its constituent words are associated with patterns of usage that allow them to convey information about particular aspects of the world. It is this substantive fact about a sentence that we discover when we discover which belief it can be used to express. And it is therefore this substantive fact about a sentence that we need to discover in order to establish that it is truth-apt.

We are now in a position to identify the main problem with Minimal Moral Realism. Minimal Moral Realism assumes the truth of minimalism about truth, and so buys into the minimalist's assumption that truth-aptitude is itself a minimal matter. But this assumption is mistaken. "Keeping promises is right" may indeed be a meaningful sentence of English of the appropriate grammatical type to figure in the antecedents of conditionals, propositional attitude contexts, and the like, but it does not follow from this alone that it can be used to give the content of people's beliefs. Indeed, as we will see, many argue that there is a principled reason for supposing that such a sentence could not give the content of anyone's belief.

EXPRESSIVISM AND INTERNALISM

We now know what would have to be the case for sentences like "Torturing babies is wrong" and "Keeping promises is right" to be capable of being true or false, strictly speaking. The words contained in these sentences – words like "right" and "wrong" – would have to be associated with patterns of usage that make it plain what information about the world people's use of them is intended to convey. The question to ask is therefore whether the patterns of usage associated with the words "right" and "wrong" have this feature. Can we give an account of the information about the world that the use of such words is intended to convey? Many people argue that we cannot.

They begin by noting the very striking fact that people's moral views tell us something about their dispositions to action. For example, it would be extremely puzzling if, having announced your firm conviction that the right thing to do is to give money to Oxfam, you then claimed utter indifference to actually giving money to Oxfam when the opportunity arose. Perhaps your indifference could be explained away. Depression and weakness of will can, after all, sap our desire to do what we think is right. But, absent some such explanation, it seems that your indifference would give the lie to your announced conviction. It would reveal you to be a hypocrite. This is why, when it comes to expressing moral views, actions speak louder than words.

This striking fact is called the *internalism constraint* (Hare 1952: Chapter 1; Blackburn 1984: 187–9). According to internalists, there is an internal or necessary connection between the moral judgements we make and our motivations. If true, internalism places a constraint on the proper use of moral sentences. It tells us that it is a constraint on the proper use of "Torturing babies is wrong" that someone who sincerely utters it is averse to torturing babies, at least other things being equal (in other words, absent depression, weakness of will, and the like). Likewise, it tells us that it is a constraint on the proper use of "Keeping promises is right" that someone who sincerely utters it desires to keep promises, at least other things being equal.

Expressivists seize on the truth of internalism and ask the obvious question. How could the proper use of moral sentences be constrained by the truth of internalism if they could be used to give the contents of people's beliefs? After all, when we consider sentences that can uncontroversially be used to give the contents of people's beliefs – sentences like "Snow is white," "London is north of Paris," "If you waste your time in school then you will diminish your life prospects in the future," and the like – we note that they can all be used by people perfectly sincerely *no matter what* pattern of desire and aversion these people have. Why should there be any difference with moral sentences?

For example, it is not a constraint on the proper use of the sentence "If you waste your time in school then you will diminish your life prospects in the future" that someone who sincerely utters this sentence desires people to waste their time in school, or is averse to people wasting their time in school, or is indifferent to people wasting their time in school. The belief that wasting your time in school will diminish your life prospects in the future can quite happily co-exist with any of these attitudes. Moreover, we find this same pattern of possibilities when we consider any other sentence that can uncontroversially be used to express the content of people's beliefs. So, Expressivists ask, why don't we find that same pattern of possibilities in the case of the sentences "Torturing babies is wrong" and "Keeping promises is right," if they too express beliefs? Why can't the belief that keeping promises is right co-exist perfectly happily with the desire to keep promises, aversion to keeping promises, and indifference to keeping promises? What is it about this belief, if there is any such belief, that makes it require the presence of a desire to keep promises? Isn't that an astonishingly peculiar feature for this particular belief to have?

The answer, according to Expressivists, is that we don't find that same pattern of possibilities because the sentences "Torturing babies is wrong" and "Keeping promises is right" *cannot* be used to give the contents of anyone's beliefs (Jackson, Oppy, and Smith 1994). They cannot be used to give the contents of anyone's beliefs because there are no such beliefs for anyone to express. Beliefs are states that give information about the world. As such, they can co-exist with any pattern of desire, indifference and aversion. So since people's moral views cannot co-exist with any pattern of desire, indifference and aversion, it follows that the proper role of the sentences people use when they tell us about their moral views cannot be to express such states. The proper role of "Torturing babies is wrong" is rather to express aversion to torturing babies, and the proper use of "Keeping promises is right" is to express the desire to keep promises, not to express any belief.

Accordingly, Expressivists hold that moral sentences, when properly understood, are really on a par with other uncontroversially non-truth-apt sentences, sentences like "Hooray for the Chicago Bulls!" The latter sentence is non-truth-apt not because of its surface syntax, according to Expressivism, but rather because it is properly used to express a pro-attitude towards the Chicago Bulls, rather than any belief about the Chicago Bulls. Likewise, sentences about actions being right and wrong are non-truth-apt because they are properly used to express desires and aversions with regard to those actions, not beliefs about them. When we say of moral sentences that they are true or false, and when we talk of moral beliefs, we are therefore at best speaking loosely, not strictly. Strictly speaking, moral sentences cannot be true or false. They cannot be true or false; they cannot be used to convey information about the way anything is. Strictly speaking, there are no moral beliefs for anyone to express.

Expressivists are thus best seen as offering a challenge to both moral realists and Nihilists. They challenge both these theorists to explain how the use of moral sentences could be constrained by the truth of internalism if their proper use was to convey information. What information is it such that, in order to possess that information, you have to have certain desires or aversions? Expressivists intend this question to be rhetorical. Even so, many opponents of Expressivism – both moral realists and Nihilists – have tried to answer the challenge. But in order properly to answer the challenge we can now see that they must do more than simply stamp their feet and insist that moral sentences *can* be used to give the contents of beliefs. They must specify, in precise terms, what the content of these beliefs is. Let's focus in on a particular example of an attempt to do just that.

NATURALISTIC MORAL REALISM

As I said at the outset, I am quite confident that torturing babies is wrong, and I am quite willing to say so by using the English sentence "Torturing babies is wrong." But if my use of this sentence expresses some belief I have about torturing babies, then it is fair and reasonable to ask what the content of that belief is. What feature of the world would make it true that torturing babies is wrong? It might be thought that we could just give the glib answer: torturing babies would have to have the feature of being wrong. But it turns out that I have to be able to say much more than this.

If there is some feature of torturing babies that makes it true that torturing babies is wrong, then, in giving an account of that feature, we are constrained by our conception of the world in which we live. This means, in turn, that we are constrained by the truth of *naturalism*, the view that the world is amenable to study through empirical science. This is because, given the success of the empirical sciences in providing explanations of various aspects of the world, it is extremely plausible to hold that the world is *entirely* amenable to study through the empirical sciences. Naturalism accordingly entails that the only features we have any reason to believe objects have are one and all naturalistic features, features which are themselves posits, or composites of posits of empirical science. The upshot is therefore that, if any form of moral realism is true at all, then it must be a form of Naturalistic Moral Realism (Railton 1993a, 1993b).

Naturalistic Moral Realism holds not only that some of the sentences that we use to make moral claims are capable of being true and false, and that some really are true, but also that what makes the true ones true are naturalistic features of the world, features amenable to understanding in scientific terms. If moral features exist at all then, given the truth of naturalism, it follows that they too must be features that can be discovered either directly by observation, or by inference from observational information. Moral beliefs must therefore have naturalistic contents, for only so could they be made true by naturalistic features of the world.

We can now ask a more specific version of the question we asked earlier. If, as Naturalistic Moral Realists suppose, the sentence "Torturing babies is wrong" can be used to give the content of a belief, then what *naturalistic feature* does someone with this belief thereby believe torturing babies to have? This is the question Naturalistic Moral Realists must answer. Moreover, they must answer this question by appealing to some constraint on the way in which we use moral words. There must be some constraint on our use of moral words that makes these words apt to pick out a natural feature of acts. It is not difficult to see what that constraint might be.

By all accounts it is a conceptual truth that the moral features of acts *supervene* on their naturalistic features: two acts which are identical in all of their natural features must be alike in their moral features as well. It thus follows that if we acknowledge that a particular act is right, but insist that another act, exactly the same in every naturalistic respect, isn't right, then we thereby mis-use the word "right." Likewise for "wrong." When we apply "right" and "wrong" to acts, we are thus constrained to do so in the belief that the acts in question have some naturalistic feature that *warrants* the ascription of "right" or "wrong." This is the *supervenience constraint* (Jackson 1997).

The fact that we are constrained to use moral words in the way just described – the fact that we are constrained to ascribe moral features in virtue of naturalistic features – requires an explanation, however. Why can't we say that acts are alike in all naturalistic respects, and yet differ morally? Why can't moral features float free of naturalistic features altogether? The obvious answer, the answer favored by Naturalistic Moral Realists, is that this is because moral features *are* natural features.

If this is agreed, then the only question left to answer is *which* natural features warrant the ascription of various moral features to acts. Once we know the answer to this question then, according to Naturalistic Moral Realists, we should simply conclude that moral features are those natural features. For example, if the naturalistic feature of acts that warrants the ascription of rightness turns out to be utility maximization, then, according to Naturalistic Moral Realists, rightness *is* utility maximization. The answer to the question "Which naturalistic feature does someone with the belief that torturing babies is wrong thereby believe torturing babies to have?" will then turn out to be the feature of failing to maximize utility.

THE OPEN QUESTION ARGUMENT

Elegant though this suggestion might be, it faces a serious objection. The objection was first put forward by G. E. Moore (1903). To stick with our example, Moore agreed that acts of utility maximization might always have the feature of being right, but he insisted that we resist concluding that the properties of maximizing utility and being right are the same property. They are, he insisted, quite distinct properties. The argument he gave for this conclusion is his famous Open Question Argument.

Suppose, for reductio, that rightness and utility maximization were indeed one and the same feature of acts. Then, according to Moore, it would follow that "rightness" and "utility maximization" are analytically or a priori equivalent. But it is quite clear that "rightness" and "utility maximization" are not analytically equivalent. After all, if they were analytically equivalent then the question "This act maximizes utility, but is it right?" would have to be one whose answer is immediately obvious to anyone who understands the meanings of the words used, being equivalent to the question "This act maximizes utility, but does it maximize utility?" However, as a moment's reflection reveals, the questions clearly are not equivalent. We can, without self-contradiction, agree that an act maximizes utility but deny that it is right. It therefore follows that the question "This act maximizes utility, but is it right?" is not a *closed question* – one

192

whose answer is immediately obvious to anyone who understands the meanings of the words – but is, rather, an *open question* – one whose answer is open to reasoned argument. "Rightness" and "utility maximization" are thus not analytic equivalents. They do not pick out the same feature.

If the Open Question Argument is sound then it delivers a very strong conclusion indeed. For, as Moore pointed out, it doesn't seem to matter which of the various natural features of acts we consider. It would always be open to reasoned argument whether an act with any of the various natural features we might care to consider is right. It is, for example, an open question whether an act of keeping a promise is right, an open question whether an act which advances my own well-being is right, an open question whether acts that I desire to perform are right, and so we could go on and on. No matter which natural features we choose, it seems that it is never obvious whether an act with such features is right. It is always open to reasoned argument. So, if sound, the Open Question Argument seems to show that rightness is not identical with any natural feature of acts at all. It thus constitutes a decisive refutation of Naturalistic Moral Realism. But if we shouldn't accept Naturalistic Moral Realism, then which theory should we accept instead?

NON-NATURALISTIC MORAL REALISM

Moore himself thought, on the basis of the Open Question Argument, that we should reject naturalism altogether and admit a realm of extra, *sui generis*, non-natural properties into our ontology. Moore thus embraced *Non-Naturalistic Moral Realism*. He believed not only that some of the sentences we use to make moral claims are capable of being true and false, and that some really are true, but also that what makes the true ones true are non-naturalistic states of the world, states that elude understanding in scientific terms. Beliefs about which acts are right and wrong are thus beliefs about the non-natural features possessed by acts. Moreover, according to Moore, some such beliefs represent the world to be the way it really is. Moore was no naturalist.

However the problems with Non-Naturalistic Moral Realism are evident and overwhelming (Blackburn 1984: Chapter 6). The first problem is that it must explain how we come by knowledge of these extra, spooky, non-natural properties. Unsurprisingly, however, Moore had no explanation. He could hardly claim that we come by knowledge of them via observation, for any property knowable in that way is, by definition, naturalistic. But neither could he claim that we come by knowledge of them via inference from any of the naturalistic features of acts, for that is precisely what the Open Question Argument (allegedly) shows to be impossible. The only options left seem to multiply the mysteries. For example, we might suppose that there is some non-empirical sort of observation, a sort of spooky sixth sense which allows us to detect the presence of spooky non-natural properties. But as soon as the idea is stated it is plain that it is, in reality, too absurd even to contemplate.

The second problem for Non-Naturalistic Moral Realism is that it must explain why there aren't possible worlds in which the non-natural properties that Moore supposes to be identical with moral properties float free of the natural properties with which they are coinstantiated in actuality. And again, unsurprisingly, Moore had no explanation of why this possibility is ruled out. If non-natural properties are distinct from natural properties then, it seems, we should be able to pull them apart modally. But, given that moral properties supervene on natural properties, it follows that we cannot pull them apart modally. He was thus forced to view the supervenience of the non-natural on the natural as a brute mystery.

THE OPEN QUESTION ARGUMENT, NIHILISM, AND EXPRESSIVISM

By and large, philosophers have therefore tended to think that even if it is sound, the Open Question Argument, properly understood, gives no support whatsoever to Non-Naturalistic Moral Realism. However there has been no great consensus as to what, precisely, it shows instead.

One possibility is that though the argument succeeds in establishing the conceptual truth that we *conceive* of moral features as non-naturalistic, and hence succeeds in showing that our beliefs about which acts are right and wrong are one and all beliefs about the non-natural features possessed by acts, Moore went wrong in supposing that any such features are instantiated. Viewed in this light, what the three problems just described show is that such non-natural features are nowhere instantiated in actuality. No acts have such non-natural features, and hence all our moral beliefs are false. Accordingly, on this way of thinking about it, the proper conclusion of the Open Question Argument is not a form of moral realism, but rather Nihilism. The problem with this way of thinking about Moore's argument, however, is that it concedes the intelligibility of Moorean non-natural properties, whereas the three problems just described make it look like non-natural properties aren't really intelligible at all.

194

Another, and more popular, suggestion has therefore been to suppose that the Open Question Argument constitutes a reductio of the very idea that there are moral features (Hare 1952; Blackburn 1994). According to this suggestion, the reason we can't come by knowledge of the moral features of acts via an inference from knowledge of their naturalistic features is because that would require that there are two distinct ways the world could be – a naturalistic way and a moral way – which stand in a certain logical relation to each other. But there aren't two ways the world could be, there is only one way, a naturalistic way. The upshot, according to this suggestion, is that the claim that the world is a certain way morally isn't true, strictly speaking. The role of a moral claim isn't to represent the world as being a certain way, and hence isn't to give the content of any belief, but is rather to express desires or aversions. Thus, according to this way of thinking, the Open Question Argument constitutes a second, and many think decisive, line of argument for Expressivism.

The problem with this alternative way of thinking about Moore's Open Question Argument, however, is that it assumes that Expressivism itself somehow manages to escape the clutches of the Open Question Argument (Smith 1998). In fact, however, Expressivism itself is extremely vulnerable to a version of the argument. This is because, though Expressivism sets itself against the view that (say) "Torturing babies is wrong" is analytically equivalent to some naturalistic claim about the way the world is – for that would assume something Expressivism takes to be false, namely that wrongness is a feature of acts – it does so by insisting that sentences like "Michael judges that torturing babies is wrong" *is* analytically equivalent to some naturalistic claim: specifically, it is analytically equivalent to "Michael expresses his aversion to torturing babies." But now it seems that we can run a version of the Open Question Argument. Here is how it goes.

If "Michael judges that torturing babies is wrong" and "Michael expresses his aversion to torturing babies" were analytically equivalent then the question "Michael expresses his aversion to torturing babies, but does he judge that torturing babies is wrong?" would have to be one whose answer is immediately obvious to anyone who understands the meanings of the words used. However, as a moment's reflection reveals, the questions clearly are not equivalent. We can, without self-contradiction, agree that Michael expresses his aversion to torturing babies, but deny that he thereby judges it to be wrong. But, if this is right, then it follows that the question "Michael expresses his aversion to torturing babies, but does he judge it to be wrong?" is not a closed question – one whose answer is immediately obvious to anyone who understands the meanings of the words – but is, rather, an open question – one whose answer is open to reasoned argument. "Michael expresses his aversion to torturing babies" and "Michael judges that torturing babies is wrong" are thus not analytically equivalent. They do not pick out the same feature of the world.

Moreover, as with the earlier application of the Open Question Argument, it doesn't seem to matter which of the various natural features of Michael we consider. It would always be open to reasoned argument whether, when Michael expresses any of the various natural features we might care to consider – various complexes of desire, second-order desires, or whatever – he is thereby judging that torturing babies is wrong. If sound, the Open Question Argument therefore seems to show that Michael's judging it wrong to torture babies isn't analytically equivalent to any natural feature of Michael either. It thus constitutes a decisive refutation of Expressivism.

But now we have surely proved too much. After all, we said at the outset that the only options available are Nihilism, Expressivism, or some form of moral realism: that is, either Naturalistic or Non-Naturalistic Moral Realism. Yet what we have just seen is that, if sound, the Open Question Argument, together with ancillary premises, rules out *all* these options. That surely cannot be. The only conclusion to draw is therefore that, properly understood, the Open Question Argument is *unsound*. But where-in lies the mistake in the argument?

THE NATURALISTIC MORAL REALIST'S FIRST RESPONSE TO THE OPEN QUESTION ARGUMENT

Many contemporary Naturalistic Moral Realists argue that the flaw lies in the assumption that it somehow follows from the fact, conceding it to be a fact, that "rightness" and "the property of maximizing utility" are not analytically or a priori equivalent, that these terms pick out different features. That this is a flaw is, they insist, evident from examples with which we are familiar in empirical science (Brink 1989; Darwall, Gibbard, and Railton 1992).

For example, "Water" is not analytically or a priori equivalent to "H_2O," but empirical science teaches us that water is just H_2O. "Redness" is not analytically or a priori equivalent to "surface reflectance property α," but empirical science teaches us that redness is just a certain surface reflectance property that we will, for convenience, call "α." So, in this particular case, they argue that the Open Question Argument assumes, wrongly, that if rightness and the property of maximizing utility were one and the same property, then it would have to be an a priori truth, one discovered by reflection on the meanings of the words "rightness" and "the property of maximizing utility," but it thereby overlooks the possibility that it may be an a posteriori truth, one discovered through observation and inference. Naturalistic Moral Realists who offer this reply to the Open Question Argument therefore face a challenge. They must show how it could be an a posteriori truth that these terms pick out the same feature. Unfortunately, however, those who face up to this challenge find that they simply run into the Open Question Argument all over again.

According to many Naturalistic Moral Realists, for example, the reason it is an a posteriori truth that rightness is the property of maximizing utility is that we invoke rightness and wrongness in order to explain various empirical phenomena, and then we discover, a posteriori, that the maximization of utility occupies the relevant explanatory role. For example, they argue that since, contingently, right actions have certain effects – they are causally responsible for a tendency towards social stability, for example – so it follows that we can fix the reference of the term "right" via the description "the property of acts, whatever it is, that is causally responsible for their tendency towards social stability."

Equipped with this reference fixing description, we can then investigate acts with this effect in order to find out which feature explains this tendency. If, say, we discover that the feature that is causally responsible is the maximization of utility, then we can conclude that rightness is the property of maximizing utility. Our conclusion will then be a posteriori, not a priori.

The answer is supposed to be straightforward because the explanation involved has the same structure as those we give in other less controversial cases. Since, contingently, red objects have certain effects – they cause those objects to look red to normal perceivers under standard conditions – so it follows that we can fix the reference of "redness" via the description "the property of objects, whatever it is, that causes them to look red to normal perceivers under standard conditions." Equipped with this reference fixing description we can then investigate the acts which have this effect in order to find out which feature explains this tendency. If, say, we discover that the feature that is causally responsible is surface reflectance

197

property α, then we can conclude that redness is surface reflectance property α.

Unfortunately, however, this reply to the Open Question Argument is inadequate, and the reason why is perhaps already evident (Jackson 1997). Consider again the case of colors. True enough, we will not find a justification for thinking that redness is surface reflectance property α merely by reflecting on the meanings of the words "surface reflectance property α" and "redness." The fact that redness is surface reflectance property α is clearly something we discover a posteriori through empirical investigation. But in explaining how we come to make this discovery a posteriori, it is clear that we do in fact appeal to an a priori truth about redness. For we simply assumed that we can fix the reference of "redness" via the description "the property of objects, whatever it is, that causes them to look red to normal perceivers under standard conditions." But what sort of justification can we give for this claim? It clearly isn't supposed to be yet another a posteriori truth. Rather it is supposed to be an a priori truth, one which is either stipulated in the act of reference fixing itself or else discovered by reflection on the everyday meaning of the word "red." Either way, it is because we accept this claim a priori that we can move straight from the discovery that surface reflectance property α is the property that causes objects to look red to normal perceivers under standard conditions to the conclusion that surface reflectance property α is redness.

By analogy, then, even though it may well be an a posteriori truth that rightness is the property of maximizing utility, in the very argument we gave in support of this claim it is clear that we in fact appealed to another truth, but this time one which is supposed to be known a priori, about the relation between rightness and certain natural properties. For we simply assumed that we could fix the reference of "rightness" via the description, "the property of acts, whatever it is, that is causally responsible for their tendency towards social stability." But what sort of justification can be given for this claim? It clearly isn't supposed to be another a posteriori truth. Rather, it is supposed to be an a priori truth, one which is either stipulated in the act of reference fixing or else discovered by reflection on the everyday meaning of the word "right." Either way, it is precisely because we accept this claim a priori that we can move straight from the discovery that the property of maximizing utility is the property acts possess when they tend towards social stability to the conclusion that the property of maximizing utility is rightness.

This is an extremely important point, one which is quite devastating to those Naturalistic Moral Realists who think they can reply to Moore's Open Question Argument by insisting that, even though the terms "rightness" and "the property of maximizing utility" are not analytically or a priori equivalent, these terms none the less pick out the same feature of acts. For what they fail to remember is that Moore's Open Question Argument is supposed to refute *all* claims to the effect that "rightness" is analytically or a priori equivalent to a term ascribing natural features to acts, no matter which natural features are in question. If sound, it thus even refutes the claim that it is a priori that rightness is the property acts possess when they tend towards social stability. The alleged refutation goes like this: we can agree that an act has the property which is causally responsible for the tendency of acts towards social stability and yet, apparently without self-contradiction, deny that it is right, for it is an open question whether such acts are right, a matter for reasoned argument. "Rightness," we should thus conclude, cannot be a priori equivalent to "the property acts possess when they tend towards social stability."

This teaches us a valuable lesson. Naturalistic Moral Realists have no alternative but to face head-on the claim that we can, via the Open Question Argument, refute the claim that there is some naturalistic analytic or a priori equivalent for "rightness."

THE NATURALISTIC MORAL REALIST'S SECOND RESPONSE TO THE OPEN QUESTION ARGUMENT

Moore claims to show that there is no naturalistic claim that is analytically or a priori equivalent to any moral claim by pointing out that it is always an open question whether an act with whichever naturalistic features we care to choose has some moral feature. It is always open to reasoned argument. In order to see where this argument goes wrong, we need to think more generally about the project of conceptual analysis (Smith 1994: Chapter 2; Jackson 1997).

When we try to analyze a concept, what are we trying to do? The answer is roughly this. There are all sorts of constraints on the way we use various words. Consider color words as an example. It is a constraint on the proper use of color words that we use them to pick out properties that cause us to have certain visual experiences; a constraint that we use them to pick out features that are more reliably detected in daylight than in the dark; a constraint that people's use of them is especially likely to be defective if there is something wrong with their eyes; and so on and so forth. When we try to come up with an analytic equivalent of "x is red," our task is to come up with something that captures this complex set of constraints: that is, to come up with an account of what "redness" means that entails them. When we say that "redness" and "the property of objects that causes them to look red to normal perceivers under standard conditions" are analytically or a priori equivalent this is what we have in mind.

If this is right, however, then the success or failure of an analysis is to be judged accordingly. It is not to be judged by the obviousness of the analysis, and nor is it to be judged by whether the analysis is open to reasoned argument. Indeed, if what we have just said is right then it will of course be open to reasoned argument whether or not an analysis is successful because it will be open to reasoned argument what the complex set of constraints on the use of the word being analyzed is and whether or not this complex set is entailed by the proposed analysis.

If an account of the project of conceptual analysis along these lines is right, however, then Moore's argument evidently fails altogether to refute the claim that "rightness" has a naturalistic analytic or a priori equivalent. Consider, for example, the claim that "rightness" is analytically equivalent to "the property of acts that is causally responsible for their tendency towards social stability." It is irrelevant whether or not it is obvious that this is so; irrelevant whether it is open to reasoned argument. The only relevant question is whether, on reflection, we think that this analysis entails the complex set of constraints on the way in which we use the word "right." If it does, then it is analytically equivalent, notwithstanding the fact that it isn't obvious.

In many ways this brings us to where we are today in the moral realism debate. The Open Question Argument isn't sound, but it does make clear the enormous task that lies before Naturalistic Moral Realists. To repeat, Naturalistic Moral Realists must give a naturalistic account of the contents of moral beliefs; an account of the naturalistic feature that they take to be identical with various moral features. But what the Open Question Argument brings out is that, in doing so, they must find naturalistic features that are analytically – or, anyway, a priori – equivalent to those moral features. It need not be obvious that the naturalistic features and moral features are analytically equivalent, of course. It may be open to reasoned argument. But, at the end of the day, it must be demonstrable, on the basis of reflection on the ways in which we use moral words, that the naturalistic features they identify are one and the same as moral features.

The naturalistic theories that have been claimed to fit this bill fall into two quite distinct categories. The first are versions of Externalist Naturalistic Moral Realism (hereafter Externalist Realism) (Sturgeon 1985; Railton 1986; Brink 1989). This is the view that though we can, by reflecting on the ways in which we use moral words, find a naturalistic equivalent for the term "rightness," the naturalistic equivalent we come up with will leave it completely open whether someone who believes an act to be right will desire to perform that act, or be indifferent to performing it, or be averse to performing it. The sort of theory described earlier which claims that rightness fills a distinctive explanatory role, the role of underwriting a tendency towards social stability, is an example of such a theory. Externalist Realists thus face a dual task.

On the one hand, they must come up with an explanation of why, when we reflect on the way in which we use moral words, we should conclude that rightness has the naturalistic equivalent they posit. For example, if we consider again the theory which holds that rightness is the property of acts, whatever it is, that is causally responsible for their tendency towards social stability, Externalist Realists must tell us what it is about the way in which we use moral words that is supposed to make this particular claim seem credible. The vast literature on moral explanations is perhaps best seen as addressing this issue (Harman 1977; Sturgeon 1985; Railton 1986; Boyd 1988). As I understand it, the claim Externalist Realists make in that literature is that "rightness" is a term whose meaning is fixed by a causal explanatory theory which assigns rightness a certain characteristic explanatory role. "Rightness" is thus, in a sense, much like the term "electron." Both terms serve to pick out a feature in virtue of the characteristic causal role that that feature occupies.

On the other hand, however, Externalist Realists must also try to explain away the fact that so many people have been inclined to think that our use of moral words is subject to the internalist constraint. If what we believe, in believing an act to be right, is (say) that the act has the feature that is causally responsible for a tendency towards social stability, then why have so many people been inclined to think that possession of this belief requires a desire to perform such an act, at least other things being equal: that is absent depression, weakness of will, and the like? It is surely an entirely contingent matter whether someone with such a belief will desire to perform such an act, whether they are depressed and weak of will or not. So how did so many philosophers get it wrong for so long? For many, the very fact that Externalist Realism is incapable of capturing the internalist constraint is a decisive reason to reject the theory. But though I am inclined to agree with this objection, I do not want to rest the case against Externalist Realism wholly on it.

Suppose we grant the idea that "rightness" picks out a property in virtue of its explanatory role. Still, mustn't the explanatory role in question be one that somehow guarantees the possibility of giving a justification for acting in the way that is deemed to be right (Sayre-McCord 1988b)? After all, by all accounts, the fact that an act is right implies that there is at least some justification for performing it. Someone who says "Though it would be right to act in that way, there is no justification at all for doing it" mis-uses the word "right." Yet the most remarkable feature of Externalist Realism is that it makes this connection altogether mysterious. Focus again on the version of Externalist Realism developed above. The most remarkable feature of the suggestion that rightness is that property, whatever it is, possessed by acts that tend towards social stability must surely be that an act may conduce towards social stability but be one that there is no justification *at all* for anyone's performing. Explanatory role and justificatory potential just seem to be quite different things.

At the end of the day, then, the really difficult task facing Externalist Realism is thus to come up with an account of the explanatory role of rightness which makes that role connect in some constitutive way with the possibility of giving a justification. Until Externalist Realists come up with such an account, their theory will look like it fails to capture one of the most important constraints on the way in which we use moral words.

INTERNALIST NATURALISTIC MORAL REALISM

This brings us to what seems to me to be the most plausible version of moral realism. Internalist Naturalistic Moral Realists (hereafter Internalist Realists) agree with Externalist Realists that we can characterize rightness in terms of its distinctive explanatory role, but they hold that the explanatory role characteristic of rightness is, broadly speaking, that of eliciting desire under certain idealized conditions of reflection. Consider a specific version of the theory, by way of illustration (Smith 1994).

According to this version of the theory, rightness is that feature, whatever it is, that we would desire our acts to possess if our desires formed a set that is maximally informed, coherent and unified. The Internalist Realist's claim is that this analysis of rightness finds support in the way in which we use moral words. Nor is it difficult to see what reasons they might give. After all, as we have just seen, when we say that acting in a certain way in certain circumstances is right we thereby imply that there is some justification for our acting in that way in those circumstances. But facts about what there is a justification for doing, in various circumstances, are in turn plausibly thought to be facts about what we would advise ourselves to do if we were better placed to give ourselves advice: that is, more precisely, they are plausibly thought to be facts about what we would desire ourselves to do in those circumstances if our desires were immune to rational criticism. That is just what the theory says.

Of course, it might be thought that there are other ways of thinking about justification. But Internalist Realists argue that this particular analysis of the notion is amply supported by various other ways in which we use moral words. For example, it is agreed on nearly all sides that moral knowledge is a relatively a priori matter, at least in the following sense: if you equip people with a full description of the circumstances in which someone acts, then they can figure out whether the person acted rightly or wrongly by just thinking about the case at hand. Someone who claimed that it would be impossible to figure out what is right by just thinking about the circumstances of action would be mis-using the word "right." Internalist Realists argue that this is well explained by the analysis just offered. It is because we can subject our desires about what is to be done in various circumstances to critical evaluation by just reflecting on our desires that moral knowledge seems to be such a relatively a priori matter.

Internalist Realists also claim that the fact that there is a connection between what it is right to do and what there is a justification for doing in turn explains the internalist constraint on the use of moral words. Suppose you believe that a certain act available to you is one which you would desire yourself to perform if you had a set of desires that was maximally informed and coherent and unified. You are then arguably under some rational pressure to have a corresponding desire. After all, desiring to act in the way you believe you would want yourself to act if you had a maximally informed and coherent and unified desire set coheres better with, or fits better with, or makes more sense in the context of, that belief, than would either being averse or indifferent to acting in that way. The coherence of your psychology thus seems to demand the desire of you.

Internalist Realists insist that it should therefore come as no surprise at all that those who believe that acting in a certain way would be right will desire to act in that way, at least absent the effects of depression, weakness of will and the like. Indeed, they argue that their analysis serves to reveal the essential nature of depression, weakness of will and the like.

As psychological conditions that can undermine the connection between moral belief and desire, depression, weakness of will and the like share a common feature: they are all conditions with the inbuilt potential to create psychological incoherence. No surprise that, absent the conditions that make for that sort of incoherence, people will desire to act in the ways that they believe they would want themselves to act if they had a maximally informed and coherent and unified desire set.

SHOULD AN INTERNALIST NATURALISTIC MORAL REALIST BE A RELATIVIST?

For these and other reasons, Internalist Realists think that their own theory is therefore a vast improvement on Externalist Realism. There is, however, an important ambiguity in the Internalist Realist's theory that still needs to be addressed. This touches on the issue of relativism.

Rightness is supposed to be that feature, whatever it is, that we would desire our acts to possess if our desires formed a set that is maximally informed, coherent and unified. But is the idea supposed to be that the "we" referred to in the analysis includes all rational creatures? In other words, is the idea that we would all converge in the desires we would have under idealized conditions of reflection? Or does the "we" include only some subset of the rational creatures? Does it include, say, me and those who desire things similar to the things that I actually desire? In other words, are contingent and rationally optional culturally induced differences in our actual desires supposed to make convergence in the desires we would have under conditions of idealized reflection impossible?

If the latter, then the theory is relativistic (Harman 1975, 1985). According to Relativistic Internalist Naturalistic Moral Realism, when we say that actions of a certain sort are right what we are really saying is a subset of rational creatures – those who have desires like our own – are such that they would desire that we act in that way if they had desires that formed a maximally informed, coherent, and unified set. However we thereby allow that other perfectly rational creatures may differ from us. This needn't force us to think that their acting in that way wouldn't be right as well. If we believe that we would desire them too to act in that way under idealized conditions of reflection then of course we will believe that acting in that way would be right for them, too. The crucial point is simply that their having corresponding desires as part of their idealized desire set is no part of what makes our claim that it is right for them so to act true. On the alternative analysis, by contrast – that is, according to

Non-Relativistic Internalist Naturalistic Moral Realism – their possession of such desires too is required for the truth of our claim (Smith 1994).

But of these two versions of the Internalist's theory it seems to me that the relativistic version is manifestly implausible as conceptual analysis. How could whether or not an act is right or wrong, and hence is justified or unjustified, the paradigm of a non-arbitrary fact about an act, be grounded in something so arbitrary as whether or not someone happens to have certain contingent and rationally optional culturally induced desires? The very idea seems to involve a contradiction. Yet this is the conclusion to which the Internalist who buys into relativism is committed.

The non-relativistic version of the theory, by contrast, holds that such facts are grounded in something that is itself appropriately non-arbitrary. Acts are right or wrong depending on whether, notwithstanding any contingent and rationally optional culturally induced differences in our actual desires, we would all desire or be averse to the performance of such acts if we had a set of desires that was maximally informed, coherent and unified. Underlying this form of Internalism is thus a wonderful picture of ourselves and our relations to other people. At the very deepest level – that is, in that idealized possible world in which we all have a set of desires that is maximally informed, coherent and unified – we share common aims simply in virtue of our nature as rational beings. No one is beyond the pale, not, at any rate, if they remain susceptible to rational argument. Even the most wretched may be reachable.

Notwithstanding how wonderful this picture is, however, it may be mere illusion. The truth of the non-relativistic version of Internalism depends on more than mere conceptual analysis, it depends, as well, on the substantive fact that *there is* a set of desires that we would all converge upon if we had a set of desires that was maximally, informed, coherent and unified. Even if the conceptual analysis is impeccable, absent the power of rational argument – that is, absent the power of information, together with considerations of coherence and unity – to elicit common desires in us, the non-relativistic version of Internalism entails that there are no moral facts at all.

The proper conclusion to draw is thus that even the very best version of moral realism is sub judice, something about which we will be convinced only to the extent that we are confident that the arguments we give ourselves for desiring as we do are arguments that should convince the arbitrary rational person to desire likewise. And, of course, experience teaches that that kind of confidence is difficult to maintain. The unfortunate tendency of the media to portray people from other cultures as radically different from each other, as though they don't even share a common tendency to believe and desire on the basis of reflection as opposed to superstition, let alone a common tendency to desire alike after reflecting, doubtless plays a significant role. Even convinced Non-Relativistic Internalist Naturalistic Moral Realists will therefore continue to feel the pull of Nihilism in their more pessimistic moments.

REFERENCES

Blackburn, S. 1984: *Spreading the Word*. Oxford: Oxford University Press.

——— 1993: "Circles, Finks, Smells and Biconditionals," *Philosophical Perspectives*, 7: 259–79.

——— 1994: *Essays in Quasi-Realism*. New York: Oxford University Press.

Boyd, R. 1988: "How to be a Moral Realist," in G. Sayre-McCord, ed., *Essays on Moral Realism*. Ithaca, NY: Cornell University Press. 181–228.

Brink, D. 1989: *Moral Realism and the Foundations of Ethics*. Cambridge: Cambridge University Press.

Carroll, L. 1872: *Alice's Adventures in Wonderland and Through the Looking Glass*, ed. R. L. Green. Oxford: Oxford Paperbacks.

Darwall, S., A. Gibbard, and P. Railton 1992: "Toward *Fin de Siècle's* Ethics: Some Trends," *Philosophical Review*: 115–89.

Gibbard, A. 1990: *Wise Choices, Apt Feelings*. Oxford: Clarendon Press.

Hare, R. M. 1952: *The Language of Morals*. Oxford: Oxford University Press.

Harman, G. 1975: "Moral relativism defended," *Philosophical Review*: 3–22.

——— 1977: *The Nature of Morality*. Oxford: Oxford University Press.

——— 1985: "Is There a Single True Morality?," in D. Copp and D. Zimmerman, eds., *Morality, Reason and Truth*. Totowa, NJ: Rowman and Allanheld.

Horwich, P. 1990: *Truth*. Oxford: Blackwell.

——— 1992: "Gibbard's Theory of Norms," *Philosophy and Public Affairs*: 67–78.

Jackson, F. 1997: *From Metaphysics to Ethics*. Oxford: Oxford University Press.

Jackson, F., G. Oppy, and M. Smith 1994: "Minimalism and Truth-aptness," *Mind*: 287–302.

Mackie, J. L. 1977: *Ethics: Inventing Right and Wrong*. Harmondsworth, UK: Penguin.

Moore, G. E. 1903: *Principia Ethica*. Cambridge: Cambridge University Press.

Nietzsche, F. 1887: *The Genealogy of Morals*; trans. W. Kaufman and R. J. Hollingdale, *On the Genealogy of Morals and Ecce Homo*, ed. W. Kaufman. New York: Random House Vintage Books. 1967.

Railton, P. 1986: "Moral Realism," *Philosophical Review*: 163–207.

——— 1993a: "What the Noncognitivist Helps Us to See the Naturalist Must Help Us to Explain," in J. Haldane and C. Wright, eds., *Reality, Representation and Projection*. Oxford: Oxford University Press. 279–300.

——— 1993b: "Reply to David Wiggins," in J. Haldane and C. Wright, eds., *Reality, Representation and Projection*. Oxford: Oxford University Press. 315–28.

Sayre-McCord, G. 1988a: "The Many Moral Realisms," in G. Sayre-McCord, ed., *Essays on Moral Realism*. Ithaca, NY: Cornell University Press.

_____ 1988b: "Moral Theory and Explanatory Impotence," in G. Sayre-McCord, ed., *Essays on Moral Realism*. Ithaca, NY: Cornell University Press. 256–81.

Smith, M. 1994: *The Moral Problem*. Oxford: Blackwell, 1994.

_____ 1998: "Ethics and the A Priori: A Modern Parable," *Philosophical Studies*: 149–74.

Sturgeon, N. 1985: "Moral Explanations," in D. Copp and D. Zimmerman, eds., *Morality, Reason and Truth*. Totowa, NJ: Rowman and Allanheld. 49–78.

Wright, C. 1992: *Truth and Objectivity*. Cambridge, MA: Harvard University Press.

11

Does the Evaluative Supervene on the Natural?

One of the few claims accepted by nearly everyone writing about the nature of value is that the evaluative features of things supervene on their natural features. Take any two persons, actions, characters, or states of affairs that are identical in all of their naturalistic features: every naturalistic feature that is a feature of the one is a feature of the other, and vice versa. These two persons, actions, characters, or states of affairs must be identical in evaluative respects as well. There can be no evaluative difference without a naturalistic difference. So, at any rate, it is said.

Those who flout the supervenience requirement when they make evaluative judgements are supposed thereby to reveal themselves to be incompetent in their use of evaluative terms. The supervenience of the evaluative on the natural thus purports to operate as a conceptual constraint on evaluative judgement. This too is accepted by nearly everyone writing about the nature of value. Given that supervenience operates as a conceptual constraint on evaluative judgement, it follows that the right way of thinking about an evaluative theory, at least in its most abstract form, is as a mapping of natural features onto evaluative features. An evaluative theory, in its most abstract form, is thus simply a long list of supervenience conditionals, conditionals such as "If objects have natural features N then they have evaluative features E," "If objects have natural features N^* then they have evaluative features E^*," and so on.

Not everyone is convinced that the evaluative does supervene on the natural, however. In recent work, James Griffin has expressed his misgivings in the following terms. "Supervenience is often regarded as an indisputable fact about value that we must come to terms with. I doubt, though, that values are supervenient. I put it inconclusively because I think that, for reasons I shall come to, it is not easy to say."[1] Griffin then goes on to provide a number of reasons for thinking that the supervenience of the evaluative on the natural demands, at the very least, serious rethinking, if not outright rejection.

Griffin's attack on the claim that the evaluative supervenes on the natural comes as a welcome prompt. As with many theses put forward as candidate conceptual truths in philosophy, and subsequently accepted as such by philosophers quite generally, it is not until someone asks "Why?" that we begin to think more carefully about what, exactly, the thesis we profess to accept really amounts to. When we ask ourselves what the thesis is, and why we believe it, we all too often discover how inadequate the answers we come up with really are. The candidate conceptual truth is just an empty form of words with no clear content. So we discover all too often. But, I will argue, it is not what we discover when we ask what it means to say that the evaluative supervenes on the natural.

The chapter is in seven main sections. In the first three sections I characterize the natural features upon which evaluative features are supposed to supervene. In the fourth section I consider, and reject, a further restriction on the class of natural features, a restriction proposed by Griffin. In the fifth section I consider, and argue against, Griffin's suggestion that a commitment to the supervenience of the evaluative on the natural requires commitment to a bogus fact/value gap. In the sixth section I provide an argument for the claim that the evaluative supervenes on the natural. And then in the seventh and final main section I explain what I take myself to have shown and what I take myself not to have shown. In a brief conclusion, I summarize the main points made in the chapter.

1. A TRIVIALIZING DEFINITION OF "NATURAL"

We are told that the evaluative features of things supervene on their natural features. But what makes something a natural feature? Without an adequate answer to this question the supervenience thesis will not even get off the ground.

It might be thought that we can afford to be relaxed about this. Perhaps we should just say that the natural features of things are those that we would all ordinarily agree they have as part of our everyday commerce with them: the painfulness of the feeling I have in my neck, the telling of an embarrassing joke about someone behind his back, the writing of certain words, and so on and so forth. They are, if you like, the features that we commonsensically ascribe to persons, acts, states of affairs, and the like. But, given the role that the concept of the natural has to play in a statement of the supervenience thesis, it seems to me that we need something much more constrained than this. The problem is that, if our conception of the natural is too relaxed, then the claim that the evaluative features of things supervene on their natural features is in danger of utter trivialization.

Suppose, for example, we are very relaxed. Because "is good" functions grammatically as a predicate, it follows that we can move back and forth between saying "Bloggs leads a good life," on the one hand, and "The life Bloggs leads has the property of being good," on the other. Though utterly pleonastic, it thus looks as though we commonsensically ascribe the feature of being good to lives.[2] But then, if to be a natural feature is to be a property that we commonsensically ascribe to objects, it seems that being good turns out to be a natural feature in its own right. It is a natural feature simply in virtue of the fact that "is good" functions grammatically as a predicate. The claim that there can be no difference between the value of two objects if they have the same natural properties then turns out to be utterly trivial, because the difference in value *itself* amounts to a difference in natural features.

Given that this completely trivial doctrine is not what is intended by the claim that the evaluative supervenes on the natural, it follows that we need to come up with a more circumscribed conception of the natural. While talk of evaluative features may be utterly pleonastic, talk of natural features cannot be: not, at any rate, if we wish to formulate a non-trivial supervenience thesis.

2. A BETTER DEFINITION OF "NATURAL"

We began with the idea that the natural features of things are those that we would all ordinarily agree they have as part of our everyday commerce with them. This idea can be developed in a more circumscribed way if we insist, commonsensically I think, that the features of objects that we would all ordinarily agree they have as part of our everyday commerce with them are those to which we need to appeal in *causally explaining* our commerce with them.

In essence this is what G. E. Moore had in mind when he suggested that the natural features of objects are those that are the subject matter of the natural sciences.[3] Or, rather, it is what Moore had in mind provided we have a very liberal conception of what it is for something to be a natural science, a conception according to which, as Griffin usefully puts it, "a natural science is any systematic set of empirical regularities" (V 306).

Thus, according to Moore's suggestion, as his suggestion is developed by Griffin, natural properties are best thought of as those properties of objects – including those ordinary, everyday, properties that we ascribe to macroscopic objects – that figure in statements of empirical regularities.

Note how commonsensical this suggestion really is. The painfulness of the feeling I have in my neck, the telling of an embarrassing joke about someone behind his back, the writing of certain words, and so on, all these turn out to be natural features, just as we said they were initially. They are all natural features because they are all properties that figure in empirical regularities. The pain causally explains my going to the doctor. The telling of the embarrassing joke about someone behind his back causally explains the subsequent shock that he experiences when he hears about it. The writing of certain words causally explains the acquisition of someone else's belief as regards the content of those words when he reads them. And so we could go on. Moore's suggestion, as developed by Griffin, thus delivers up as natural features a set of features that is easily recognizable as the ordinary, everyday, features of objects with which we have commerce.

We are now in a position to state a non-trivial supervenience thesis. Any two objects that are alike in those of their features that figure in empirical regularities – that is any two objects that are such that every property that figures in an empirical regularity that is a property of the one is a property of the other, and vice versa – must be alike in their evaluative features as well. Unfortunately, however, the thesis so stated also presupposes something that some might think is false. It presupposes, after all, that properties that do not figure in empirical regularities make no difference at all to value. But, once it is admitted that properties that do figure in empirical regularities can make a difference to value, it might be thought that we have to admit that properties that do not figure in empirical regularities, but that at least could have figured in such a regularity, can make a difference to value as well. Let me illustrate this point with an example.[4]

Imagine that in the actual world we believe property P to be the most beautiful feature we have ever seen. Of course, since we have managed to form a belief about P, it follows that P does figure in some sort of empirical regularity in the actual world. But now imagine that P is also instantiated in a possible world in which it does not figure in any empirical regularity. What should we say about P in that possible world? It seems at least conceivable – at least on the line of objection that I am presently considering – that we should say that the most beautiful feature we have ever seen is instantiated in the imagined possible world. If what made P beautiful was not the fact that it figured in any empirical regularity, but rather just its intrinsic nature, then the fact that it does not figure in an empirical regularity in that world seems to be neither here nor there.

If this is correct, however, then we have a potential counterexample to the supervenience thesis just stated. Imagine a pair of objects that are identical in all of the properties they have that figure in empirical regularities. In addition, however, imagine that one of these objects also has P and that the other lacks P, where P is a property that figures in no empirical regularity at all. If the situation is as described above, then we must surely suppose that these two objects will differ in their value, notwithstanding the fact that they are identical in all of those of their features that figure in empirical regularities. They will differ in their value because one of them – the one with P – will have a feature that is the most beautiful we have ever seen (though presumably we will not see it, if it figures in no empirical regularity) and the other – the one without P – will not.

Can we modify the definition of a natural property suggested by Moore and developed by Griffin so as to avoid this objection? It seems to me that we can. We can retreat to the view that what is crucial to the idea of a natural property is not the fact that natural properties *do in fact* figure in an empirical regularity – whether or not P figures in an empirical regularity is, after all, an extrinsic fact about it, a matter of whether or not it happens to be instantiated in a regular pattern throughout space and time – but rather the fact that it *could* figure in an empirical regularity. P may not figure in an empirical regularity in fact, but it should count as a natural property anyway, in the terms required by the supervenience thesis, because it would if it were instantiated in a possible world in which it was part of a regular pattern. A natural property, let us say, is thus any property that could figure in an empirical regularity; or, as I shall put it from here on, any property that is *such as to* figure in an empirical regularity.

Armed with this amended account of what it is to be a natural property, the modified supervenience thesis can be stated in the following terms. Any two objects that are identical in those of their features that are such as to figure in empirical regularities – that is, any two objects that are such that every property that is such as to figure in an empirical regularity that is a property of the one is a property of the other, and vice versa – must be identical in their evaluative features as well. The modified supervenience thesis differs from the thesis stated earlier in that it assigns no special significance to the properties that do in fact figure in empirical regularities. What is important, from the point of view of value, is whether objects are alike in those of their properties that are such as to figure in empirical regularities: that is, those of their properties that do or could figure in such regularities.

The supervenience thesis so stated is still non-trivial provided it is a non-trivial fact about evaluative features, if it is a fact about them at all, that they are such as to figure in empirical regularities. And this assumption in turn seems to be very plausible. Certainly the fact that evaluative features are such as to figure in empirical regularities does not follow trivially from the superficial grammar of evaluative language. If we think that evaluative features are such as to figure in empirical regularities, then, it seems, that would have to be something we come to believe as a consequence of some non-trivial argument, an argument that proceeds by allowing us to identify evaluative features with features whose status as natural features is established independently.[5]

This is just as it should be. The supervenience thesis itself should not rule out the possibility of a non-trivial argument for the claim that evaluative features are natural features. Evaluative naturalism is a possible position on the metaethical landscape, after all. All supervenience requires is that, if evaluative naturalism is true, then it needs to be shown to be true by some such non-trivial argument. Evaluative naturalism cannot follow trivially from the definition of "naturalism." It seems that this is indeed the case if we define natural features as those that are such as to figure in empirical regularities.[6]

3. A FURTHER RESTRICTION ON THE CLASS OF NATURAL PROPERTIES

There remain some ambiguities in the supervenience thesis, ambiguities that need to be removed before we go any further. In removing these ambiguities we will see the need further to restrict the class of the natural upon which the evaluative can plausibly be said to supervene.

The supervenience thesis has us doing pair-wise comparisons of objects with the same natural features. But are we allowed to consider any pair of objects, without regard to the possible worlds in which those objects happen to exist, or are we restricted to comparing pairs of objects where both objects exist in the same possible world? In other words, does the supervenience thesis purport to tell us that objects with the same natural properties, even objects in different possible worlds from each other, have the same value? Or does it tell us that, within a single possible world, pairs of objects with the same natural properties cannot differ in value? The latter allows that an object with those same natural properties in another possible world may have a different value. The former precludes this. The latter is an *intra-world* supervenience claim. The former is an *inter-world* claim.

The only plausible answer – the answer I assumed in my previous remarks about beauty – is that the supervenience thesis is an inter-world claim, not merely an intra-world claim. To suppose otherwise is to suppose that the mere fact that an object happens to exist in *this* particular possible world as opposed to *that* particular possible world can somehow make a difference to its value, independently of the features it has in those worlds that could be possessed by objects in other possible worlds. This, after all, would seem to be the only reason available to explain why, on the intra-world claim, objects with the same natural features in different possible worlds can differ in value. But this seems incoherent on the face of it.

The reason is that particularity itself is entirely arbitrary, from the evaluative point of view. The fact that my life is Michael Smith's life, say, cannot be what makes mine a good life or a bad life, because it could make such a difference only if being Michael Smith's life was somehow a special feature of a life, a feature that is special in a way that being Joe Bloggs's life or John Doe's life is not. But the fact that a life is Michael Smith's life seems to be of no consequence or significance in and of itself. Of course, the fact that my life has other features – the fact that it is a life with a certain amount of pleasure and pain in it, a life in which there have been certain successes and failures, and so on – could be such as to make my life something special. The features that make my life something special might even uniquely pick my life out in actuality. But it is consistent with this that the fact that the life that has these features in actuality is Michael Smith's life is evaluatively irrelevant. Someone else's life in another possible world could have precisely these features.[7]

It therefore seems to me that a ban on particularity is a further constraint that needs to be placed on the ordinary, everyday, features that count as natural features, in the sense required by the supervenience thesis. Value cannot supervene on facts about particularity, so, in the sense of "natural" required by the supervenience thesis, no natural features can be defined in terms of particulars.[8] But, if this is right, then it follows immediately that the fact that an object happens to exist in *this particular possible world*, as opposed to *that particular possible world*, must also be irrelevant to the value of that object. In other words, if an object is good or bad then it must be so in virtue of its possession of features that could be possessed by objects in other possible worlds. It follows that the supervenience of the evaluative on the natural is an inter-world supervenience claim, not merely an intra-world claim.[9]

There is another related ambiguity in the supervenience thesis as well. As we are now understanding the supervenience of the evaluative on the natural, it has us doing pair-wise comparisons of all possible objects, even objects that exist in different possible worlds from each other. For each of these pairs it purports to tell us that they cannot differ in their evaluative properties if they are exactly alike in their natural properties, where natural properties are those that are such as to figure in empirical regularities, and that, further, are not defined in terms of particulars. (From here on I take this last qualification as read.) But when we talk of those of an object's properties that are such as to figure in empirical regularities, we might have in mind two quite different things.

On the one hand, without regard to the possible world in which the object we are considering happens to exist, we might have in mind those of its properties that are such as to figure in empirical regularities in a particular possible world: the particular properties that happen to be such as to figure in empirical regularities in actuality, say. If we think of an object's natural properties in this way, then what the supervenience thesis tells us is that the only properties that can make a difference to an object's value, in any possible world, are those that happen to be such as to figure in empirical regularities in actuality. Two objects in any possible world that are exactly alike in respect of these properties – those that happen to be such as to figure in empirical regularities in the actual world, say – are alike in their evaluative properties no matter what other properties they possess. Other properties – properties that these objects have that are such as to figure in empirical regularities in the possible world in which these objects exist, for example, but not in actuality – are irrelevant to the value of those objects.

On the other hand, when we talk about those of an object's properties that are such as to figure in empirical regularities, we might have in mind all of those properties, whatever they might happen to be, that are such as to figure in empirical regularities in the possible world in which the object we are considering happens to exist. If we were to understand what an object's natural properties are in this way, then the supervenience thesis would tell us that any two objects that are exactly alike in respect of the properties they possess, where these properties are chosen from among those that are such as to figure in empirical regularities in the

215

possible worlds in which they happen to exist, must be alike in respect of value. On this way of thinking, the properties that are such as to figure in empirical regularities in the actual world are not a privileged set with regard to value. Any properties that are such as to figure in empirical regularities in any possible world can potentially make a difference to the value of an object in that possible world.

Once we spell out this ambiguity in the notion of a natural property, it is, I think, plain that the only plausible way to interpret the supervenience thesis is as the claim that objects that are alike in all of their natural properties in the second of the two ways just described, not the first, must be alike in respect of their value. To think otherwise is once again to suppose that the mere fact that properties happen to be such as to figure in empirical regularities in a particular possible world – the actual world, say – is somehow important from the point of view of value. But the fact that properties happen to be such as to figure in empirical regularities in a particular possible world seems once again to be an evaluatively irrelevant fact about them. To suppose that they can alone contribute to value is once again to suppose that particularity can make a difference to value.

It is important to note that this is not to deny that we might eventually come to the conclusion that the only properties that can contribute to the value of an object are properties that happen to figure in empirical regularities in, say, the actual world. For example, in the course of constructing a theory of prudential value, we might convince ourselves that certain properties that figure in empirical regularities in the actual world – pleasure and pain, say – are the only *possible* sources of intrinsic value of a life. For this reason we might go on to conclude that the value of any possible life supervenes on facts about properties that happen to figure in empirical regularities in the actual world: any two possible lives that are identical in terms of certain properties that happen to figure in empirical regularities in the actual world – specifically, pleasure and pain – are identical in value.

The important point about this way of coming to the conclusion that certain properties that happen to figure in empirical regularities in the actual world are especially significant from the point of view of value, however, is that what makes them especially significant is not the fact that they happen to figure in empirical regularities in the actual world, but rather the fact that they emerge as significant in the most plausible theory of prudential value. The latter fact, unlike the former, is an evaluatively significant fact about a property *par excellence*. Prior to constructing a theory of prudential value, then, we should leave it as an open question whether there are sources of intrinsic value that are not present in the actual world, but that are present only in other possible worlds in virtue of the empirical regularities in which those properties are such as to figure in those worlds. That is, we should leave it an open question whether we are cut off from all sorts of sources of intrinsic value in our lives by the fact that the properties that happen to be such as to figure in empirical regularities in the actual world are only some among the many possible such properties. The supervenience thesis itself must, therefore, be interpreted in the second of the two ways described, not the first.

Let me sum up the argument so far.

I have tried to spell out the claim that the evaluative supervenes on the natural in a non-trivial way. In essence this has required me to spell out what a natural property is in such a way that it is a non-trivial fact about evaluative features that they are natural properties, if indeed evaluative features are natural properties (indeed, if evaluative features are features at all, in anything other than a pleonastic sense). My suggestion has been that natural properties are all and only those properties that are such as to figure in empirical regularities, with the further proviso that, in characterizing these properties, we mention no particulars. Given this account of what natural properties are, we should understand the claim that the evaluative supervenes on the natural in terms of the following inter-world supervenience claim.

Consider any pair of objects in any two possible worlds. If every non-particular property that is such as to figure in an empirical regularity in the possible world in which the first object exists, and that happens to be a property of the first object, both is a property that is such as to figure in an empirical regularity in the possible world in which the other object exists, and happens to be a property of that other object, and vice versa (that is, if every non-particular property that is such as to figure in an empirical regularity in the possible world in which the second object exists, and happens to be a property of the second object, both is a property that is such as to figure in an empirical regularity in the possible world in which the first object exists, and happens to be a property of the first object), then, if the first object has a certain evaluative feature, so does the second, and vice versa (that is, if the second object has a certain evaluative feature, so does the first).

My aim in the sections that follow is further to clarify and defend the claim that the evaluative supervenes on the natural in this sense. Though, as we will see in the next section, stronger supervenience claims might be true, these stronger supervenience claims are not plausibly thought to be conceptual truths. The supervenience thesis just stated is the strongest that can plausibly be suggested to be a conceptual truth. So, at any rate, I want to argue.

4. DO WE NEED TO ADD A FURTHER RESTRICTION ON THE CLASS OF NATURAL PROPERTIES?

Griffin thinks that the supervenience thesis I have just described needs to be further constrained in order to be interesting. But he thinks that further constraining the thesis is problematic because, once we add the further constraint that is required, the supervenience thesis looks false.

The further constraint Griffin thinks the supervenience thesis requires is outlined in the following passage.

It is part of the definition of supervenience, as it stands, that the properties supervened upon are specified according to kind, and are of a different kind from the supervening properties. And the specification makes the relation non-tautological: the properties supervened upon are not defined as "any properties, regardless of type, relevant to something's having the supervening property" (e.g. in the present case, relevant to being valuable), but as being of one independently specified kind (e.g. in the present case, natural properties). But I think that something yet stronger is intended. We do not, in the present case, mean any natural property at all, but only ones that appear in explanatory regularities at the natural level, and those explanatory regularities mention kinds of spatial and temporal relations but do not mention such particulars as, say, occurring today and in Parks Road, Oxford. But I think that we have to go somewhat further and add a relevance requirement. . . . What we are interested in is whether values supervene not on any natural properties, but some subclass of the natural, a subclass relevant to something's being valuable. Though it is not easy to specify the subclass, I think we should accept the relevance limitation that it represents. Most moral philosophers do. (V 314–15)

The constraint is thus to be a further constraint on the class of natural properties. The natural properties on which the evaluative supervene are a "subclass of the natural": those "relevant to something's being valuable."

Griffin's reason for thinking that a relevance limitation of this sort is required in order to make the supervenience thesis interesting is explained in a later passage.

Can we supply difference in prudential value without any difference in relevant natural properties? I think that the answer is unclear. If we could mention any natural property to establish a difference, then we could always, though uninterestingly, come up with one. Smith's poetry is a genuine accomplishment; Jones's poetry, just as long, varied, innovative, and so on, is not. But Smith and Jones must at least have written in different-coloured ink or in different places. But these differences will not do; we need properties that are "relevant" in the sense explained earlier. (V 317)

The reason we need to add a relevance limitation is thus supposed to be that, without it, the claim that the evaluative supervenes on the natural is uninteresting. It is uninteresting because we can always "though uninterestingly" come up with a naturalistic difference between any two objects whose value we wish to compare.

But once we add the relevance limitation Griffin thinks that the claim that the evaluative supervenes on the natural looks like it might well be false. The passage just quoted continues as follows: "can we supply difference in prudential value without any difference in relevant natural properties? I think that the answer is unclear. . . . It is the relevance limitation in particular that seems to me to introduce a measure of doubt. A lot that is natural is not relevant, and a lot that is relevant is not natural" (V 317). Griffin thus concludes that the supervenience of the evaluative on the natural suffers from a fatal flaw. With the relevance limitation on natural properties the supervenience thesis seems to be false. But without it it is uninteresting. The defender of the supervenience thesis should therefore choose their poison.

Quite a lot needs be said in response to this argument.

Griffin claims that the supervenience thesis looks to be false once we add the relevance limitation. His reason for thinking this is that, as he puts it, "a lot that is natural is not relevant, and a lot that is relevant is not natural" (V 317). The way his argument develops, it is plain what he means. Once we add the relevance limitation to the properties on which evaluative features supervene, we open the door to the possibility that other *evaluative* features are relevant. But, while this last idea might have some independent plausibility – I discuss the idea at some length in section 7 below – I do not see how Griffin thinks it can be embraced by someone who accepts his official definition of what it is for a property to be relevant. According to his official definition, the relevant properties are a *subclass of the natural*. But it follows immediately from this that *only* natural properties can be relevant. Nothing can be a member of a subclass of the natural, after all, that is not a member of the class of the natural.[10]

Next consider Griffin's suggestion that the supervenience thesis without the relevance limitation is uninteresting. His reason for thinking this is that we can always supply a naturalistic difference between two objects that we think differ in value, and that we must therefore think differ in naturalistic features, if the supervenience thesis is correct. Suppose, as in the example he considers, we are comparing the poetry that Smith writes with the poetry that Jones writes, and we think that Smith's is superior. "Smith and Jones must at least have written in different coloured ink or in different places" (V 317). But why does Griffin think that the supervenience thesis puts any constraint at all on our relative assessments of the value of the poetry that Smith writes and the poetry that Jones writes?

Remember that the supervenience thesis without the relevance limitation that I have characterized above is an *inter-world* supervenience claim. It tells us that two objects with exactly the same naturalistic features, even objects in different possible worlds, must be exactly alike in terms of their evaluative features. It is, therefore, consistent with this inter-world supervenience thesis that no other object in the actual world has exactly the same naturalistic features as the poetry that Smith writes in the actual world. So perhaps Griffin is right that Smith's and Jones's poetry will not have the same naturalistic features. But it does not follow from this that the inter-world supervenience thesis is thereby made uninteresting.

What would make the inter-world supervenience uninteresting is if there were no *possible* object with exactly the same natural features as the poetry that Smith writes. But, given just a principle of plenitude about possibilia, we know that there most certainly is a possible world in which there is poetry written by someone else, not Smith, with exactly the same naturalistic features as the poetry that Smith writes. And what the inter-world supervenience thesis that I have characterized above tells us is that, if Smith's poetry has a certain value, then so does this other person's poetry in this other possible world. Griffin's claim that without a relevance limitation the supervenience thesis becomes uninteresting thus seems to me to lapse.

But not only does Griffin's reason for adding a relevance limitation lapse; it seems to me that he was quite wrong to suggest that we should even consider adding a relevance limitation in the first place. The supervenience thesis that we are trying to state is supposed to be a conceptual truth. The question we must, therefore, ask in deciding whether or not to add a relevance limitation is thus not whether most moral philosophers would accept a supervenience thesis with a relevance limitation, but rather whether such a supervenience thesis would be a plausible candidate for a conceptual truth. For that to be so we would have to be able to defend the particular relevance limitation we came up with as a conceptual truth.

But any particular relevance limitation we might come up with would surely be a substantive evaluative truth, one that reflects our commitment to one particular evaluative theory rather than another.[11] And, worse still, there are substantive views about the nature of value, views that it seems to me we should not rule out as based on *conceptual* confusion, according to which no relevance limitation at all is defensible. What I have in mind are the views defended by particularists.[12]

According to particularists about value, the very best we can do when we try to construct an evaluative theory is to supply an endless list of supervenience conditionals: a mapping of every possible total way objects could be naturalistically onto evaluative features. This is because, according to particularists, the evaluative difference any particular naturalistic feature makes depends on the other naturalistic features it occurs in combination with: any naturalistic feature could make an evaluative difference to the value of an object if it was in suitable combination with other natural features.

But, if particularists about value are right, then it follows immediately that no relevance limitation is defensible. After all, a relevance limitation purports to tell us that some naturalistic features are irrelevant to an object's value, whereas particularists tell us that every naturalistic feature is relevant in some context or other. They therefore hold that facts about the value of a life, say, really are sensitive to *every single* naturalistic feature that that life possesses, features that might well go back to the Big Bang. Nothing short of the endless list of inter-world supervenience conditionals of the sort characterized above, supervenience conditionals with endlessly complex naturalistic antecedents detailing every single naturalistic feature a life possesses, will therefore be guaranteed to provide the correct mapping of naturalistic features of lives onto facts about the value of lives. So particularists claim, at any rate.

What Griffin's suggestion that we add a relevance limitation to the supervenience thesis thus seems to me to reflect is his implicit commitment to generalism about value. According to generalists, if we were to state the endless list of inter-world supervenience conditionals linking every possible way a life could be naturalistically with the value of the life so characterized, then a higher-order pattern would be discernible. This pattern could itself be stated in the form of a shorter list of inter-world supervenience conditionals, conditionals that provide a mapping from some subset of a life's natural features onto its evaluative features. For example, at the other extreme from particularism, a generalist might hold that a single pattern is discernible, a pattern according to which, say, the value of a life is always and only sensitive to facts about the pleasure and pain in that life. Notwithstanding all of the other naturalistic differences between lives, pleasure and pain might be the only relevant naturalistic features when it comes to value. So a generalist – a generalist who is in effect a monist rather than a pluralist – might say.

As it happens, my inclination is to agree with Griffin that generalism about value is more plausible than particularism. Most moral philosophers would agree. That is why they would accept a supervenience conditional with a relevance limitation. Generalism seems to be more plausible than particularism, because, as I see it, we do in fact seem to be able to discern higher-order patterns in the endless list of inter-world supervenience conditionals that we have reason to believe are true. But the crucial point for present purposes is that I do not think that generalism is any sort of conceptual truth about value, and nor, it seems to me, do most moral philosophers. Rather, if it is a truth at all, it is a truth we discover by attempting, and succeeding, in the task of discerning such higher-order patterns: that is, by attempting and succeeding in the task of constructing monistic, or at least not radically pluralistic, evaluative theories. It therefore seems to me that it would be quite wrong to add a relevance limitation to the inter-world supervenience thesis that I have characterized. Such a limitation would simply undermine the thesis's claim to operate as a *conceptual* constraint on evaluative judgement.

5. THE SUPERVENIENCE THESIS AND THE FACT/VALUE GAP

Another of Griffin's misgivings about the claim that the evaluative supervenes on the natural is that it presupposes a bogus fact/value gap.

How valuable a thing is *must* depend upon what it is like. If there is a difference in supervening property, how could it *not* show up in a difference in base properties? But this is where the dubiousness of the separation of fact and value . . . matters. To regard some properties as "base" suggests that *they* are where it all happens and that valuing is something entirely different – a human response, say, or a rather mysterious epiphenomenon. To contrast a thing's "value" with "what it is like" suggests that values have no hand in what it is like. Then, of course, our strong pro-supervenience intuition is easily explainable: things are valuable because, and only because, of what goes on in the (natural) world. But this picture begs the central question: what are the boundaries of the *world* or *reality* or *fact*? Once one has reason to doubt that those boundaries simply coincide with those of the natural world, and once one sees how much goes into a value concept

222

besides the natural (indeed, how relatively unimportant the natural component is compared to the rest), then our pro-supervenience intuition starts to weaken. (V 316–17)

But does the supervenience thesis I have described make any presuppositions at all about the boundaries of the world or reality or fact? I do not think so. As far as I can see, the supervenience thesis is consistent both with realism about evaluative features, and with irrealism, and it is also consistent both with the idea that the world is naturalistic, and with the idea that the world has non-naturalistic features.

Consider a supervenience conditional of the form "Objects with natural features N have evaluative features E" that someone might accept. One possibility is that acceptance of this supervenience conditional amounts to a disposition to express approval – or disapproval or whatever else the judgement that something is E might be supposed to express – towards objects with N. Irrealists who give this interpretation of what it is to accept the supervenience conditional do indeed believe in a fact/value gap of the sort that Griffin rejects. They believe that the world contains all and only natural features, and that there is no place in the world for evaluative features. But another possibility is that acceptance of the conditional amounts to a belief that objects with one property, N, have another property, E. Realists who give this interpretation of what it is to accept the supervenience conditional hold that evaluative features are part and parcel of the world, and so of reality. They therefore hold that there are evaluative facts. It thus seems to me quite wrong for Griffin to suggest that a commitment to supervenience itself requires us to contrast "a thing's 'value' with 'what it is like'," and so "suggests that values have no hand in what it is like." Acceptance of the supervenience conditional is consistent with both realism and irrealism.

Is it possible, though, for a realist who is committed to the supervenience thesis to deny that "the boundaries of the *world* . . . simply coincide with those of the natural world"? Or does a commitment to the supervenience thesis require the realist to suppose that, since there are evaluative properties, so it follows that these properties are really just natural properties? Griffin might suggest that this is the presupposition he wants us to question, the presupposition of *naturalism*. But it seems to me that a realist's commitment to the supervenience of the evaluative on the natural simply does not all by itself require her to identify evaluative properties with natural properties. Evaluative naturalism only follows given an additional premise. As it happens, the additional premise required does seem to me to be very plausible. But it is an additional premise all the same, one that some reject. For this reason it also seems to me wrong to suppose that a commitment to the supervenience of the evaluative on the natural, together with realism, entails evaluative naturalism. In order to see that this is so, let me spell out the various steps in the argument from realism about evaluative features, together with a commitment to the supervenience of evaluative on the natural, to evaluative naturalism.

Suppose we have a long list of all the conditionals that map every possible way things could be naturalistically onto evaluative features. We could then in principle collect together all of the different ways things are naturalistically that map onto one particular evaluative feature – all of the different ways of living a life, naturalistically characterized, that map onto that life's being good, for example – and then disjoin them, and then rewrite the whole statement as a biconditional linking that disjunctive set of natural features with that particular evaluative feature. In this way, a claim like "Lives have natural features N or N^* or N^{**} or ... or N^{***} if and only if those lives are good" can be seen to be entailed by the long list of supervenience conditionals of the form "If lives have natural feature N then they are good." But, if this is right, then, in the light of the metaphysical principle banning necessary connections between distinct existences, it follows that a life's being good simply is its having naturalistic features N or N^* or N^{**} or ... or N^{***}. The properties must be one and the same, because there is no possible world in which an object has the one property but fails to have the other, and vice versa. They cannot be distinct.

In this way realism, together with supervenience, can lead to evaluative naturalism. But, as should now be plain, an additional premise is indeed required for this argument to go through. The additional premise is the metaphysical principle banning necessary connections between distinct existences. Without this metaphysical principle, the argument for evaluative naturalism is a *non-sequitur*. The realist who rejects this principle is therefore free to embrace an enriched conception of reality as comprising both natural features, on the one hand, and metaphysically distinct but necessarily connected evaluative features, on the other, evaluative features that play no causal role. In this way someone committed to both evaluative realism and the supervenience of the evaluative on the natural can deny that "the boundaries of the *world* ... simply coincide with those of the natural world." They can be non-naturalists.

224

6. SUPERVENIENCE AS THE DENIAL THAT EVALUATIVE CLAIMS CAN BE BARELY TRUE

My task thus far has been to clarify what it means to say that the evaluative supervenes on the natural. Though I have not yet explicitly said why we should believe this claim to be true, I do hope that what I have said thus far makes it at least look plausible. The time has come, however, to give a more positive argument.

The claim that the evaluative supervenes on the natural divides into two parts. The first part is the claim that the evaluative is *supervenient*; the second part is a claim about what the evaluative supervenes on – namely, the *natural*. Let me consider these two parts in turn. As regards the first part, the relevant fact seems to me to be that it is simply incoherent to suppose that evaluative claims could be *barely* true. Evaluative claims must always be *made true* by other claims. Because evaluative claims are always made true by other claims, it follows that, in possible worlds that agree in the truth of all of the same claims that make evaluative claims true, the same evaluative claims will be true. This is all it means to say that the evaluative is supervenient.

Note that the fact that evaluative claims cannot be barely true is reflected in ordinary evaluative practice. Suppose I say that a particular life is good, but then look totally flummoxed when asked to provide the features of the life that make it good. Perhaps I say, "You clearly don't understand. It isn't made good by *other* features. *It's just good!*" If I am using "good" as an evaluative term, then I would plainly violate the rules that govern the use of the word "good." When I say of a life that it is good, using "good" as an evaluative term, I thereby incur an obligation to say why my ascription of goodness to that life is appropriate in the light of the features that the life possesses. If the life is good, these are the features of the life that make it good.

This is not to deny that I might have all sorts of difficulties in saying which features of a life I judge to be good make it good. But, if I use "good" as an evaluative term, the pressure I would feel under to overcome these difficulties, and so to provide an account of the properties that make it good, is sufficient to prove the point. Having made the claim that a life is good, I am under conceptual pressure to admit that it is made good by other properties it possesses, and so to provide an account of such properties if needs be. In this way, ordinary practice bears out the fact that claims about the goodness of a life cannot be barely true. Ordinary practice bears out the fact that the evaluative is supervenient.

When Griffin discusses the way in which we justify evaluative claims, he in effect concedes that we always incur an obligation to say what it is about an object that has a certain value that makes it true that it has that value. However, in his view, we might simply cite other evaluative features. What he denies is thus not the claim that the evaluative is supervenient. Rather he denies the claim that what the evaluative is supervenient on is the natural. Here is a representative passage.

If I am a Fool-like person living for day-to-day pleasures and meet a Socratic sort who strikes me as making something of his life, I might start on [a process of] radical reflection.... Does accomplishing something with one's life make it prudentially better? What is accomplishment? I should then be embarked on the search for the definition of the possible value. I should have to use value-rich vocabulary to focus on it: accomplishment is roughly the achievement of the sort of value that gives life weight and point. But, then, having isolated it, I should have to decide whether the apparent value is really a value, or, rather, since the search for a definition already brings in value rich language, these two processes – definition of the putative value and decision about its value – go hand in hand. (V 302)

Griffin's idea in this passage seems to be that the Fool-like person can succeed in justifying to himself the claim that the Socratic sort's life is good by citing the fact that the life she leads is a life of accomplishment. But, given that accomplishment itself is defined in value-rich terms, it follows that the Fool-like person succeeds in saying what makes the Socratic sort's life good only by mentioning another evaluative feature of her life. Admittedly, it is a more specific evaluative feature than the feature of being good. But it is still an evaluative feature for all that.

It thus appears that, though Griffin agrees that evaluative claims are never barely true, and though he agrees that it follows from this that evaluative claims are always made true by other claims, the other claims that he thinks make evaluative claims true are themselves further, more specific, evaluative claims. Evaluative features are, therefore, supervenient in the following sense: more general evaluative features supervene on more specific evaluative features. In this way he leaves himself free to deny that the features evaluative features supervene on are natural features. But, while this might initially seem plausible, I think it looks decidedly less plausible once we subject it to closer examination.

Let us agree that accomplishment is defined in value-rich terms, and let us also agree that the Fool-like person can justify the claim that the Socratic sort's life is good by citing the fact, if it is a fact, that her life is a life of accomplishment. The problem is that, since the claim that the Socratic sort's life is a life of accomplishment is an evaluative claim, it follows that it cannot plausibly be supposed to be barely true either – true but not in virtue of anything. The claim that her life is a life of accomplishment thus stands in need of something to make it true, but so far the Fool-like person has not told us what that thing is. True enough, *if* the Socratic sort's life is a life of accomplishment, then it is a good life. But *is it* a life of accomplishment? What is it about the Socratic sort's life that makes that claim true? The Fool-like person clearly does not understand what it is to make an evaluative claim if he simply says, "You don't understand. The Socratic sort's life isn't made a life of accomplishment by *other* features it possesses. *It's just a life of accomplishment!*"

At this point Griffin will presumably agree but then insist that the Fool-like person can say that what makes it true that the Socratic sort accomplishes something with her life is the truth of *yet other* evaluative claims about her life. Perhaps she lives a life in which she gives *good* philosophical arguments; and so on. My reply will then be the same. True enough, *if* the Socratic sort lives a life in which she gives good philosophical arguments, and so on, then she accomplishes something with her life. But *is it* a life in which she does these things? Since these are evaluative claims about her life, they cannot be barely true either. So what makes them true?

Griffin might say that the Fool-like person can say that what makes the claim that the Socratic sort lives a life in which she gives good philosophical arguments, and so on, is the truth of yet other evaluative claims about her life. Perhaps she lives a life in which she writes articles that display her understanding. . . . At this point, however, as Griffin himself notes, it is not clear that we have not broken through a crucial barrier. A characterization of a life such as this – a life in which articles are written that display understanding – seems as though it might itself be a characterization of a life in terms of naturalistic features (V 318). After all, understanding does seem to be something that fairly straightforwardly figures in empirical regularities. (It is because she understands various complex philosophical issues that the Socratic sort is in demand to give lectures.) But, if this is wrong, and understanding is not a naturalistic feature, then my reply will be the same as before.[13] True enough, *if*. . .

If this line of questioning is followed to its logical conclusion, then it seems to me simply irresistible to suppose that the Fool-like person will eventually have to admit that something in the sphere of the natural is what makes true the evaluative claims he makes about the Socratic sort's life. In this particular case, for example, if he has not already appealed to a natural feature in saying that the Socratic sort writes articles that display her understanding, then he will eventually have to appeal to such features in any case, because what makes it true that the Socratic sort lives a life in which she writes articles that display her understanding is evidently the fact that she writes the particular words that she writes in those articles. (Likewise, what makes it true that the Socratic sort understands various complex philosophical issues is the fact that she is disposed to think and say the particular things she is disposed to think and say about them.)

Once this is agreed, however, the crucial point has been established. What makes the Socratic sort's life good is the fact that she lives a life in which she does things like writing the particular words that she writes. The evaluative claim about the Socratic sort's life is made true by a claim about the natural features of her life after all. Evaluative features therefore supervene on natural features, not merely on more specific evaluative features. The halfway house Griffin wants to occupy cannot be occupied.

In fact, much the same conclusion can be reached from another direction. Focus on a different example, not on the value of a life, but on the value of an act. People do things that add value to their lives, and they do things that diminish the value of their lives. But it is a truth of action theory that, though agents do all sorts of wonderful things, and all sorts of awful things, they are able to do these things only in so far as there are things that they can *just do*, movements they can make with their bodies (or, in the case of mental acts, thoughts they can have, or whatever) that have the effects that are wonderful or awful in the various ways that they are. What makes it true that they do wonderful or awful things is thus the fact that they make movements with their bodies (or think the thoughts they think, or whatever). But the fact that they make movements with their bodies (or think the thoughts they think) is the paradigm of a feature of their lives that is such as to figure in an empirical regularity.[14]

Viewed from this perspective, the idea that more general evaluative features supervene on more specific evaluative features, but not on natural features, looks as if it requires the assumption that there is something that someone can just do, a basic act he can perform, that constitutes, all by itself, the making-true-of-an-evaluative-claim. But I cannot see how to make sense of the idea. It is as though we are to suppose that we could set ourselves to act, and believe ourselves to be (say) writing an article that displays our understanding (assuming for the moment that this is not a characterization of an act in terms of natural features), but yet suppose that whether or not we do anything with our fingers on a keyboard (or our hand on a pen, or whatever), or have thoughts with particular contents when we do, is completely irrelevant to that act that we are performing. Writing an article that displays our understanding is (we are supposed to think) something we can *just do*, not something we have to do by doing something else.

But it is just obviously false that anyone can do any such thing. Someone who does not put his fingers on a keyboard (or his hand on a pen, or whatever) will never write anything at all. Moreover, once he puts his fingers on the keyboard, it is absolutely crucial what he does with them: crucial which thoughts he has. This is because the keys he hits with his fingers fix the facts about which letters appear on the page; and the facts about which letters appear on the page, together with the facts about the ways in which those letters are used more broadly in the community, fix the facts about the meaning of what is on the page; and the meaning of what is on the page fixes whether he has managed to display any understanding at all. The evaluative features of acts must, therefore, supervene on natural features. They must supervene on natural features because all acts are, at bottom, bodily movements with certain characteristic causes – desires, beliefs, thoughts – bodily movements that in turn cause effects in a naturalistic world. These are one and all natural features *par excellence*.[15]

7. METAPHYSICS VERSUS EPISTEMOLOGY

Let me make it plain what I do and do not take myself to have shown.

I do take myself to have shown that Griffin is wrong to suppose that, even though the evaluative features of things do supervene, they supervene only on other more specific evaluative features of those things. If the life of the Socratic sort of person is good, then so is the life of any other person, in any other possible world, whose life is an exact duplicate in every naturalistic respect of the Socratic sort's life. This is because evaluative claims cannot be barely true, but have to be made true by facts about naturalistic features.

What I have not shown, however, is that we could ever give a compelling argument for the truth of any particular supervenience conditional – any particular claim about which naturalistic features of a life are such that any life with those features is a good life – without appealing to all sorts of other evaluative features. In fact, I suspect that we would need to appeal not just to other evaluative features, but probably to other supervenience conditionals as well. This is because the task of justifying a particular supervenience conditional and the task of (partially) constructing an evaluative theory are one and the same task. But constructing an evaluative theory is a reflective equilibrium process, a matter of bringing our various evaluative commitments into a harmonious relationship with each other. There is, therefore, no process of giving such a justification that somehow isolates the supervenience conditional being justified from others, and so from evaluative claims more generally.

Sometimes it seems to me that Griffin's real reason for rejecting the idea that the evaluative supervenes on the natural is his appreciation of this fact. It is as though he asks, "If in order to justify a particular supervenience conditional linking a natural feature with an evaluative feature we have to appeal to various ancillary evaluative commitments we have, then how can we seriously suppose that the presence of that natural feature is sufficient, *all by itself*, for the presence of that evaluative feature?" But, of course, that is precisely what appeal to our various ancillary evaluative commitments justifies us in believing. Consider an analogy.

In order to justify my belief that, if it rains tomorrow, then the football match will be cancelled, I may have to appeal to the source of my belief. Let us suppose I was told that this is what will happen by someone who is trustworthy, and that reflection on this fact is enough for me to feel justified in holding the belief. But just as in this case there is no temptation at all to suppose that rain tomorrow must not really be sufficient, all by itself, for the cancellation of the football match – that really what is required is *both* rain tomorrow *and* the trustworthiness of my informant (as though the officials in charge of the football match could care less about my informant!) – so the fact that we have to appeal to various ancillary evaluative claims in justifying a particular supervenience conditional should not tempt us to suppose that the natural features mentioned in the antecedent of that conditional are not really sufficient for the evaluative features mentioned in the consequent. They are sufficient. It is just that, if we are to believe this to be so, then we have to have other evaluative beliefs as well.

The crucial point thus seems to be that we need to distinguish sharply between, on the one hand, the reasons we might have for believing that evaluative features supervene on natural features, and, on the other hand, the reasons we might have for believing that some particular supervenience conditional linking natural features with evaluative features is true. I have been talking exclusively about the former, not at all about the latter. My argument has been that the reasons we have for believing that the evaluative supervenes on the natural are conceptual. But much of what Griffin has to say in opposition to the claim that the evaluative supervenes on the natural makes me think that he is really more interested in the latter, and not so much in the former. Whereas his interests seem to be more broadly epistemological, mine have been more narrowly metaphysical.

8. CONCLUSION

There are many different interpretations we could give to the claim that the evaluative supervenes on the natural. I have argued for a particular interpretation, an interpretation according to which all of those non-particular features objects have that are such as to figure in empirical regularities are supposed to be sufficient for whatever evaluative features they have. All possible objects with the same such features must have the same value.

We have seen that commitment to a supervenience claim of this kind is consistent with both particularism and generalism about value; that it is neutral with regard to the debate between evaluative realists and irrealists; and that, among evaluative realists, it is neutral as regards the debate between evaluative naturalists and non-naturalists. Moreover, we have seen that the reason we have for believing that the evaluative does indeed supervene on the natural in this way is that it is a conceptual truth that evaluative claims cannot be barely true. They must be made true by other claims, and what they must be made true by are claims about naturalistic features.

I said at the outset that one of the few claims accepted by nearly everyone writing about the nature of value is that the evaluative features of things supervene on their natural features. Notwithstanding Griffin's misgivings, it seems to me that we have seen good reason to believe that this is true.

NOTES

Thanks to Roger Crisp, Richard Holton, Brad Hooker, and Frank Jackson for very helpful comments on a draft of this chapter.

1. J. Griffin, "Values: Reduction, Supervenience, and Explanation by Ascent" in David Charter and Kathleen Lennon, eds., *Reduction, Explanation, and Realism* (Oxford: Clarendon Press, 1992), 316. Hereafter V.
2. Steve Schiffer talks about pleonastic properties in his *Remnants of Meaning* (Cambridge, MA: MIT Press, 1987), 51.
3. G. E. Moore, *Principia Ethica* (Cambridge: Cambridge University Press, 1903), 40–1. It is noteworthy that David Wiggins, who seems to accept Moore's account of the distinction between the natural and the non-natural, goes on to claim that

non-natural properties *can* figure in causal explanations: see his "Postscript," in *Needs, Values, Truth* (Oxford: Blackwell, 1987), 355. Is this a real disagreement between Wiggins and me? I do not think so. Rather I suspect that Wiggins's claim reflects a conservative conception of what it is for something to be a natural science, coupled with a liberal conception of the properties that can figure in causal explanations.

4. See Mark van Roojen, "Moral Functionalism and Moral Reductionism," *Philosophical Quarterly*, 46 (1996), 77–81.

5. For an account of just how non-trivial the argument would have to be, see section 5. There I discuss whether the supervenience thesis has any bearing on the debate between evaluative realists and irrealists, and the debate between those realists who are evaluative naturalists and those realists who are non-naturalists. My claim is that the supervenience of the evaluative on the natural is consistent with all these views. For the purposes of understanding the supervenience thesis, talk of evaluative features is utterly pleonastic.

6. Is the category of the natural vague, when it is so characterized? Griffin thinks it is (V 306). Let us suppose we agree. It is important to realize that it need not follow from this that it is vague whether or not evaluative features supervene on natural features. Suppose that evaluative features do supervene on certain features whose status as natural is vague. It will be vague whether evaluative features supervene on natural features only if the features whose status as natural is vague do not themselves supervene on features whose status as natural is determinate. See also n. 10 below.

7. The modern champion of this constraint is, of course, R. M. Hare. See his discussions of universalizability in *The Language of Morals* (Oxford: Clarendon Press, 1952), and, in more recent times, in *Moral Thinking* (Oxford: Clarendon Press, 1981).

8. Note that the ban on particularity is indeed a *further* ban. It does not follow straight from the fact that natural features are those that are such as to figure in empirical regularities. There is, after all, an empirical regularity connecting persistently and belligerently asking Joe Bloggs questions with giving Joe Bloggs a headache. Persistently and belligerently asking questions of Joe Bloggs, as opposed to John Doe, is the feature of acts we need to appeal to if our aim is causally to explain giving Joe Bloggs, as opposed to John Doe, a headache.

9. In *Spreading the Word* (Oxford: Clarendon Press, 1984), Simon Blackburn seems to suggest that the supervenience of the moral on the natural is an intra-world supervenience claim (p. 184). In fact, Blackburn would not disagree with the point just made in the text, however. Blackburn's point is that those who fail to apply "good" to objects with the naturalistic features that in fact make them good need betray no failure of competence in their use of evaluative concepts. There is, then, a possible world in which someone without conceptual confusion applies "good" to objects with natural properties that do not make them good. But, he says, people would betray a failure of competence if they both claimed that objects with certain naturalistic features were good, and yet failed to go on to apply "good" to all possible objects with all and only the same naturalistic features. Blackburn's point about conceptual competence is thus evidently consistent with – indeed, it presupposes – the point just made in the text, which is that it is a conceptual truth that, if objects with certain naturalistic features are good in the actual world,

then all possible objects with all and only those same naturalistic features are likewise good. For an irrealist account of what it is to accept a supervenience conditional, see the discussion in section 5 below.

10. It might be thought that Griffin's real concern at this point is, as he puts it elsewhere, "the fuzziness of the notion of the natural" (V 310). But, if he is concerned with vagueness, then he did not need to add a relevance limitation in order to bring that concern out. Even without a relevance limitation we can see that, if the evaluative supervenes on a class of properties whose status as natural is vague, then it will be vague whether, in virtue of supervening on those properties, the evaluative meets the supervenience condition. But remember what I said in n. 6 above.

11. One of the questions Griffin is concerned to answer is how we are to distinguish one kind of value from another (V 310–11, n. 14). How, for example, do we distinguish prudential values from moral values? Do we not need a relevance limitation in order to do this? The answer to this question is much the same as I have just said in the text. The difference between the moral and the prudential is extremely vague, and that vagueness in part reflects the fact that there is no conceptual barrier to people holding different substantive moral and prudential theories from each other, theories that draw the border between the moral and the prudential at different places. It therefore seems to me to be best if we do not distinguish prudential values from moral values at the most abstract conceptual level, but rather allow that distinction to get fixed by the substance of the theories that people happen to hold. For an example of just how vague we might have to be in order to distinguish the moral from the non-moral, see my own characterization of the difference between moral reasons and non-moral reasons in Chapter 6 of *The Moral Problem* (Oxford: Blackwell, 1994).

12. See, e.g., Jonathan Dancy, "Ethical Particularism and Morally Relevant Properties," *Mind*, 92 (1983), 367–85, and also his *Moral Reasons* (Oxford: Blackwell, 1993), Chapters 4, 5, 6.

13. Here we recall the discussion in notes 6 and 10 above of the idea that the class of natural properties is vague.

14. For a discussion of the point in action theory, see Donald Davidson, "Agency," repr. in his *Essays on Actions and Events* (Oxford: Clarendon Press, 1980).

15. In Frank Jackson's terms the point can be put this way. We must suppose that the evaluative supervenes on the natural because we know, in advance, that we never need to appeal to evaluative features in order to discriminate between possibilities: natural features suffice for that purpose. Jackson makes the point in Chapter 5 of his *From Metaphysics to Ethics: A Defence of Conceptual Analysis* (Oxford: Clarendon Press, 1998).

12

Objectivity and Moral Realism: On the Significance of the Phenomenology of Moral Experience

1. MACKIE'S ERROR THEORY

In Chapter 1 of *Ethics: Inventing Right and Wrong* (hereafter E), John Mackie makes two claims: firstly, that we ordinarily conceive of values as "objectively prescriptive" features of the world, and, secondly, that, as a matter of fact, the world contains no such features.[1] Central to Mackie's discussion is thus the relationship between a conceptual claim and an ontological claim. It is *because* our concept of value is the concept of an objective and prescriptive feature of the world, and thus a part of our ontology, that we can make the ontological claim that nothing *like that* figures in our ontology. Mackie thus adopts an "error theory" about moral value. Our moral thought embodies a commitment to evaluative realism but, in being so committed, we are in error.

In "Values and Secondary Qualities" (hereafter VASQ), John McDowell offers a potentially devastating critique of Mackie's error theory.[2] He argues that Mackie ascribes to common sense a conception of the objectivity of values that makes the idea of an objectively prescriptive value incoherent, and obviously so – no surprise, according to McDowell, that there is nothing *like that* in our ontology. McDowell thinks that we should therefore be suspicious of Mackie's claim that common sense has such a conception of value; better to think that, according to common sense, values are objective in a rather different sense. Embracing this alternative conception of the objectivity of values enables us to see not only that the idea that there exist objectively prescriptive values is coherent but also, according to McDowell, that the claim that there do exist such values is plausibly true.

McDowell may be right to criticize Mackie's own version of the conceptual claim. However the analogy with secondary qualities is itself potentially misleading. Once we correct the analogy in the appropriate way – a way suggested by Mackie himself – we see that there is no straightforward move from McDowell's own version of the conceptual claim to the conclusion that there do exist objectively prescriptive values. An error theory may be on the horizon yet. So, at any rate, I will argue.[3]

2. MCDOWELL'S REJECTION OF THE ERROR THEORY

McDowell agrees with Mackie's "phenomenological thesis" that when we have moral experience we seem to be confronted with objectively prescriptive features of the world (VASQ: 110). However, according to McDowell, Mackie goes on to argue that there are no such features only because he mistakenly thinks that, in order to be objective, values would have to be objective in one of the senses in which primary qualities are objective: that is, "objective" in a sense that contrasts with the sense in which secondary qualities are "subjective." McDowell explains the distinction as follows:

A secondary quality is a property the ascription of which to an object is not adequately understood except as true, if it is true, in virtue of the object's disposition to present a certain sort of perceptual appearance: specifically, an appearance characterizable by using a word for the property itself to say how the object perceptually appears. Thus an object's being red is understood as obtaining in virtue of the object's being such as (in certain circumstances) to look, precisely, red. (VASQ: 111–12)

Such a conception of secondary qualities may rightfully count them as subjective because, according to it, our concept of a secondary quality just is the concept of a disposition to produce certain subjective states – in this case, perceptual appearances. We could put the point by saying that our concept of a secondary quality is the concept of a property having an "internal relation" to perceptual appearances.[4] McDowell claims that this feature of secondary quality concepts contrasts with a feature of our primary quality concepts:

In the natural contrast, a primary quality would be objective in the sense that what it is for something to have it can be adequately understood otherwise than in terms of dispositions to give rise to subjective states. (VASQ: 113)

Thus, according to McDowell, since we can understand what it is for something to have primary qualities in terms other than what it is for them to present certain perceptual appearances – in the theoretical terms dictated by geometry, or physics, for instance – so our conception of what it is for something to have such properties does not tie their presence or absence constitutively to the possibility of their presenting a certain sort of perceptual appearance.[5] We could put the point by saying that our concept of a primary quality *is not* the concept of a property enjoying the "internal relation" to perceptual appearances enjoyed by the secondaries. Such a conception of primary qualities may therefore rightfully count them as objective, by contrast with the earlier account of secondary qualities.

Let's now return to Mackie's idea that values are "objectively prescriptive" features of the world. McDowell agrees with Mackie that if our concept of value were the concept of a property that is objective in the primary quality sense just described then it would be impossible for evaluative thought to have "the internal relation to 'attitudes' or the will that would be needed for it to count as evaluative" (VASQ: 110), and hence there could be no objectively *prescriptive* values.[6] However, for reasons that should now be apparent, he expresses a certain incredulity at Mackie's suggestion that the fact that there are no objectively prescriptive values in this sense is any sort of *discovery* (VASQ: 113). For the sense in which we are to suppose that values are objective is defined in a way that *contrasts with* the idea that the concept of the relevant property bears an internal relation to a subjective state. What it would be to conceive of a value as objective is thus, *inter alia*, to conceive of the denial of what it would be to conceive of it as prescriptive. Thus if Mackie were right that we conceive of value as an objectively prescriptive feature of the world, in the primary quality sense of "objectivity," then what he tries to pass off as an empirical discovery about the world is really something that we can trace to an incoherence in our evaluative thought; indeed, an incoherence that lies very close to the surface.

For his part McDowell thinks the implausibility of the idea that ordinary moral thought is guilty of so grotesque an incoherence constitutes a *reductio* of Mackie's version of the conceptual claim. He thus suggests that we conceive of value as a property that is objective in a different sense, a sense in which we conceive primary and secondary qualities to be alike with respect to objectivity: that is, "objective" in the sense of being "there to be experienced" (VASQ: 113–14). For once we see that there is no obstacle to supposing that there really are secondary qualities, properties that really are there to be experienced which we conceive in terms of a relation to our perceptual states, we see that there is no obstacle to there really being values, properties that are there to be experienced which we conceive in terms of a relationship to the will. That is, we see that there is no obstacle to there really being values, objectively prescriptive features of the world. On this account of the matter, ordinary moral thought is not to be convicted of the kind of error of which Mackie convicts it. Ordinary moral experience may yet be veridical. How plausible is McDowell's response to Mackie?

The suggestion is that we ordinarily conceive of values as objective in the sense of being "there to be experienced." But what does McDowell say in support of his claim that *that* is part of our conception of value? And, even if we grant him that, why does he think that it is so clear that values, so conceived, really are there to be experienced? It will be helpful if we first consider these questions in the case of colour, and then compare and contrast the case of value. What does McDowell say in support of his claim that we conceive of colour as a property that is there to be experienced? And even if we grant him that, why does he think that it is so clear that colours really are there to be experienced? I begin by considering the second question first.

3. MCDOWELL ON THE OBJECTIVITY OF COLOUR

Let's digress for a moment. In *The Nature of Morality* (hereafter TNOM) Gil Harman suggests that, in these terms, we have reason to believe that a property really is there to be experienced only if we need to posit an object's having such a property in order to give a satisfying explanation of our experiences.[7] Mackie, too, endorses this explanatory test for whether something really is a property of an object.[8] Mackie and Harman differ, however, over the proper status of colours, given the explanatory test. Mackie thinks that colours fail the explanatory test. Harman thinks that they pass. Who is right?

There is strong prima-facie reason to think that colours fail the explanatory test. For, as Harman points out, in order to explain our experiences, it seems that we need make no mention of the colours of objects. It suffices that we appeal to the "physical characteristics of surfaces, the properties of light, and the neurophysiological psychology of observers" (TNOM: 22). Indeed, it is for this very reason that Mackie thinks colours fail the explanatory test. Why, then, does Harman think that colours none the less pass the test? Harman thinks that colours pass the test because they will

237

covertly have been mentioned in giving such explanations; for, in his view, "facts about colour are . . . reducible to facts about physical characteristics of perceived objects, facts about light, and facts about the psychology and perceptual apparatus of perceivers" (TNOM: 14).

However a little reflection reveals this move to be wholly illegitimate. What entitles Harman to believe that we can give such a reduction at this stage of the argument? After all, such a reduction itself *presupposes* that we are entitled to think of colours as properties that really are there to be experienced in the first place, otherwise there would be nothing there to reduce. But then we have to ask what our reason is for presupposing that, given that the explanatory test suggests otherwise.[9]

It is important to see the inadequacy of the explanatory test to this task in the present context, because at one point McDowell seems to suggest, in the spirit of Harman, that, properly applied, it is the explanatory test that delivers the result that secondary qualities, conceived of as dispositions to elicit certain experiences, are properties of objects that are there to be experienced. Here is what he says:

A "virtus dormitiva" objection would tell against the idea that one might mount a satisfying explanation of an object's looking red on its being such as to look red. The weight of the explanation would fall through the disposition to its structural ground. Still, however optimistic we are about the prospects for explaining colour experience on the basis of surface textures, it would be obviously wrong to suppose that someone who gave such an explanation could in consistency deny that the object was such as to look red. The right explanatory test is not whether something pulls its own weight in the favoured explanation (it may fail to do so without thereby being explained away), but whether the explainer can consistently deny its reality. (VASQ: 117–18)

McDowell is right that if we have reason to think that colours are dispositions of objects – if that is our *concept* of colour – then the fact that we need mention only the ground of the disposition, not the disposition itself, in our explanations, does nothing to undermine the claim that the object really has the disposition.[10] This is why, when he imagines someone conducting the explanatory test, he says that they will not consistently be able to deny the reality of colours. But if we are to take seriously his suggestion that this is meant to be an interpretation of how properly to conduct an *explanatory test* for whether a property really is there to be experienced, then the remark seems altogether irrelevant. For the reality of colours seems then to have been determined prior to administering the explanatory test by whatever gave the tester the conviction that our concept of colour is the concept of such a disposition, a disposition that objects possess.

Another way of putting the same point is this. Someone who denies that colours are properties of objects need not deny that objects *have* these dispositions, all he has to deny is that colours *are* such dispositions (that our concept of colour is the concept of such a disposition). In the case of both values and secondary qualities, John Mackie denied precisely this.[11]

The upshot is that, even if we do conceive of colour as a property that is there to be experienced, this conjoined with the explanatory test will not clearly yield the result that colours really are there to be experienced. If we had reason to believe that we conceive of colours as there to be experienced because, contrary to Mackie, we conceive of them as dispositions, then that would certainly help yield the result that colours really are there to be experienced. But that in turn just makes us wonder why anyone should think that we conceive of colour as such a disposition. It is time to go back to the first question. What does McDowell say in support of his claim that we conceive of colour as a property that is there to be experienced?

What we have just seen is that, in order to argue for the claim that colours are there to be experienced it will not be enough for McDowell to argue that we conceive of colours as being there to be experienced. He needs to argue for something else besides, perhaps for the claim that our concept of colour is the concept of a certain kind of disposition, perhaps for the claim that the explanatory test is not the only test for whether a property really is there to be experienced. What does he have to say as regards these matters?

As far as I can see, the only remark of relevance is the following, made in passing:

Secondary-quality experience presents itself as perceptual awareness of properties genuinely possessed by the objects that confront one. And there is no general obstacle to taking that appearance at face value. (VASQ: 112)

Talk of how secondary quality experience "presents itself" is talk about the phenomenology of such experience. As I understand it, McDowell is therefore claiming that the phenomenology of secondary quality experience is *representational*. Now this certainly seems plausible. For if we were asked to make an unreflective judgement about our secondary quality experience, we would certainly describe it in apparently representational terms. That is, we would say that such experience is the *experience of coloured objects*. And this in turn certainly suggests that we conceive of colours as there to be experienced. For it is a necessary condition of such descriptions being apt that we have such a conception of colours. Thus, to the extent that facts about our use of language are useful "surrogates" for talk about the phenomenology of our experience, McDowell seems to be right that the phenomenology of secondary quality experience supports the idea that we conceive of colour as a property that is there to be experienced (VASQ: 110 and fn. 2).[12]

I will have more to say about this "phenomenological" argument presently. For the moment, however, I want to concentrate on a different point: the way the argument just given interacts with the ideas of giving a dispositional analysis of colour concepts and coming up with a different test for whether a property really is there to be experienced.

Remember we just saw that in order to argue for the conclusion that colours really are there to be experienced McDowell has to do more than simply argue for the claim that we conceive of colours as properties that are there to be experienced. For when we conjoin that claim with, say, the explanatory test, colours seem not to turn out to be properties that are there to be experienced. However the argument just given suggests a different test for whether colours really are there to be experienced.

Suppose we concede the phenomenological claim that colours seem to be there to be experienced. Then, in order to show that colours really are there to be experienced, we need simply to be able to draw the is/seems distinction for them and show that they satisfy the "is": that is, show that objects do not *merely seem* to be coloured. Enter the dispositional analysis. For it is precisely the role of the "in normal perceivers" and "in certain conditions" clauses of the analysis to explain the various ways in which we might be mistaken about the colours an object has on the basis of our experience, and hence to allow us to draw the distinction between an object's really being coloured and merely seeming to be so. Indeed, it would seem to be this McDowell has in mind when he says that "there is no general obstacle" to taking the "appearance" of representation in secondary quality experience "at face value" (VASQ: 112 and fn. 8). There is no general obstacle because the dispositional analysis provides us with the materials to take the appearance at face value: that is, make the is/seems distinction.

Unfortunately, however, there is an obstacle. For even if we grant McDowell that the phenomenology of colour experience gives us reason to think that our concept of colour is the concept of a property that is there to be experienced, and concede he is right that if we can make an is/seems distinction then we can take this appearance at face value, and concede he is right that if we could give a dispositional analysis of our colour concepts then that would give us a way of making an is/seems distinction, we must not let him simply assume that giving a dispositional analysis of our colour concepts would be an appropriate way of making an is/seems distinction for colours. After all, if we could give a dispositional analysis of our shape concepts then that would enable us to make the is/seems distinction for shapes. However, as McDowell himself emphasizes, it would be totally inappropriate to analyse our shape concepts dispositionally, for shape concepts "can be adequately understood otherwise than in terms of dispositions to give rise to subjective states" (VASQ: 113). Thus we make the is/seems distinction for shapes in non-experiential terms, in terms of our geometrical concept of shape. McDowell therefore has to provide a further *argument* for the claim that it would be appropriate to give a dispositional analysis of our colour concepts.

McDowell seems to recognize this, for he does provide an argument of sorts for the dispositional analysis. However the argument he provides does not really help. For what he says is that the phenomenology of colour experience presents objects to us not merely as being coloured, but also as possessed of "qualities that could not be adequately conceived except in terms of how their possessors would look" (VASQ: 113). Thus, according to McDowell, "colours figure in perceptual experience . . . as essentially phenomenal qualities of objects," *as* dispositions to look certain ways (VASQ: 113). However, this is likely to convince no one. The phenomenology is being asked to do too much.

Recall McDowell's suggestion that we can read the fact that we conceive of colours as properties that are there to be experienced off from the phenomenology of our colour experience. As I have said, this claim has some plausibility, for we would certainly unreflectively describe our colour experience in representational terms as the experience of coloured objects. However the further claim that we can read the fact that we conceive of colours as dispositions to produce certain experiences off from the phenomenology of our colour experience is surely quite simply incredible. For we have no disposition whatsoever unreflectively to describe our colour experience in these terms at all. The idea of colour as a disposition is thus, in the very best sense of the word, a "philosopher's" idea.

Of course, McDowell may agree with this. For he may think that colours figure in experience as being however the correct analysis of colour concepts says they are – adding, *sotto voce*, that according to the correct analysis colours are dispositions. But then all the work is being done by the additional claim, the claim for which we want to see an argument, an argument McDowell simply fails to provide.

Can we provide an argument on McDowell's behalf? We can certainly sketch an argument. Note that there are all sorts of platitudes about colour, platitudes like "Things don't usually look the colour they are in the dark," "If you want to see what colour something really is, take it into the daylight," "If your eyes aren't working properly, you might not be able to tell what colour things are," and so on. Indeed, the phenomenological claim made earlier is another platitude about colour: "Objects that we see seem all to be coloured." And then there are platitudes about the nature of colours, and the relations between them, "There's no such thing as transparent matt white," "Red is more similar to orange than to blue," and the like. And there are also platitudes about the sense specific nature of colours, as when we say "Blind people don't really know what colours are like," "A normal person can tell an object is red just by looking at it, but not just by touching it or smelling it," and the like. These platitudes about colour play a certain crucial role in our coming to master colour vocabulary. For we master colour vocabulary precisely *by* coming to treat remarks like these *as* platitudinous. Of course, to say that they are platitudinous is not to say that we couldn't be argued into giving one or another of them up, perhaps by being made to see that one or another is in tension with other platitudes. But it is to say that we will give them up only with the greatest reluctance. For to give up on these platitudes wholesale would be to give up on talking about *colours* altogether.

If an account along these lines of what it is to have mastery of colour terms is right, then, it seems to me, a certain natural picture emerges of what would be involved in giving a dispositional analysis of our colour concepts. It would be to argue that the dispositional analysis *best encapsulates*, or is the *best systematization of*, our platitudes about colour.[13]

Arguing convincingly that this is so would, of course, be an enormous task. Doing so would require that we see implicit in the platitudes about colour just mentioned the idea that there is a privileged kind of perceiver, and a privileged set of conditions in which that person perceives, such that the colour experiences had by that perceiver in those conditions represent the colours of objects as they are. I do not myself think that this task is impossible, however I do not intend to attempt the task here.[14] For I am not so interested in whether a dispositional analysis of colour concepts is correct. What interests me is rather the plausibility of the strategy just outlined as a response to the original problem.

Remember, the problem was to argue for the following pair of claims: "Our concept of value is the concept of a property of objects that is there to be experienced" and "Objects really have such properties." The detour via colour has served its purpose if it has shown us a coherent and non-question-begging way of arguing for these claims. For whether or not, in the case of colour, we can support the crucial premise that our concept of colour is properly to be given a dispositional analysis, we may plausibly be able to argue for the corresponding premise in the case of value. Let's therefore consider the argument by analogy for the claim that values are properties of objects that are there to be experienced.[15]

4. ARE VALUES OBJECTIVE IN McDOWELL'S SENSE?

The argument is to proceed in two stages. In the first stage we are to argue that our concept of value is the concept of a property that is there to be experienced. The argument for this is to be phenomenological. We are to argue that evaluative experience presents itself to us as the experience of properties genuinely possessed by the objects that confront us. This phenomenological argument is to yield the conclusion that objects *seem* to have evaluative properties. In the second stage we are to argue for the is/seems distinction by showing that, according to the best systematization of our platitudes about value, values are dispositions to elicit certain attitudes in us under certain conditions: that is, our concept of value is the concept of such a disposition. Let's consider the two stages in turn.

Many think that this argument is doomed from the start. Thus, for instance, Chris Hookway has recently remarked that unlike the case with colours, it "does not seem obvious" to him at all that "we would all agree that we experience values as 'there to be experienced'."[16] And I am sure that he is right, at least in the sense that there are those who reject the claim – he cites Simon Blackburn. However I suspect that Hookway's pessimism is somewhat premature. In order to see why, let's remind ourselves what it means to think of a property as being there to be experienced.

To say that we conceive of a property as being there to be experienced is, you will recall, to say that that property may figure in the representational content of an experience (section 3). Now we have seen that to say that the phenomenology of our experience supports this conclusion about a property is to make a rather minimal claim. It is to say merely that we would unreflectively describe our experiences as experiences of that property: that is, in apparently representational terms. The crucial question is therefore whether we would unreflectively use moral words in the predicate position in describing our evaluative experiences. If we would then it seems that we do have reason to believe that we conceive of values as being there to be experienced.

Put like this, however, it is not at all clear that, despite what they may say about the "phenomenology" of moral experience, philosophers do not all agree that we do experience values as being there to be experienced. For who denies that we would unreflectively describe the experience we have when, say, we witness a wilful murder in apparently representational terms: that is, as the experience of a wrong act? Even Blackburn agrees, for he himself admits that moral discourse has a "realist-seeming *grammar*."[17]

Now no doubt Blackburn would protest at this point. For he has urged that since the realist-seeming grammar of moral discourse can be explained without supposing that there are, nor even that we believe that there are, any values, so that grammar cannot properly be used in an argument for the existence of values.[18] But this is to put the cart before the horse. The most natural explanation of the realist-seeming grammar is surely here, as it is elsewhere, that the realist-seeming grammar reflects the way we take things to be – perhaps even, if we are lucky, the way things are. *If we can make this most natural explanation out* – that is, if we can make sense of the claim that there are values, perhaps even make sense of the claim in such a way as to make it come out true – then what reason do we have *not* to suppose that there are values?

Of course, there may be some principled reason why the preferred explanation of the realist-seeming grammar of an area of discourse cannot be made out in a particular case. Blackburn himself offers several arguments for just this conclusion in the case of values.[19] But such arguments presuppose, rather than undermine, the legitimacy of *preferring* the more natural explanation of the realist-seeming grammar, the explanation that takes the realist-seeming grammar at face value. Consequently, if the more natural explanation can be made out, as McDowell claims it can in the case of values, then we will have a vindication of the realist-seeming grammar that ought to be acceptable to Blackburn on his own terms.[20]

It seems, then, that the claim that we conceive of value as a property that is there to be experienced finds support from the realist-seeming grammar of the discourse we use in describing our evaluative experience. I want now to argue that we can find additional reasons for accepting this conclusion. For the fact that values may figure in the representational content of experience manifests itself more directly in the phenomenology of evaluative experience.

In order to see what I have in mind here, contrast the experiences we have when we are disposed, on the basis of experience, to judge that something is red, and the experiences we have when we are disposed, on the basis of experience, to judge that something is nauseating.[21] The contrast is illuminating because, as I understand it, though we clearly hold that being red is part of the representational content of our experiences of red objects, we are less comfortable, indeed, perhaps not disposed at all to hold that being nauseating is part of the representational content of our experiences of the nauseating (though, as we shall see, that we are not so disposed at all is not essential for the point that I am making). Moreover, and this is important, we take this to be so despite the fact that we unreflectively describe our experiences of the nauseating in apparently representational terms – that is, *as* experiences of the nauseating – and thus despite the realist-seeming grammar. We need to ask why there is this difference and whether moral experience is, in the relevant respect, more like the experience of red or the experience of the nauseating.

What is it like to experience something as red? It is commonplace that when we experience something as red the colour seems to be, as we say, "out there, on the object." This appearance shows up in the nature of our experience in the fact that our attention is drawn away from our own bodies, and indeed away from the intrinsic character of our experience itself altogether, and is focussed instead on the object of our experience. The relevant point is best seen by contrasting the experience of the nauseating, for in experiences of the nauseating our attention is very much focussed on an aspect of our own inner life. To the extent that we focus on the object at all, we fix on it merely as cause of what is inwardly experientially salient: that is, merely as cause of the easily identifiable combination of an uncomfortable feeling in the stomach, and a kind of giddiness located behind the eyes. When we experience something as nauseating our attention is thus very much focussed on something that is "in here, in my body."

Why is there this difference in facts about where our attention is focussed? Why do giddiness and feelings of nausea not play a role in experiences of the nauseating analogous to the role played by visual sensations in experiences of colours? Here is a suggestion.

Facts about the focus of our attention are not themselves primitive. They may be explained. For it is significant that we have rich resources in our practice of colour ascription for correcting our experiential evidence as to whether some object is red. Is there a red light shining on it? Would I get a better look at it if I took it out into the daylight? Are my eyes functioning properly? And so on. This should come as no surprise. They are, after all, just the platitudes about colour mentioned earlier that allow us to provide for the is/seems distinction. And the fact that we can make an is/seems distinction for colours is thus reflected in the *nature* of our colour experience. It reflects itself in the fact that we experience colours as properties whose existence is not merely constituted by our colour experience. This, we might say, is what it is to have our attention focussed "out there" rather than "in here" on features of our own experience.

Contrast the experience of the nauseating. It is significant that there is no rich set of resources in our practice of calling things "nauseating" for correcting our experiential evidence as to whether something really is nauseating. And, because this is so, experiences of the nauseating present themselves as experiences of something whose existence is largely constituted by our feelings of nausea. We might say that this is what it is to have our attention focussed "in here" on features of our own experience rather than "out there" on the object.

It should now be apparent why it does not matter for the purposes of this argument whether in the end we would say that the nauseating may figure in the representational content of an experience or not. For what we have said suggests that there will be a spectrum of cases between the clearly representational in this sense, the experience of colour, say, and the clearly non-representational in this sense, say, the experience of pain.[22] It is not important where the nauseating figures on this spectrum. What is important is rather that focussing in the difference between the red and the nauseating enables us to see that there is such a spectrum, and what it is about an experience that determines where it figures on the spectrum: the richness or paucity of the associated platitudes that allow us to adopt a critical perspective on our experience so making for an is/seems distinction.[23]

Consider now evaluative experience. If we do not conceive of values as being there to be experienced, if they cannot figure in the representational content of our experience, then we should surely expect this to reflect itself in the phenomenology of our evaluative experience. The question thus becomes whether evaluative experience is more like the experience of red or the experience of the nauseating.

Suppose we judge a wilful murder to be wrong on the basis of experience. Where is our attention focussed? If evaluative experience were like experience of the nauseating, then we would expect our attention to be focussed partially outward, partially inward, much as with the experience of the nauseating: outwardly on the features of the murder that make us, now inwardly, feel so disapproving (or whatever) towards it. But this is surely phenomenologically quite false. Our attention need not be focussed at all on an aspect of our own inner life. Indeed, there may be no *feelings* of disapproval to focus on. Rather, when we judge a wilful murder to be wrong, our attention may be wholly focussed, as it were, "out there" on features of the murder itself.

If the suggestion made above is correct then we should be able both to confirm and explain the fact that this is where our attention is focussed by reference to the platitudes associated with mastery of moral terms. And, indeed, we can. For there exists in our evaluative practices a rich set of resources for correcting our unreflective judgements about the value of objects, and thus of discounting or redirecting our consequent attitudes of approval and disapproval. For example: "In making moral judgements it is important to consider the matter from perspectives other than your own," "If you disagree with someone in your moral judgements then at least one of you is making a mistake," "Being taken in by an ideology is a sure-fire way of making mistaken value judgements." "It's sometimes useful to check your value judgements with those you admire," "Depression can make you blind to the value of things," and so we could go on.

Indeed, I doubt that Hume himself would have disagreed with this. In order to see why, consider once again the much quoted passage from which the "wilful murder" example is taken:

Take any action allowed to be vicious: wilful murder, for instance. Examine it in all lights, and see if you can find that matter of fact or real existence which you call vice. In whichever way you take it, you find only certain passions, motives, volitions and thoughts. There is no other matter of fact in the case ... the vice entirely escapes you, as long as you consider the object. You never can find it until you turn your reflexion into your own breast, and find a sentiment of disapprobation, which arises in you, towards this action. ... So that when you pronounce any action or character to be vicious, you mean nothing, but that from the constitution of your own nature you have a feeling or sentiment of blame from contemplation of it.[24]

For one remarkable, yet little mentioned, feature of this passage is that Hume is precisely trying to focus our attention away from where it is naturally focussed when we judge a wilful murder to be wrong: that is, away from the murder itself, and on to an otherwise quite unnoticed "calm passion" he supposes to arise in us. Hume did not fail to notice this aspect of the phenomenology of evaluative experience, the aspect that undermines a conception of moral experience as non-representational.

He did notice it, and tried quite literally to explain it away. In this respect Hume seems to have been more aware of the phenomenological barrier to denying that we conceive of value as being there to be experienced than are his contemporary followers.

Let us recap. We have been concerned so far with the first stage of the argument for the existence of values, the claim that we experience values as being there to be experienced. We have seen that this claim finds support from the realist-seeming grammar of our unreflective descriptions of our evaluative experience and from the fact that the phenomenology of the experience of value seems more like the phenomenology of an experience with representational content than an experience without such content. It is time to consider the second stage of the argument.

In the second stage we are to argue that there really are values by providing for this is/seems distinction and by showing that values fall on the side of the "is." We are to do so by arguing that, according to the correct analysis of evaluative concepts, values are dispositions to elicit certain attitudes in us under suitable conditions. The task is once again the enormous one of showing that the dispositional analysis best encapsulates, or provides the best systemization of, our platitudes about value.

Now I do not want to underestimate the difficulty of this task. Rather, I want to join with others in emphasizing two related problems we face in undertaking it, for two serious sources of disanalogy now present themselves.

First, whereas the platitudes governing colour terms suggest that the "privileged" conditions in which a "privileged" perceiver's colour experiences represent objects as being the colours that they are are conditions in which, at the very least, the perceiver has *causal contact* with a coloured *object*, the platitudes governing values suggest no such thing. For it seems entirely consistent with the platitudes governing moral terms that we could decide what is right and wrong without being in causal contact with any right or wrong *acts*; for we merely have to think about the non-moral features an action may have in order to decide whether an act with those features would be right or wrong.[25]

Now I do not think that this is devastating for McDowell's argument by analogy. Rather, what it does is undermine any serious sense in which we can talk of "moral perception" – perception is, after all, a *causal* process – and thus any serious sense in which we can model moral knowledge on perceptual knowledge. This does not undermine the force of the argument by analogy, however, for to say of an act that it is wrong may still be to say of it that it has a certain non-moral feature, and that reflection upon that non-moral feature elicits a certain attitude in us under suitable conditions. Such an analysis allows that we may discover whether actions are right or wrong by merely reflecting upon their non-moral features. The argument by analogy may thus be disconnected from a perceptual model of moral knowledge.

There is, however, a second and potentially more worrying feature of disanalogy.[26] For whereas the platitudes governing colour ascriptions may seem to suggest a quasi-statistical conception of what a "privileged" condition and a "privileged" perceiver are, the platitudes governing values suggest no such thing. Indeed, there seems to be a problem in getting the requisite distance from our moral vocabulary itself in explaining what a "suitable" condition is, or who "we" are, in such a way as to make true the claim that an act with some non-moral feature is valuable just in case reflection upon that non-moral feature elicits a certain attitude in "us" under "suitable" conditions. Is there any answer that could plausibly hope to give the truth conditions of ascriptions of value except the answer that "we" are those who accept the correct moral principles and that conditions are "suitable" when we can apply these principles without error? If not, then the idea that we have given any kind of *analysis* of value is simply a sham. We have come full circle.

I do not want to attempt a solution to this problem just yet. Rather I want to digress for a moment. For it is important to notice that there is yet another sense in which we might think that values are objective, a sense quite different from the sense in which values would turn out to be objective even if this argument were to go through. I have in mind the idea that moral requirements are objective in the sense of being requirements of reason. There is good reason to believe that John Mackie supposed values to be objective in just this sense. Surprisingly, by focusing on the idea that values are objective in this sense we come across a traditional answer to the question of how to specify the "suitable" conditions and "us" clauses in the dispositional analysis.

5. MACKIE ON THE OBJECTIVITY OF VALUE

John Mackie certainly talked of values as being like primary qualities. However, it is significant that alongside such talk we find a different, perhaps incompatible, way of explicating the idea of the objectivity of value. Here are some examples:

A categorical imperative ... would express a reason for acting which was un-conditional in the sense of not being contingent upon any present desire of the agent.... Kant himself held that moral judgements are categorical imperatives ... and it can plausibly be maintained at least that many moral judgements contain a categorically imperative element. So far as ethics is concerned, my thesis that there are no objective values is specifically the denial that any such categorical imperative element is objectively valid. The objective values which I am denying would be action-guiding absolutely, not contingently (in the way indicated) upon the agent's desires and inclinations. (E: 29)

Another way of trying to clarify this issue is to refer to moral reasoning or moral arguments.... Let us suppose that we could make explicit the reasoning that supports some evaluative conclusion, where this conclusion has some action-guiding form that is not contingent on desires or purposes or chosen ends. Then what I am saying is that somewhere in the input to this argument – *perhaps in one or more of the premises, perhaps in some part of the form of the argument* – there will be something which cannot be objectively validated – *some premise which is not capable of being simply true, or some form of argument which is not valid as a matter of general logic*, whose authority or cogency is not objective, but is constituted by our choosing or deciding to think in a certain way. (E: 29–30 – my emphasis)

For these passages suggest that when Mackie claimed that, according to common sense, values are objectively prescriptive he had in mind the sense of "objectivity" that we associate with *rationalism*. But what exactly is that sense?

The characteristic rationalist thesis is that moral norms, if there are any, reduce to norms of practical reason. Thus, according to the rationalist, just as fully rational creatures either believe that q when they believe that p and that $p \rightarrow q$ or give up believing p or $p \rightarrow q$ (that is, conform their beliefs to *modus ponens* and *modus tollens*), and desire to Ψ when they desire to Φ and believe that they can Φ by Ψ-ing (that is, conform their desires to the principle of means–ends, Kant's hypothetical imperative), so, for example, if they are morally required to Ψ when someone is in pain and they can relieve his pain by Ψ-ing, fully rational creatures form the desire to Ψ when they believe that someone is in pain and they can relieve his pain by Ψ-ing (that is, conform their desires to the principle of limited altruism).[27] If morality requires some limited form of altruism then, according to the rationalist, the principle of limited altruism is a principle of reason on all fours with *modus ponens* and *modus tollens* and the principle of means–ends. According to the rationalist moral judgements are thus objective in this sense: they are expressive of reasons for action that are binding on rational creatures as such.[28]

Note how different this sense of the objectivity of value is from the idea that moral values are objective in the sense in which primary qualities are objective, the sense that contrasts with the sense in which secondary qualities are supposed to be subjective. For the rationalist says nothing to make us think that we can have a conception of what a moral value is other than as a disposition to elicit certain subjective states. This will be important in what follows (section 6).

Moreover, note how different this sense of the objectivity of value is from the sense in which primary and secondary qualities are alike objective, "objective" in the sense of being "there to be experienced." For the rationalist says nothing to make us think that value is there to be experienced. For all he tells us moral experience may not be representational. Indeed, moral judgements may not properly be thought of as ascriptions of properties to objects, they may rather have the semantic form of, say, imperatives: indeed, *categorical* imperatives.

Mackie thought that the objectivity of moral judgements in this sense, the rationalist's sense, was part of our *common-sense* conception of moral value. Is that plausible? I believe that it is, for, as I see it, rationalism is simply an attempt to articulate much that is platitudinous about moral practice.

Consider, for example, the phenomenology of moral choice. Think of what it is like to act on one desire, rather than another, in the context of some moral conflict. Does it seem that we are simply being, as it were, led around by the strongest desire? No. It seems that we choose to act on one desire rather than another for reasons; that we come to desire to act in one way rather than another because we think that acting in that way is more appropriate, the course of action supported by the best reasons. Acting in that way is not more appropriate, not supported by the best reasons, simply because that is what *we* happen to desire to do.[29]

The rationalist offers us a plausible way of making sense of this aspect of the phenomenology. He suggests that when we come to desire to act in one way rather than another we do sometimes do so for reasons. To take the schematic example just mentioned, he suggests that we may form the desire to Ψ because of our appreciation of the reasons: that is, because we believe that someone is in pain and we can relieve his pain by Ψ-ing. The transition from these beliefs to the desire to Ψ is, he suggests, a rational transition on a par with forming the belief that q on the basis of the beliefs that p and that $p \rightarrow q$. The rational appropriateness of desiring to relieve pain is not a matter of our simply finding ourselves, contingently, desiring to relieve pain.

Rationalism enables us to make good sense of other platitudinous features of moral practice as well. For example, as we have already seen, it is a platitude that if A claims that Φ-ing is worthwhile, and B claims otherwise, then, when the value in question is moral value, at most one is right. Argument ensues: "What are your reasons for believing that Φ-ing is worthwhile? Display them to me so that I too can see the value in Φ-ing." If such reasons are not forthcoming then A's assumption isn't just that he hasn't been given reason to believe that Φ-ing is worthwhile, he will assume that B's belief is ungrounded; that in having such a belief he is mistaken or in some other way in error. Contrast the case where the disagreement in question does not concern something of moral value, but concerns a mere matter of taste: say, whether ice cream is good to eat. In this case we are quite happy to resolve the apparent conflict by making it *merely* apparent, thereby preserving the cognitive integrity of each agent. Eating ice cream may be good from the point of view of A but not from the point of view of B. Both may be right. However, finding such hidden relativities and making both right seems never to be the appropriate way of resolving an apparent conflict when the value in question is moral value. As the point is sometimes put, moral disagreement is *disagreement*, not mere *difference*.[30]

Rationalism enables us to give substantive content to these platitudes about moral disagreement. For to say that when A claims that Φ-ing is worthwhile and B claims otherwise at most one is right is, according to the rationalist, merely to insist that at most one of A's and B's claims reduces to a norm of reason. And to say that at least one of A and B is making a mistake or is in some other way in error is merely to acknowledge that the beliefs of at least one of A and B are contrary to a norm of reason, merely to insist that at least one is being, in some way, irrational.

I am not saying that the rationalist's explanation of these platitudes is compulsory. But it is certainly a coherent explanation, one that seems to me to be very difficult to resist once we begin to take seriously the cognitive implications of moral choice and moral disagreement.

In summary, there is good reason to believe that when John Mackie said that values are objectively prescriptive he had in mind that they are objective in the sense in which the rationalists claim moral judgements to be objective: "objective" in the sense of being expressive of reasons for action that are binding on rational creatures as such.[31] Moreover, it is plausible to think, as Mackie did, that it is part of our common-sense conception of value that moral judgements are objective in just the sense.

For rationalism enables us to make sense of much that is platitudinous about moral judgement and practice.

6. MACKIE'S ERROR THEORY AGAIN

Let us return to the substantive issue. What we have just seen is that we can give a phenomenological argument for the claim that values are objective in the sense of being expressive of reasons that are binding on rational creature as such. And what we saw earlier is that we can give a different phenomenological argument for the claim that values are objective in McDowell's sense, the sense of being there to be experienced. That suggests that both claims to the objectivity of values can be found in ordinary moral thought: that is, both claims find support in our platitudes about value.

Now recall the role of our platitudes about value in coming up with an analysis of our evaluative concepts. The question that immediately arises is whether a single analysis could capture both kinds of platitude; that is, whether ordinary moral thought is, in this respect, coherent. I want to suggest that it may well be. Indeed, I want to suggest that the idea of the objectivity of moral judgement in the rationalist's sense gives us a way of completing the dispositional analysis, and thus filling out the idea of the objectivity of value in McDowell's sense.

Remember, according to the dispositional analysis an act with a certain non-moral feature is valuable just in case reflection upon that non-moral feature would elicit a certain attitude in "us" under "suitable" conditions (section 4). And recall that we faced a problem in completing the account, for we have yet to give some sort of plausible and non-circular gloss on who "we" are, or what makes conditions "suitable." But now the rationalist appears to have offered us an answer. For remember that his is a *reductive* theory. In his view, the "us" in whom attitudes are supposed to be elicited is thus simply all rational creatures – no circularity there – and the "suitable" conditions in which to take the attitudes elicited in us to be indicative of value are simply those conditions in which our evaluative reasoning, and hence our desires, are controlled by the particular norms of practical rationality to which moral norms reduce, the categorical requirements of reason – no circularity there, either. So, if the rationalist is right, then we can have it that our conception of value is *both* the concept of a property that is there to be experienced, *and*, given that the idea is that rational creatures will not differ in the attitudes that are elicited in them

253

in the appropriate conditions, our concept of value is also the concept of a property which, when ascribed to an act, say, is expressive of reasons for action that are binding on rational creatures as such. It thus seems that we can give a single dispositional analysis of our concept of value that has some claim to capturing the platitudes about value that support the objectivity of value in both McDowell's and Mackie's senses.

Once we see that this is so, however, we are bound to ask the final, crucial question. If this is our conception of value, are there any values so conceived? Is our moral experience veridical?

As is perhaps already evident, this turns, in part, on whether the rationalist is right that there are norms of practical reason to which we can reduce the norms of morality. If there are such norms, it follows that there are non-moral features of acts that elicit certain attitudes in us when our thinking is in accordance with such norms, and so there are values. But if, as John Mackie thought, the rationalist is wrong, then we may well have to face up to the fact that none of our evaluative concepts are instantiated. And that, of course, is just identical with the conclusion that John Mackie reached in the first place.

Of course, since the arguments for and against rationalism are conducted on a priori grounds, so it follows that the error, if error there be in our ordinary moral thought, is not empirically discoverable. To that extent John Mackie was wrong. But it should not be thought that, for that reason, the error would amount to some sort of surface incoherence, the kind of incoherence McDowell thought there would have to be if we were to take seriously Mackie's idea that values are objectively prescriptive. For the very fact that the debate between the rationalists and the anti-rationalists has remained moot for so long indicates that any problem that may exist with the idea of norms of practical reason to which we can reduce moral norms lies rather deep beneath the surface of ordinary thought about such matters. The error may well be discoverable a priori, but it may be unobvious for all that.

If the argument in this final section has been on the right track then it seems to me that, for all that John McDowell tells us, John Mackie may well have been right to convict ordinary moral thought and experience of a pervasive error. Indeed, in reaching this conclusion, my suspicion is that John Mackie displayed a greater sensitivity to the phenomenology of moral experience than many of us may have thought he did. For he appreciated, as so many of us now don't, the extent to which ordinary moral talk presupposes a conception of value as built upon a secure rational foundation. If we want to resist the Error Theory then it seems to me that we have no choice but to tackle head on the widespread assumption that no plausible account can be given of how morality could be erected on that basis.[32, 33]

NOTES

1. John Mackie, *Ethics: Inventing Right and Wrong* (Harmondsworth: Penguin, 1977).

2. John McDowell, "Values and Secondary Qualities," in T. Honderich, ed., *Morality and Objectivity* (London: Routledge & Kegan Paul, 1985): 110–29.

3. In VASQ McDowell tells us that Mackie's response to the position McDowell adopts "used to be, in effect, that it simply conceded his point" (p. 121). He goes on to ask whether Mackie is right to claim that the position he outlines "is at best a notational variant . . . of [Mackie's] own position?" In essence my aim is to defend Mackie's contention that, for all McDowell says, it may well be.

4. Let me enter a caveat here. I am prepared to go along with McDowell's talk of our concept of redness being the concept of a disposition of an object to look red. However, insofar as I do, I want it to be understood as not prejudging whether our concept of a disposition of an object to look red is itself the concept of a property of an object that causes it to look red. Leaving this question open allows us to entertain the possibility that secondary qualities are identical with their categorical bases. On this matter see Gareth Evans, "Things Without the Mind," in Zak van Straaten, ed., *Philosophical Subjects: Essays Presented to P. F. Strawson* (Oxford: Clarendon Press, 1980), esp. p. 95; Martin Davies and Lloyd Hymberstone, "Two Notions of Necessity," in *Philosophical Studies* (1980): 1–30; Colin McGinn, *The Subjective View* (Oxford: Oxford University Press, 1983), p. 14, n. 13.

5. Compare Evans, "Things Without the Mind," part III; McGinn, *The Subjective View*, Chapter 7.

6. Note McDowell's assumption that it is sufficient, in order to capture the prescriptivity of value, that we define our evaluative concepts in terms of a relation to the will. Unfortunately, matters are more complex. Not just any old definition of value in terms of the will will do, at least not if the "prescriptivity" of value requires a necessary connection of some sort between *judging* a course of action to be right and being motivated accordingly. See, e.g., David Lewis's explanation of why his own definition of value in terms of a relation to the will fails to provide for that sort of connection in his "Dispositional Theories of Value," *Proceedings of the Aristotelian Society*, Supplementary Volume (1989), pp. 114–16. However, in my "Dispositional Theories of Value," *Proceedings of the Aristotelian Society*, Supplementary Volume LXII (1989), pp. 89–111, I argue that that sort of connection can be captured by a definition of value in terms of a relation to the will provided we make certain further assumptions.

7. Gilbert Harman, *The Nature of Morality* (New York: Oxford University Press, 1977), Chapter 1.

8. John Mackie, *Problems from Locke* (Oxford: Clarendon Press, 1976), pp. 17–18.

9. Harman's own response to this problem seems to get him into more trouble. For when he comes to justify his belief that colours are properties of objects that are

there to be reduced, as he realizes he must, he does so by insisting that colours really pass the explanatory test after all. Here is what he says:

> We will still sometimes refer to the actual colours of objects in explaining colour perception, if only for the sake of simplicity. . . . It may be that the reference to the actual colour of the object in an explanation . . . can be replaced with talk about the physical characteristics of the surface. But that would greatly complicate what is a simple and easily understood explanation. That is why, even after we come to be able to give explanations without referring to the actual colours of objects, we will still assume that objects have actual colours and that therefore facts about the actual colours of objects are somehow reducible to facts about physical characteristics of surfaces and so forth, even though we will (probably) not be able to specify the reduction in any but the vaguest way. (TNOM: 22)

Thus, says Harman, we will believe that colours are there to be reduced because we will still invoke colours in giving ordinary explanations; that is, because colours still pass the explanatory test. But I thought the problem was supposed to be that colours seem to fail the explanatory test!

10. Indeed, it seems to me that we should then quite rightly insist that the "virtus dormitiva" objection is misplaced; that colours do causally explain our experiences. For relevant considerations, see Frank Jackson and Philip Pettit's comments on what they call "programme explanations," as against "process explanations," in their "Functionalism and Broad Content," *Mind* (1988) 97: 381–400.

11. For Mackie's discussion of the dispositional theory of value, see *Hume's Moral Theory* (London: Routledge), pp. 73–4.

12. Indeed, it seems to me that McDowell's point here closely resembles Crispin Wright's idea, in *Truth and Objectivity* (Cambridge, MA: Harvard University Press, 1992), that it is the syntactic potentialities of the sentences that we use in an area of discourse that gives support to the idea that the sentences in that area of discourse are truth-assessable.

13. The account of what it is to give an analysis proposed here is supposed to be reminiscent of David Lewis on the analysis of mental state concepts: see his "How to Define Theoretical Terms" and "An Argument for the Identity Theory," reprinted in his *Philosophical Papers*, Vol. I (Oxford: Oxford University Press, 1983); "Psychophysical and Theoretical Identifications," in *Australasian Journal of Philosophy* 50 (1972): 249–58. It should be evident from this account of what it is to give an analysis why the phenomenology of colour experience, what it is like to have such experience, gives the experiencer no special insight into the proper analysis of colour concepts. For someone who has colour experience need not even have contemplated, let alone gone through, the laborious process of trying to give system to our platitudes about colour.

14. John Campbell and Mark Johnston argue against such an analysis in John Haldane and Crispin Wright, eds., *Reality, Representation and Projection* (Oxford: Oxford University Press, 1993), pp. 257–68 and 85–130. See my reply to Campbell in "Colour, Transparency, Mind-Independence," in the same book, pp. 269–77.

15. It is, I hope, clear from what has been said why I do not think that someone impressed by the idea of an argument by analogy for realism about values has any need to deny many of the substantial disanalogies between values and secondary qualities. For some suggested disanalogies, see Simon Blackburn, "Errors and the Phenomenology of Value," in T. Honderich, ed., *Morality and Objectivity*

(London: Routledge & Kegan Paul, 1985), pp. 13–15. For a response to some of these, see section II of Crispin Wright's "Moral Values, Projection and Secondary Qualities," in *Proceedings of the Aristotelian Society*, Supplementary Volume (1988) LXII, pp. 1–26. However, as we will see in the next section, certain disanalogies are more worrying than others.

16. Christopher Hookway, "Two Conceptions of Moral Realism," in *Proceedings of the Aristotelian Society*, Supplementary Volume (1986), pp. 189–205.

17. Blackburn, "Errors and the Phenomenology of Value," p. 5. Compare once again Crispin Wright's idea. Blackburn should agree that the syntactic potentialities of the sentences that we use in moral discourse give support to the idea that such discourse is truth-assessable.

18. Blackburn, "Errors and the Phenomenology of Value," p. 5.

19. Simon Blackburn, *Spreading the Word* (Oxford: Oxford University Press), pp. 182–8.

20. McDowell's theory seems tailor-made to answer those who argue that it is impossible to take the realist-seeming grammar of moral discourse at face value. For certainly the most popular argument given for this conclusion is that the realist-seeming grammar is inconsistent with the prescriptivity of value. I discuss this argument further in my "Dispositional Theories of Value," *Proceedings of the Aristotelian Society*, Supplementary Volume (1989), pp. 89–111.

21. Simon Blackburn first led me to think about the significance of contrasts like this. More recently, Steve Stich and Mark Johnston have stressed their importance to me. Blackburn's example was the funny, Stich's was the yummy. The example of the nauseating used in the text comes from Johnston, and the substance of what follows owes much to discussions with him. (I am not sure whether he agrees with my conclusions.)

22. It might be objected that contrary to what I say here the experience of pain is representational, for it represents part of the subject's body as being a certain way. This is why I have said that the experience of pain is not representational "in the relevant sense." For, in these terms, an experience is representational in the relevant sense only if the way it represents something as being is not wholly constituted by our experience of its being that way – such is not the case with the experience of pain.

23. I suspect that the existence of such a spectrum helps explain why secondary qualities are not all on a par. Why, for instance, is there a difference in our modal judgements about the *colours* objects would possess if our perceptual apparatus were to change as against the *tastes* objects would have if our perceptual apparatus were to change? Why do tastes seem more "mind-dependent" than colours? My suggestion is that colours and tastes differ in this respect because of the differences in the associated corrective platitudes.

24. David Hume, in L. A. Selby-Bigge, ed., *Treatise of Human Nature* (Oxford: Clarendon Press, 1968), pp. 468–9. Originally published 1740.

25. Compare Simon Blackburn's objection to the idea that values are analogous to secondary qualities in his "How to Be an Ethical Antirealist," in P. French, T. Uehling Jr., and H. Wettstein, eds., *Midwest Studies in Philosophy* (Notre Dame: University of Notre Dame Press, 1987), pp. 361–75. McDowell is not unaware of the point: see VASQ, pp. 118–20.

26. Here I follow a line of argument presented most forcefully in Wright, "Moral Values, Projection and Secondary Qualities."

27. I am here simply assuming that rationalists will endorse such a principle of limited altruism. The precise content of the principle is, of course, not important for present purposes. What is important is rather its form and status. For a discussion of these matters, see my "Reason and Desire," *Proceedings of the Aristotelian Society* 88 (1987–8), pp. 243–56.

28. As Tom Nagel puts it, moral requirements are "inescapable." See his *The Possibility of Altruism* (Princeton, NJ: Princeton University Press, 1970), Chapter 1.

29. I discuss this matter further in "Dispositional Theories of Value."

30. See McGinn, *The Subjective View*, p. 152.

31. Tom Nagel discusses this aspect of Mackie's concern in his *The View From Nowhere* (Oxford: Oxford University Press, 1986), p. 144.

32. In this connection, it is worthwhile considering Mackie's own reason for rejecting rationalism. That reason, you will recall, is that the norms of reason to which the rationalist seeks to reduce moral norms – the principle of limited altruism, for instance – are not "valid as a matter of general logic" (E: 30). As he puts it later: "Disagreement on questions in history or biology or cosmology does not show that there are no objective issues in these fields for investigators to disagree about. But such scientific disagreement results from speculative inferences or explanatory hypotheses based on inadequate evidence, and it is hardly plausible to interpret moral disagreement in the same way. Disagreement about moral code seems to reflect different people's adherence to and participation in different ways of life" (E: 36). This objection should not impress us however. For note that we could similarly object to any principle of *inductive* logic that underwrites the validity of some scientific inference that it does not satisfy the standards of *deductive* logic. For a good discussion of this point, see Paul Edwards, "Russell's Doubts about Induction," J. O. Urmson, "Some Questions Concerning Validity," and Wesley Salmon, "Rejoinder to Barker and Kyburg," all in R. Swinburne, ed., *The Justification of Induction* (Oxford: Oxford University Press, 1974). I discuss the prospects for rationalism in *The Moral Problem* (Oxford: Blackwell, 1994).

33. I would like to thank Simon Blackburn, John Campbell, Jonathan Dancy, Robert Gay, Mark Johnston, Mark Kalderon, David Lewis, Steve Stich, Jay Wallace, and Crispin Wright for many helpful comments.

13

In Defence of The Moral Problem: *A Reply to Brink, Copp, and Sayre-McCord*

The comments on and criticisms of *The Moral Problem* offered in the articles by David Brink, David Copp, and Geoffrey Sayre-McCord convince me that my book would have been much better – clearer, less likely to mislead, more likely to convince – if only I had been able to read their articles before putting pen to paper (well, finger to keyboard, actually).[1] Unfortunately, this was not to be, and so *The Moral Problem* exists in its present form. The question on which I wish to focus is just how serious their objections to the main line of argument pursued in *The Moral Problem* really are.

Although the criticisms advanced are often very different, there are several points on which they are more or less agreed: the argument I give for the claim that moral judgements must themselves conform to a practicality requirement at the very least needs more spelling out; the account I give of the fully rational agent requires more justification; my claim that our beliefs about our normative reasons, and our moral beliefs, have the content that I say that they have requires more in the way of defense; and my claim that our evaluative beliefs, even when their content is conceived of in the way I suggest, can rationally produce desires in us requires more in the way of clarification and defense as well. There are other complaints too, but these seem to be the main ones.

Brink, Copp, and Sayre-McCord are doubtful that a defense can be provided of all the various claims that need to be defended for the argument to go through, but it seems to me that their reasons for thinking that this is so are mistaken. I will not respond to each of them in turn. Rather, I will restate what I take the main line of argument in the book to be, and then I will comment on each of the various criticisms of that argument at the appropriate juncture. My hope is that, by proceeding in this way, I will manage to show just how well the argument hangs together and how well supported the various steps are. I close with some comments about the book's title.

I. WHAT IS THE MORAL PROBLEM?

I say that there is a central, organizing problem in meta-ethics, and that this problem can be brought out in the following three apparently inconsistent propositions.

1. Moral judgements of the form "It is right to φ" express a subject's beliefs about an objective matter of fact.
2. If someone judges it right that she φs, then, other things being equal, she is motivated to φ.
3. An agent is motivated to act in a certain way just in case she has an appropriate desire and means-end belief, where belief and desire are, in Hume's terms, distinct existences.

(Of course, to say that an agent is motivated to φ is consistent with saying that she is motivated, more strongly, not to φ.) My reason for characterizing the problem in terms of these three propositions is that they seem to be the three very weakest propositions which can plausibly be said to capture the different demands that the wide variety of theorists working in meta-ethics think of themselves as trying to satisfy.

David Brink does not like my statement of the problem, so he begins by restating it.[2] The crucial difference between his statement of the problem and mine is that he thinks my second proposition is too weak to capture the commitments of non-cognitivists. He tells us that they accept the much stronger claim that moral judgement entails motivation. In other words, he removes my "other things being equal" clause. Of course, if some non-cognitivists accept his stronger claim, then it follows that they also accept my weaker claim as well, so we do not yet have a reason to prefer his statement of the problem to mine, not at any rate if the weaker claim states a connection between moral judgement and motivation that other non-cognitivists think is already too strong for a cognitivist to accommodate.

Brink's reason for preferring his statement of the problem to mine is that, as he sees things, the only arguments possible for non-cognitivism are based on the stronger claim. This is an interesting suggestion, but not one with which non-cognitivists themselves all seem to agree. Indeed, as Brink himself concedes in a footnote, perhaps the best-known non-cognitivist writing today, Simon Blackburn, does not accept the stronger claim.[3] (Gibbard seems not to accept it either.[4]) This is because Blackburn seems to think that moral claims express an agent's second-order desires, not their first-order desires: desires *about* motivations, not motivations themselves. In other words, Blackburn seems to think of moral claims as expressions of the sorts of desires that Harry Frankfurt, too, thinks constitute our valuings: reflectively formed desires about the motivations we are to have.[5]

This seems to me to count decisively in favor of my own original statement of the moral problem, rather than Brink's restatement of it. For while Blackburn's view about the nature of moral judgement is inconsistent with Brink's stronger claim about the connection between moral judgement and motivation, it certainly appears to be consistent with my weaker statement of that connection. Moreover, it is plain why Blackburn should think that the weaker claim still suffices for an argument for noncognitivism.

What the "other things being equal" clause allows, after all, is the possibility of an agent's dissociation or alienation from her values, the sort of dissociation or alienation that Frankfurt describes: an agent's values are those things she really wants, in some sense, not just those things she happens merely to find herself wanting. If this is right, however, then the question naturally arises as to the nature of the psychological state that gives expression to an agent's values, where these carry with them the possibility of such dissociation and association. Just as an agent's desires can diverge from her values, her values can also shape her desires: they can have a rational impact on what she wants. But what sort of psychological state can have such an impact? Frankfurt and Blackburn both seem to think that the only psychological state capable of playing this role – that is, capable of both telling us what an agent really wants, on the one hand, and having a rational impact on her desires, on the other – is a reflectively formed higher-order desire: a desire about which motivations she is to have. No cognitive state could simultaneously tell us what an agent really wants and be such as to have a rational impact on her first-order desires, or so they seem to think.[6]

It is perhaps worth remarking that Brink himself seems to think that my initial statement of the problem makes it too easy for me to come up with a novel solution that accepts all three propositions, unlike any of the standard solutions, which require that we reject one or another of them. As David Copp's and Geoffrey Sayre-McCord's contributions to this symposium make clear, however, they at least most certainly do not agree with Brink. Nor, it must be said, do most commentators.[7] People by and large seem to think that my initial statement of the moral problem, and my subsequent explanation of its intractability in the first four chapters, is *so* successful that it should come as no surprise that my own solution to the problem fails. I would therefore be happy enough if I could come up with a reconciliation of my three relatively weak propositions, a reconciliation that demonstrates where these commentators have gone wrong.

II. TWO KINDS OF REASON

The central plank in my reconciliation of these three propositions lies in the distinction between justifying or normative reasons, on the one hand, and explanatory or motivating reasons, on the other. This distinction is made in Chapter 4 of *The Moral Problem*.

Normative reasons are considerations, or facts, that rationally justify certain sorts of choices or actions on an agent's behalf. They are propositions of the form "Acting in such-and-such a way in so-and-so circumstances is desirable." Motivating reasons, on the other hand, are psychological states with the potential to explain an agent's action teleologically, and perhaps also causally. They are pairs comprising desires and means–end beliefs. (Of course, as David Brink notes, to say that an agent has a motivating reason to do something is not to say that her reason is over-riding. An agent may have a desire to act in a certain way, but have a stronger desire to act in another.) With this distinction between normative reasons and motivating reasons in place, the first step in the argument for reconciliation lies in a claim about the nature of normative reasons and the relationship in which they stand to motivating reasons.

The claim I defend is that normative reasons, if there are any, are both objective and practical. They are objective in the sense that, via a conversational process involving rational reflection and argument, we are each able to come up with an answer to the question, "What do we have normative reason to do if we are in such and such circumstances?" and our answers to this question, provided we have each reflected properly, will all be one and the same. We will all converge on an answer of the form "It is desirable that we do so-and-so in such-and-such circumstances." And normative reasons are practical in the sense that someone who believes that she has a normative reason to act in a certain way in certain circumstances will have a motivating reason to act in that way in those circumstances, at least absent weakness of will and the like: that is, absent various forms of practical irrationality. (The idea of "practical irrationality" is left intuitive at this stage in the argument. It gets made more precise later.) I argue for these two claims by providing an analysis of normative reasons that lays bare just how and why it is that normative reasons are both objective and practical. The analysis is provided in Chapter 5, the main positive chapter of *The Moral Problem*.

III. THE ANALYSIS OF NORMATIVE REASONS

The core idea is that facts about our normative reasons for action – that is, facts about what it is desirable for us to do – are facts about what we would advise ourselves to do if we were perfectly placed to give ourselves advice. Everything therefore turns on what "good advice" amounts to.

Spelling this core idea out just a little, my suggestion is that when we say of an agent, A, that she has a normative reason to, say, keep a promise in certain circumstances C, what we are saying is that, in nearby possible worlds in which A has a set of desires that are completely beyond reproach, from the point of view of reasoned criticism, A desires that, in those possible worlds in which she finds herself in circumstances C, she keeps her promise. These desires constitute "advice" in a sense similar to the sense in which the instruction "Throw the ball!" said to yourself as you watch yourself play basketball on a video, counts as advice to yourself. If we call the possible world in which A has such desires the "evaluating" world, and if we call the possible world in which A is in circumstances C the "evaluated" world, then my proposal is that facts about A's normative reasons in the evaluated world are constituted by facts about the desires she has in the evaluating world about what she is to do in the evaluated world.

As a shorthand, I say that the desires A has in the evaluating world – desires which are completely beyond reproach, from the point of view of reasoned criticism – are those she has in a state of full rationality. The idea of full rationality employed in the analysis – the idea of being beyond reproach from the point of view of reasoned criticism – clearly needs to be spelled out in greater detail. My suggestion is that to be fully rational an agent must not be suffering from the effects of any physical or emotional disturbance, she must have no false beliefs, she must have all relevant true beliefs, and she must have a systematically justifiable set of desires, that is, a set of desires that is maximally coherent and unified. Furthermore, I argue that it is part of what we mean when we say that a set of desires is systematically justifiable that the desires that are elements in that set are desires that other people too would have if they had a systematically justifiable set of desires. Fully rational agents converge in the desires that

263

they have, and converge by definition, because it is part of what we mean by the rational justification of our desires that people who have such desires have a justification for them that other people also could see to be a justification. A justification for one agent to adopt a desire to act in a certain way in certain circumstances is justification for another to adopt a desire to act in that way in those circumstances as well.[8]

Note that the convergence required is very circumscribed. There is no suggestion that fully rational people will all have the same tastes in food, and clothes, and basketball teams. On the contrary, they will presumably be at least as culturally and individually diverse as many human beings throughout history have been. The claim is rather that they will all converge in their desires about what is to be done in highly specific circumstances. Characterize a choice situation in its entirety – "What would we desire ourselves to do in a situation in which the external circumstances are thus and such (list them completely) and we have these and those desires and beliefs and other mental states (list them completely)?" – and, I say, fully rational creatures will all converge on a desire that the very same course of action be pursued.

Thus, for example, fully rational creatures may well all converge on a desire that in circumstances in which we have acquired a desire to cheer for the Chicago Bulls through a certain process of enculturation, we act on that desire and cheer for the Bulls; that in circumstances in which we have acquired a desire to cheer for the L. A. Lakers through a certain process of enculturation, we act on that desire and cheer for the Lakers; and so on and so forth. But there will be this sort of convergence only if fully rational creatures regard it as permissible for people to have and act on such desires, that is, only if they are at least indifferent to people having such desires, and in favor of their acting on them once they have them. Whether or not fully rational creatures will in fact have this pattern of attitudes is always a substantive question, one which can be answered only by going through the process of constructing a maximally informed and coherent and unified desire set and seeing what the elements of that set are. In certain cases it seems not too far-fetched to suppose that there would be an aversion to people having the desires they happen to have and an aversion to their acting on the desires they happen to have even once they have them. For example, use your actual desires as the basis on which to construct the possible world in which you have a fully rational set of desires and then contemplate the evaluated possible world in which you just so happen to have a desire to destroy the whole world in preference to scratching your little finger. I suspect that you will find yourself, as I find myself, with a strong aversion to your having this desire, and an equally strong, if not stronger, aversion to your acting on this desire in possible worlds in which you have it. But in the case of cheering for a basketball team there may well be indifference to our having a desire to cheer for one team or another, and a desire that the desire to cheer for a particular team be acted on once had.

The claim that fully rational creatures would all converge in their desires is a strong claim, and I offer the following defense of it. I say that to think otherwise – that is, to suppose that our concept of what constitutes a rational justification could be radically relative in some way to the interests or desires of those who make claims about what is rationally justified, so that the considerations that rationally justify relative to that agent may fail to justify relative to another – is to suppose, quite incoherently, that something completely arbitrary – the mere fact that a particular agent who is making a claim about rational justification happens to have the contingent interests or desires that she happens to have – could in some way constitute a normative fact: a fact about rational justification. But this is incoherent because the only decisive point we can make about normativity is that arbitrariness, as such, always undermines normativity. A normative fact, whatever it is, thus cannot be constituted by something which is itself completely arbitrary. This means, in turn, that if facts about the considerations that rationally justify are constituted by the desires of fully rational agents at all, then they must be constituted by facts about the desires these fully rational agents would all converge upon. Only so can we be sure that these desires are not, in their turn, completely arbitrary.

IV. OBJECTIONS TO THE ANALYSIS OF NORMATIVE REASONS

David Copp objects to my analysis. In particular, he objects to my suggestion that a fully rational agent would have all true beliefs.[9]

Copp thinks that, given the way in which we ordinarily use the term "rationality," it is wrong to say of someone who has certain false beliefs – those that it was reasonable for her to acquire in her circumstances – and wrong to say of someone who fails to have all true beliefs, that she is irrational. I myself would have thought that the term "rationality" is almost entirely a philosopher's term of art. But, in any case, I am not sure that anything hangs on my use of the word "rationality."

My suggestion is that an agent's normative reasons are constituted by facts about the desires she would have in a possible world in which she is perfectly placed to give herself advice, and I say that this, in turn, is the possible world in which her desires are beyond reproach, from the point of view of reasoned criticism: the evaluating world in which her desires are maximally informed and coherent and unified. Provided I am right that we would ordinarily say that someone who is mistaken or ignorant *is not* perfectly placed to give advice, and hence that the desires she has which are based on her false beliefs or ignorance *are not* immune from reasoned criticism aimable at those who do not reach this standard of perfection, my account of what we are saying when we say of someone that they have a normative reason seems to survive intact. And I do seem to be right. "You are ignorant" and "You are mistaken" seem to be paradigms of the forms that such reasoned criticism can take. It is irrelevant to the appropriateness of these forms of criticism that the ignorance and mistakes are reasonable relative to the agent's less-than-perfect circumstances. Facts about the desires of people who are criticizable in these ways could thus hardly constitute facts about our normative reasons.

It seems to me that I could therefore agree with Copp that I shouldn't have used the words "fully rational" as a shorthand in describing the state that we are in when we are immune from reasoned criticism. I could agree because nothing in the argument hangs on the use of those particular words. Everything hangs on the detailed characterization I give of that state itself. Copp says nothing to suggest that this characterization is wrong.

Copp's other objection to my analysis is that since we can have conflicting normative reasons – normative reasons of potentially different weights to act in inconsistent ways in the same circumstances – it follows that I am committed to thinking that fully rational agents have to have conflicting desires corresponding to each of these conflicting normative reasons.[10] He says that nothing I say justifies this claim, and that nothing I say could justify this claim because, according to an alternative picture that he finds attractive, the fully rational agent "might have no desire at all" to do the thing "she thinks she has a reason to do . . . because she thinks she has a better reason overall not to do it."[11] I agree with Copp that I am committed to thinking that fully rational agents have desires corresponding to each of the normative reasons that there are.[12] But the justification for supposing this to be so in the present context is not hard to find.

After all, what does Copp mean when he says of a fully rational agent that "she thinks the reason to do" something and also "thinks she has a better reason overall not to do" that thing? I was trying to give an analysis of the content of such thoughts, whether they are had by fully rational agents or by us, not to *presuppose* an account of the content of such thoughts. Thus, as I see things, we absolutely must think of the fully rational agent as having conflicting desires because therein lies the story of what her thoughts as regards what she has reasons to do are all about. What makes true the fact that she has conflicting reasons, and what makes true her claims about the relative weights of these reasons, are thus the facts about the relative strengths of her conflicting desires. Copp's alternative picture leaves an explanatory residue at precisely the place where I am offering an explanation. Perhaps he has an alternative account of the content of normative reason claims, one which squares with his alternative picture. But if he does then it will be the plausibility of his alternative account, not the plausibility of the alternative picture, which will constitute an objection to my account of the content of normative reason claims. The alternative picture he finds attractive has no independent appeal.

Sayre-McCord objects to my analysis as well.[13] He is unhappy at my idea that desires can exhibit relations of coherence and unity. Moreover, even if he were to be persuaded on this point, he tells us that he would then be unhappy at my idea that a more coherent and unified set of desires is a more rational set, in the sense of being less liable to reasoned criticism. He argues by counter-example.

As it happens, Sayre-McCord has a desire to eat coffee ice cream. He admits that if he acquired a more general desire to eat ice cream of all flavors, then this desire, once in place, would indeed provide a rationale for his desire to eat coffee ice cream. It would provide a kind of unifying principle in his resultant desire set. But even if he were to acquire such a desire, and even if we were to agree that his overall desire set would exhibit more in the way of unity, in some sense, Sayre-McCord wants to know why we should agree that it has become a more rational set of desires, in the sense of being less liable to reasoned criticism. If anything, he tells us, the acquisition of such a desire looks to be completely irrational, an instance of a kind of desire-fetishism. Why should anyone who desires to eat coffee ice cream feel under any sort of rational constraint to desire to eat ice cream of all flavors? The idea is absurd.

The idea is absurd. But I do not find Sayre-McCord's suggestion that my analysis somehow supports the idea very persuasive. Indeed, I suspect that it is his treatment of the counter-example that is defective rather than my analysis. One reason for thinking this is that if his treatment worked at all it would prove far too much. Suppose we switch from talk of our desires for particular things, and of trying to find a more coherent and unified set of desires by adding desires for more general things to our overall desire

267

set, to talk of our evaluative beliefs concerning particular situations or activities, and trying to find a more coherent and unified set of evaluative beliefs by adding evaluative beliefs which concern more general states of affairs to our overall belief set. Now consider the following parody of Sayre-McCord's treatment of his counter-example.

Sayre-McCord judges it desirable to eat coffee ice cream. If he were to acquire the belief that eating ice cream of all flavors is desirable then this belief, once in place, would indeed provide a rationale for the belief that it is desirable to eat coffee ice cream, in the sense of providing a unifying principle in his resultant belief set. But it seems perverse to suppose that the belief set that comprises the more general evaluative belief is more rational, in the sense of being less liable to reasoned criticism. Indeed, the more general evaluative belief seems rather fetishistic. Why should anyone who believes it desirable to eat coffee ice cream feel under any rational constraint to believe it desirable to eat ice cream of all flavors? The idea is absurd.

True enough. But it does not follow from this that our evaluative beliefs are quite generally incapable of exhibiting relations of coherence and unity, nor does it follow that when they do exhibit such relations they are not made less liable to reasoned criticism. All that follows is that this *particular* way of trying to secure more in the way of coherence and unity among Sayre-McCord's evaluative beliefs – that is, by adding the belief that it is desirable to eat ice cream of all flavors – spectacularly *fails* to add more in the way of coherence and unity. And the reason why is plain enough. It has to do with the subject matter of these particular evaluative beliefs.

When we attempt to secure more in the way of coherence and unity among our evaluative beliefs we begin by looking at all of the different things we believe to be desirable and then we ask ourselves whether there is a more general evaluative belief we could add to our overall belief set which is such that, by adding it, our overall set would make more sense. In Sayre-McCord's case, let's assume that he begins with the beliefs that it is desirable to eat coffee ice cream, to eat dim sum, to eat pork rinds, and so on and so forth. We are therefore to imagine him asking whether there is any more general evaluative belief he could add to his overall belief set which is such that, by adding it, his overall set of beliefs about what it is desirable to eat would make more sense. The answer that seems most plausible is that there is indeed such a belief. The belief he should add is the belief that it is desirable to eat whatever he enjoys eating. Adding this belief will ensure that his overall belief set makes more sense, and so make it less liable to reasoned criticism, because if the new belief were added he would no longer be liable to the charge of making arbitrary distinctions: "How can you believe that it is desirable to eat coffee ice cream, and dim sum and pork rinds, but yet not believe it desirable to eat chicken tenderloin sandwiches? You agree that it is equally enjoyable to eat all of them. It makes no sense!" In order to resist the charge he would need either to acquire the belief that it is desirable to eat chicken tenderloin sandwiches or else to make finer-grained distinctions, distinctions that make *more* sense of his beliefs about what it is desirable to eat.

This account of how more in the way of coherence and unity can be achieved among Sayre-McCord's evaluative beliefs seems to me to translate well into a story of how more in the way of coherence and unity could be achieved among his desires. When we attempt to secure more in the way of coherence and unity among our desires we likewise begin by looking at all of the different things we desire and then we ask ourselves whether there is a more general desire we could add to our overall desire set which is such that, by adding it, our overall set of desires would make more sense. In Sayre-McCord's case, let's assume that he begins with the desires to eat coffee ice cream, to eat dim sum, to eat pork rinds, and so on and so forth. We are therefore to imagine him asking whether there is any more general desire he could add to his overall desire set which is such that, by adding it, his overall set of desires about what to eat would make more sense. The answer that seems most plausible is that there is such a desire: the desire to eat whatever he enjoys eating. Adding this desire will indeed ensure that his overall desire set makes more sense, and so make it less liable to reasoned criticism, because if the new desire were added he would no longer be liable to the charge of making arbitrary distinctions: "How can you desire to eat coffee ice cream, and dim sum and pork rinds, but not desire to eat chicken tenderloin sandwiches? You agree that it is equally enjoyable to eat all of them. It makes no sense!" In order to resist the charge he would need either to acquire the desire to eat chicken tenderloin sandwiches or else to make finer-grained distinctions, distinctions that make *more* sense of his desires about what to eat.

The example so far considered is fairly trivial, but the point gleaned from it readily generalizes. Imagine someone with certain beliefs about the desirability of distributions of benefits and burdens (or desires about such distributions): she believes that it is desirable (desires) that Adam, Bob, and Charlie get x, and that David gets x minus y. This woman can most certainly ask herself whether there is a more general evaluative belief (desire) which she could add to her overall belief (desire) set which is such that, by adding it, her set of beliefs (desires) taken together as a whole would make more sense. When she reflects and tries to extract a feature from giving x to Adam, Bob, and Charlie which makes the best sense of her beliefs that it is desirable (desires) that each of them gets x, we can readily imagine that the feature she extracts is a feature possessed by David too: being in desperate need, say. In this way she can come to discover that her evaluative beliefs (desires) are not maximally coherent and unified. Reflection can lead her to believe that it is desirable (desire) to distribute benefits and burdens in accordance with desperate need, and so undermine her belief that it is desirable (desire) that David, who is in desperate need as well, gets only x minus y, whereas others who are equally in desperate need get x. By trying to make the best sense out of her overall set of evaluative beliefs (desires), she can in this way be led to see that she had made an arbitrary distinction between David and the others.

I am therefore left unconvinced by Sayre-McCord's claim that desires do not exhibit normatively significant relations of coherence and unity in their own right. Our desires, taken together as a whole set, can be made to make more or less sense depending on which desires we add to, or subtract from, the set. As far as I can see, this is on all fours with a similar process in which we try to make sense of our evaluative beliefs. Notwithstanding the differences between evaluative beliefs and desires, making sense of our desires, and making sense of our evaluative beliefs, is thus all much of a muchness.[14]

Sayre-McCord would not be happy with this reply because, quite independently of his counter-example, he has a more general and abstract problem with the idea that desires exhibit normatively significant relations of coherence and unity. The problem is that the *explanation* of the pressure toward coherence in the case of desire, if such exists, would have to be very different from the explanation in the case of belief. The pressure toward coherence in the case of our empirical beliefs arises from the fact that we interact causally with a world which is systematic and unified. For this reason, as Sayre-McCord puts it, "more general beliefs have as their content considerations that both serve as evidence for the truth of the lower level claims and find support themselves from their being able to explain (what the person takes to be) other facts."[15] But this explanation of the pressure towards coherence among our empirical beliefs most certainly does not carry over to the realm of desire. So what explains that pressure? Absent a plausible explanation, we should reject the idea that desires exhibit such relations.

But the problem with this line of thought is that there is simply no requirement that we explain the pressure towards coherence among our desires on the model of the pressure toward coherence among our empirical beliefs. This is because, even within the realm of belief, the pressure toward coherence comes from other sources. Consider beliefs about what is a priori true. It would be absurd to suppose that what explains the pressure toward coherence among them is that we interact causally with a set of a priori truths which are systematic and unified. This is because, whatever facts about what is a priori true are, they most certainly are not facts with which we causally interact. So what does explain the pressure toward coherence and unity in the case of our beliefs about what is a priori true? Here it seems to me that we note a pleasing parallel.

Once it is agreed that facts about what is a priori true do not cause our beliefs, many people conclude that all there is left to make our beliefs about what is a priori true, true, if they are true at all, are facts about constructions, that is, roughly speaking, facts about the beliefs about what is a priori true that we would all converge on if we were to subject our initial beliefs about what is a priori true to a reflective equilibrium process and so came up with a maximally informed and coherent and unified set of beliefs about what is a priori true. According to this view of the a priori, the pressure towards coherence in the case of beliefs about what is a priori true is thus not so much explained as assumed. Different sets of beliefs we might have about what is a priori true simply can make more or less sense. In the case of desires it seems to me that we should say much the same thing. Facts about what we have normative reason to do are constructed facts: they are facts about the desires we would all converge on if we were to come up with a maximally informed and coherent and unified set of desires. The pressure towards coherence is not so much explained as assumed. Different sets of desires we might have simply can make more or less sense.[16]

Sayre-McCord has another line of objection to my analysis as well, one which in effect concedes that desires exhibit relations of coherence and unity.[17] The concession isn't very helpful to me, however, because, as he sees things, it is our evaluative beliefs which exhibit relations of coherence and unity in the first instance, with our desires only getting to count as exhibiting relations of coherence and unity by being desires which match these evaluative beliefs. Why desires should count as exhibiting relations of coherence and unity by being desires which match evaluative beliefs is something that Sayre-McCord never explains. (Brink would presumably resist this idea, in so far as he speaks on behalf of his principled amoralist.) Sayre-McCord's objection does not require him to give such an explanation, however, because his objection is simply that we need to get the order of priority in which we explain the unity and coherence among our evaluative beliefs and desires right. In his view, we have to explain the coherence and unity among our evaluative beliefs first and then see coherence and unity among our desires as derivative from this. I see things the other way around.

I must confess that I am not quite sure what to say about this objection. In part this is because, as I explain in Chapters 2 and 5 of the book – and as Sayre-McCord himself emphasizes in his description of my position – I am not inclined to think that I have provided a reductive analysis of desirability. This is not to say that I wouldn't love to have provided a reductive analysis: I most certainly would! The point is simply that I am not sure whether such an analysis can be had. Moreover, I am not sure that such an analysis is needed in order to solve the problem I take myself to be trying to solve, the problem of reconciling the three propositions. This in turn complicates questions concerning orders of priority.

Metaphysically, since I hold that facts about desirability are simply facts about the desires that we would have in the possible world in which we have a maximally informed and coherent and unified desire set, it follows that, given that our evaluative beliefs are beliefs about these desires, so I assign priority to relations of coherence and unity among our desires. But epistemologically, if the analysis is not fully reductive, I see no real objection to assigning priority to our evaluative beliefs instead.

In other words, when someone asks how we might come to know what we would desire if we had a maximally informed and coherent and unified set of desires, it seems to me that we might well feel free to say "By seeing what we would desire in a possible world in which we had a maximally informed and coherent and unified set of evaluative beliefs." We should feel free to say this because once we use our evaluative beliefs to locate the possible world in which we have a maximally informed and coherent and unified set of desires we can simply help ourselves to the structural relations that our desires bear to each other in that world and insist that it is the fact that our desires bear these structural relations to each other that constitutes their exhibiting maximal coherence and unity.

The failure to provide a reductive analysis can in this way be seen to be of merely epistemological significance. It is, if you like, a limitation on the expressive power of our actual language that we cannot directly characterize the structural relations among our desires that constitute their exhibiting maximal coherence and unity in a way that will be useful for doing moral epistemology. But that is neither here nor there from the point of view of the metaphysics. Let's now return to Sayre-McCord's objection.

If his point is that the relations of coherence and unity among our evaluative beliefs are epistemologically prior to the relations of coherence and unity among our desires, then it seems to me that we can agree with him. We can agree with him because this provides him with no objection to the analysis. But if, on the other hand, his point is that the relations of coherence and unity among our evaluative beliefs are metaphysically prior to the relations of coherence and unity among our desires, then it seems to me that I simply have to record my disagreement with him. I disagree with him and I see nothing in what he has said to support that metaphysical claim. Indeed, what he says seems to me all best read as being about the epistemology of desirability.

V. USING THE ANALYSIS TO EXPLAIN THE PRACTICALITY OF BELIEFS ABOUT NORMATIVE REASONS

Armed with the analysis of normative reasons I argue that it is easy to see why agents who believe that they have a normative reason to, say, keep a promise in certain circumstances C are motivated to keep their promise in C, at least absent weakness of will and the like: that is, absent practical irrationality. The explanation comes at the end of Chapter 5.

Consider those who believe that they would desire that they keep a promise in circumstances C if they had a maximally informed and coherent and unified set of desires, and who also desire that they keep a promise in C, and compare them with another group of people who have the belief but lack the desire. It seems to me that the first group plainly has a psychology that, in this respect at any rate, exhibits more in the way of coherence than the latter. There is a disequilibrium or dissonance or failure of fit involved in the latter psychology, where there is equilibrium or consonance or fittingness involved in the former. Rationality, in the sense of this sort of coherence, is thus on the side of agents whose desires match their beliefs about the normative reasons they have. Exhibiting this sort of coherence is what practical rationality consists in, and failing to exhibit it is what practical irrationality consists in.

If this is right, however, then note that we not only have an explanation of why people who fail to desire what they believe they have a normative reason to do are practically irrational, but that we also have an explanation of the mechanism by which practically rational agents can come to desire to do what they believe they have a normative reason to do. Agents whose psychologies exhibit this sort of coherence — that is, those whose psychologies include a tendency toward such coherence — will have desires that match their beliefs about their normative reasons, whereas those whose psychologies do not exhibit this sort of coherence may fail to have such desires. Beliefs about normative reasons, when combined with an agent's tendency to have a coherent psychology, can thus cause agents to have matching desires.[18]

VI. OBJECTIONS TO THE EXPLANATION OF THE PRACTICALITY OF BELIEFS ABOUT NORMATIVE REASONS

Copp and Sayre-McCord have serious misgivings about this step in the argument.[19] Sayre-McCord has two objections, but one of his objections can be dealt with rather swiftly.

The objection is that I have not demonstrated that there is any incoherence at all involved in an agent's believing that they would desire that they keep a promise in circumstances C if they had a maximally informed and coherent and unified set of desires and yet failing to desire that they keep a promise in C. But the reason Sayre-McCord says this is because he was not persuaded that our desires, as opposed to our evaluative beliefs, exhibit any normatively significant relations of coherence and unity at all: remember again his counter-example concerning his desire to eat coffee ice cream. Since we have already seen reason to reject this counterexample, and to embrace the idea that our desires can exhibit normatively significant relations of coherence and unity, I will put this objection to one side. Our desires, taken together, can make more or less sense. Because this is so there evidently is incoherence of a sort — a kind of dissonance or disequilibrium or failure of fit — involved in failing to desire something that you believe you would desire if you had a maximally informed and coherent and unified set of desires. This desire also makes a certain sort of sense, given the belief.

The main objection both Copp and Sayre-McCord have to this step in my argument is that, as they see things, I cannot move from the claim that the proper analysis of facts about what it is desirable to do is to be given in terms of facts about what we would want if we had a maximally informed and coherent and unified set of desires to the claim that an agent's beliefs about what it is desirable to do are beliefs about what they would want if they had a maximally informed and coherent and unified set of desires. This, they say, is a fallacy. Copp insists that I am violating a norm of intentional logic to the effect that analytic equivalents cannot be substituted inside belief contexts. He then goes on to offer me a way out, but finds that the way out he offers me won't work. He concludes that the argument is therefore doomed.

I agree with Copp that the way out he offers to me won't work. The trouble is, however, that what I have claimed to be providing all along is an account of the *content* of claims about normative reasons. That is what my analysis purports to be. Let's put to one side whether I succeed in that task. The point is that if I *do* succeed in that task then there is no objection to my substituting that content inside belief contexts. If the content of claims about normative reasons is what I say it is then my belief that it is desirable to φ in C *is* my belief that φing in C is what I would want myself to do if I had a maximally informed and coherent and unified desire set. There are not two beliefs here, just one.

This merely postpones what might now seem to be the real objection, however. Think of an analogy. Though it is indeed a priori and necessary that seven is the cube root of 343, we would surely hesitate in attributing the belief that there are the cube root of 343 apples in the fruit bowl to my eight-year-old son Sam, even though we would have no hesitation in ascribing to him the belief that there are seven apples in the fruit bowl. The reason is that there appear to be quite different levels of conceptual sophistication required for people to have the two beliefs. Sam has the concept of there being seven apples in the fruit bowl, and even 343 apples in the (in that eventuality, overflowing!) fruit bowl, but he doesn't have the concept of there being the cube root of any number of apples, because he doesn't know what a cube root is. Despite the fact that it is priori and necessary that seven is the cube root of 343, then, we cannot ascribe beliefs whose content we would ordinarily give by using the number 7 by substituting in the cube root of 343.

In terms of this analogy, the real objection to my argument can now be put like this. Copp and Sayre-McCord can at this point agree, for the sake of argument, that I have shown that it is a priori and necessary that it is desirable for me to φ in C if and only if I would desire myself to φ in C if I had a maximally informed and coherent and unified set of desires. Their objection is that, even so, it doesn't follow that my belief that it is desirable for me to φ in C is just the belief that I would desire myself to φ in C if I had a maximally informed and coherent and unified set of desires. In order to show that this is so – in order to secure the "belief-identity" thesis, as Copp calls it – I would have to show that the concepts are one and the same. But the concepts are evidently different. So this crucial step in the argument fails.

Have I, or have I not, shown that the concepts of being desirable and being something that I would desire if I had a maximally informed and coherent and unified set of desires are one and the same? It seems to me that I have indeed shown that they are the same. Think again about the way in which I suggested, in Chapter 2, that we need to proceed, as philosophers interested in the content of our moral beliefs. This is the procedure that I followed when, in Chapter 5, I attempted to come up with a content for our beliefs about normative reasons.

What we believe, when we believe that it is desirable to φ in circumstances C, is a function of what we mean, quite generally, when we judge things to be desirable. Note immediately that we can distinguish between two things. On the one hand, there is what we mean by our desirability judgements. On the other there is what we believe we mean by our desirability judgements. These two can and do come apart. Someone can have all sorts of false beliefs about what they mean by their desirability judgements, but, ex hypothesi, their false beliefs do not infect what they believe when they believe something to be desirable, nor do they infect what they judge when they judge something to be desirable. What people believe and judge, when they believe and judge something to be desirable, is fixed by what they mean, not by what they believe themselves to mean.

How, then, do we determine what we mean by our desirability judgements, as opposed to what this or that person merely believes that we mean? The answer I defend in Chapter 2 of *The Moral Problem* is that we need to look at the role played by our desirability judgements in our mental economy. We need to look at what we are willing and able to infer that something is desirable from, and we need to look at what we are willing and able to infer from the fact that something is desirable, and we need to look at any other conditions on the appropriate use of desirability judgements as well, any constitutive connections with other mental states, for example. The meaning of our desirability judgements is, if you like, simply equivalent to whatever it is that has these inferential and quasi-inferential potentials.[20]

What we need to do then, as philosophers interested in figuring out what desirability judgements mean, is to come up with a description of these inferential and quasi-inferential potentials, and then to construct, as a content for our desirability judgements, whatever content it is which is such that our desirability judgements' having that content would best explain the various inferential and quasi-inferential roles that such judgements have. To repeat: this is because there is nothing for the content of our judgements to be but whatever best explains these roles. My suggestion in Chapter 5 of the book is that when we go through this procedure in the case of judgements about normative reasons we should conclude that my belief that it is desirable to φ in C has, as its content, the proposition that φing in C is what I would want myself to do if I had a maximally informed and coherent and unified desire set. I suggest that this content best explains the inferential and quasi-inferential roles that seem to me to be played by desirability judgements.

In order to have a telling objection to my argument, at this stage, Copp and Sayre-McCord thus really need to provide some reason for thinking either that the content that I say best explains these inferential and quasi-inferential roles doesn't really best explain them, or that even though it does best explain these roles, the content of beliefs about normative reasons isn't what best explains these roles, or else they need to come up with something else along these general lines. Only so will they engage with the argument at all. As far as I can see Copp does not specifically address these issues. He simply asserts that I have not given the content. I do not know how to reply to him beyond reiterating the point that, given the way in which I came up with the analysis, it seems to me that I have given the content. Sayre-McCord does address these issues, however, for he argues that the very method that I use to prove the equivalence – granting, remember, only for the sake of argument that I have provided a necessary and a priori equivalence – itself shows why someone who possesses the concept of a normative reason need not possess the concept of what would be desired in a situation in which they had a maximally informed and coherent and unified set of desires. His reason for thinking this is as follows.

When, as philosophers, we come up with a description of the various inferential and quasi-inferential dispositions of someone who is competent with the concept of a normative reason, Sayre-McCord points out that we might well find that we have to use concepts that they don't possess. It is as if, in describing the inferential dispositions of Sam, and his grasp of the number system, we found the need to use our concept of a cube root. This needn't undermine the a priori and necessary status of any of the equivalences we come up with, on the basis of our description of these inferential and quasi-inferential dispositions. When Sam believes that there are seven apples in the fruit bowl it is indeed a priori and necessary that what he believes is equivalent to the claim that there are the cube root of 343 apples in the fruit bowl. But just as it would be wrong to conclude that Sam believes that there are the cube root of 343 apples in the fruit bowl, Sayre-McCord claims that it is wrong for me to conclude that our beliefs about our normative reasons are beliefs about what we would desire ourselves to do if we had a maximally informed and coherent and unified set of desires. A fact about us, as philosophers, might be the source of the complexity of the analysis, not any fact about those who possess the concept of a normative reason.

I certainly feel the force of this objection. Although I am confident that the complexity in the analysis I have offered is not merely a function of something that I brought to the analytic enterprise, as a philosopher, I am not quite sure how to prove that this is so. One point to keep in mind, however, as we think about this issue, is that once it is agreed that the complexity of a concept is fixed by that degree of conceptual complexity, whatever it is, that is required in order best to explain the inferential and quasi-inferential dispositions possessed by someone who is competent with a concept, we should be very wary of trusting any of our own pre-theoretical convictions about the complexity of our concepts. Our pre-theoretical convictions might be quite misleading. The only thing that can be trusted as a guide to the complexity of our concepts is the structure implicit in the inferential and quasi-inferential dispositions possessed by someone who is competent with these concepts: the various discriminations and the like that those competent with the concepts are disposed to make.

But, as I see things, it is precisely this fact about those who possess the concept of a normative reason that explains the complexity in the analysis that I provide. Those who are competent with the concept of a normative reason really are sensitive in their application of the concept to the way in which failures of information can undermine normative reason claims; they really are sensitive in their application of the concept to the way in which the unavailability of a certain sort of ideal justification – a lack of coherence and unity – can undermine normative reason claims; and they really are sensitive in their application of the concept to the way in which a failure to be motivated in accordance with allegedly accepted normative reason claims, at least absent practical irrationality, can undermine the genuineness of the acceptance of the normative reasons claim. Those who fail to exhibit these sensitivities are not properly competent in their use of the concept of a normative reason. What justifies our attribution to them of the complex concept of what they would desire if they had a maximally informed and coherent and unified set of desires is thus that their possession of this concept best explains these discriminative abilities that they manifest in their judgements and inferences.

Here, then, lies the crucial difference between those who possess evaluative concepts and those like Sam who, while they possess the concept of there being seven apples in the fruit bowl, do not possess the concept of there being the cube root of 343 apples in the fruit bowl. There is nothing in Sam's discriminatory behavior that obliges us to ascribe to him the concept of a cube root. But there is something in the discriminatory behavior of those who possess evaluative concepts that obliges us to ascribe to them the concept of what they would want if they had a maximally informed and coherent and unified set of desires. For this reason, it seems to me wrong to suppose, as Sayre-McCord supposes, that the source of the complexity in the analysis that I propose lies in our need, as philosophers, to use sophisticated concepts in order to describe the inferential and quasi-inferential dispositions of those who possess the less sophisticated concept of a normative reason. The source of the complexity lies in facts about those who possess evaluative concepts themselves.[21]

The upshot at this crucial juncture of the argument is thus that neither Copp nor Sayre-McCord gives us any reason to doubt that the analysis I provide of a normative reason can be substituted in to give the content of the beliefs we have about normative reasons. If this is right, however, then, for the reasons already given, we can now readily explain why agents who believe that they have a normative reason to act in a certain way are motivated to act in that way, at least absent practical irrationality. Coherence augurs in favor of desiring to act in a certain way in certain circumstances when you believe that you would desire yourself to act in that way in those circumstances if you had a maximally informed and coherent and unified desire set. A failure to have such a desire constitutes a kind of incoherence. This kind of incoherence is what practical irrationality is.

VII. USING THE ANALYSIS TO EXPLAIN THE OBJECTIVITY OF NORMATIVE REASONS

So far I have explained why normative reasons, analyzed in the way I suggest, are practical. But the analysis allows us to explain more than that. It allows us to explain why normative reasons, if there are any, are objective as well.

According to the analysis if there exist any normative reasons at all then, under conditions of full rationality, we would all of us converge in the desires we have as regards what is to be done in certain highly specific circumstances. This is because, via a conversational process involving rational reflection and argument, we would be able to justify our desires, where a justification sufficient to convince one fully rational agent to adopt a desire is a justification sufficient to convince another to adopt it too, and this, in turn, is because only such a justification could guarantee that facts about normative reasons are not arbitrary. The objectivity of normative reason claims consists in no more or less than the fact that these desires possess such a justification.

Note that we do not need to make any extravagant assumptions about our psychological powers in order to see how we might in fact come up with such a justification of our desires. We need simply to be able to engage in the imaginative process of making our desires maximally informed, unified, and coherent, and to be disposed, in so doing, to respond appropriately should we discover that the desires that others come up with when they, too, engage in this imaginative exercise are different from ours. We need to see ourselves as in disagreement with these others and to be willing and able to provide further arguments in support of our own desires, or else to change our desires in response to the arguments that they offer in defense of theirs. Far from these being extraordinary psychological abilities, they are very ordinary abilities, abilities that we take each other to have as a matter of course in the give and take of everyday life.

VIII. USING THE ANALYSIS OF NORMATIVE REASONS TO EXPLAIN THE NATURE OF MORAL REQUIREMENTS

Given this analysis of normative reasons we are in a position to move on to the final stage of the argument. At this stage we use the analysis of normative reasons to reconcile the three propositions.

The claim I make in Chapter 6 is that we can give an analysis of moral facts – that is, in particular, facts about rightness and wrongness – in terms of facts about normative reasons. If this is right then the reconciliation is effected. For normative reasons are themselves both objective and practical, and so offer a satisfying way of reconciling all three propositions. The analysis of moral facts in terms of normative reasons proceeds as follows. First of all, we find out what all of our normative reasons are. Next we look to see whether any of these have the peculiar features of *moral* reasons: that is, we look to see whether there are any normative reasons that are other-regarding, or which require us to ascend to an egalitarian plateau, or which require us to promote human flourishing, or whatever else might be thought to be the distinctive feature of moral, as opposed to non-moral, reasons. Such an analysis seems to me to be simply irresistible given that moral facts do indeed purport to provide us with objective reasons for acting.

IX. OBJECTIONS TO THE EXPLANATION OF THE NATURE OF MORAL REQUIREMENTS

This is precisely where David Copp, and more especially David Brink, want to dig in and resist my argument. In fact, Brink gives a whole battery of arguments for rejecting my claim that moral facts can be analyzed in terms of facts about normative reasons.

For example, Brink notes that, in my view, whenever someone believes that an act is morally required, what they believe is that there is a normative reason to perform that act. As he points out, however, many philosophers claim that there is no normative reason to act morally, and, again as he points out, they offer arguments of the following sort in support of this claim: since morality admits of impartial conceptions, and practical reason admits of agent-centered conceptions, so it follows that it must be at least conceptually possible for someone to hold an impartial conception of morality and an agent-centered conception of practical reason. Brink draws the conclusion that it therefore cannot be the case that there is a constraint on the *content* of our beliefs about morality, and about practical reason, that forces them always to march in step: both must be impartial or both must be agent-centered. Otherwise, we are committed to holding that these philosophers' beliefs are incoherent.[22]

But, as I see things, all that Brink is talking about here is the beliefs that various philosophers have about what we all mean when we say that there is a normative reason to act in a certain way, and that we are morally required to act in a certain way. Brink points out, perfectly correctly, that some philosophers think that we mean very, very different things in these two cases – that is the point that these philosophers try to establish in the argument that Brink describes – and they therefore think that beliefs about moral requirements and beliefs about normative reasons are quite different beliefs. But what I was talking about wasn't what philosophers can and do believe about what we mean when we believe acts to be morally required, or what philosophers can and do believe about what we mean when we believe that there is a normative reason to act in a certain way, but rather about what we mean. I am, of course, committed to thinking that those philosophers whose beliefs about what we mean are different from my own are wrong. Moreover, the fact that so many philosophers disagree with me does give me pause for thought. Perhaps it is me who is wrong. My beliefs about what we mean are not guaranteed to be true. But the fact that I disagree with them should give them pause for thought as well, because perhaps they are the ones who are wrong. The point is that the mere fact of our disagreement about what we mean when we talk about what is morally required, or what there is normative reason to do, gives us no purchase on who is right and who is wrong.[23]

Another of Brink's objections is that people like me who hold the view that facts about moral requirements are just facts about normative reasons overlook the fact that it is appropriate to use the term "reason" in connection with requirements of etiquette. "There is every reason in the world for you to wear a tie when you give a paper at the APA!" one of my colleagues protested when he saw me wearing a shirt buttoned at the neck, but without a tie. But all he meant by this use of the term "reason" is that wearing a tie to give a paper at the APA is a well-entrenched behavioral norm or convention. It need not, and as he used the term "reason" most certainly did not, signal that he thought I was in any sense irrational for failing to wear a tie. He could consistently agree that I have no normative reason to wear a tie. Likewise, Brink suggests, moral facts might simply be behavioral norms or conventions like requirements of etiquette. Even though it is appropriate for us to say that moral requirements provide us with objective reasons he tells us that the use of the term "reason" here, properly understood, has nothing to do with "reasons" in the sense of requirements of rationality. Reasons, here, are not normative reasons.[24]

Brink is right that this alternative needs to be eliminated, and, as it happens, I do discuss it at some length in Chapter 3 of *The Moral Problem*. What I argue there is that a conventional account of morality is unacceptable because it tries to explain the normative force of morality in terms of something that is essentially arbitrary. In order to see that this is so, we need to look a little more closely at one of the best worked out accounts of behavioral norms or conventions on offer. This is the account Brink himself appeals to, the account of behavioral norms provided by H. L. A. Hart in his seminal account of the conditions under which social rules exist in *The Concept of Law*.[25]

According to Hart's account, the existence of a behavioral rule in a group is constituted by a behavioral regularity in the group, a behavioral regularity that is kept in place by the activity of a special sub-group of those to whom the rule applies, a sub-group who adopt the "internal point of view" on the rule. What Hart means by this is very weak. For example, it would suffice for a sub-group's having an internal point of view on the rule that it is in their interests to act in accordance with the rule, and that it is in their interests to get others to do so as well. As Hart tells the story, the activity of this special sub-group helps constitute the rule because they not only follow the rule themselves but are appropriately motivated to play the crucial role of eliciting the behavioral conformity of others to the rule as well. They play this role by dealing out punishments and rewards, punishments and rewards that they can justify to themselves and to each other, given their common interest, but which they might not be able to justify to those who they punish and reward. If those they punish and reward do not see any normative reason to act in accordance with the rule – imagine that acting in accordance with the rule does not happen to be in *their* interests – then they will simply see the punishments and rewards as thoroughly and unjustifiably coercive.

As is perhaps already evident, whatever its merits as an account of the existence of social rules like rules of etiquette, there is a crucial feature of Hart's story about what makes for the existence behavioral rules that disqualifies it as an account of what makes for the existence of *moral* requirements. In Hart's story it is entirely arbitrary and contingent that the sub-group whose activity gets to fix the content of the rules happens to be the group that it is, and it is arbitrary and contingent that they happen to have the interests that they have. Different people have different interests, in Hart's story, and would therefore help constitute quite different social rules if they happened to be a part of the coalition which dealt out the punishments and rewards. It therefore follows that the content of the rules depends on who, among the members of the social group, is such that their activity gets to constitute the prevailing rules. On plausible assumptions they will be the most powerful group in the society.

But while this might be a good account of what makes for the existence of requirements of etiquette – for it does indeed seem that their content can be entirely arbitrary and contingent in just this way, fixed by the interests of a powerful group – as an account of what makes for the existence of moral requirements it is fundamentally at odds with a conceptual truth about moral requirements. The content of moral requirements, if such requirements exist at all, cannot be so utterly arbitrary and contingent. Moral requirements, if they exist at all, are not mere reflections of power. At best, such a conventional story could therefore be used to debunk the existence of moral requirements. It could not possibly constitute an account of what it is for something *really* to be morally required. Though

Brink announces his own attraction to the conventional story, he does not explain how he would defend it against this objection. I therefore see no attraction in his suggestion that the use of the term "reason" in connection with moral requirements simply marks the existence of a convention or behavioral norm.

Brink has another argument against my claim that we can analyze moral facts in terms of facts about normative reasons. Since our beliefs about our normative reasons give rise to corresponding motivations, at least absent practical irrationality, it follows that if moral facts can be analyzed in terms of facts about normative reasons then our beliefs about what we are morally required to do must also give rise to corresponding motivations, at least absent practical irrationality. Brink argues against this last claim via a *modus tollens*. A principled amoralist is someone whose beliefs about what he is morally required to do, even when he is not suffering from practical irrationality – that is, even when he is suffering from no incoherence of the kind described earlier in spelling out the practicality of normative reasons – need not give rise to any corresponding motivations. So the claim that moral beliefs entail corresponding motivations, absent practical irrationality, must be false. Beliefs about what we are morally required to do are therefore not beliefs about our normative reasons. Copp, too, seems attracted to an argument along these lines.[26]

In Chapter 3 of the book I in effect argue against Brink's *modus tollens* by *reductio*. Assume, for *reductio*, that what makes someone a "principled amoralist" is that he may have beliefs about what he is morally required to do and yet not be motivated even when he is not suffering from the sort of incoherence described earlier. Given Brink's account of what makes someone a principled amoralist, it follows that we can simply define a class of moralists: moralists are people whose motivations do follow reliably in the wake of their beliefs about what they are morally required to do, at least when they are not suffering from the sort of incoherence described earlier.[27] Thus, even though Brink denies the following:

The Practicality Requirement on Moral Judgement: If an agent judges it right to do something then she is motivated accordingly, at least absent practical irrationality,

for he thinks that the mere possibility of principled amoralists provides a counter-example to this requirement, he is committed to agreeing with the following:

The Claim about Moralists: If a moralist judges it right to do something then she is motivated accordingly, at least absent practical irrationality.

Brink is committed to the Claim about Moralists, and so is Copp for that matter, by the mere fact that we can *define* the class of moralists in the way described. But, as I will argue, this presents them with a problem.

The problem is that anyone like Brink and Copp who accepts the Claim about Moralists needs to say why they accept it. I accept the Claim about Moralists, and I can clearly state why. I accept it because it is entailed by the Practicality Requirement on Moral Judgement. Anyone capable of making a moral claim is a moralist. No problem. But why do Brink and Copp accept it? To be sure, as we have already said, we can simply define the class of "moralists" so as to make the Claim about Moralists come out true. But the very fact that we can do this, and *there are* many moralists out there in the world – that is, people whose motivations follow reliably in the wake of their moral judgements – so ensuring that the class of moralists is not empty, means that we need to say what it is about them that makes them such that their moral judgements bring along corresponding motivations, at least absent practical irrationality.

Remember, I say that the Claim about Moralists is true because of something about the nature of *moral judgement:* moral judgements are analyzable in terms of beliefs about our normative reasons, analyzed in the way I suggest. Brink and Copp cannot give this answer. They must say that the Claim about Moralists is true because of something about the nature of *moralists.* So what is it about the nature of a moralist that explains the truth of the Claim about Moralists? Why is it that there are moralists whose motivations change when they are led to change their minds about morality?

The only answer I could think of when I wrote *The Moral Problem,* on behalf of those who reject the Practicality Requirement, is that moralists change their motivations in this way because what makes someone a moralist is the fact that they are simply so disposed that they change their desires given that they change their moral beliefs. But, given that this disposition cannot be the sort of rational disposition that makes the Practicality Requirement on Moral Judgement true – the sort of tendency toward coherence described earlier – because it seems that *would* require the moral belief to be a belief about a normative reason, the suggestion has to be rather that the moralist's disposition is a contingent, rationally optional, feature of their psychology. In other words, the moralist is someone who simply desires, contingently, to do what is right.

But now think of the explanation we have been offered. The idea is that the very fact that so many of us reliably change our motivations after we have been convinced to change our minds about moral matters shows that our primary motivation, the one that drives all the others, is our desire to do what we believe to be right. My objection to this is that I simply don't see how to square this with our commonsense idea of moral virtue.

Under the conditions of uncertainty about what is of value that we all operate, it seems to me that common sense demands that we recognize certain qualities of mind in people, qualities of mind that reflect a sort of talent for the enterprise of moral discovery in which we are all engaged. This is our commonsense idea of moral virtue. Morally virtuous people, at least as we commonsensically think about them, are those who are especially careful and thoughtful in the formation of their moral beliefs; they have a demonstrated ability to be open and sensitive to a range of important considerations that others are inclined to overlook; they aren't dogmatic but are willing to enter into the point of view of others and sometimes to change their minds when they are persuaded by a good argument; and, importantly, their concerns shift with shifts in their moral judgements: they don't say "Oh yes, I see. You're right. I am obliged to do that. I was wrong. But I just don't feel any inclination to do it. I still feel like doing what I used to think I was obliged to do."

No doubt there is more to the commonsense idea of moral virtue than this, but what I have already said is enough for present purposes. For note that our commonsense idea of morally virtuous people makes them fall into the class of moralists. It follows that, on the way of thinking to which those who reject the Practicality Requirement on Moral Judgement are committed, morally virtuous people too must have as their primary source of moral motivation a desire to do what is morally required. When morally virtuous people believe it right to, say, look after the well-being of their family and friends, then they will therefore have an instrumental desire to look after the well-being of their family and friends. But if the only mechanism that exists for causing and sustaining moral motivation in the face of revisions of their beliefs about what they are morally required to do is the desire to do what is morally required, then it seems that not only will they have an instrumental concern for their family and friends, but that they will positively eschew any non-instrumental concern.

After all, a non-instrumental desire to look after family and friends wouldn't be kept in check by the desire to do the right thing under conditions of moral belief revision. It would simply remain and produce a motivational conflict, a conflict which one side should win. The desire to do what is morally required would then have to be weighed against the non-instrumental desire to look after family and friends, and, unhappily, it might lose. On this picture of the moralist, there is therefore always the potential for an agent who acquires non-instrumental desires to do the various things which he believes to be morally required to be led astray. Better, it would seem, not to acquire such desires at all. Better if you are morally virtuous, anyway.

But this seems to me to fly in the face of too much that we ordinarily think about moral virtue. We normally assume that morally virtuous people are possessed of appropriate sensitivities and sympathies. Indeed, we normally assume that what ultimately moves them are the very features of their acts that they believe make them right. Thus, if what they believe makes an act right is the fact that it serves the well-being of their family and friends, then we normally assume that what ultimately moves them is that very fact: that is, the fact that their act serves the well-being of their family and friends. If what they believe makes an act right is that it maximizes happiness and minimizes suffering, then we normally assume that what ultimately moves them is that very fact: that is, the fact that their act maximizes happiness and minimizes suffering. And so we could go on. This is part of what makes them morally virtuous, on the ordinary view. Morally virtuous people are, inter alia, those who are ultimately moved, noninstrumentally, by what they take to be the right-making features themselves, and when they revise their moral beliefs, their sensitivities shift accordingly.

This is certainly the picture of things that we get from the view I hold, given that I accept the Practicality Requirement on Moral Judgement. I say a moral judgement is a belief about what we would want ourselves to do if we had a maximally informed and coherent and unified set of desires. It thus comes as no surprise that we acquire a non-instrumental desire to, say, maximize happiness and minimize suffering when we believe it right to do so. If we believe that we would have a non-instrumental desire that we act so as to maximize happiness and minimize suffering if we had a maximally informed and coherent and unified set of desires, and if our overall psychology tends toward coherence, then we will indeed acquire a non-instrumental desire to maximize happiness and minimize suffering. Moreover, if we revise our belief about what we would non-instrumentally desire if we had a maximally informed and coherent and unified set of desires – let's say we acquire the belief that we would non-instrumentally desire ourselves only to look after our nearest and dearest – then that same tendency towards coherence will make the non-instrumental desire to maximize happiness and minimize suffering disappear at the very same time as it makes us acquire a non-instrumental desire to look after our nearest and dearest. For this reason, I say that morally virtuous people are indeed motivated by the very features of their acts that they take to be right-making features themselves.

But it is hard to see how someone who rejects the Practicality Requirement can accept this ordinary view. If morally virtuous people are ultimately moved by a desire to do the right thing then they are moved, ultimately, by a feature that the right-making features of their acts possess: the feature of being a right-making feature. Only so can they guard against the moral danger of being led astray by non-instrumental desires to do things which they no longer believe to be morally required. But to think this is to suppose that morally virtuous people are, in a quite straightforward sense, alienated from the features of acts that they believe make them right. In desiring to do what is right for the sake of its being the right thing to do, rather than for the sake of the very feature that they believe makes it the right thing to do itself, the people we have to think of as morally virtuous, on this alternative conception, desire something that is not of any moral significance at all, as far as I can see. They seem precious, overly concerned with the moral standing of their acts when they should instead be concerned with the features in virtue of which their acts have the moral standing that they have. Indeed, as I say in *The Moral Problem*, they seem to have a moral fetish. If a rejection of the Practicality Requirement on Moral Judgement commits us to a view which has us saying something so obviously false about the motivations of morally virtuous people, then, as I see things, that constitutes a *reductio* of that view. This, in turn, provides us with a reason to accept the Practicality Requirement. But if we must accept the Practicality Requirement then Brink is wrong to suppose that there are principled amoralists. His *modus tollens* collapses.

Brink and Copp both seem to agree that this would be a *reductio*, if the argument worked. But they do not think that by rejecting the Practicality Requirement they are committed to the false view about the motivations of morally virtuous people that I describe. Instead of saying, as I suggest, that moralists possess a desire to do the right thing, they both suggest what makes someone a moralist is the fact that they have a desire to acquire non-istrumental desires to perform acts with right-making features. They both think that this allows them to avoid the *reductio*. For imagine a morally virtuous agent who believes it right to look after her family and friends. Brink and Copp rightly think that if such an agent has a desire to acquire a non-instrumental desire to perform acts with right-making features, then this second-order desire together with their moral belief will cause them

288

to desire, *non-instrumentally*, to look after her family and friends. It thus is not the case that they are committed to the false view that morally virtuous people are ultimately motivated by the fact that their acts have right-making features, rather, when they act, they are motivated by the features that they believe to be right-making features themselves.[28]

Sure enough, when they act, they are appropriately motivated. But what ultimately moves them, as moralists? All Brink and Copp have managed to do is to reorient the fetish that their so-called morally virtuous people possess. It isn't now about their actions. Rather it is about themselves and their own desires. As I described them they were ultimately motivated by a desire that their acts have right-making features, not by the features that they believed to be right-making features themselves. This seems to me to be perverse, and Brink and Copp apparently agree. But as Brink and Copp describe morally virtuous people they are ultimately motivated by the fact that they have non-instrumental desires to perform acts with right-making features, not by the fact that they have non-instrumental desires to perform acts with the features that they believe to be the right-making features themselves. The desire I described as a fetish, and which they agree sounds perverse, but which they deny a morally virtuous person possesses, is thus on all fours with the desire that they ascribe to the morally virtuous person. They should therefore agree that the morally virtuous person they describe sounds equally precious, equally self-absorbed, equally fixated on something that isn't of any moral significance: the moral standing of the contents of his first-order desires, rather than the features in virtue of which his first-order desires have the moral standing that they have. We therefore still have a *reductio* of the view that they are led to embrace once they reject the Practicality Requirement on Moral Judgement.

In fact, however, by this stage of the argument Brink and Copp are in a much more vulnerable position than this suggests. For once it is agreed that I have both defined the class of normative reasons and demonstrated the way in which these normative reasons are at once both objective and practical – in other words, once we have rehearsed all the arguments and counter-arguments and replies to the counter-arguments in the way in which we have here – the argument for the Practicality Requirement on Moral Judgement that we have just discussed, and which I give in Chapter 3 of *The Moral Problem*, turns out really to be just a sideshow. There are independent and more compelling reasons to believe that moral claims are claims about normative reasons, and so subject to the Practicality Requirement.

Suppose, as Brink at least is prepared to concede, that some normative reasons defined in the way I define them do exist, and suppose further that after reflection we come to the conclusion that there is just one such reason and that its content corresponds to the principle of utility. That is, suppose that if we were fully rational we would all of us converge upon a single desire: the desire that we act so as to maximize happiness and minimize suffering in every possible situation we ever face. Suppose further that we come to believe that this is so and for good reasons. Could Brink, or Copp, seriously suggest that even though this normative reason exists, and even though we believe it to exist, nevertheless we would still believe that the question whether there are any moral facts is a *different* question? That seems quite incredible to me.

If, in fact, everyone has a normative reason to maximize happiness and minimize suffering in every possible situation, and if we came to believe this to be so, then it seems to me that the existence of this normative reason would structure our thinking about every single action, decision, policy, and relationship that we ordinarily take to be structured by morality. Moreover, once our thinking had been structured by this normative reason it seems to me that there would be no residue, no possible object of interest or concern left, to be structured by whatever Brink and Copp seem to think the moral facts are.

A normative reason to maximize happiness and minimize suffering in every situation, if such a reason exists, therefore seems to me to be an excellent candidate for a moral fact. Another excellent candidate would be a series of normative reasons corresponding in their content to Ross's seven prima facie duties.[29] Another excellent candidate would be an endless list of normative reasons, each tailor-made to a situation, corresponding in their content to particularist stories about the actions of virtuous people in those situations.[30] And so we might go on. The crucial point is that if any of these would be *excellent* candidates for a moral fact, if only they existed, then it follows that in the here and now, when we do not know whether such normative reasons exist or not, we have no choice but to suppose that they are the sorts of things that we are looking for in looking for moral facts.

In short, moral facts should be analyzed in terms of facts about normative reasons, and so be thought of as subject to the Practicality Requirement, because as soon as you realize that facts about normative reasons could, for all we know at present, have distinctively moral content, you see that no other way of thinking about moral facts would be in the least conceptually satisfying. It is the excellence of normative reasons, defined in the way I define them, as candidates for moral facts, that should in the end force us to admit that we have really been thinking of moral facts as facts about such normative reasons all along. Once you have glimpsed the rationalist's heaven, you simply can't bring yourself to look back.

X. CONCLUSION

Despite the many ways in which I agree with David Brink and David Copp and Geoffrey Sayre-McCord that various of the claims I make in *The Moral Problem* require more in the way of elucidation and defense, at the end of the day I am therefore left thinking that the elucidation and defense can be given. The basic line of argument I pursue in the book seems to me to survive in pretty much the form in which I initially presented it.

None of this is to say that *The Moral Problem* constitutes any sort of proof of the existence of moral facts, of course. I don't think that anyone could prove that there are moral facts, in the sense of providing a compelling deductive argument for their existence. Nor do I think we should expect such a thing either, in so far as we aim at understanding ourselves and our relationship to morality. Nihilistic thoughts are a central part of the human condition in their own right. A deductive proof of the existence of moral requirements would make that fact hard to understand. My main concern in the book, and here as well, has been the more modest one of saying what moral facts would be like if there were any. According to the account I have offered, the existence of moral facts is not so wild as to make engaging in moral reflection pointless. But nor is there any guarantee that reflection will deliver the goods.

Once the contestable nature of moral facts, as I conceive of them, is agreed upon, it seems to me that the particular suggestion I make about their nature is well placed not just to solve the meta-ethical problem that has been up for discussion thus far, but that it also helps to diagnose and solve that same problem, viewed now as a problem lying at the very core of first-order ethics. This is why, despite Sayre-McCord's misgivings, I continue to think that *The Moral Problem* is so aptly named. He says that when he thinks of "*the* moral problem" he thinks of "rampant cruelty, systematic injustice, moral indifference, maybe even the paltry supply of simple human decency," not the meta-ethical problem that I am concerned to solve.[31] These are what I think of, too. But when I think of the worst-case scenario for the cause of these, I think of the meta-ethical problem that I am concerned to solve.

This is because skepticism about morality is itself largely fueled by meta-ethical reflection of the sort I describe, and moral skepticism itself can be a very, very bad thing. As I argue in *The Moral Problem*, what meta-ethical reflection suggests, at least initially, is that the very idea of being morally required to act in some way or other is all a total sham: nothing could be everything a moral requirement purports to be. When people become convinced moral skeptics for this sort of reason *and then* go on to acquire an indifference to the suffering of others, as so many certainly do, the problems the rest of us face become acute. The problems become acute because those who are indifferent don't agree that we say anything of significance when we try to engage them in a first-order moral argument in the attempt to talk them out of their indifference. The cause of this particular first-order moral problem, then, is not the fact that moral thought *is* incoherent, as Sayre-McCord represents me as thinking in a footnote, but rather the fact that it is *believed* to be incoherent when it is not.

The only way to solve this first-order moral problem, it seems to me, is to demonstrate, as best we can, how being subject to moral requirements flows from inescapable features of what it is to be a thinking, reflective, rational creature, the sort of creature that someone who is indifferent must admit themselves to be in so far as they base their indifference on rational reflection about the nature of morality. This is what the analysis of moral requirements in terms of facts about our normative reasons allows us to do. For, if I am right, moral requirements are just normative reasons accessible to any rational creature capable of engaging in rational reflection. It therefore follows that there is no problem at all involved in sustaining the thought that there at least might be some moral requirements, moral requirements that we have access to on the basis of the same sort of reasoning that allows any other rational creature access to them. And it also follows that there is no problem at all involved in sustaining the thought that once any rational creature forms a belief about what they are morally required to do – that is, a belief about what they have a normative reason to do – that belief makes certain rational demands on their cares and concerns, and therefore on their actions.

Once we think of moral requirements in the way I suggest, it thus turns out that, to the extent that we really do believe that there are moral requirements, we should think that those whose indifference is fueled by moral skepticism are in danger of giving up on being thinking, reflective, rational creatures. This itself should convince most people not to have the attitude. People can and should pull themselves together. Those whom it doesn't convince – that is, those who are willing to give up on being thinking, reflective, rational creatures, at least as regards what they have normative reason to do – plainly aren't convincible by any form of rational argument that we can bring to bear against them. They will therefore remain a part of the problem we face in first-order moral theorizing, but only in the more ordinary sense of being a fixed part of its subject matter. We should think of them as like wild animals, creatures with whom we cannot reason but whose activity has the potential to have all sorts of bad effects on others. Their behavior therefore needs to be managed in ways which respect, as much as possible, their own capacity for pain and suffering.[32] Dealing with such people seems to me to present us with as vexing a first-order moral problem as we are likely to find, a problem whose true nature only becomes clear once we realize how firmly rooted it is in their own meta-ethical reflection.

NOTES

I would like to thank Richard Arneson for very helpful comments on a draft of this chapter, and Paul Hurley for arranging the original APA book symposium.

1. David Brink, "Moral Motivation"; David Copp, "Belief, Reason, and Motivation: Michael Smith's *The Moral Problem*"; Geoffrey Sayre-McCord, "The Metaethical Problem," all in *Ethics*, 108, 1997. These articles all discuss Michael Smith, *The Moral Problem* (Oxford: Blackwell, 1994).

2. Brink, pp. 4–5.

3. Ibid., n. 5.

4. Allan Gibbard, *Wise Choices, Apt Feelings* (Oxford: Clarendon, 1990).

5. Simon Blackburn, *Spreading the Word* (Oxford: Oxford University Press, 1984), and *Essays in Quasi-Realism* (Oxford: Oxford University Press, 1993); Harry Frankfurt, "Freedom of the Will and the Concept of a Person," *Journal of Philosophy* 68 (1971): 5–20.

6. In effect, this amounts to the idea that since our valuing something can have a rational impact on our first-order desires, so our valuings must be such as to obey what Jay Wallace calls the "desire-in desire-out" principle. Wallace's discussion of the "desire-in desire-out" principle appears in his "How to Argue about Practical Reason," *Mind* 99 (1990): 267–97. If we think of valuing as second-order desiring then it does indeed obey this principle.

7. I am thinking in particular of Tom Hurka's review of *The Moral Problem*, "Between Belief and Desire," in the *Times Literary Supplement* (October 27, 1995), but a similar line of thought can be found in James Dreier's review in *Mind* (105 [1996]: 363–67), Christian Piller's Critical Notice in *Australasian Journal of Philosophy* (74 [1996]: 347–67), Jonathan Dancy's Critical Notice in *Ratio* (9 [1996]: 171–83), and Ingmar Persson's Critical Notice in *Theoria* (61, pt. 2 [1996]: 143–58). In his Critical Study of *The Moral Problem*, "Smith's Moral Problem," in *Philosophical Quaterly* (46 [1996]: 508–15), Stephen Darwall is more sympathetic than the

others – perhaps unsurprisingly, given that he is the only reviewer tempted by the sort of rationalism that tempts me – but he, too, thinks that the arguments I provide are flawed in various ways.

8. See also n. 16 below.
9. Copp, p. 44.
10. Ibid., pp. 45–46.
11. Ibid.
12. When we do moral psychology it is crucial to suppose that this is so. See Philip Pettit and Michael Smith, "Practical Unreason," *Mind* 102 (1993): 53–79; "Brandt on Self-Control," in *Rationality, Rules and Utility*, ed. Brad Hooker (Boulder, CO.: Westview, 1993); Jeanette Kennett and Michael Smith, "Philosophy and Commonsense: The Case of Weakness of Will," in *Philosophy in Mind*, ed. Michaelis Michael and John O'Leary-Hawthorne (Dordrecht: Kluwer, 1994); Michael Smith, "Normative Reasons and Full Rationality: A Reply to Swanton," *Analysis* 56 (1996): 160–68.
13. Sayre-McCord, pp. 75–76.
14. This idea is made to do considerable work when we bring the account of what it is to judge something desirable to bear on issues of freedom and responsibility. See esp. Philip Pettit and Michael Smith, "Freedom in Belief and Desire," *Journal of Philosophy* 93 (1996): 429–49; Michael Smith, "A Theory of Freedom and Responsibility," in *Ethics and Practical Reason*, ed. Garrett Cullity and Berys Gaut (Oxford: Oxford University Press, 1997).
15. Sayre-McCord, p. 75.
16. The analogies between this sort of account of what is a priori true and our beliefs about what is a priori true, on the one hand, and facts about what there is normative reason to do and our desires, on the other, seem to me to go very deep. For example, once it is agreed that facts about what is a priori true are facts about constructions – facts about the beliefs about what is a priori true that we would all converge on if we were to subject our initial beliefs about what is a priori true to a reflective equilibrium process and so came up with a maximally informed and coherent and unified set of beliefs about what is a priori true – note that one very popular argument for skepticism about the truth of beliefs about normative reasons, understood in the way I suggest, looks like it should carry over and be an argument for skepticism about the truth of our beliefs about what is a priori true as well. "After all," the objection goes, "if there are any a priori truths at all then it follows that we would all converge in our beliefs about what is a priori true if we had a maximally informed and coherent and unified set of such beliefs." But surely such a convergence in our beliefs about what is a priori true is unlikely. Consider two people who have rather different beliefs about what is a priori true from each other to begin with, prior to engaging in the reflective process. Shouldn't we suppose that what one of them ends up believing to be a priori true, after subjecting *their* beliefs to a reflective equilibrium process, will be radically relative to the beliefs that *they* had to begin with? Absent the causal regulation of their various beliefs by the one set of a priori truths – that is, given the constructivism – the answer must be yes. We should therefore conclude that there are no a priori truths at all, on the grounds that there are no beliefs as regards what is a priori true that we would all converge upon if we had

a maximally informed and coherent and unified set of such beliefs. But I take it that the answer to this question is relatively straightforward in the case of beliefs about what is a priori true on this view. Given that, on this view, people have to converge in their beliefs about what is a priori true for any claim about what is a priori true to be true at all so it follows that, if we wish to interpret people as having beliefs about what is a priori true where some such beliefs are indeed true, then we simply have to so interpret them that they would converge if they had a maximally informed and coherent and unified set of such beliefs. Though people can therefore have quite different beliefs about what is a priori true from each other to begin with, prior to engaging in a reflective process, we have no choice but to interpret them in such a way that the differences between them would slowly cancel out as they came closer and closer to having a maximally informed and coherent and unified set of beliefs about what is a priori true. This suggests a parallel reply to the same argument for skepticism about the truth of beliefs about what we have normative reason to do. Given that people have to converge in the desires they would have if they had a maximally informed and coherent and unified set of desires for any claim about what there is normative reason to do to be true at all so it follows that, if we wish to interpret them as having beliefs about what there is normative reason to do where some such beliefs are true, then we simply have to so interpret them that they would converge if they had a maximally informed and coherent and unified set of desires. Although people can therefore have quite different desires from each other to begin with, prior to engaging in a reflective process, we have no choice but to interpret them in such a way that the differences between them would slowly cancel out as they came closer and closer to having a maximally informed and coherent and unified set of desires. Of course, none of this is to say that there is good reason to interpret people so that it turns out that some of their beliefs about what there is normative reason to do are true, any more than it shows that there is good reason to interpret them so that it turns out that some of their beliefs about what is a priori true, conceived of in the way discussed here, are true. The crucial point is simply that worries about the possibility of a convergence are in both cases irrelevant to that decision. Convergence can be secured, if it needs to be. Arguments for skepticism must therefore come from elsewhere.

17. Sayre-McCord, p. 76.
18. It is the causal power of the tendency towards coherence that allows us to reject the "desire-in desire-out" principle: see note 6 above. Note that those whose psychologies exhibit this sort of coherence may still fall far short of *full* rationality: that is, their desires may not yet be *maximally* informed and coherent and unified. For though people who both believe that they would desire that they keep a promise in circumstances C if they had a maximally informed and coherent and unified desire set, and who also desire that they keep a promise in C, have a psychology that, in a certain respect, exhibits more in the way of coherence than those who have the belief but lack the corresponding desire, they might still have a psychology that, in other respects, fails to exhibit coherence and unity. Such would be the case if, for example, their belief that they would desire that they keep a promise in C if they had a maximally informed and coherent and unified desire set was *false*. For then, precisely because they have a desire that matches

their *false* belief about their normative reasons – that is, precisely because their psychology exhibits the sort of coherence that we have been talking about thus far – they thereby have a desire that they would not have if they had a maximally informed and coherent and unified desire set, and so their overall psychological state cannot be *maximally* coherent. This is my reply to James Dreier's central objection to *The Moral Problem*; see note 7 above.

19. Copp, p. 39; Sayre-McCord, pp. 77, 81–82.
20. In *The Moral Problem*, I say, "Whereas mastery of a mastered concept requires knowledge-how, knowledge of an analysis requires us to have knowledge-that about our knowledge-how" (p. 38). The point I had in mind is the one described in the last two paragraphs. Knowledge of an analysis is a belief we have about what we mean by a particular concept we possess. It is philosophers' knowledge par excellence. Our possession of that concept, by contrast – and therefore our meaning by it just what we do – is fixed otherwise: namely, by the inferential and quasi-inferential dispositions we possess.
21. For an alternative treatment of these issues, one which might suit my purposes just as well, see Philip Pettit's "Practical Belief and Philosophical Theory," *Australasian Journal of Philosophy*, 76, 1998: 15–33.
22. Brink, pp. 18–19.
23. Perhaps Brink's thought here is like the idea I attributed to Copp and Sayre-McCord earlier on. Perhaps he wants to draw a distinction between what we all mean when we talk about what is morally required, or what there is a normative reason to do, on the one hand, and what follows a priori from what we all mean on the other. If so then he might even admit that there could be an a priori argument that proves that what we are morally required to do is what we have a normative reason to do. He would simply deny that it follows from this that the two mean the same thing. If this is Brink's view, however, then my reply is the same as the earlier reply to Copp and Sayre-McCord.
24. Brink, pp. 20–21, note 21.
25. H. L. A. Hart, *The Concept of Law* (Oxford: Clarendon, 1961), cited in Brink, note 20.
26. Brink, p. 18; Copp, p. 52.
27. In *The Moral Problem* I call these people "good and strong-willed," a piece of terminology I now regret. I first introduced the new terminology "moralist" in "The Argument for Internalism: A Reply to Miller," *Analysis* 56 (1996): 175–84.
28. Brink, pp. 27–28 (this is how I understand Brink's talk of the regulative role of moral beliefs); Copp, pp. 50–51.
29. W. D. Ross, *The Right and the Good* (Oxford: Oxford University Press, 1930).
30. John McDowell, "Virtue and Reason," *Monist* 62 (1979): 331–50; David McNaughton, *Moral Vision* (Oxford: Blackwell, 1988); Jonathan Dancy, *Moral Reasons* (Oxford: Blackwell, 1993).
31. Sayre-McCord, p. 55.
32. Here I find myself in agreement with P. F. Strawson in his "Freedom and Resentment," in *Free Will*, ed. Gary Watson (Oxford: Oxford University Press, 1982).

14

Exploring the Implications of the Dispositional Theory of Value

Suppose, just for the sake of argument, that the version of the dispositional theory of value that I myself prefer is correct (see, for example, Smith 1989, 1994a, 1997; compare Lewis 1989, Johnston 1989): when a subject judges it desirable for p to be the case in certain circumstances C, this is a matter of her believing that she would want p to be the case in C if she were in a state that eludes all forms of criticism from the point of view of reason – or, for short, and perhaps somewhat misleadingly (Copp 1997), if she were fully rational.[1] More precisely, if still somewhat misleadingly, let's suppose that when a subject judges it desirable that p in C this is a matter of her believing that, in those nearby possible worlds in which she is fully rational – let's call these the "evaluating possible worlds" – she wants that, in those possible worlds in which C obtains – let's call these the "evaluated possible worlds" – p obtains.

Once we have supposed this to be so it is, I think, extremely tempting to suppose that we have thereby either explicitly or implicitly taken a stand on certain crucial debates in meta-ethics: tempting to suppose that we must be cognitivists as opposed to non-cognitivists; relativists as opposed to non-relativists; and realists as opposed to irrealists. We must be cognitivists because we have supposed that evaluative judgement is a species of belief. We must be relativists because we have supposed that the truth conditions of a subject's evaluative beliefs are fixed by whatever that subject would want if she were fully rational, and hence are relative to what that subject herself actually desires: the contents of different subjects' evaluative beliefs must be different from each other simply because they are beliefs of different subjects. And we must be realists because there is every reason to suppose that there are facts about what different subjects want in possible worlds like the evaluating world, possible worlds in which they are fully rational; every reason to suppose, in other words, that some such beliefs are true. The realism that is thus implied contrasts not with the kind of irrealism defended by non-cognitivists, but with that defended by cognitivists like John Mackie who thinks that we should all be error theorists about value (Mackie 1997).

Notwithstanding the very understandable temptation to think that all of this is so, I will argue that the implications of the dispositional theory are either different or, at the very least, much less clear. Though the dispositional theory does give us grounds on which to make a case for cognitivism, I will argue that making that case requires that we appeal to certain controversial supplementary premises (§1). As regards relativism, I will argue that the dispositional theory not only has no such implication, but that, on its face, it commits us, if anything, to non-relativism (§2). And as regards realism, I will argue that the dispositional theory leaves it very much an open question whether realism or irrealism is true. That debate, too, turns on the truth of certain supplementary, and highly controversial, premises (§3).

1. THE DISPOSITIONAL THEORY AND COGNITIVISM

Since the issue that divides cognitivists from non-cognitivists is, by definition, whether evaluative judgements are expressions of belief (the cognitivists' view) or some non-belief state, a state of desire or whatever (the non-cognitivists' view), it may seem inevitable that, having taken it as given that a subject's judging desirable is a matter of her believing that she would have certain desires if she were fully rational, we must be cognitivists. Inevitable though it might appear, however, it seems to me this line of reasoning is mistaken.

Consider the following, much shorter, argument for cognitivism, by way of comparison.

> Premise: When a subject judges it desirable for p to be the case in certain circumstances C, this is a matter of her believing that it is desirable for p to be the case in C.
> Conclusion: A cognitivist theory of desirability judgements is correct.

Now I take it that no one will find this argument convincing. The problem is not that the premise is false. The premise, being simply a correct report of the way in which we use the English word "belief," is true. The problem is rather that, precisely because this is why the premise is true, it is too weak to establish the truth of the desired conclusion. Moreover the reason why this is so should be evident. Quite generally, the mere fact that we ordinarily describe things in certain ways does nothing to show that those descriptions apply to those things strictly speaking. The mere fact that we ordinarily describe certain people as "pigs," for example, does nothing to show that they are pigs strictly speaking. It shows, at most, that they are like pigs in certain respects. Likewise, then, the mere fact that we ordinarily describe people as having evaluative beliefs does nothing to show that the attitudes thus described are beliefs strictly speaking either. It shows, at most, that the attitudes are like beliefs in certain respects. This is something that can be agreed by cognitivists and non-cognitivists alike.

The question that naturally arises is what more we need to establish in order to show that evaluative judgements express beliefs strictly speaking. In order for the attitudes that people have when we ordinarily describe them as having evaluative beliefs to be beliefs strictly speaking, the sentences that we use to give the "contents" of these attitudes – sentences like "It is desirable for p to be the case in C" – must be truth-apt. Belief is, after all, the attitude of taking something to be a certain way, and specifying one of the ways that something could be is the distinctive role of a truth-apt sentence (Jackson, Oppy, and Smith 1994). It is this that cognitivists and non-cognitivists disagree about. Non-cognitivists think that there is a compelling reason to think that these sentences do not purport to say how things are (Hare 1952; Blackburn 1984). Non-cognitivists insist that those who use these sentences properly must, at least absent practical irrationality, be in some sort of non-cognitive state – a motivational state, or a state of approval – and the only way in which this could be so is if the function of these sentences wasn't to say how things are, but was rather to express that very non-cognitive state. It follows, at least as the non-cognitivists see things, that though we do not violate any rules of English usage when we describe those who are disposed to make evaluative judgements as having "evaluative beliefs," this must be understood as loose talk (Smith 1994b; Blackburn 1998). The attitudes in question, though like beliefs in certain respects, are not beliefs strictly speaking.

Let's now return to the original argument. If what we have just said is right then the mere fact that we would ordinarily describe a subject as "believing" that she would want p to be the case in certain circumstances C if she were fully rational does nothing to show that this attitude is a belief strictly speaking either. This too is so only if the sentence we use to give the "content" of this attitude – the sentence "Subject S would want p to be the case in circumstances C if she were fully rational" – is truth-apt; in other words, only if the function of the sentence is to specify a way that things could be. Here, too, cognitivists and non-cognitivists might therefore disagree. Non-cognitivists might insist that the very same consideration that shows that the sentence "It is desirable for p to be the case in C" is not truth-apt shows that the sentence "Subject S would want p to be the case in circumstances C if she were fully rational" is not truth-apt either (Blackburn 1998). In other words, they might argue that the connection between the state that one is in when one is disposed to make that judgement and some sort of non-cognitive state – a motivation, or a state of approval – shows that the role of the sentence is to express that non-cognitive state. If they were right about this we would once again have to conclude that we only speak loosely when we say that subjects believe that they would want p to be the case in C if they were fully rational. Strictly speaking they would not be in a state of belief at all. They would be in a non-cognitive state.

The upshot is thus that, even if we grant that a subject's judging desirable is a matter of her believing that she would have certain desires if she were fully rational, it simply doesn't follow that we thereby commit ourselves to the truth of cognitivism. In order to establish the truth of cognitivism we must establish the truth of further supplementary premises. Specifically, we must establish that the function of the sentence "Subject S would want p to be the case in circumstances C if she were fully rational" is to specify a way that that subject could be. Moreover, in order to do this without begging the question against the non-cognitivists we must establish something else as well, namely, that when subjects have beliefs about themselves being that way, whatever that way is, their beliefs have the kind of connection with non-cognitive attitudes – with motivating attitudes, or attitudes of approval – that non-cognitivists say no belief can have.

Can these supplementary premises be provided? It seems to me that they can, but this is of course all very controversial. As I see things, the claim that a subject is fully rational – where, remember, in the present context this is just to say that the subject is in a state that eludes all forms of criticism from the point of view of reason – entails a set of quite specific claims about the way that that subject is.

For example, following Bernard Williams's lead, we must suppose that the fact that a subject's desires are based on ignorance or error is, at one and the same time, a determinate way that those desires are and, for that very reason, a criticism of those desires from the point of view of reason (Williams 1980). This is because someone who was perfect, from the point of view of reason, would be omniscient and make no mistakes. But, if this is right, then it follows that there is at least one counter-example

300

to the quite general non-cognitivist suggestion that to say that a subject's desires are liable to criticism from the point of view of reason is not to specify a way that those desires are, but is rather to express a desire about, or some other non-belief attitude towards, those desires being a certain way. Indeed, it would seem to be completely irrelevant whether those who use the term "fully rational" happen to desire people not to have desires that are based on ignorance or error, or whether they happen to have any other non-cognitive attitude towards them. Instead it seems to be analytic that desires based on ignorance and error are liable to criticism from the point of view of reason.

Once we see that this is so an obvious question presents itself. Are there other ways a subject's desires can be which, as such, make those desires criticizable from the point of view of reason? And the answer, as I see things, is that there most certainly are. To say that a subject has a desire set that, as a whole, exhibits incoherence, for example, or to say that she has a desire set which, as a whole, exhibits a lack of unity, is equally a specification of a way that that desire set can be and a criticism of that desire set from the point of view of reason. Again, it would seem to be completely irrelevant whether those who use the term "fully rational" happen to desire people to have desires that are coherent and unified, or whether they have any other non-cognitive attitude towards them. Someone who claimed that, according to their usage of the words "rational criticism," to say of a set of desires that they lack coherence and unity isn't a form of rational criticism is someone who simply doesn't understand what rational criticism is. It would therefore seem once again to be analytic that a desire set that lacks coherence or unity is, as such, a desire set that is liable to criticism from the point of view of reason.[2]

How might non-cognitivists try to resist this line of argument? Following a suggestion made by Geoffrey Sayre-McCord, they might profess not to understand what is meant by the terms "coherence" and "unity" when these terms are applied to sets of desires (Sayre-McCord 1997). Alternatively, following a suggestion made to me by Sigrún Svavarsdóttir in conversation, they might agree that they can understand what is meant, but only if the terms "coherent and unified" as applied to sets of desires are taken to mean something like "co-satisfiable," an interpretation which is of little help given that desires that do not form a coherent and unified set in this sense – that is, desires that do not constitute a co-satisfiable set – are hardly, as such, criticizable from the point of view of reason.

But neither of these responses seems to me to be very plausible. When applied to sets of beliefs the terms "coherence" and "unity" are plainly comprehensible as specifying ways that those sets of beliefs can be. The relations that hold between desires when the terms "coherence" and "unity" are applied to them are, as I will go on to argue, plainly relations of exactly the same kind as these. As such it is, I think, hard to take seriously the objections of both those who profess not to understand what is meant by the terms "coherence" and "unity" when these terms are applied to sets of desires, and those who wish to offer an idiosyncratic interpretation of the terms, an interpretation that has nothing to do with the possibility of criticism from the point of view of reason.

In order to see that the terms "coherent" and "unified" really do specify ways that sets of beliefs can be, consider various sets of beliefs that combine, on the one hand, ordinary observational beliefs together with, on the other, beliefs about the behaviour of theoretical entities, theoretical entities whose behaviour is supposed to explain those observations. It is, I take it, completely uncontroversial that some of these sets of beliefs will exhibit more or less in the way of coherence and unity than other sets. Moreover I take it that when we so describe sets of beliefs we plainly specify a way that these beliefs are. We would perhaps have difficulty specifying in terms other than "coherent" and "unified" what that way is – the concepts of coherence and unity are perhaps, in this respect, rather like recognitional concepts – and the classifications might be vague at the borders, but, at least after allowing for these peculiarities, it seems to me that we would have little difficulty in principle in providing an interpersonally agreed ordering of the various sets of beliefs from those that exhibit most in the way of coherence and unity to those that exhibit least. To this extent being coherent and being unified would seem to be ways that these sets of beliefs can be. Moreover, to say that a set of beliefs is a way such that it exhibits less rather than more in the way of coherence and unity is simultaneously a criticism of that set of beliefs from the point of view of reason. It is analytic that, at least other things being equal, a more coherent set of beliefs is less liable to criticism from the point of view of reason, and the same goes for a set of beliefs that is more unified.

If this is right, however, then it seems plain that much the same can be said about sets of evaluative judgements. Consider the variety of sets of judgements that combine what Rawls calls our considered evaluative judgements – these are evaluative judgements about rather specific situations in which we have the greatest confidence – together with various alternative sets of judgements that we might make about general evaluative principles, general evaluative principles which are supposed to justify these considered judgements (Rawls 1951). In this case, too, it seems that

302

we can order the sets from those that exhibit most in the way of coherence and unity to those that exhibit least. There is, in other words, nothing about the nature of the relations that exist between the judgements themselves, whether those judgements are best thought of as expressing beliefs or desires, that requires us to suppose that these relations aren't of the very same kind as the relations that exist between the sets of beliefs just considered. In this case, too, then, it seems that being coherent and being unified specify ways that these sets of judgements can be. Moreover in this case, too, to say of a set of evaluative judgements that it exhibits less rather than more in the way of coherence and unity is simultaneously a criticism of that set of judgements from the point of view of reason. It is analytic that, at least other things being equal, a more coherent set of evaluative judgements is less liable to criticism from the point of view of reason, and the same goes for a set of evaluative judgements that is more unified.

Finally, consider the relations that exist between the various sets of desires that we get if, for each set of evaluative judgements of the kind just mentioned we substitute a specific desire that A Φs in circumstances C for each specific evaluative judgement of the form "It is desirable that A Φs in circumstances C," and we substitute a general desire that (x) (x Ψs in circumstances C′) for each general evaluative judgement expressible in the form "(x) (It is desirable that x Ψs in circumstances C′)." Once we have granted that the various sets of evaluative judgements of the kind just mentioned exhibit relations of coherence and unity, it seems to me that there is no alternative but to suppose that the isomorphic sets of desires just described exhibit those same relations of coherence and unity. In this case, too, it seems that we must suppose that being coherent and unified specify ways that these sets of desires can be. In this case, too, to say of a set of desires that it is a way such that it exhibits less rather than more coherence and unity is simultaneously a criticism of that set of desires from the point of view of reason.

The upshot is that those who deny that claims of the form "Subject S would want that p be the case in circumstances C if she were fully rational" specify a way that things could be look to be on very shaky ground. To say that S would have certain desires if she were fully rational is to say that she would have those desires if she had a set of desires that eludes all forms of criticism from the point of view of reason, and, so far, we have seen that this entails that her desire set would have to be certain quite specific ways: maximally informed, coherent, and unified. Though we haven't yet been given any reason to suppose that this provides an exhaustive account of the ways that S's desire set would have to be to be fully rational, we have so far been given no reason to suppose that such further conditions as we might add wouldn't simply be further specifications of ways that sets of desires have to be in order for them to count as fully rational. Though this does not constitute a decisive proof of cognitivism, it should at least be agreed that a cognitivist account of subjects' judgements about what they would want if they were fully rational looks to be on the cards. Pro tem, then, we should suppose that such judgements express not just beliefs loosely speaking, but beliefs strictly speaking.

I said above that if we aren't to beg the question against the non-cognitivists then, in order to show that evaluative judgements really do express beliefs strictly speaking, we would have to show not just that there is a way that someone takes things to be when they believe that they would desire p to be the case if they were fully rational, but also that their taking things to be that way has the kind of necessary connection with motivation that non-cognitivists insist evaluative judgements have. We must show, in other words, that, absent practical irrationality, a subject who believes that she would desire p to be the case in C if she were fully rational does indeed desire that p in C. Can this argument be given? Though this too is controversial (Shafer-Landau 1999), it seems to me that the argument can indeed be given (Smith 2001).

Imagine a case in which a subject comes to believe that (say) she would desire that she abstains from eating sweets in the circumstances of action that she presently faces if she had a maximally informed and coherent and unified set of desires, but that she doesn't have any desire at all to abstain. She desires to eat sweets instead. Now consider the pair of psychological states that comprises her belief that she would desire that she abstains from eating sweets in the circumstances of action that she presently faces if she had a maximally informed and coherent and unified set of desires, and which also comprises the desire that she abstains from eating sweets, and compare this pair of psychological states with the pair that comprises her belief that she would desire that she abstains from eating sweets in the circumstances of action that she presently faces if she had a maximally informed and coherent and unified set of desires, but which also comprises instead a desire to eat sweets. Which of these pairs of psychological states is more coherent?

The answer would seem to be plain enough. The first pair is much more coherent than the second. There is disequilibrium or dissonance or failure of fit involved in believing that you would desire yourself to act in a certain way in certain circumstances if you had a maximally informed and coherent and unified desire set, and yet not desiring to act in that way.

304

The failure to desire to act in that way is, after all, something that you yourself disown; from your perspective it makes no sense, given the rest of your desires; by your own lights it is a state that you would not be in if you were in various ways better than you actually are: more informed, more coherent, more unified in your desiderative outlook.[3] There would therefore seem to be more than a passing family resemblance between the relation that holds between the first pair of psychological states and more familiar examples of coherence relations that hold between psychological states. Coherence would thus seem to be on the side of the pair that comprises both the subject's belief that she would desire that she abstains from eating sweets in the circumstances of action that she presently faces and the desire that she abstains from eating sweets.

If this is right, however, then it follows immediately that if the subject is rational, in the relatively mundane sense of having and exercising a capacity to have the psychological states that coherence demands of her, then, at least abstracting away from such other dynamic changes in her beliefs as might occur for evidential reasons (Arpaly 2000), that subject will end up having a desire that matches her belief about what she would want herself to do if she had a maximally informed and coherent and unified desire set. In other words, in the particular case under discussion, she will end up losing her desire to eat sweets and acquiring a desire to abstain from eating sweets instead. Subjects' beliefs about what they would want if they were fully rational thus seem both to be beliefs strictly speaking and to be beliefs which have the kind of necessary connection with motivation that non-cognitivists insist evaluative judgements have. Absent practical irrationality – that is to say, absent a failure either to have or to exercise the capacity to have the psychological states that coherence demands of her – a subject who believes that she would want p to be the case in C if she had a maximally informed and coherent and unified desire set will indeed desire p to be the case in C. The non-cognitivists' reasons for supposing that evaluative judgements are not beliefs strictly speaking therefore seem, in the end, to be unconvincing.[4]

2. THE DISPOSITIONAL THEORY AND RELATIVISM

Let's now suppose not just that when a subject judges it desirable that p be the case in certain circumstances, C, this is a matter of her believing that she would want that p be the case in C if she were fully rational, but also that, for the reasons just given (§1), these states are beliefs strictly speaking. Once we grant this it is, I think, extremely tempting to suppose that we thereby commit ourselves to the truth of relativism (Johnston 1989). Here is why.

Consider two people, A and B, who appear to have the same evaluative belief, the belief that it is desirable that p. Given the equivalence what A believes is that she, A, would desire that p if she, A, had a set of desires that is maximally informed and coherent and unified. But what B believes, by contrast, is that he, B, would desire that p if he, B, had a set of desires that is maximally informed and coherent and unified. A's and B's beliefs thus have quite different truth conditions. A's belief is made true by the desires that she would have, never mind about B's, and B's by the desires he would have, never mind about A's. If this is right, though – that is, if A's and B's beliefs do indeed have different truth conditions – then the appearance that they have the same belief, when they each believe that it is desirable that p, is misleading. A is more accurately represented as believing that it is desirable$_A$ that p, and B as believing that it is desirable$_B$ that p. The suggested equivalence thus seems to imply the truth of relativism.

Tempting though this line of thought is, we should, I think, resist it. In order to see why, it will be helpful to work through an example of a particular substituend for "p" in the belief that it is desirable that p. To anticipate, my argument will be that once we pay due regard to three facts about values – the fact that value is universalizable, the fact that value can be either neutral or egocentric, and the fact that some neutral values and egocentric values are commensurable – it becomes plain that evaluations not only are not, but that they could not be, relative in the way that has just been suggested. If anything, these considerations suggest that we are committed to a non-relativist conception of value.

Imagine someone, A, with a belief whose content we might initially think she should express in the following sentence:

It is desirable that my$_A$ children fare well.

where the subscript to the "my" simply serves to make it explicit whose children are being referred to. Given the equivalence, this amounts to A's having a belief whose content she could express in the following sentences:

I$_A$ would want that my$_A$ children fare well if I$_A$ had a set of desires that is maximally informed and coherent and unified.

Complications immediately arise, however.

It is, after all, a conceptual truth that evaluations are one and all universalizable. It therefore follows that specific evaluations, like this one, must be derivable from more universal beliefs to which agents are committed.

We must therefore ask which universal evaluation A is committed to simply in virtue of having the belief that it is desirable that her own children fare well. In other words – and, remember, we are supposing equivalently – we must ask which universal evaluation A is committed to simply in virtue of having the belief that she would want that her children fare well if she had a set of desires that is maximally informed and coherent and unified.

One possibility is that A is committed to a universal evaluative belief with the following content:

(x) (It is desirable that x's children fare well)

or, perhaps equivalently:

(x) (I_A would want that x's children fare well if I_A had set of desires that is maximally informed and coherent and unified)

But while this might be one possibility, it certainly isn't the only possibility. It simply assumes that A assigns neutral, or non-egocentric, value to the welfare of people's children – assumes, in other words, that A believes it equally desirable that her own children fare well and that other people's children fare well; assumes, in terms of the equivalence, that she would desire equally that her own children fare well and that other people's children fare well if she had a set of desires that is maximally informed and coherent and unified – whereas the original belief is plainly ambiguous betwen that possibility and the quite different possibility that she assigns egocentric value to the welfare of her children, and hence that the desires she would have if she had a set of desires that is maximally informed and coherent and unified would be quite specifically desires about the welfare of her own children. This, in turn, suggests that we went wrong in trying to give the content of her original belief. We should have noted that that belief is ambiguous, and insisted that it be disambiguated before we give its equivalent. Let's therefore start again.

The content of A's original belief, the belief that it is desirable that her children fare well, is ambiguous. What she has is either a belief the content of which she could express in the following sentence:

It is desirable$_A$ that my$_A$ children fare well

– this is what she believes if she assigns the welfare of her children egocentric value – or, alternatively, it might be suggested, she has a belief the content of which she could best express in the following sentence:

It is desirable that my$_A$ children fare well

which is what she believes if she assigns the welfare of her children neutral value. Because evaluations are one and all universalizable, these beliefs might then be thought to commit A to universal beliefs that she could best express in one or another of the following sentences:

(x) (It is desirable$_x$ that x's children fare well)

– this is the content of the universal belief to which she is committed if she assigns the welfare of her children egocentric value – or, alternatively,

(x) (It is desirable that x's children fare well)

which is the content of the universal belief to which she is committed if she assigns the welfare of her children neutral value.

But this can't be quite right either. If it were it would follow, implausibly, that such assignments of neutral and egocentric value to the welfare of children are radically incommensurable. Neutral value would, after all, be a completely different property from egocentric value – egocentric value would be an indexed property, whereas neutral value an unindexed property – and this in turn would mean that we couldn't sensibly ask someone who assigns both neutral value to the welfare of people's children and egocentric value to the welfare of her own children whether the egocentric value that she assigns to her own children's welfare was greater than or less than the neutral value that she assigns to their welfare, and the welfare of other people's children. The comparative concept of desirability would, after all, have to be the comparative form of either the indexed property or the unindexed property. We could only ask A questions such as whether her own children's welfare has more *egocentric* value than the egocentric value possessed by other people's children (a question the answer to which is that it plainly does, since other people's children have no such egocentric value), or whether the welfare of other people's children has more *neutral* value than that possessed by her own children (the answer to which is plainly that it doesn't, since other people's children's welfare has the same neutral value as that possessed by her own).

As I said, it seems to me that the idea that assignments of neutral and egocentric value are radically incommensurable in this way is manifestly implausible. Those who assign neutral value to the welfare of people's children and egocentric value to the welfare of their own children have no problem at all comparing these two values. Indeed, I think that most people would insist that the egocentric value that they assign to their own children's welfare is greater than the neutral value they assign to their own children's welfare, and to the welfare of the children of others. This is why they feel totally justified in giving benefits to their own children over comparable benefits to strangers. We are, however, yet to find an account of the logical form of evaluations that makes it plain just what it might mean when we make such comparative evaluative claims.

Returning to the example we have been working through so far, what this suggests, I think, is that A should express the content of her original belief in the following sentence:

It is desirable$_A$ that my$_A$ children fare well

and that in order to disambiguate this belief we must say whether it, in turn, is derived from a universal belief with the following content:

(x) (It is desirable$_x$ that x's children fare well)

– this is the content of the universal belief to which A is committed if she assigns the welfare of her children egocentric value – or, alternatively, in a universal belief with the following content:

(x)(y) (It is desirable$_x$ that y's children fare well)

This is the content of the universal belief to which she is committed if she assigns the welfare of her children neutral value. In other words, and rather naturally I think, the difference between a neutral evaluation of the welfare of a subject's children and an egocentric evaluation is that whereas the egocentric evaluation is an evaluation from that subject's own point of view, the neutral evaluation is an evaluation from everyone's point of view. Moreover, though the subscript on the desirability predicate in the neutral evaluation might look completely idle when neutral evaluations are considered in isolation from egocentric evaluations, the fact that there is such an index on the desirability predicate in the neutral evaluation is absolutely crucial when it comes to an understanding of how comparisons of neutral and egocentric value are possible. Much as I suggested above, for example, A might be committed to a comparative universal evaluative belief with the following content:

(x)(y) ((It is desirable$_x$ that x's children fare well) & (It is desirable$_x$ that y's children fare well) & (It is more desirable$_x$ that x's children fare well than that y's children fare well))

This might be why the egocentric value that A assigns to the welfare of her own children is greater than the neutral value that she assigns to the welfare of people's children quite generally, including even her own children.

Note what we have done so far. So far we have simply focussed on evaluations themselves – particular substituends for the "p" in the proposition "It is desirable that p" – and asked how, in the light of three facts about values – the facts that evaluations are universalizable, that evaluations can be assignments of either neutral value or assignments of egocentric value, and that it is at least possible for neutral value and egocentric value to commensurate – a particular subject, A, should express the content of the evaluations to which she is committed when she believes that it is desirable that her own children fare well. We are now in a position to ask what the contents of A's beliefs are, given the equivalence postulated by the dispositional theory of value.

We have seen that A's belief that it is desirable that her own children fare well is ambiguous. In terms of the equivalence, how should she express the content of the universal evaluative beliefs to which she is committed under the various disambiguations? Disambiguating in favour of the possibility that she assigns her children's welfare egocentric value, it turns out that she is committed to a universal belief with the following content:

(x) (It is desirable$_x$ that x's children fare well)

which, given the equivalence, suggests that she is committed to a belief with the following content:

(x) (x would want that x's children fare well if x had a set of desires that is maximally informed and coherent and unified)

Alternatively, disambiguating in favour of the possibility that she assigns her children's welfare neutral value, it turns out that she is committed to a universal belief with the following content:

(x)(y) (It is desirable$_x$ that y's children fare well)

which, given the equivalence, means that she is committed to a belief with the following content:

(x)(y) (x would want that y's children fare well if x had a set of desires that is maximally informed and coherent and unified)

A subject committed to a comparative evaluative belief with the following content:

310

$(x)(y)$ ((It is desirable$_x$ that x's children fare well) & (It is desirable$_x$ that y's children fare well) & (It is more desirable$_x$ that x's children fare well than that y's children fare well))

is, given the equivalence, committed to a comparative belief with the following content:

$(x)(y)$ ((x would want that x's children fare well if x had a set of desires that is maximally informed and coherent and unified) & (x would want that y's children fare well if x had a set of desires that is maximally informed and coherent and unified) & (the desire x has that x's children fare well would be stronger than the desire x has that y's children fare well))

As is perhaps already plain, when it comes to the issue of relativism, the conclusion is therefore exactly the opposite of the one that we were tempted by at the outset.

Imagine, once again, two people, A and B, both of whom believe that it is desirable that their own children fare well. Do their beliefs have the same truth conditions or different truth conditions? Since, as we have seen, A's and B's beliefs are ambiguous, the truth conditions of their beliefs depend on how we disambiguate them. Contrary to the suggestion made at the outset, however, and notwithstanding the fact that A's and B's beliefs are ambiguous, it turns out that, so long as we disambiguate them in the same way, their beliefs have the very same truth conditions. For, given universalizability, they must either both be committed to a belief with the following content:

(x) (x would want that x's children fare well if x had a set of desires that is maximally informed and coherent and unified)

– this is the belief to which they are committed if their original beliefs were about the egocentric value of their children's welfare – or, alternatively, to a belief with the following content:

$(x)(y)$ (x would want that y's children fare well if x had a set of desires that is maximally informed and coherent and unified)

– this is the belief to which they are committed if their original beliefs were about the neutral value of their children's welfare.

On the assumption that we can generalize on the basis of this example, it would thus seem to follow that, contrary to the suggestion made at the outset, one subject's evaluative beliefs are made true not just by the desires that she would have if she had a set of desires that was maximally informed and coherent and unified, but also by the desires that every other subject would have if they had a set of desires that was maximally informed and coherent and unified. Far from the suggested equivalence committing us to relativism, then, it appears that it commits us if anything to non-relativism. The truth of a subject's evaluative beliefs requires that all subjects converge in the desires they would have if they had a set of desires that was maximally informed and coherent and unified.[5]

3. THE DISPOSITIONAL THEORY AND REALISM

I said at the outset that the dispositional theory would seem to commit us not just to relativism, but also to realism. The connection between these two commitments should be plain.

We suggested initially that a subject's judgements about the desirability of p's being the case in circumstances C were made true by whether or not that subject herself would want p to be the case in C if she had a set of desires that was maximally informed and coherent and unified, never mind about what other subjects would want if they had a set of desires that was maximally informed and coherent and unified. If this were right then, since it is so plausible to think that there are some things that a particular subject would want if she had such a set of desires – this only requires that we be able to give determinate content to the relevant counterfactuals, after all – it follows that it would likewise be plausible to suppose that, since some such judgements are true, realism must be true. In other words, we could reject the possibility of an error theory of the kind argued for by John Mackie (1977). However, now that we have seen that the dispositional theory commits us not to relativism, but, if anything, to the rejection of relativism, we must reevaluate this commitment to realism.

If a subject's judgements about the desirability of p's being the case in certain circumstances C are made true not just by whether or not that subject herself would want that p be the case in C if she had a set of desires that was maximally informed and coherent and unified, but also by whether everyone else would want that p in C if they had a set of desires that was maximally informed and coherent and unified, then should we suppose that some such judgements are true? In other words, is it plausible to suppose that there are some desires that all subjects would converge upon if they had desire sets that are maximally informed and coherent and unified? Many will insist that there are no such desires (Sobel 1999). If they are right then we must conclude that realism is false. The dispositional theory, since it entails non-relativism, entails irrealism. My own view, however, is that this is all far too quick. It is unclear whether there are any desires that all subjects would converge upon if they had desire sets that are maximally informed and coherent and unified, but it is equally unclear that there are no such desires. It therefore seems to me best to suppose that the debate between realists and irrealists is yet to be resolved.

Those who think that the dispositional theory entails irrealism are, I think, impressed by a chain of reasoning much like the following. We can surely imagine two subjects, D and E, each of whom, in actuality, has a single intrinsic desire – that is, a desire that they haven't derived from some further desire that they have plus a belief about means – but a different one: let's suppose, for example, that D has an intrinsic desire that p, whereas E an intrinsic desire that q. Furthermore, since their respective desires are intrinsic, we can also imagine that each of them would retain their single intrinsic desire no matter what further information they acquired. But since there is no reason to suppose that the acquisition of any further information would lead D and E to acquire additional intrinsic desires, and since D's and E's desire sets, comprising as they do just one desire each, are already as coherent and unified as they could possibly be, it follows that D and E would not converge in their intrinsic desires even if they did have a maximally informed and coherent and unified desire set. They would still diverge. Indeed, they would still just have their respective intrinsic desires that p and that q. It therefore follows that there are no desires that everyone would converge upon if they had a maximally informed and coherent and unified desire set. The hypothetical D and E constitute the decisive counter-example. If realism requires such convergence, then realism is false.

What is wrong with this chain of reasoning? The problem lies in the premise that there is no reason to suppose that the acquisition of further information would lead D and E to acquire any additional intrinsic desires beyond their respective intrinsic desires that p and that q. To begin, let's be clear what this premise says. It says, *inter alia*, that there is no information that D and E could acquire such that, having acquired that information, they would be rationally required to acquire intrinsic desires beyond their respective intrinsic desires that p and that q. But it seems to me that the only reason we would have to accept this premise is if we were to assume, quite generally, that there are no rational principles of the following form:

It is rationally required that subjects who believe that r either give up their belief that r or acquire an intrinsic desire that s.

Yet, as we have already seen, this quite general assumption is false.

313

This is, in effect, what we discovered earlier when we saw that coherence requires subjects who believe that they would want p to be the case in circumstances C if they had a desire set that was maximally informed and coherent and unified to desire that p be the case in C (§1). We saw, in other words, that the following – an instance of the rational principle we would have to assume quite generally to be false – is in fact true:

It is rationally required that an agent who believes that she would have an intrinsic desire that p be the case in circumstances C if she had a maximally informed and coherent and unified desire set either gives up her belief or acquires an intrinsic desire that p be the case in C.

Now, to be sure, this particular claim connecting the acquisition of information with intrinsic desiring is not sufficient all by itself to show that D and E would converge in their desires. But nor is that required at this stage of the argument. All that is required is that we show what is wrong with the chain of reasoning described above that purports to prove that two hypothetical subjects, D and E, would not converge in their intrinsic desires. The crucial point, to repeat, is that once we see that the quite general assumption that there are no rational principles of the form "It is rationally required that an agent who believes that r either gives up his belief that r or acquires an intrinsic desire that s" is false – once we remind ourselves, in other words, that reflection can lead us to accept the surprising conclusion that certain instances of that principle are in fact true – then it is hard to see what, beyond dogmatic commitment, would lead anyone to think that *further* reflection won't lead us to the surprising conclusion that *more* instances of that principle are true (compare Korsgaard 1986). In particular, it is hard to see what, beyond dogmatic commitment, would lead anyone to think that further reflection won't lead us to discover that further instances of that principle, instances sufficient to show that D and E would converge in their desires, are true.[6]

At this stage it therefore seems to me that we would be wise to suspend judgement on the debate over realism versus irrealism. Perhaps further reflection will reveal that such further instances of rational principles of the form "It is rationally required that an agent who believes that r either gives up his belief that r or acquires an intrinsic desire that s" as are required in order to undergird a convergence in the desires of subjects with a maximally informed and coherent and unified desire set are true; perhaps it will not. We have little choice but to do the required reflection and see.[7]

314

REFERENCES

Arpaly, Nomy 2000: "On Acting Rationally against One's Best Judgment," in *Ethics*: 488–513.

Blackburn, Simon 1984: *Spreading the Word*. Oxford: Oxford University Press.

_____ 1998: *Ruling Passions*. Oxford: Clarendon Press.

Copp, David 1997: "Belief, Reason, and Motivation: Michael Smith's *The Moral Problem*," *Ethics*: 33–54.

Hare, R. M. 1952: *The Language of Morals*. Oxford: Oxford University Press.

Jackson, Frank, Graham Oppy, and Michael Smith 1994: "Minimalism and Truth-Aptness," *Mind*: 287–302.

Johnston, Mark 1989: "Dispositional Theories of Value," *Proceedings of the Aristotelian Society* Supplementary Volume: 139–74.

Korsgaard, Christine 1986: "Skepticism about Practical Reason," *Journal of Philosophy*: 5–25.

Lewis, David 1989: "Dispositional Theories of Value," *Proceedings of the Aristotelian Society* Supplementary Volume: 113–37.

Lillehammer, Hallvard 2000: "Revisionary Dispositionalism and Metaphysical Modesty," *The Journal of Ethics*: 173–90.

Mackie, J. L. 1977: *Ethics: Inventing Right and Wrong*. Harmondsworth: Penguin.

Rawls, John 1951: "Outline of a Decision Procedure for Ethics," *Philosophical Review*: 177–97.

Sayre-McCord, Geoffrey 1997: "The Meta-Ethical Problem: a discussion of Michael Smith's *The Moral Problem*," *Ethics*: 55–83.

Schafer-Landau, Russ 1999: "Moral judgement and normative reasons," *Analysis*: 33–40.

Smith, Michael 1989: "Dispositional Theories of Value," *Proceedings of the Aristotelian Society* Supplementary Volume: 89–111.

_____ 1994a: *The Moral Problem*. Oxford: Blackwell.

_____ 1994b: "Why Expressivists About Value Should Love Minimalism About Truth," *Analysis*: 1–12.

_____ 1997: "In Defence of *The Moral Problem*: A Reply to Brink, Copp and Sayre-McCord," *Ethics*: 84–119.

_____ 1999: "The Non-Arbitrariness of Reasons: Reply to Lenman," *Utilitas*: 178–93.

_____ 2001: "The Incoherence Argument: Reply to Shafer-Landau," *Analysis*: 254–66.

Sobel, David 1999: "Do the Desires of Rational Agents Converge?," *Analysis*: 137–47.

Williams, Bernard 1980: "Internal and External Reasons," reprinted in his *Moral Luck*. Cambridge: Cambridge University Press. 101–13.

NOTES

1. This is somewhat misleading because, whereas non-culpable ignorance plausibly constitutes a failure to achieve an ideal of reason, and so something that is in this sense criticizable from that point of view, it may not constitute what we would

315

ordinarily call a failure of rationality. For reasons that will become plain shortly I will, however, ignore these differences of meaning in what follows.

2. It should now be plain why we were right to ignore the fact that the shorthand term "being fully rational" does not mean exactly the same as "being in a state that eludes all forms of criticism from the point of view of reason" (see footnote 1 above). All that is crucial is that we can give an account of the way that subjects are when they are in the latter state. The term "being fully rational" really is just convenient, if misleading, shorthand.

3. I have just said that a subject who believes that she would desire that she acts in a certain way if she had a maximally informed and coherent and unified desire set, but who does not desire to act in that way, is in a state that she would not be in if she were in various ways *better* than she actually is: more informed, more coherent, more unified in her desiderative outlook. It is important to note that this use of the term "better" trades on an understanding of value that cannot be analysed in the way suggested by the dispositional theory, an understanding according to which it is simply analytic that a subject with a maximally informed and coherent and unified desire set is as good as she can be, and that subjects with desire sets that fall ever shorter of being maximally informed and coherent and unified are subjects who are correspondingly less good. This should perhaps come as no surprise given that being good as can be, in this sense, is simply a matter of being perfect from the point of view of reason. Hallvard Lillehammer suggests that dispositional theories that define value in terms of such a non-dispositional conception of the good give up on any claim to metaphysical modesty (Lillehammer 2000). For more on this, see footnote 6 below.

4. Another way of putting the conclusion just reached is that it is in the nature of desires that they are psychological states that are rationally sensitive to our beliefs about what we would desire that we do if we had a set of desires that was maximally informed and coherent and unified, "rationally sensitive" in the sense of being psychological states that we would acquire in the light of such beliefs given that we have a capacity to have the psychological states that coherence demands of us. As we will see later (§3), this is an important conclusion to draw, not just because it undermines one of the main arguments for non-cognitivism, but also because it undermines one of the main arguments for relativism.

5. Though I have argued for this conclusion elsewhere (Smith 1994a, 1997, 1999), note that the argument given in the text is completely new. To repeat, the argument given in the text is that the natural interpretation of the dispositional theory, given three facts about values – the fact that values are universalizable, that values can be either neutral or egocentric, and that at least some neutral values and some egocentric values are commensurable – is a non-relativist interpretation. The argument I have given in the past for the conclusion that we must give a non-relative interpretation of the dispositional theory has been that only so can we capture the non-arbitrariness of values. The argument given in the text might well prompt the question whether it is so much as possible to formulate a relativist version of the dispositional theory. Would any such formulation have to assume, implausibly, either that values are not universalizable, or that values cannot be both neutral and egocentric, or that neutral values and egocentric values are radically incommensurable? Though I will not spell out the formulation here, let me say, for the record, that I

316

do not think that this is so. It seems to me that it is possible to formulate a relativist version of the dispositional theory, albeit a very unintuitive and ad hoc version, that is consistent with the three claims about values just mentioned. Unsurprisingly, however, it also seems to me that when we spell out the relativist version of the dispositional theory that is consistent with these three claims it becomes manifest just how arbitrary value is, on such a relativist conception.

6. Hallvard Lillehammer (2000) suggests that dispositional theories that define value in terms of a non-dispositional conception of the good give up on any claim to metaphysical modesty. But there would seem to be nothing metaphysically immodest about the claims about the good made in footnote 3 above, and nor would there seem to be anything metaphysically immodest about principles of reason of the form "It is rationally required that an agent who believes that r either gives up his belief that r or acquires an intrinsic desire that s." What is true, of course, is that we do indeed find it surprising that there are true instances of a general principle of that form. But, as the argument given in §2 illustrates, perhaps the real surprise lies in the fact that the argument for that conclusion relies on such uncontroversial premises. It remains to be seen whether the arguments given for any further instances that we might discover rely on such similarly uncontroversial premises.

7. I would like to thank John Broome, David Estlund, and Philip Pettit for helpful conversations while I was writing this paper.

15

Internalism's Wheel

If an agent judges that she morally ought to φ in certain circumstances C then, according to internalists, absent practical irrationality, she must be motivated, to some extent, to φ in C.[1] Internalists thus accept what I have elsewhere called the "practicality requirement on moral judgement."[2] Externalists deny this.[3] They hold that agents may not be motivated to any extent to act in accordance with their moral judgements, and this without any irrationality on their behalf.

Internalism has traditionally been thought to function as a high-level conceptual constraint on moral judgement, accounts of which are supposed to be assessed, *inter alia*, by the extent to which they can explain and capture its truth. Unfortunately, however, on closer inspection this doesn't amount to much in the way of a constraint. There are many different theories about the nature and content of moral judgement that aspire to explain and capture the truth embodied in internalism, and these theories share little in common beyond that aspiration.

Worse still, as I will argue in what follows, these theories are perhaps best thought of as lying around the perimeter of a wheel, much like Fortune's Wheel, with each theory that lies further on along the perimeter representing itself as motivated by difficulties that beset the theory that precedes it. The mere existence of Internalism's Wheel need not pose a problem for internalists, of course. They may believe that the truth about ethics lies wherever Internalism's Wheel stops spinning. But a problem evidently does arise if Internalism's Wheel is in perpetual motion, for then the truth about ethics presumably lies nowhere at all on Internalism's Wheel.

Let me now confess. I am an internalist, but an internalist who is worried, deep down, by the thought that Internalism's Wheel is indeed in perpetual motion. Since externalism, too, seems to me to be seriously flawed – as I have argued elsewhere, externalism is committed to an implausible moral psychology[4] – the conclusion I see looming is thus wholescale moral skepticism. Endless cycles of Internalism's Wheel augur in favour of the view that moral concerns are, quite literally, incoherent.

In sections I through V, I state the arguments against various internalist accounts of moral judgement. I describe examples of the theories that lie around Internalism's Wheel, and I explain why each of these theories is able to represent itself as motivated by problems that beset the theory that precedes it. By the end of section V we will have come full circle. Internalism will look like it is in deep trouble. But then, in section IV, I reassess this situation. I argue, though only rather tentatively, that one of the theories we considered has fewer difficulties and more advantages than the others. As I see it, if there is truth to be found in ethics at all, it is here that that truth lies.[5]

I. EXPRESSIVISM

Faced with theories that occupy various points around the perimeter of a wheel, it is of course quite arbitrary where we start. But let us begin with the theory whose claims about morality are most outlandish, for then the fact that we manage to argue ourselves in a circle will seem all the more remarkable. We therefore turn Internalism's Wheel to expressivism.

Like the early emotivists, expressivists tell us that when we make claims like "A morally ought to φ in circumstances C" we are not saying anything about the way things are, but are rather expressing certain emotions or feelings we have about the way things are to be. Our judgement is an expression of our desire that A φs in C, and perhaps also an expression of our desire that others too desire that A φs in C. This view of moral judgement has radical implications. It entails, for example, that moral claims are not truth-assessable, and that, lacking as they do any truth conditions, we must therefore give the semantics of moral claims exclusively in terms of their expressive function.

But why would anyone believe this radical view of moral judgement? In *Spreading the Word* Simon Blackburn tells us that internalism itself provides the reason.

Evaluative commitments are being contrasted with other, truth-conditional judgements or beliefs. This contrast means that to have a commitment of this sort is to hold an attitude, not a belief, and that in turn should have implications

319

for the explanation of people's behaviour. The standard model of explanation of why someone does something attributes both a belief and a desire to the agent. The belief that the bottle contains poison does not by itself explain why someone avoids it; the belief coupled with the normal desire to avoid harm does. So if moral commitments express *attitudes*, they should function to supplement beliefs in the explanation of action. If they express beliefs, they should themselves need supplementing by mention of desires in a fully displayed explanation of action (fully displayed because, of course, we often do not bother to mention obvious desires and beliefs, which people will presume each other to have). It can then be urged that moral commitments fall in the right way of the active, desire, side of this fence. If someone feels moral distaste or indignation at cruelty to animals, he only needs to believe that he is faced with a case of it to act or be pulled towards acting. It seems to be a conceptual truth that to regard something as good is to feel a pull towards promoting or choosing it, or towards wanting other people to feel the pull towards promoting or choosing it. Whereas if moral commitments express beliefs that certain truth-conditions are met, then they could apparently co-exist with any kind of attitude to things meeting the truth-conditions. Someone might be indifferent to things which he regards as good, or actively hostile to them.[6]

Simple though it might be, however, this argument raises all sorts of problems.

Internalism is the premise from which expressivism is supposed to follow. But how does Blackburn formulate this premise? He tells us that internalism is the "conceptual truth" that "to regard something as good is to feel a pull towards promoting or choosing it, or towards wanting other people to feel the pull towards promoting or choosing it." But far from this being a conceptual truth, the one expressed by internalism, it is no truth at all.

The "is" suggests a biconditional, but the biconditional is false in both directions. It is, after all, a commonplace that drug addicts, and others who are alienated from their projects, may want to promote, or want other people to promote, certain outcomes, without regarding those outcomes as good. They need not suppose that their projects have any normative significance whatsoever.[7] And it is also a commonplace that depressives, and others suffering from emotional disturbances, may regard outcomes as good which, because of their depression or emotional disturbance, they have no desire whatsoever to promote. Projects which they suppose to have normative significance may leave them unmoved.[8] Contrary to Blackburn, then, it is the case that "someone might be indifferent to things which he regards as good, or actively hostile to them."

Note that these examples do not undermine the truth of internalism as that doctrine was spelled out at the very beginning of this paper, however. Internalism is the view that an agent who judges something good should feel a pull towards promoting it, whether or not she does in fact. The examples are helpful, as they allow us to give commonsense content to this idea. They suggest that someone who makes moral judgements without being motivated must be suffering from compulsion, or weakness, or depression, or emotional disturbance or something similar. These constitute manifestations of practical unreason that can defeat the connection between moral judgement and motivation even if internalism is true.[9]

Once we remember that internalism posits a normative connection between moral judgement and motivation we see immediately that expressivism is unable to say anything by way of an explanation of it. If when an agent regards something as good she needn't be motivated at all to promote it, it cannot be the case that her regarding it as good is an expression of her motivation. At best, it seems, her judgement is the expression of a motivation she *should* have. But a motivation that should be had need not be a psychological state that even exists to be expressed. Internalism therefore seems to suggest that, contrary to expressivism, moral judgements are not expressions of motivations at all.[10]

Nor should this conclusion be surprising. There are, after all, quite independent reasons for thinking that moral judgements express beliefs rather than desires, and that the explanation of internalism should therefore concern the connection between moral belief and desire, not the constitution of moral judgement by desire. The independent reasons are familiar from the work of Peter Geach.[11] We already mentioned the fact that expressivists are committed to the view that someone who says, for example, "It is wrong to kick cats," is not saying something that is truth-assessable. Instead, they tell us, it is as if she were saying "Boo for kicking cats!" But, as Geach points out, this is a difficult view to maintain. After all, why do the sentences we use when we make moral judgements have so many of the features of ordinary truth-apt sentences? And why do they have so few of the features of the sentences that are overtly expressive?

Consider an utterance of "The sentence 'It is wrong to kick cats' is true" by way of example. Why is it perfectly permissible to say this when it is not permissible to say "The sentence 'Boo for kicking cats!' is true"? The sentence "Boo for kicking cats!," which is overtly expressive, behaves like an expressive sentence. It resists embedding in contexts, like "The sentence '____' is true" that might otherwise have been thought to be the exclusive preserve of truth-assessable sentences. But the sentence

321

"It is wrong to kick cats" behaves for all the world like a truth-assessable sentence rather than an expressive sentence. It embeds in just this and other similar contexts: "A believes that _____," "If _____ then *p*," and so on.

Expressivists therefore face the enormous difficulty of explaining, in expressive terms, how and why moral sentences function like ordinary truth-apt sentences that are used to express the contents of beliefs, rather than like overtly expressive sentences which are used to express emotions.[12] Some expressivists, like Blackburn himself, have confronted this task fairly and squarely. It must be said that they have met with at best limited success, however.[13] The fact that they have not yet come up with a convincing explanation does not mean that no such explanation is forthcoming. It does, however, make pessimism about their success seem appropriate. It therefore seems wise to assume that moral sentences express beliefs rather than desires. So Internalism's Wheel turns.

II. SPEAKER RELATIVISM

We are now looking for a theory that can explain two things. First, it must give an account of what moral beliefs are beliefs about – that is, it must give their truth conditions – and, second, it must use that account to explain the normative connection between moral belief and motivation. James Dreier's speaker relativism, a close relative of expressivism, attempts just these tasks.[14]

The kind of relativism I advocate is roughly this: the content of a moral term in a context is a function of the affective attitudes of the speaker in the context. Thus, "x is good" means "x is highly evaluated by the standards of system M," where M is filled in by looking at the affective or motivational states of the speaker and constructing from them a practical system.[15]

In deciding whether someone's claim that something is good is true we are thus to use the content of the speaker's affective or motivational states to construct a system of rules of evaluation, and then we are to measure the extent to which that thing accords with these rules. The sentence "x is good," as uttered by the speaker, is true just in case x scores well, false otherwise.

The "roughly" is important, however, for Dreier immediately goes on to qualify his analysis. The affective or motivational states of the speaker out of which we construct a practical system are not those the speaker actually has, but rather those she "normally" has.[16] This qualification is made in response to examples, like those we have already considered, of agents who make moral judgements without being motivated: cases of addiction, alienation, depression, emotional disturbance and the like. In the sense in which Dreier uses the term "normal," these are to be considered abnormal cases. Let's grant this for the time being.

Given his relativist account of the content of a moral belief Dreier gives the following explanation of internalism. Internalism tells us that agents who believe they morally ought to φ in circumstances C are either appropriately motivated or practically irrational. But when a speaker says that she morally ought to φ in C she describes φ-ing in C as meeting certain standards, standards which are determined by her motivations in the normal case. It therefore follows that, in the normal case, she will be appropriately motivated. Indeed, in the normal case, a speaker's judgement that she morally ought to φ in C will be *both* an expression of her belief that φ-ing in C is highly evaluated by her moral system *and* an expression of her desire to φ in C.

Dreier's explanation depends crucially on the idea of a normal condition. Though he admits he doesn't know how to specify this idea rigorously, he is confident that we do have an "independent grip" on what normal conditions are, and that we will therefore not be reduced to defining them as the "circumstances under which a person is motivated by what she believes to be good."[17] Unfortunately, however, the little he says about the independent grip we have is discouraging.

It is clear to me that if everyone in a community behaves in a certain way, then that behaviour is normal in the community, and if a person has a certain state of character for all of her life, then behaviour flowing from that state is normal for her.[18]

According to Dreier "everyone" and "always" are thus supposed to imply "normal." Normality is thus a *statistical* matter. The real question is therefore whether a statistical conception of normality can play the role required in spelling out the content of a moral belief.

An agent's desires in normal conditions are supposed to fix the content of her moral system. But there seems to be no conceptual barrier to the idea of someone who lives the whole of her life in an alienated, depressed, or emotionally disturbed state – someone whose normal desires, given a statistical gloss on "normal," for this reason run contrary to the content of both her moral beliefs and her moral system. And nor does there seem to be any conceptual barrier to the idea of an entire community of such agents. Yet there would have to be such conceptual barriers if the content of an agent's moral system, and so the content of her moral beliefs, were fixed by her desires in the normal case, as Dreier understands normality.

The fact that Dreier appeals to statistical notions in giving the cognitive content of a moral judgement undermines his explanation of internalism as well. The connection between moral belief and motivation posited by internalism is, after all, a normative connection. But because he appeals to a statistical conception of normality in explaining that connection, Dreier's theory entails that there is at best a "generally speaking" or "for the most part" connection – a connection which, even if it were in place, would be entirely lacking in normative significance.

It might be thought that these objections are superficial, and that Dreier could easily amend speaker relativism to overcome these difficulties.[19] But I want now to argue that this is not the case. My argument for this conclusion requires only a very uncontroversial assumption: namely, that whatever account we give of the cognitive content of a moral judgement, that account must enable us to make sense of the distinction between justified and unjustified uses of coercive power. My argument is to be that speaker relativism undermines this uncontroversial assumption.

Imagine a conversation between two people, A and B. B says to A "You morally ought to ϕ in C," and A replies "It is not the case that I morally ought to ϕ in C," Let's suppose further that this conversation takes place in a context in which B is in a position to coerce A, and that B says, by way of justifying his use of coercive power, "I morally ought to force you to ϕ in C." A denies this, saying "You morally ought not to force me to ϕ in C."

As described this conversation is, of course, abstract and schematic. But it does allow us to bring out a crucial point. At least as we ordinarily see things, if what B says is true then it follows that his use of coercive power over A is indeed justified, and that in turn must entail that B's use of coercive power can be conceptualized in a way that makes it seem very different from the power exercised by, say, a thug or a gangster. A gangster who holds a gun at his victim's head and demands "Your money or your life" is *simply* forcing his will upon his victim against his victim's wishes. B, by contrast, is not simply forcing his will upon A against A's wishes, at least not if his use of coercive power is justified. Whatever account we give of the cognitive content of moral judgement, then, it must not turn out that cases of justified coercion – that is, cases like that described in which B's judgement that he morally ought to force A to ϕ in C are true – are not substantively different from cases involving a gangster and

324

his victim. Unfortunately, however, this is just what happens if we accept speaker relativism.

Consider once again the abstract conversation just described. According to speaker relativism B says that A's ϕ-ing in C is highly evaluated by moral system M, where the content of M is determined by B's affective attitudes. A's reply is that it is not the case that A's ϕ-ing in C is highly evaluated by moral system M*, where the content of moral system M* is determined by A's affective attitudes. B insists that his forcing A to ϕ in C is highly evaluated by moral system M, where the content of M is determined by B's affective attitudes, and A's reply is, once again, that it is not the case that B's forcing A to ϕ in C is highly evaluated by moral system M*, where the content of moral system M* is determined by A's affective attitudes.

As should now be evident, however, A and B are, potentially at any rate, not even contradicting each other. A's talk is all about a moral system whose content is fixed by his, A's, affective attitudes, whereas B's is all about a moral system whose content is fixed by his, B's. It is therefore possible that B may even be brought to agree with A that it is not the case that A's ϕ-ing in C, and B's forcing A to ϕ in C, are highly evaluated by moral system M* where the content of M* is determined by A's affective attitudes, and that A may be brought to agree with B about how these acts are evaluated by moral system M. It is possible because, on speaker relativist assumptions, it is both a conceptual and an empirical possibility that A's and B's affective attitudes simply differ in crucial respects.

This is all deeply problematic, however, at least given the assumption that an analysis of the cognitive content of a moral judgement must allow us to preserve the commonsense distinction between justified and unjustified use of coercive power. For that distinction simply collapses under the speaker relativist's analysis. The gangster is supposed to be unjustified in his use of coercive power because he is *simply* forcing his will upon his victim against his victim's wishes. B's use of coercive power is supposed to be different, at least if his claim that he morally ought to force A to ϕ in C is true. But B's use of coercive power is not different – or not if we accept the speaker relativist's analysis of moral claims. The truth of B's claim that he morally ought to force A to ϕ in C requires just that B's forcing A to ϕ in C is highly evaluated by a moral system whose content is fixed by his, *B's*, affective states, and, at least as I understand it, that is just a fancy way of saying that the truth of B's claim requires that B's will is to force A to ϕ in C. A's will on this issue is simply different from B's, just as the victim's wishes differ from the gangster's. A and B thus look for all the world, in relevant respects at any rate, like a victim and a gangster. Their wills simply conflict. The distinction between justified and unjustified use of coercive power has collapsed. Internalism's Wheel therefore turns again.

III. HARMAN'S MORAL RELATIVISM

We are now looking for a theory that can explain three things. First, it must give an account of what moral beliefs are beliefs about; second, it must use that account to explain the normative connection between moral belief and motivation; and third, it must use that account to explain the distinction between justified and unjustified uses of coercive power. Speaker relativism is in fact closely related to another theory which does make some headway in this regard, Gilbert Harman's version of moral relativism.[20]

Harman begins by distinguishing "inner judgements," judgements about what people ought to do, from "outer" judgements, judgements to the effect that this or that person is evil. He then focusses on inner judgements, judgements of moral obligation, as opposed to outer judgements, evaluations of people's characters, in order to advance the following "soberly logical thesis." When we say of someone, A, that she morally ought to ϕ in certain circumstances C, Harman tells us that the logical form of what we say is best captured by treating "ought" not as a three-place predicate – "Ought (A, ϕ, C)" – as perhaps it seems, but rather as a four-place predicate – "Ought (A, ϕ, C, M)." What this means is, roughly, that given A has motivating attitudes M, attitudes shared by the speaker, and given that she is in circumstances C, ϕ-ing is the course of action for A that is supported by the best reasons.

In order better to understand Harman's analysis, and to see how it differs from Dreier's, we need to focus on which motivating attitudes he has in mind. He tells us he has in mind "intentions to adhere to a particular agreement on the understanding that others also intend to do so," where the agreement is not supposed to be an overt ritual or ceremony, but rather, as he puts it, simply an "agreement in intentions."[21]

It is enough if various members of a society knowingly reach an agreement in intentions – each intending to act in certain ways on the understanding that the others have similar intentions.

Moreover, as he immediately concedes, the precise content of these intentions may be difficult to specify. Such intentions may "in various ways

326

be inconsistent, incoherent, or self-defeating."[22] But this, too, he thinks his analysis can easily accommodate.

> Moral reasoning is a form of practical reasoning. One begins with certain beliefs and intentions, including intentions that are part of one's acceptance of the moral understanding in a given group. In reasoning, one modifies one's intentions, often by forming new intentions, sometimes by giving up old ones, so that one's plans become more rational and coherent – or, rather, one seeks to make all of one's attitudes coherent with each other.[23]

When Harman says that "ought" judgements are made relative to a set of motivating attitudes, he therefore seems to have in mind those intentions to act in certain ways, on the understanding that others also have such intentions, that are part of the set of intentions that the speaker and the agent in question would have if their intentions and other attitudes formed a maximally coherent and rational set.[24]

Let me digress for a moment. Harman labels this a set of "intentions," but the label seems quite inappropriate. His basic idea is that a speaker's claim that an agent A morally ought to φ in C is made true, if it is true, by the fact that both the speaker and A would have a pro-attitude – as I would prefer to call it – towards A's φ-ing in C if they had a maximally coherent and rational set of pro-attitudes, each on the understanding that the other would have similar pro-attitudes (from now on I will omit this qualification). Let's call the possible world in which the speaker and A have a maximally coherent and rational set of pro-attitudes the "evaluating world," and the possible world in which A is in circumstances C, the possible world that both the speaker and A are evaluating, the "evaluated world."[25] We can then restate Harman's basic idea as follows. A speaker's claim that an agent A morally ought to φ in C is made true, if it is true, by the fact that the speaker and A *in the evaluating world* each have a pro-attitude towards A's φ-ing in C *in the evaluated world*. If this is right, however, then it should be clear that these pro-attitudes are not properly labelled "intentions" at all, at least not if an agent's intentions are psychological states that are crucially concerned with her own possibilities for action. For there is no necessity that the pro-attitudes the speaker and A have in the evaluating world, the world in which they are maximally rational, about what is to be done in the evaluated world, the world in which A is in circumstances C, have any connection at all with their own possibilities for action in the evaluating possible world. Their intentions in the evaluating world are, after all, a function of their view of their own circumstances, circumstances they face in the evaluating world. But the circumstances A faces in the evaluated world may be completely different. From now on I will therefore omit any mention of intentions in describing Harman's view. I will say, instead, that as he sees things, the truth of moral claims is relative to shared pro-attitudes. Here ends the digression.

Harman's version of moral relativism differs from Dreier's in several key respects. First, though Harman, like Dreier, makes a speaker's own pro-attitudes part of the truth conditions of her claims about what other agents morally ought to do, the pro-attitudes in question are not those the speaker normally has, where "normality" is a statistical matter, but rather those that she would have if she were to come up with a maximally coherent and rational set of such attitudes. Harman thus explicitly defines "morally ought" in normative terms, for the attitudes agents would have if they were maximally coherent and rational are those they rationally should have. Second, in striking opposition to Dreier's speaker relativism, Harman also makes the pro-attitudes of those about whom a speaker is speaking part of the truth conditions of a speaker's claims about what people morally ought to do. The first difference is crucial for the explanation Harman can give of internalism. The second is crucial for the account he can give of the distinction between justified and unjustified uses of coercive power.

Consider the explanation of internalism. If an agent believes that she would have a pro-attitude towards φ-ing in C if she had a maximally coherent and rational set of pro-attitudes then she does indeed seem practically irrational if she doesn't actually have a pro-attitude towards φ-ing in C. Coherence is, after all, on the side of psychologies that combine an agent's believing that she would have a pro-attitude towards φ-ing in C if she had a maximally coherent and rational set of pro-attitudes with her actually having a pro-attitude towards φ-ing in C, rather than psychologies that include that belief but lack the corresponding pro-attitude. Agents whose psychologies evolve in accordance with a tendency towards coherence, then, will tend to be moved in accordance with their moral beliefs. In this way Harman's theory can explain the requisite normative connection between moral belief and motivation. Agents who have moral beliefs but lack corresponding motivations exhibit a kind of incoherence in their overall psychological state. This seems to me to be an eminently plausible explanation of internalism.[26]

Consider now the distinction between justified and unjustified uses of coercive power. Suppose B says that he morally ought to force A to φ in C, and that A denies this, saying that it is not the case that B morally ought to force him to φ in C. The question on which the justification of B's use of coercive power is supposed to turn is which of A's and B's opinions are true, which mistaken. And this is indeed the case, given Harman's analysis. If A's belief that it is not the case that B morally ought to force her to φ in C is mistaken, and the right thing for A to believe is that B morally ought to force her to φ in C, then it must be the case that both A and B would share the very same pro-attitudes towards B's use of coercive power if they had a maximally coherent and rational set of such attitudes. There is therefore a relatively straightforward sense in which B's use of coercive power against A is not merely a matter of B forcing his will on A, for his use of coercive power is also, in a sense, a matter of his forcing A's will upon A. B is simply doing what A would want done to himself if he, A, had a maximally coherent and rational set of pro-attitudes. As with the explanation of internalism, this seems to me an eminently plausible explanation of the difference between justified and unjustified uses of coercive power.

Have we therefore found the theory we have been looking for? Unfortunately we have not, for we have so far failed to discuss a crucial part of Harman's theory: the theory of outer moral judgements. When I said at the beginning that Harman distinguishes inner from outer judgements I didn't explain what outer judgements were, I simply gave his example: judgements to the effect that someone or other is evil. Now that we have his theory of inner moral judgements before us, however, the difference between inner and outer moral judgements is easy to explain.

A moral judgement made by a speaker about another person whose truth requires certain pro- and con- attitudes on the part of both the speaker and the person spoken of is, according to Harman, an *inner* moral judgement. Harman thinks that all claims about what people morally ought to do are inner judgements. But a moral judgement made by a speaker about another person whose truth requires no such attitudes on the part of the person spoken of is an *outer* moral judgement. Harman tells us that claims to the effect that this person or that is evil are outer judgements. Roughly speaking, then, judgements of moral obligation are inner judgements, character assessments are outer judgements.

Harman illustrates the need for a theory of outer moral judgements by considering what we can legitimately say about Adolph Hitler. According to Harman, Hitler was beyond the "motivational reach" of the moral considerations we use to condemn him.[27] Given Harman's theory of inner judgements it is literally false to say of Hitler that he did what he morally ought not to have done when he ordered the extermination of the Jews. It is false because it is not the case that Hitler, like us, would have had a con- attitude towards his doing so if he had had a maximally coherent and rational set of such attitudes. The true claims Hitler could make about his moral obligations may therefore be completely different from the true claims we could make about ours. This is why Harman calls his theory a form of moral relativism. However, despite the fact he thinks this form of moral relativism is true, Harman insists that we can and do rightly condemn Hitler on moral grounds. This is because we can and do rightly say of Hitler that he is evil, where the truth of this claim requires nothing from a maximally coherent and rational Hitler in the way of suitable pro- or con-attitudes.

Harman thus adds a theory of outer judgements to his theory of inner judgements because of the inherent *limits* of the latter. But is the theory of outer judgements plausible? I do not think so. For one thing, it forces us to suppose that various logical relations which we would ordinarily suppose to hold between inner and outer judgements fail to hold. For example, we would ordinarily suppose that "A is evil" entails "A is disposed reliably to do what A morally ought not to do"; that this is true simply in virtue of the meanings of the words used. But Harman's theory tells us that the entailment is fallacious. Hitler may be evil even though he is not disposed to do what he morally ought not to do, as the first requires less for its truth than the second. Yet what would be our reason for supposing someone is evil, if not that he is disposed reliably to do what he morally ought not to do? A theory that provides uniform truth conditions for inner and outer judgements therefore seems preferable to a theory like Harman's that provides different truth conditions.[28]

Worse still, Harman's theory of outer moral judgements cannot play the role it needs to play in his overall theory of morality. Its role is to provide a set of moral judgements we can legitimately make about people, like Hitler, about whom we cannot legitimately make inner moral judgements. But why do we need to be able to make such judgements? We need to be able to make such judgements in order to be able to condemn their behaviour on moral grounds, so justifying our stand against them and, ultimately, our use of coercive power. But precisely because outer judgements differ from inner moral judgements in the way they do, we are unable even to make a coherent distinction between justified and unjustified use of coercive power simply in their terms.

Imagine trying to justify our use of coercion against Hitler by claiming that he is evil. What makes this claim true, if it is true, according to Harman? Presumably this claim has the same truth condition as a claim about what people morally ought to do *minus* the requirement that the person spoken of shares our pro- attitudes. Here we resort to a theory more like speaker relativism. We coerce Hitler because, as we see things, coercion is in accordance with the maximally coherent and rational set of pro- attitudes we would have. Hitler resists because, as he sees things, the extermination of the Jews is in accordance with the maximally coherent and rational set of attitudes he would have. Since, by Harman's lights, there is no sense in which either of us may suppose that our attitudes are rationally preferable to the other's, our justifiably coercing Hitler collapses, under analysis, into a case of our forcing our (maximally coherent and rational) will upon Hitler against his (maximally coherent and rational) wishes. Coercion justified by outer moral judgements therefore looks, in relevant respects at any rate, just like unjustified coercion.

Harman's moral relativism must therefore be rejected. His theory does, however, suggest how further progress might be made. Harman adds a theory of outer judgements to his theory of inner judgements because of what he perceives to be the inherent *limits* of the latter. As he sees things it is a conceptual truth that we are only able to make inner judgements about those whose maximally coherent and rational attitudes would be similar to our own. This seems right. But he also thinks that, as a matter of fact, different people's maximally coherent and rational sets of attitudes would all too often be very different from each other. This means that we will sometimes be unable to make inner judgements by way of criticizing the behaviour of those we want to criticize. However, granting the conceptual point, we should question the relevance of his empirical claim. Our task is to give an account of what moral beliefs are beliefs about. Surely the only relevant issue is therefore whether, when we make moral judgements, we in effect *presuppose* that we would all end up with the same pro- and con-attitudes if we each had a maximally coherent and rational set of such attitudes. The truth of this presupposition is neither here nor there. Internalism's Wheel therefore turns yet again, this time to a theory according to which we make just this presupposition.

IV. THE NON-RELATIVE VERSION OF THE DISPOSITIONAL THEORY OF VALUE

The non-relative version of the dispositional theory of value holds that claims about moral obligations and character assessments alike require that we would all of us converge upon the same set of pro- and con-attitudes if we each came up with a maximally coherent and rational set of such attitudes.[29] According to this theory all the moral judgements we ever make are therefore inner judgements. To say that we morally ought to φ in circumstances C requires that we would all of us have suitable pro-attitudes towards φ-ing in C if we had a maximally coherent and rational set of pro- and con-attitudes, and character assessments require a convergence in maximally coherent and rational attitudes as well because, according to this view, they are analysable in terms of judgements of moral obligation: to say that someone is evil is to say, *inter alia*, that he is disposed reliably to do what he morally ought not to do.

Unlike Harman's moral relativism the dispositional theory is therefore a non-relativist moral theory. It is non-relativist because the effect of the convergence requirement is to ensure that the truth of moral claims is independent of the peculiar pro- and con-attitudes of both those who make such claims and those about whom such claims are made. This is crucial for the explanation the theory is able to give of the distinction between justified and unjustified uses of coercive power. Thus, to take Harman's example, even though Hitler may have a con-attitude towards our preventing him from exterminating the Jews, and even though he may believe that this attitude would survive in a maximally coherent and rational set of such attitudes, in supposing that he morally ought not to do so we assume that his beliefs are false. When we coerce Hitler we therefore take ourselves not simply to be forcing our own maximally coherent and rational wills upon him against his maximally coherent and rational wishes, we take ourselves also to be forcing his own maximally coherent and rational will upon himself. Justifiably coercing Hitler thus does not collapse, under analysis, into a mere clash of wills.

The non-relative version of the dispositional theory of value offers us a straightforward explanation of the truth of internalism as well. Indeed, its explanation is the same as that made available by Harman's theory. Internalism is true because coherence is on the side of psychologies that combine an agent's believing that she would have a pro-attitude towards φ-ing in C, if she had the maximally coherent and rational set of pro- and con-attitudes all agents would converge upon, with actually having a pro-attitude towards φ-ing in C, rather than on the side of psychologies that include that belief but lack the corresponding pro-attitude. A mismatch between moral belief and motivation is therefore a kind of incoherence.

The non-relative version of the dispositional theory of value thus seems to explain the three things we want explained: it gives us an account of the cognitive content of a moral judgement, it uses that account to explain the normative connection between moral belief and motivation, and it uses that account to make a coherent distinction between justified and unjustified uses of coercive power. The theory pays a significant price for these explanations, however. For note how strong the convergence requirement really is.

The truth of the claim that we morally ought to φ in C requires that we would all of us have a pro-attitude towards φ-ing in C, if we had a maximally coherent and rational set of pro- and con-attitudes, not merely *contingently*, but *necessarily*. The convergence requirement must be understood in this way because a weaker, contingent, convergence requirement, which entails simply that:

1. In the actual world we would all have maximally coherent and rational sets of pro- and con-attitudes with the same content, the content of our moral obligations, but there is another possible world in which different agents have maximally coherent and rational sets of pro- and con-attitudes with different content.

is simply inconsistent with two further claims, claims we cannot reject, namely:

2. There is a combined possible world that contains both us as we actually are and them as they are in their world.

and

3. It is coherent to suppose that we would be justified in coercing them in the combined possible world.

This set is inconsistent because, as we have seen, the very coherence of the distinction between justified and unjustified uses of coercive power requires that the parties involved would each have attitudes with the same content if they had maximally coherent and rational sets of attitudes. Only so can the justified use coercive power be a matter of inflicting the coerced's own will upon them. The truth of (1) and (2) would therefore undermine the truth of (3). It follows that we must therefore reject (1). The convergence requirement must be necessary, not merely contingent.

According to the dispositional theory, then, in making moral judgements we presuppose that, *necessarily*, if we had a maximally coherent and rational set of pro- and con-attitudes we would all have attitudes with the same content. Of course, the dispositional theory is simply an analysis of the cognitive content of a moral judgement. It tells us what would have to be the case for moral claims to be true, it does not tell us whether any such claims are true. The theory is therefore consistent with an *error theory* of moral judgement, consistent with the claim that moral judgements are all based on a *false* presupposition: namely, that we would all converge on the same set of pro- and con-attitudes if we had maximally coherent and rational sets of such attitudes.[30] But a dilemma now looms large.

On the first horn the concepts of "maximal coherence" and "rationality" are given their ordinary everyday meaning. But then the objection is that it is simply implausible to suppose that something so obviously false – namely, that we would all have attitudes with the same content if we had maximally coherent and rational sets of pro- and con-attitudes – could be presupposed not just to be true, but necessarily true, by everyone who makes moral judgements. Think again about Hitler. Isn't it just obvious that he would not have the same attitudes as us if we both had maximally coherent and rational sets of attitudes? If so then it is implausible to suppose, as the dispositional theory supposes, that ordinary folk, when they moralise about Hitler, make the utterly preposterous presupposition that he would.

On the other horn of the dilemma the plausibility of the presupposition is granted, but only because it is assumed that we further presuppose something capable of explaining its truth: specifically, that a set of pro- and con-attitudes counts as maximally coherent and rational only if they are pro- and con-attitudes had towards doing what morally ought and ought not to be done respectively. But if this is part of what we presuppose in presupposing that there would be a necessary convergence in our maximally coherent and rational sets of pro- and con-attitudes then the non-relative version of the dispositional theory of value has clearly been abandoned. Facts about our moral obligations are being thought of as independent, thus far unanalyzed, facts. In order to have a theory that is credible at all, then, it seems that we must abandon the dispositional theory and look for an account of the cognitive content of moral judgements which posits independent facts about our moral obligations. Internalism's Wheel therefore turns to such a theory.

V. MORAL PLATONISM

Moral platonism is the view of moral facts John Mackie ascribes to common sense in his *Ethics: Inventing Right and Wrong*. According to this view, the concept of a moral feature is the concept of an "objectively prescriptive" feature of acts and characters.[31] These features are prescriptive in that it is part of their nature to elicit desire from those who recognize them. They are objective in that they elude analysis in subjective terms. Moral claims are not made true by facts about speakers or those spoken of, in the manner of Dreier's or Harman's theories. Nor are they made true by facts about rational creatures as such in the manner of the non-relative version of the dispositional theory of value. They are made true by independent moral facts.

Let's grant, for the time being, the coherence of the moral platonist's conception of moral facts as objectively prescriptive features. Once we grant him this, he can explain the truth of internalism: internalism is true because of what it means to say that a moral belief is a belief about a "prescriptive" feature of the world. He can also explain the coherence of the distinction between justified and unjustified uses of coercive power: coercion is justified whenever it is morally obligatory, where being morally obligatory is an objectively prescriptive feature of an act of coercion, a feature that eludes analysis in subjective terms; being justified thus does not reduce, under analysis, to facts about anyone's will. And, finally, he can explain the necessary convergence in maximally coherent and rational sets of pro- and con-attitudes: such attitudes converge because they are, by definition, formed in response to the objectively prescriptive features of things. The real question we must address is therefore whether we should grant the platonist the coherence of his conception of moral facts.

Consider the platonist's idea that moral features are objective. Moral claims are not supposed to be made true by facts about speakers or those spoken of, in the manner of Dreier's or Harman's theories, and nor are they supposed to be made true by facts about the pro- and con-attitudes of maximally coherent and rational creatures either, in the manner of the non-relative version of the dispositional theory of value. Moral facts are independent facts, facts that elude analysis in subjective terms. The platonist therefore seems to be conceiving of moral facts in the way in which many philosophers suppose we might conceive of *primary* qualities, as opposed to *secondary* qualities.[32] However, as John McDowell points out, it is difficult to square the idea that moral facts are objective in this sense with the idea that they are also prescriptive.

For it seems impossible – at least on reflection – to take seriously the idea of something that is like a primary quality in being simply there, independently of human sensibility, but is nevertheless intrinsically (not conditionally on the contingencies of human sensibility) such as to elicit some "attitude" or state of will from someone who becomes aware of it.[33]

Indeed, the idea of an objectively prescriptive feature looks like a contradiction. Insofar as they are objective they must be conceived of independently of any effects they might have upon rational agents. But insofar as they are prescriptive they must be conceived of in terms of a very particular effect they have upon rational agents: namely, their impact upon a rational agent's pro-attitudes.[34]

Worse still, the idea that moral features might be objective and independent of facts about human subjects in the sense in which the primary qualities of objects are objective and independent of facts about human subjects sits best with a *causal* model of moral knowledge, an account according to which moral knowledge is perceptual, or a matter of inference to the best scientific explanation, with moral facts playing a crucial causal role in the generation of that knowledge. But moral knowledge − or, at any rate, knowledge of fundamental moral truths or general principles − is a relatively a priori matter, and, however we are to conceive of a priori knowledge in general, it seems quite inappropriate to suppose that we gain such knowledge via causal contact with the a priori truths. If this is right, however − that is, if the platonist is not entitled to say that moral facts are independent of rational agents in the sense of being the cause of moral knowledge in the manner of primary qualities − then it simply isn't clear how he is to give an account of the sense in which he takes moral facts to be independent of facts about human subjects. His account of independence loses all content.

We must therefore conclude that the moral platonist's conception of moral facts is indeed incoherent. And there is worse to come. For moral platonism is simply the latest in a series of theories all which have tried, and failed, to give an account of what moral beliefs are beliefs about. These theories form a spectrum, from the extreme subjectivism of speaker relativism to the equally extreme objectivism of moral platonism. What should we conclude from the fact that they all fail? Many would have us draw the conclusion that moral judgements do not express moral beliefs at all. According to these theorists we should suppose instead that moral judgements express a psychological state of a kind more suited to entering into a direct explanation of the truth that lies in internalism: an emotion, or a feeling, or a desire. Internalism's Wheel therefore turns once more, or so they tell us. But, as our discussion makes plain, if we were to embrace this conclusion we would simply be arguing ourselves around in a circle. We would be led back to expressivism, and then on around Internalism's Wheel once more. Perhaps we should therefore draw the more pessimistic conclusion that the very idea of a moral judgement is incoherent. Or perhaps not.

Have the objections to the various theories really been as forceful as they have been portrayed to be? I do not think so. The weakest, as I see it, is the objection to the non-relative version of the dispositional theory of value, the view that we morally ought to φ in C just in case we would all of us converge, and necessarily so, upon a desire that we φ in C if we had a maximally coherent and rational set of pro- and con- attitudes. The objection takes the form of a dilemma. Either the concepts of maximal coherence and rationality are given their ordinary everyday meanings, in which case it is simply incredible to suppose that anyone would ever make moral judgements, presupposing as they do such a manifest falsehood, or else these concepts are to be defined in terms of independent facts about moral obligations, in which case we have to abandon the dispositional theory in favour of moral platonism. But as I see it neither horn of the dilemma does justice to our ordinary concepts of coherence and rationality. There is a third alternative in between.

In order to find out what our moral obligations are, let's agree that we initially have no alternative but to consider what we would all end up having pro- and con- attitudes towards in so far as our sets of pro- and con- attitudes come closer to maximal coherence and rationality in the most uncontroversial sense of these terms. But then, in order to find out whether one or another of us has a maximally coherent and rational set of pro- and con-attitudes, in the fullest possible sense, let's agree that we initially have no choice but to consider whether one or another of us has a set of attitudes that have, as their content, our moral obligations, as we ordinarily take them to be. There is no contradiction here. Rather we should conclude that neither concept, neither maximal coherence and rationality on the one hand nor moral obligation on the other, can be wholly understood except in terms of the other. Our ordinary, everyday, concepts of maximal coherence and rationality, and moral obligation, must rather be *inter-defined*.

On this way of seeing things the task before us, in coming up with a complete account of the cognitive content of a moral judgement, is thus to see whether we can extend our most uncontroversial ways of understanding of coherence and rationality so as to make plausible the idea that maximally coherent and rational creatures, as we newly understand these notions, would all converge upon a set of pro-attitudes towards their moral obligations. And this task in turn requires that we amend and precisify, wherever necessary, our ordinary everyday understanding of what our moral obligations are so as to bring our moral obligations more in line with the sorts of pro- and con-attitudes we would have if we had a maximally coherent and rational set, as these are newly understood.[35]

The fact that we need to play these two ideas off against each other in this way, that neither concept can be wholly understood except in terms of the other, means that in moral philosophy there is no clear line to be drawn between the tasks of conceptual analysis and substantive moral theorising. And indeed, as partial confirmation of this idea, note that it is in terms of such a play-off between the two ideas of a maximally coherent and rational set of pro- and con- attitudes on the one hand, and a moral obligation on the other, that we can perhaps best understand the appeal of many of the devices employed in contemporary normative ethics: the ideal observer,[36] the veil of ignorance,[37] the role-reversal test,[38] the agreements of idealised contractors,[39] and the like. For these devices can each be seen as different ways of giving content to the idea that our moral obligations derive from a procedure whereby we rationally justify our desires, where that procedure in turn aims to capture or model our susceptibility as rational creatures to the legitimate claims made against us by others, given a suitable characterisation of "legitimate."

Of course, as perhaps these examples make plain, no attempt to enrich our understanding of our concepts of coherence and rationality so as to make plausible the idea that we would all converge upon a set of pro-attitudes towards our moral obligations if we had a maximally coherent and rational set of such attitudes is guaranteed to succeed. The devices described are all controversial as interpretations of rationality, and, in some cases at least, indeterminate in the substantive conclusions they deliver. Indeed, there is no guarantee that any such attempt will succeed. But that is simply to reiterate the point that the dispositional theory, even if it is cast in a non-reductive mould in the way I am suggesting, leaves open the possibility of an error theory. Our concepts of a maximally coherent and rational set of pro- and con- attitudes on the one hand, and a moral obligation on the other, may resist being brought into equilibrium with each other. But, if they do, then the right conclusion to draw is that neither of these concepts makes any real sense. Showing that this is so would, however, be an enormous task. In effect it would require showing that no progress can be made in normative ethics.

A complete defence of the suggestion I am making here would require more in the way of argument. We would need to show, at the very least, that the project of conceptual analysis does not itself force us to take a reductive, as opposed to a non-reductive, route. Providing these further

338

arguments would, however, take us way beyond the scope of the present paper. I here simply assume that these arguments can be provided.[40] But once we clear the way for non-reductive analyses of the kind envisaged, and help ourselves to analyses of moral obligation in terms of rationality and rationality in terms of moral obligation, it should be clear that the dispositional theorist can avoid the dilemma foisted upon him by the moral platonist. The platonist is right to insist that reduction is implausible, but wrong to suppose that the alternative to reduction is to conceive of moral facts as wholly independent of our maximally coherent and rational attitudes.

Somewhat tentatively, then, my conclusion is that the non-reductive, non-relative version of the dispositional theory of value provides a stable stopping point for Internalism's Wheel. That is good news for internalists, of course. But it should also be good news for those interested in substantive moral issues as well. For even though, as we have seen, the theory is so far consistent with the possibility of an error theory, it does at least tell us the task we must undertake if we are to show that the error theory is mistaken, and the task it tells us to undertake looks by no means to be impossible. Indeed, it looks to be the same as the task of substantive moral theorising itself.[41]

NOTES

1. See W. D. Falk, " 'Ought' and Motivation," *Proceedings of the Aristotelian Society* 48 (1948); G. Harman, "Moral Relativism Defended," *Philosophical Review* 85 (1975); J. L. Mackie, *Ethics: Inventing Right and Wrong* (Harmondsworth: Penguin, 1977); J. McDowell, "Are Moral Requirements Hypothetical Imperatives?," *Proceedings of the Aristotelian Society* suppl. vol., 1978; M. Platts, *Ways of Meaning* (London: Routledge and Kegan Paul, 1979); S. Blackburn, *Spreading the Word* (Oxford: Clarendon Press, 1984), Chapter 6; C. Korsgaard, "Skepticism about Practical Reason," *Journal of Philosophy* 83 (1986); M. Johnston, "Dispositional Theories of Value," *Proceedings of the Aristotelian Society* suppl. vol., 1989; M. Smith, *The Moral Problem* (Oxford: Blackwell, 1994), Chapters 1 and 3.
2. Smith, *The Moral Problem*, p. 62.
3. See W. Frankena, "Obligation and Motivation in Recent Moral Philosophy," in A. I. Melden (ed.), *Essays on Moral Philosophy* (Seattle: University of Washington Press, 1958); P. Foot, "Morality as a System of Hypothetical Imperatives," reprinted in her *Virtues and Vices* (Berkeley: University of California Press, 1978); P. Railton, "Moral Realism," *Philosophical Review* 95 (1986); D. Brink, "Externalist Moral Realism," *Southern Journal of Philosophy* suppl. vol., 1986.
4. See Smith, *The Moral Problem*, pp. 60–76. D. Copp discusses this argument in his "Moral Obligation and Moral Motivation," in J. Couture and K. Nielsen (eds.), *New Essays on Metaethics, Canadian Journal of Philosophy* suppl. vol., 1996.

5. To anticipate, the theory I defend is the non-relative version of the dispositional theory of value I argue for in *The Moral Problem*.

6. Blackburn, *Spreading the Word*, pp. 187–8.

7. Watson, "Free Agency," reprinted in G. Watson (ed.), Free Will (Oxford: Oxford University Press); Smith, *The Moral Problem*, pp. 133–4.

8. Stocker, "Desiring the Bad: An Essay in Moral Psychology," *Journal of Philosophy* 76 (1979); Smith, *The Moral Problem*, pp. 135–6.

9. See P. Pettit and M. Smith, "Practical Unreason," *Mind* (102) 1993.

10. How might expressivists reply? They might argue that moral judgements express a disposition to be motivated: a second-order desire, a desire about which first-order desires to have, not a first-order desire, a desire about what to do. They might then insist that an agent who desires that she desires that she φs in C – which is the second-order desire her judgement that she morally ought to φ in C expresses – *is* practically irrational if she doesn't desire to φ in C. But the reply is unconvincing. What the examples of heroin addiction, depression and emotional disturbance show is that the mere fact an agent desires something does not, as such, confer any special normative status on that thing. An agent may desire that she φs in C without regarding her φ-ing in C as good. The point is fully general. There is no exception for that instance of the schema where we substitute "desiring to do something" for "φ-ing." A related point is made by Gary Watson in his criticisms of Harry Frankfurt's second-order desire account of freedom of the will. See Frankfurt's "Freedom of the Will and the Concept of a Person" and Watson's "Free Agency" both reprinted in G. Watson (ed.), *Free Will* (Oxford: Oxford University Press, 1982). See also the explicit criticism of second-order desire accounts of weakness of will in J. Kennett, "Decision Theory and Weakness of Will," in *Pacific Philosophical Quarterly* 72 (1991).

11. Geach, "Assertion," *Philosophical Review* 75 (1965).

12. C. Wright has argued, wrongly as it seems to me, that functioning like an ordinary truth-apt sentence is all there is to being a truth-apt sentence: see his *Truth and Objectivity* (Cambridge, MA: Harvard University Press, 1992). A general discussion of this issue can be found in M. Smith, "Why Expressivists About Value Should Love Minimalism About Truth"; J. Divers and A. Miller, "Why the Expressivist About Value Should Not Love Minimalism About Truth"; P. Horwich, "The Essence of Expressivism"; and M. Smith, "Minimalism, Truth-Aptitude and Belief" (all in *Analysis* 54 [1994]), and in F. Jackson, G. Oppy, and M. Smith, "Minimalism and Truth-Aptness," *Mind* 103 (1994).

13. Blackburn's attempts can be found in his *Spreading the Word*, Chapter 6; "Attitudes and Contents," *Ethics* 98 (1988); "Realism, Quasi or Queasy?," in J. Haldane and C. Wright (eds.), *Reality, Representation and Projection* (Oxford: Oxford University Press, 1994). Decisive replies to Blackburn can be found in B. Hale's "The Compleat Projectivist," *Philosophical Quarterly* 36 (1986), and "Can There Be a Logic of Attitudes?" and "Postscript," both in Haldane and Wright. See also C. Wright, "Moral Values, Projection and Secondary Qualities," in *Proceedings of the Aristotelian Society* suppl. vol., 1988.

14. J. Dreier, "Internalism and Speaker Relativism," *Ethics* 101 (1990). As Dreier himself puts it: "I have some sympathy for emotivism and other noncognitive

meta-ethical theories. Relativism flows naturally from them, and speaker relativism is in a way their child" (p. 14).

15. Dreier "Internalism and Speaker Relativism," p. 9.
16. Dreier, "Internalism and Speaker Relativism," pp. 9–14.
17. Dreier, "Internalism and Speaker Relativism," p. 13.
18. Dreier, "Internalism and Speaker Relativism," p. 14.
19. At one point Dreier suggests a sophistication of his theory which might be thought to address just these difficulties: "I started by allowing the speaker's actual motivational states to determine completely the relevant moral system. The modification in response to counterexamples to crude internalism allowed the moral system to be picked out by the speaker's motivations under normal conditions. The sophisticated relativist will look to what Westermark called the 'retributive emotions.' So elements of the system will be rules which are such that if the speaker violates them he will tend to feel guilty; if others violate them he will tend to feel indignation; and so forth" ("Internalism and Speaker Relativism," p. 24). The ideas of guilt and indignation might be thought to introduce an appropriately normative element into the picture while allowing Dreier's basic idea to remain the same. According to this more sophisticated theory, when a speaker says that she morally ought to φ in C she is saying that φ-ing in C is highly evaluated by system M, where M is a system of rules whose content is filled in by looking at the causes of her feelings of guilt and indignation. The following principle is therefore analytic: if an agent believes that it is morally right to φ in C then either she is motivated to φ in C or she feels guilty. It might be thought that this principle is equivalent to the truth embodied in internalism. However, this more sophisticated theory is no improvement if, as it seems to me, feelings of guilt cannot be understood except as the feelings we have when we believe that we have done something wrong, for then the derived principle, which is supposed to be equivalent to internalism, is the following: if an agent believes she morally ought to φ in C then either she is motivated to φ in C or she has the feelings that accompany her belief that she has done the wrong thing. Since internalists and externalists can both accept this principle it is obviously not equivalent to internalism.
20. Harman, "Moral Relativism Defended."
21. Harman, "Moral Relativism Defended," p. 13.
22. Harman, "Moral Relativism Defended," p. 16.
23. Harman, "Moral Relativism Defended," p. 20.
24. Let me here acknowledge that my interpretation of Harman goes beyond anything he explicitly says in the text. I assume, perhaps wrongly, that Harman thinks that once I have engaged in a process of moral reasoning I am still able to make judgements about what my earlier, less coherent, self morally ought to have done, because both my earlier, less coherent, self and my later, more coherent, self make moral judgements relative to the same set of intentions: namely, the maximally coherent and rational set. An alternative view is that we always make moral judgements relative to the intentions we in fact have. The drawback of this alternative is that, once I have engaged in a process of moral reasoning, I may be unable to make judgements about what my earlier, less coherent, self morally ought to have done. This will be the case if the process of reasoning has led me

to adopt different intentions. My interpretation of Harman thus has the virtue of making moral reasoning a means by which we can adopt a critical perspective on our less coherent and rational selves, a means by which we can discover what we morally ought to have done.

25. For a futher development of this idea see my "Internal Reasons," *Philosophy and Phenomenological Research* 55 (1995).

26. See also my "Internal Reasons."

27. Harman, "Moral Relativism Defended," p. 8.

28. Here I find myself in agreement with David Brink: "This distinction between inner and outer judgements may seem somewhat puzzling. If morality's practical or action-guiding character establishes a connection between moral considerations and reasons for action, shouldn't we expect all moral judgements to imply the existence of reasons for action? Are character assessments any less 'inner' than ascriptions of obligation? . . . Indeed, Harman's distinction is incoherent if it should turn out that moral properties of character can be specified in terms of the relation between an agent's character and the fulfillment or failure to fulfill different obligations that the agent has." Brink, "Moral Realism Defended," in L. Pojman (ed.), *Ethical Theory: Classical and Contemporary Readings* (Belmont, CA: Wadsworth Publishing Company, 1989), p. 44.

29. Smith, *The Moral Problem*, especially Chapters 5 and 6. Other versions of the theory are defended by D. Lewis and M. Johnston in their contributions to the "Dispositional Theories of Value" symposium in *Proceedings of the Aristotelian Society* suppl. vol., 1989.

30. Compare Mackie, *Ethics*, Chapter 1.

31. Mackie, *Ethics*, p. 35.

32. See especially C. McGinn, *The Subjective View* (Oxford: Clarendon Press, 1985), Chapter 2.

33. J. McDowell, "Values and Secondary Qualities," in T. Honderich (ed.), *Morality and Objectivity* (London: Routledge and Kegan Paul, 1985), p. 111.

34. M. Smith, "Objectivity and Moral Realism: On the Significance of the Phenomenology of Moral Experience," in Haldane and Wright, p. 237.

35. The idea should sound familiar from J. Rawls, "Outline of a Decision Procedure for Ethics," *Philosophical Review* 50 (1951).

36. R. Firth, "Ethical Absolutism and the Ideal Observer," *Philosophy and Phenomenological Research* 12 (1952).

37. J. Rawls, *A Theory of Justice* (Cambridge, MA: Harvard University Press, 1971), Part 1.

38. R. M. Hare, "Ethical Theory and Utilitarianism," in A. Sen and B. Williams (eds.), *Utilitarianism and Beyond* (Cambridge: Cambridge University Press, 1982).

39. Harman, "Moral Relativism Defended"; T. M. Scanlon, "Contractualism and Utilitarianism," in Sen and Williams.

40. I attempt to provide these arguments in *The Moral Problem*, Chapter 2.

41. Thanks to John O'Leary-Hawthorne and Brad Hooker for helpful comments.

16

Evaluation, Uncertainty, and Motivation

Evaluative judgement has a decidedly Janus-faced character.

On the one hand, when an agent judges her performance of some action to be desirable it seems that she thereby conveys her normative perspective on the world, her assessment of the importance of acting in the way in question. This assessment is one in which she might have more or less confidence, and for which she might have more or less justification. In this respect an agent's evaluative judgements seem to give expression to her beliefs. On the other hand, however, when an agent judges that some action is desirable she also appears to be in a state that has the potential to lead her all the way to action, at least in so far as she is rational. No additional desire to (say) do whatever it is that she happens to value doing is needed. In this respect an agent's evaluative judgements seem to give expression to her desires.

The Janus-faced character of evaluative judgement sets the agenda for much contemporary meta-ethics. Cognitivists take it as read that they can accommodate the belief-like features of evaluative judgement, and then confront the problem of trying to account for the potential to lead all the way to action that beliefs with that sort of content must have (Brink 1989; Scanlon 1998). Non-cognitivists do the reverse (Gibbard 1990; Blackburn 1998). They take it as read that they can accommodate the desire-like features of evaluative judgement, and then face the problem of trying to account for the potential for justification and rational defence that such motivational antecedents must therefore have. The usual manifestation of this is the attempt non-cognitivists make to explain the truth-apt appearance of the sentences we use when we give linguistic expression to our evaluative commitments.

One remarkable feature of these maneuvers by cognitivists and non-cognitivists alike is thus that they tend to treat the belief-like and the desire-like features of evaluative judgement pretty much in isolation from each other. For example, and to repeat, non-cognitivists take it for granted that they can accommodate the desire-like features of evaluative judgement – take it for granted, in other words, that an agent's evaluative commitments, being just a set of desires as they see things, explain her actions – and then proceed to discuss how they can accommodate the belief-like features. My own view, however, and hence the argument of much of this paper, is that the tendency to treat the belief-like and the desire-like features of evaluative judgements in isolation from each other is a mistake. The belief-like features of evaluative judgement are, I will argue, quite complex, and these complexities play a crucial role when it comes to understanding the way in which an agent's values explain her actions (see also Humberstone 1987). The crucial question for cognitivists and non-cognitivists is thus whether they can accommodate these complexities.

This chapter is in four main sections. In the first I explain what the complexities of the belief-like features of evaluative judgement are. In the second section I say a little about how these complexities impact on the way in which an agent's values explain her actions. In the third I say how a particular cognitivist account of evaluation, the account that I myself prefer, handles these complexities. And then in the fourth and final section I say a little about how these complexities might be handled by non-cognitivists. To anticipate, cognitivists handle the complexities well, non-cognitivists appear to handle them badly.

1. THREE FEATURES OF EVALUATIVE JUDGEMENT

Commonsense tells us that, in so far as they are belief-like, evaluative judgements have three quite different features. Two of these are features that such judgements share with beliefs quite generally. The third is a feature that is distinctive of evaluative judgements in particular. Let me describe each of these three features in turn.

The first feature of an evaluative judgement is the level of confidence a subject has that things are evaluatively as she judges them to be. For example, a subject might think it very unlikely that (say) being honest is desirable in itself, but much more likely that being knowledgeable is desirable in itself, and even more likely still that experiencing pleasure is desirable in itself. This is, as I said, a feature that evaluative judgements share with beliefs quite generally. To take a non-evaluative example, a subject might think it very unlikely that the sun will explode tomorrow, but much more likely that it will rain tomorrow, and even more likely still that there will be a football match tomorrow.

The fact that subjects can have different levels of confidence in both evaluative and non-evaluative judgements alike is important, because it reminds us that the level of confidence that a subject has in certain of her evaluative judgements is a product of both a level of confidence she has in another evaluative judgement and the level of confidence she has in a non-evaluative judgement. For example, the level of confidence a subject has that her riding on a roller coaster is desirable might be a product of two levels of confidence: first, her level of confidence in the non-evaluative judgement that her riding on a roller coaster would lead her to experience pleasure, and, second, her level of confidence in the evaluative judgement that experiencing pleasure is desirable. Importantly, however, the levels of confidence that subjects have in certain of their evaluative judgements are not in this way the products of the confidence they have in other evaluative judgements and the confidence they have in some non-evaluative judgement. The level of confidence a subject has in the judgement that pleasure is desirable in itself is like this. It is this kind of evaluative judgement, a judgement of intrinsic or fundamental or non-derived value, which will be the focus of discussion in the remainder of this chapter.

How do we measure the different levels of confidence subjects have in their evaluative judgements? Differences in subjects' levels of confidence is the sort of thing that gets revealed in how much they would be willing to bet on one outcome as opposed to another under circumstances of forced choice. It would perhaps be difficult to construct an appropriate betting situation that would reveal the different levels of confidence that subjects have in the claims they make about what is of intrinsic value, but the basic idea should in principle be clear enough. Facts about subjects' different levels of confidence are thus, as we might put it, synchronic facts about their evaluative judgements. In referring back to this feature of evaluative judgements later, I will call this their "Certitude."

The second feature of evaluative judgement, another that such judgements share with beliefs in general, concerns how stable a subject's confidence that things are evaluatively the way that she judges them to be is under the impact of incoming information and reflection. For example, though a subject might be equally confident that (say) experiencing pleasure is desirable in itself and being autonomous is desirable in itself, her confidence in the former might be very stable under the impact of incoming information and reflection, whereas her confidence in the latter is very unstable.

As I said, this too is a feature that evaluative judgements share with beliefs in general. Again, to take a non-evaluative example, though a subject might have the very same level of confidence – or, as we might say, the very same degree of belief – in the proposition that the Sydney Swans is the most talented Australian Rules football team and the proposition that her son is a responsible supermarket employee, her degree of belief in the proposition that her son is a responsible supermarket employee might be very stable under the impact of incoming information and reflection, whereas her degree of belief in the proposition that the Sydney Swans is the most talented Australian Rules football team is much more unstable. Though nothing much in the way of incoming information and reflection would change her confidence in the proposition that her son is a responsible supermarket employee all that much – perhaps the evidence is already in – all sorts of incoming information would radically change her confidence in the proposition that the Sydney Swans is the most talented Australian Rules football team.

Whereas facts about subjects' levels of confidence are fixed synchronically by how much they would bet on the propositions they accept under circumstances of forced choice, facts about how stable the levels of confidence in the propositions subjects accept is under the impact of incoming information and reflection are plainly fixed diachronically. They are fixed by changes in how much subjects would be willing to bet on one outcome as opposed to another over time. In order to be able to refer back to this feature of evaluative judgement later, let's call this their "Robustness."

The third feature of evaluative judgements on which I wish to focus is a feature of such judgements in particular. When a subject judges that (say) both experiencing pleasure and being autonomous are desirable in themselves, it is always relevant to ask how desirable she judges each of these features to be: which she judges to be more desirable. The best way to fix on this feature of evaluative judgements is to imagine the perspective of people who are omniscient, for we are then able to abstract away from any differences due to Certitude. As between two outcomes, in one of which they are autonomous to a certain extent, and in the other of which they experience a certain amount of pleasure, how autonomous would people who are omniscient have to imagine themselves being, as compared with experiencing how much in the way pleasure, in order for them to be indifferent? Intuitively, the idea is, the less autonomous they would have to imagine themselves being, and the more they would have to imagine themselves experiencing in the way of pleasure, in order to be indifferent between being autonomous to that extent as opposed to experiencing that amount of pleasure, the more desirable they would thereby be taking autonomy to be and the less desirable they would thereby be taking experiencing pleasure to be. In order to refer back to this feature later, let's call this feature of evaluative judgements their "Importance."

Let me sum up what we have said so far. We have distinguished three different features commonsense tells us evaluative judgements have, in so far as they have belief-like features: Certitude, Robustness, and Importance. I suggested at the outset that these three features are crucially important when it comes to understanding the way in which an agent's values explain her actions. We are now in a position to see why that is so.

2. THE ROLE OF THE THREE FEATURES IN THE EXPLANATION OF ACTION ON THE BASIS OF VALUES

Our initial statement of the desire-like feature of an evaluative judgement was that, in so far as agents are rational, we expect them to be motivated to do what they judge it desirable to do. However, as is perhaps now evident, this initial statement is far too crude. It is far too crude because it abstracts away from Certitude, Robustness, and Importance as features of evaluative judgement, whereas commonsense tells us that the motivations of a rational agent will plainly be crucially dependent on these features. In order to be more accurate we must therefore state the desire-like features of evaluative judgements in the following rather more complicated terms.

To begin with, in so far as they are rational, agents will be more strongly motivated to do that which they judge it more desirable to do, as between options about which their confidence levels are the same. In other words, in the terms introduced in the previous section, at a time, the strengths of a rational agent's different motivations will reflect such differences as might exist in relative Importance, abstracting away from differences in Certitude. For example, if a rational agent is equally confident that experiencing a certain amount pleasure is desirable in itself and that being autonomous to a certain degree is desirable in itself, but judges that being autonomous to that degree is more desirable than experiencing pleasure to that extent, then she will be more strongly motivated to be autonomous to that degree than to experience pleasure to that extent.

Second, in so far as they are rational, agents are more strongly motivated to do that about which they are more confident, as between options which they judge to be equally desirable. In other words, in the terms introduced in the previous section, at a time, we expect the strength of a rational agent's different motivations to covary with such differences as might exist in Certitude, abstracting away from differences in Importance. For example, if a rational agent judges that experiencing pleasure to a certain extent and being knowledgeable to a certain extent are equally desirable, but she is much more confident that experiencing pleasure to that extent is desirable than she is that being knowledgeable to that extent is desirable, then she will be more strongly motivated to experience the pleasure than she is to be that knowledgeable.

Finally, in so far as they are rational, the stability of agents' motivations over time covaries with the stability of their evaluative judgements. In other words, in the terms introduced in the previous section, over time, we expect the stability of a rational agent's motivations to track Robustness, abstracting away from such differences as might exist in Importance and Certitude. For example, if a rational agent judges it desirable to a certain degree to experience pleasure, and if her confidence level is stable under the impact of information and reflection, then the strength of her motivation to experience pleasure will be stable under the impact of information and reflection, and if a rational agent judges it desirable to a certain degree to be autonomous, and if her confidence level waxes and wanes under the impact of information and reflection, then the strength of her motivation to be autonomous will wax and wane under the impact of information and reflection too.

We now have before us our more complicated formulation of the desire-like features of evaluative judgement. To repeat, this more complicated formulation of the desire-like features of evaluative judgement is mandated by the three features that evaluative judgement are supposed to have, according to commonsense. It thus follows that, to the extent that a theory about the nature of evaluative judgement is unable to give a satisfactory account of the three features, and the roles that they play in the explanation of action, that theory fails to accord with commonsense. The question we must ask ourselves is thus whether cognitivists and non-cognitivists are equally able to make room for these three features of evaluative judgement and whether they are also equally able to accommodate the crucial roles played by these three features when it comes to understanding the way in which an agent's values explain her actions.

In the next section I consider how a particular cognitivist account of evaluation, the account that I myself prefer, makes room for the three different features and accommodates the different roles they play in the explanation of action. In the section after that I say a little about how

348

non-cognitivists might attempt to make room for these three different features and accommodate their different roles.

3. HOW A COGNITIVIST CAN MAKE ROOM FOR THE THREE FEATURES OF EVALUATIVE JUDGEMENT AND ACCOMMODATE THE DIFFERENT ROLES THAT THEY PLAY IN THE EXPLANATION OF ACTION

We need to begin at the beginning. Cognitivists must, first and foremost, come up with a plausible account of what it is that an agent believes when she judges some action to be desirable.

It seems to me helpful, in this connection, to start from the more or less common sense assumption that for an agent to believe that her acting in a certain way in certain circumstances is desirable is for her to believe that her so acting is advisable: that is, a matter of her believing that she would advise herself to perform that act in those circumstances if she were herself in circumstances in which she was best placed to give herself advice (Smith 1995). This is the appropriate place to start because the fact that one would give oneself such advice in such circumstances clearly has normative force. Two questions then spring naturally to mind. First, what are these circumstances in which agents are best placed to give themselves advice, and second, what fixes the content of the advice that the agents in those circumstances would give to themselves?

The answer to the first question is, I suggest, that agents are best placed to give themselves advice when their psychologies have been purged of all cognitive limitations and rational failings. The answer to the second question, the question about the content of the advice that agents would give to themselves, is then that the content of such advice is fixed by the contents of the desires that they would have about what they are to do in the circumstances of action about which they are seeking advice, were their psychologies thus purged. In other words, when I judge my performance of a certain action to be desirable that amounts to my believing that my performance of that act is advisable, where that, in turn, amounts to my believing that I would want myself so to act if I had a desire set that was purged of all cognitive limitations and rational failings.

If something like this is along the right lines then all we need in order to get a full-blown analysis of desirability is to give an account of the conditions that need to be met by a desire set which is devoid of cognitive limitations and rational failings. My suggestion in this regard, developing an idea of Bernard Williams's (1980), is that for a desire set to be devoid of cognitive limitations and rational failings is for it to be one which meets certain descriptive-cum-normative conditions: specifically, it is for one's desire set to be maximally informed and coherent and unified (Smith 1994). If we call the possible world in which the agent has the desires that she actually has in the circumstances of action she faces the "evaluated" world, and the possible world in which she has that set of desires that is maximally informed and coherent and unified the "evaluating" world, then, the suggestion is, what it is desirable for her to do in the evaluated world is fixed not by what, in the evaluated world she wants herself to do in the evaluated world, and not by what, in the evaluating world, she wants herself to do in the evaluating world, but rather by what, in the evaluating world, she wants herself to do in the evaluated world. This, accordingly, is the property that an agent must believe her act to have when she values the performance of that act.

Once this is agreed, it seems to me that there is no difficulty at all in seeing, at least in broad terms, why valuing has the Janus-faced character noted at the outset. Since valuing is a matter of having certain beliefs about what is desirable, where desirability is in turn a matter of what the agent would want herself to do if she had a set of desires that was maximally informed and coherent and unified, it should come as no surprise at all to learn that her values convey her normative perspective on the world; that she might be more or less justified in the beliefs that she thus has; that she might therefore have more or less confidence in the things she believes; and that her levels of confidence might be more or less stable under the impact of information and reflection. An agent's evaluative beliefs are, after all, just a species of belief, so the reason that these features are features of evaluative beliefs is that they are features of beliefs quite generally.

But nor should it come as any surprise to learn that an agent who values acting in a certain way has a belief that is capable of both causing and rationalizing certain desires without the aid of any further desire, a desire such as, for example, the desire to do what she values. In order to see that this is so, imagine a case in which, on reflection, you come to believe that (say) you would desire that you experience pleasure in the circumstances that you presently face if you had a maximally informed and coherent and unified set of desires, but imagine further that you don't in fact have any desire at all to experience pleasure in these circumstances. Now consider the pair of psychological states that comprises your belief that you would desire that you experience pleasure in the circumstances that you presently face if you had a maximally informed and coherent and unified set of desires together with the desire that you experience pleasure in these circumstances, and compare this pair of psychological states with the pair that comprises your belief that you would desire that you experience pleasure in the circumstances that you presently face if you had a set of desires that was maximally informed and coherent and unified together with an aversion – or just indifference – to experiencing pleasure in these circumstances. Which of these pairs of psychological states is more coherent?

The answer would seem to be plain enough. The first pair is much more coherent than the second. There is disequilibrium or dissonance or failure of fit involved in believing that you would desire that something obtain if you had a maximally informed and coherent and unified desire set, and yet being averse to the prospect of that thing's obtaining. The aversion is, after all, something that you yourself disown. From your perspective it makes no sense, given the rest of your desires. By your own lights it is a state that you would not be in if you were in various ways better, in the sense of being more rational, than you actually are: more informed, more coherent, more unified in your desiderative outlook. There would therefore seem to be more than a passing family resemblance between the relation that holds between the first pair of psychological states and more familiar examples of coherence relations that hold between psychological states. Coherence would thus seem to be on the side of the pair that comprises both the belief that you would desire that you experience pleasure in the circumstances that you presently face and the desire that you experience pleasure.

If this is right, however, then it follows immediately that if you are rational, in the relatively mundane sense of having and exercising a capacity to have the psychological states that coherence demands of you, then you will end up having a desire that matches your belief about what you would want if you had a maximally informed and coherent and unified desire set. In other words, in the particular case under discussion, you will end up losing your aversion or indifference to experiencing pleasure, and acquiring a desire to experience pleasure instead. The belief that you would desire that things be a certain way if you had a set of desires that was maximally informed and coherent and unified would thus seem able to cause you to acquire a corresponding desire when it operates in conjunction with the capacity to have coherent psychological states. Moreover, because acquiring the desire makes for a more coherent pairing of psychological states, it would seem to follow that the desire thus caused is rationalized as well. Finally, note that no causal role at all needs to be played by any desire in the explanation of the acquisition of this

351

desire. All that is required is the exercise of the capacity to have coherent psychological states, a capacity whose exercise is ubiquitous across both the cognitive and the non-cognitive realms.

That, at any rate, is the story in broad outline. But once we see the story in broad outline it seems to me that we can also see why the more complex features that our evaluative beliefs can have impact on our desires in the way that they do. In order to see why this is so let's consider the three features: Certitude, Robustness, and Importance. Consider Importance first.

Suppose an agent believes that if she had a maximally informed and coherent and unified desire set then she would desire that she experiences a certain amount of pleasure in the circumstances that she presently finds herself in, but she also believes that she would have a stronger desire that she be autonomous to a certain degree in these circumstances. In other words, more intuitively, suppose that she believes that being autonomous to that degree is more important than experiencing that amount of pleasure. What does coherence require of her?

Coherence plainly demands of her not just that she has desires both to experience that amount of pleasure and to be autonomous to that degree in the circumstances in which she presently finds herself, but that the relative strength of her desires matches the relative strength of the desires she believes she would have: demands of her, in other words, that her desire to be autonomous to that degree be stronger than her desire to experience that amount of pleasure. The argument for this is simply a more sophisticated version of the argument given above.

Consider the quadruple of psychological states that comprises the agent's belief that she would have a desire of a certain strength that she experiences the relevant amount of pleasure in the circumstances in which she presently finds herself if she had a maximally informed and coherent and unified desire set, and the belief that she would have a somewhat stronger desire that she be autonomous to the relevant degree in these circumstances, together with a desire that she experiences pleasure in these circumstances and a correspondingly stronger desire that she be autonomous. This quadruple of psychological states would seem to exhibit more in the way of coherence than the quadruple of psychological states that comprises those beliefs together with (say) a stronger desire that she experiences pleasure and a weaker desire that she be autonomous.

Now consider Certitude. Imagine the agent just described with the beliefs just described, but let's suppose further that while she has a certain high degree of confidence that she would desire that she experience pleasure in the circumstances in which she presently finds herself if she had a maximally informed and coherent and unified desire set, her confidence that she would have a somewhat stronger desire that she be autonomous in the circumstances that she presently finds herself is somewhat lower. In other words, put more intuitively, though she believes that being autonomous is more important than experiencing pleasure, she is far more confident of her assessment of the value of experiencing pleasure than she is of her assessment of the value of being autonomous. What does coherence demand of her in this case?

Again, it seems plain enough that we could construct a similar comparison of quadruples of psychological states to show that coherence demands of her that the relative strengths of her desires to be autonomous and experience pleasure matches the relative strengths of the desires she believes that she would have that she be autonomous and experience pleasure, but this time, as discounted by her different levels of confidence. Indeed, we can even imagine the level of confidence that she would desire that she be autonomous being so low, as compared with her level of confidence that she would desire that she experiences pleasure, that, notwithstanding the fact that she believes that her desire that she be autonomous would be stronger than her desire that she experience pleasure, coherence may even demand of her that her actual desire that she experience pleasure be stronger than her desire that she be autonomous.

Consider, finally, Robustness. Imagine the agent just described, with the confidence levels just described, but let's suppose further that the higher level of confidence she has that she would desire that she experience pleasure in the circumstances in which she presently finds herself if she had a maximally informed and coherent and unified desire set diminishes over time under the impact of information and reflection, and that her lower level of confidence that she would have a somewhat stronger desire that she be autonomous in the circumstances that she presently finds herself increases over time under the impact of information and reflection. What does coherence demand of her over time in this case? The answer is, again, plain. Coherence demands of her over time that her actual desires that she experience pleasure and be autonomous shift in their relative strengths so that they reflect, at each moment, the appropriate mix of believed strength and level of confidence.

We have thus seen that at least one cognitivist account of evaluative judgement, the account that I myself prefer, can not only make room for the three features of such judgements that we described earlier, and accommodate the different roles that these features play in the explanation of action, but that it can also do so in a straightforward and intuitive way. This particular cognitivist account thus squares extremely well with commonsense. The question we must now ask is whether the same can be said for a non-cognitivist account of evaluative judgement.

4. CAN A NON-COGNITIVIST MAKE ROOM FOR THE THREE FEATURES OF EVALUATIVE JUDGEMENT AND ACCOMMODATE THE DIFFERENT ROLES THAT THEY PLAY IN THE EXPLANATION OF ACTION?

How might a non-cognitivist attempt to make room for Certitude, Importance, and Robustness as features of evaluative judgement? The answer to this question is crucially important. For without an answer to this question they are plainly unable to accommodate the different roles that these features play in the explanation of action.

Non-cognitivists hold that a subject's evaluative judgements are expressions not of her beliefs about the ways things are in evaluative respects, but are rather expressions of her desires that things be a certain way in non-evaluative respects. The judgement that experiencing pleasure is desirable in itself, for example, is claimed by non-cognitivists not to be the expression of a belief about an evaluative property, desirability, that is possessed by the experience of pleasure, but rather to be the expression of the desire to experience pleasure, or some other, similar, non-belief state.

It thus follows that unlike cognitivists, who can explain at least one of the three features of evaluative judgements, namely Importance, in terms of a feature of the world – think again of the explanation given above according to which Importance is a matter of desirability, conceived of as a property that can be possessed by things which are desirable, where this in turn is a matter of the differential strengths of the desires that a subject would have if she had a maximally informed and coherent and unified desire set – and only have to explain the remaining two features of evaluative judgements, namely, Certitude and Robustness, in terms of a structural feature of the psychological state that such judgements express, non-cognitivists must attempt to explain all three features in terms of structural features of the psychological state that such judgements express. Certitude, Importance, and Robustness must one and all reduce, in some yet to be specified way, to structural features of the desires that non-cognitivists tell us we have in so far as we have evaluative commitments.

Here, however, looms a problem. For what structural features do desires possess? As far as I can see, desires possess just two structural features

354

that look like they will be of any use in the present connection. Desires differ from each other in terms of their strength: a subject's desire that she experiences a certain amount of pleasure might be weaker than, as strong as, or stronger than, her desire that she enjoys a certain degree of autonomy, for example. And the strength of an agent's desires may vary over time under the impact of information and reflection: at one time a subject's desire that she experiences a certain amount of pleasure might be weaker than her desire that she enjoys a certain degree of autonomy, for example, but, under the impact of information and reflection, at a later time her desire that she experiences a certain amount of pleasure might be stronger than her desire that she enjoys a certain degree of autonomy.

Now consider a very flat-footed form of non-cognitivism, just to make the problem that looms vivid, a form of non-cognitivism according to which a subject's judgement that experiencing a certain amount of pleasure is desirable is an expression of her desire that she experiences pleasure, and whose judgement that being autonomous to a certain degree is desirable is an expression of her desire that she enjoys that degree of autonomy. Since subjects' desires can vary in strength, that degree of strength can represent something, presumably either Importance or Certitude, and since the strength of the subjects' desires over time can vary under the impact of information and reflection, that too can presumably represent something, presumably Robustness. But this leaves one thing, either Importance or Certitude, not represented at all. The problem that looms, then, is that a non-cognitivist seems not to have the resources to accommodate all three features of evaluative judgement that we commonsensically ascribe to them. They can accommodate either Importance and Robustness, or Certitude, and Robustness, but not all of Importance, Certitude, and Robustness.

At this point it might be thought that non-cognitivists should simply insist that we not consider such a flat-footed version of their theory. It is worthwhile considering this response. Instead of holding that an evaluative judgement expresses a first-order desire, what happens if we hold that an evaluative judgement expresses a second-order desire? It might be thought that we could then represent both Importance and Certitude, in addition to Robustness, in the following terms.

A subject who judges that it is desirable to experience a certain amount of pleasure, and who also judges that it is desirable to be autonomous to a certain degree, and who judges, as well, that experiencing that amount of pleasure is less desirable than being autonomous to that degree, is someone who desires to desire that she experiences that amount of pleasure,

355

and desires to desire that she be autonomous to that extent, and, in addition, the suggestion might be, she is someone whose desired desire that she experiences pleasure is weaker than her desired desire that she be autonomous. Importance, it might be claimed, can in this way be represented by the strength of the desired desire. Certitude, it might then be thought, could be represented by the relative strengths of the second-order desires themselves. In other words, a subject whose desire that she desires that she experiences a certain amount of pleasure is stronger than her desire that she desires that she be autonomous is someone who is more confident about the value of pleasure than she is about the value of autonomy. Robustness could then be explained as before in terms of the diachronic sensitivity of the second-order desires to information and reflection.

Speaking for myself, I must say that I don't find this less flat-footed version of non-cognitivism very compelling. Why should we suppose that Importance maps onto the strength of the desired desire, and Certitude onto the strength of the second-order desire itself, rather than vice versa? The assignment seems arbitrary, and, for that reason alone, difficult to believe. But there is another, and more striking, problem with the suggestion as well. For it is difficult to see how to square the proposed account of Certitude and Importance with the observation that a subject who is less certain about the value of autonomy and more certain about the value of pleasure may none the less be rationally required to desire to be autonomous more than she desires to experience pleasure because of her assignments of relative desirability.

In order to see why, consider a subject who has a strong desire that she has a weak desire that she experiences pleasure, and a weak desire that she has a strong desire that she be autonomous. According to the proposal under consideration, this is supposed to amount to her having a certain level of confidence that experiencing pleasure is desirable to a certain degree and a lesser level of confidence that being autonomous is desirable to a greater degree. But whereas, intuitively, it should be possible for the relativities in the levels of confidence and desirability to be such that the subject is rationally required to have a stronger first-order desire that she be autonomous and a less strong first-order desire that she experience pleasure, there doesn't seem to be any way for the fact that her desired desire to be autonomous is strong, as compared with her desired desire that she experience pleasure, to have any effect whatsoever on what it is rational for such a subject to first-order desire more. The simple fact is that she wants more strongly to have a weak desire to experience pleasure, which seems to entail that, in cases of conflicts between values, greater confidence will always determine what it is rational for a subject to want most.

Now, of course, since I have only considered two versions of non-cognitivism it would doubtless be premature to conclude that non-cognitivists are unable to make room for Certitude, Importance, and Robustness as features of evaluative judgements. But, assuming for the moment that that is right, and I must say that that is my suspicion, note that it follows not just that non-cognitivism is therefore unable to make room for all of the features of evaluative judgements that commonsense tells us such judgements have in so far as they are belief-like, but that it also follows that non-cognitivism is unable to give an adequate account of the way in which an agent's values explain her actions. For, as we saw earlier, and as we just saw, commonsense tells us that the three features play a crucial role in our understanding of the explanatory connection that obtains between an agent's values and her actions. When it comes to the explanation of action, less confidence that something is more desirable may well trump greater confidence that something is less desirable, and greater confidence that something is less desirable may well trump lesser confidence that something is more desirable. It therefore follows that non-cognitivism is unable to accommodate either the belief-like or the desire-like features of evaluative judgements.

CONCLUSION

As I said at the outset, evaluative judgements have a decidedly Janus-faced character, and this Janus-faced character sets the agenda for much contemporary meta-ethics. Cognitivists take it as read that they can accommodate the belief-like features of evaluative judgement, and then confront the problem of trying to account for the potential to lead all the way to action that beliefs with that sort of content must have. Non-cognitivists take it as read that they can accommodate the desire-like features of evaluative judgement, and then face the problem of trying to account for the potential for justification and rational defence that such motivational antecedents must therefore have.

The argument of this paper has been, in essence, that this tendency that cognitivists and non-cognitivists alike have to treat the belief-like and the desire-like features of evaluation in isolation from each other is a mistake. The belief-like features of evaluative judgement are complex – in so far as they are belief-like – evaluative judgements have three distinct

357

features: Certitude, Importance, and Robustness – and these complexities play a crucial role when it comes to understanding the way in which an agent's values explain her actions. The crucial question for cognitivists and non-cognitivists is whether they can accommodate these complexities.

My argument has been that at least one form of cognitivism, the form that I myself prefer, can accommodate the complexities. It therefore succeeds in giving a plausible account of both the belief-like and the desire-like features of evaluative judgement. Moreover I have also offered some reasons for supposing that non-cognitivism is not so well placed to accommodate these complexities. If I am right then, contrary to popular belief, non-cognitivism is unable to accommodate either the belief-like or the desire-like features of evaluative judgement. I leave it for the non-cognitivists themselves to tell us why this is wrong.

REFERENCES

Blackburn, Simon 1998: *Ruling Passions*. Oxford: Clarendon Press.
Brink, David O. 1989: *Moral Realism and the Foundations of Ethics*. New York: Cambridge University Press.
Gibbard, Allan 1990: *Wise Choices, Apt Feelings*. Oxford: Clarendon Press.
Humberstone, Lloyd 1987: "Wanting as Believing," *Canadian Journal of Philosophy*, 17(1): 49–62.
Scanlon, Thomas 1998: *What We Owe to Each Other*. Cambridge, MA: Harvard University Press.
Smith, Michael 1994: *The Moral Problem*. Oxford: Blackwell.
Smith, Michael 1995: "Internal Reasons," *Philosophy and Phenomenological Research*, 55(1): 109–31.
Williams, Bernard 1980: "Internal and External Reasons," reprinted in his *Moral Luck*. Cambridge: Cambridge University Press. 1981.

NOTE

This paper was first presented at the British Society for Ethical Theory annual conference held in Glasgow, July 2001. Subsequent versions were presented at Stanford University; at the Research School of Social Sciences, Australian National University; at Flinders University; and at Monash University. Thanks to all of those who participated in the lively discussions that took place at these sessions. I would also like to thank the many people who listened to the basic idea behind this paper over several years. I am especially grateful to Simon Blackburn, Michael Bratman, Mark Greenberg, Lloyd Humberstone, Frank Jackson, James Lenman, Philip Pettit, Michael Ridge, and Jack Smart.

17

Ethics and the A Priori:
A Modern Parable

It was a pleasant, sunny day, the sort of day Cog and Noncog always hoped for when they arranged to have lunch. They settled themselves down to eat, Cog with his regular choice, soup and salad, and Noncog with his standard order of fish and chips.

Noncog was unusually quiet. He had had another terrible morning wondering how to explain the role of the sentence "It is desirable to eat snails" in the conditional statement "If it is desirable to eat snails then Cog will know all about it." His official view, which he had defended in print for some time, was that when people sincerely utter evaluative sentences they do not express their beliefs, but rather express their desires. Noncog had thus argued that, contrary to appearances, sentences like "It is desirable to eat snails" are not really truth-assessable, and that this particular sentence therefore means pretty much the same as "Hooray for eating snails!" He had to admit, though, that such sentences certainly *appeared* truth-assessable, which is why he had been worrying about its appearance in the conditional statement. How could the sentence figure in the antecedent of the conditional if it wasn't truth-assessable? Interpreting the conditional statement quite literally he was obliged to see it as meaning "If hooray for eating snails then Cog will know all about it," which didn't seem to make any sense at all. He had therefore spent the entire week trying to come up with some alternative interpretation of what the statement means, an interpretation that does make sense. Perhaps in being disposed sincerely to utter the conditional statement he was disposed to express some other desire – but if so, which? If another interpretation of the statement was to be had, apart from the nonsensical one, it had most certainly eluded him so far that week. The whole experience had been rather depressing.

Cog, who knew all about his friend's troubles that week, was keen to get him to forget about all that, at least for the time being. He looked forward to their philosophical discussions over lunch, and, for reasons of his own, he was determined that this day would be no exception.

"We at least agree about this much," said Cog, trying to sound as engaging as he could. "The world contains only natural properties and relations, properties and relations that are the subject matter of the natural or the social sciences."

"Here here," said Noncog, picking up his glass of water, and offering a toast, "I'll drink to that." He wondered whether Cog was going to tell him all about his latest views on physicalistic reductionism.

"So what you are trying to figure out, and what I should try to figure out too," Cog continued, "is what the role of evaluative discourse is in this naturalistic world."

"So far so good," Noncog said, his interest sparked. He had heard Cog talk about evaluative discourse once before, but it was very amateurish. He had excused him at the time, as he knew that Cog was a newcomer to the subject. But he thought that perhaps the time had come for him to be enlightened a little. Teaching Cog the basics of meta-ethics would take his mind off the more technical problems he had been thinking about all morning. "I fear that our agreement will end here, however," he added.

"Really?" Cog replied, somewhat taken aback. "I thought we'd agree about much more. Why do you say that that's all we'll agree about?"

"Well," said Noncog, "from what I've heard you say before I assume you think that when we engage in evaluative discourse we express our beliefs about the ways things are in evaluative respects. Is that right?"

"Right," agreed Cog.

"So by your own lights and mine this means that for evaluative discourse to be at all kosher – that is, for any of our beliefs to be true – the beliefs in question would have to be beliefs about the ways things are naturalistically. So, tell me: do you think that some of our evaluative beliefs are true?"

"Yes I do," said Cog, "and I know that this means I have to defend the claim that evaluative beliefs are one and all beliefs about the ways things are naturalistically. But I have thought about it and I am quite prepared to do that."

"Yes I suppose you are Cog," Noncog replied patiently. "But the idea that evaluative beliefs are beliefs about the ways things are in some naturalistic respect is quite incredible. Let me tell you: after years and years of hearing people attempt to provide such naturalistic equivalents the fact is that they always face a dilemma. Either they say something manifestly false about the content of evaluative claims, or they make a possibly true first-order evaluative judgement. What they never provide is what they claim to provide: a naturalistic equivalent of an evaluative claim."

Cog looked puzzled. "I'm not sure I understand what you mean."

"You'll see," said Noncog, just a little patronisingly. "Go ahead and tell me which naturalistic belief you think I express when I say of a particular act that it is desirable. It will be plain enough which horn of the dilemma you're impaled on."

"Well, as it happens," Cog began boldly, sounding every bit as naive as Noncog thought he was, "as I say, I've thought about it for a bit, and I'm inclined to think that you are expressing your belief that that act maximises happiness and minimises suffering."

"What you mean is you think that what makes a judgement about the rightness of an act true is whether or not that act maximises happiness and minimises suffering. But that's evidently a first-order evaluative claim, Cog, because . . ."

Cog interrupted him immediately. "No. I mean just what I said."

"You mean you really think that a belief to the effect that an act is desirable is a belief to the effect that that act maximises happiness?" Noncog asked, incredulous.

"Yes, that's my hunch."

"You think that these are one and the same belief? You think you can demonstrate via some sort of conceptual or a priori argument that what I literally mean when I say an act is desirable is that it maximizes happiness and minimises suffering?"

Cog was determined to stand his ground. "Again, yes I do."

Noncog scoffed. "This is ridiculous. You are telling me that all of those deontologists who say 'That act is desirable, but it doesn't maximise happiness and minimise suffering' are contradicting themselves? Surely they say that without contradiction. If they are making a mistake at all theirs is a first-order evaluative mistake, not a mere verbal blunder!"

But this was one of the responses Cog had thought about, and he was having nothing of it. "I am not sure why you think it is so obvious that they aren't contradicting themselves. After all, analytic truths are rarely obvious. Even the standard examples like 'bachelor' means 'unmarried male' aren't obviously true. Indeed, not only is this particular example not obviously true, it isn't true at all! Male newborn babies aren't bachelors, because they aren't of a marriageable age. So at the least we would need to say that 'bachelor' means 'unmarried male of a marriageable age.' But even this claim isn't yet obviously true either because it isn't at all obvious what it means. Whether someone is of a marriageable age depends, after all, on whether they are of the minimal age for people to marry, and this is a normative matter. The norms may be moral or legal. But which are they? Or is the term 'bachelor' ambiguous? In order to make the meaning or meanings of 'bachelor' plain we would need to find out. Moreover, whether the norms are moral or legal, they may vary from one society to another. So when we say of someone that he is a bachelor, which society's norms do we have in mind? Are they the norms of the society that the person belongs to? Or are they the norms of the society of the person who is uttering the sentence? Or are they norms which vary from context of utterance to context of utterance, depending on conversational cues? Again, in order to make the meaning or meanings of 'bachelor' plain we would need to find out. And how do we find out? We need to think about all of the different ways in which it is appropriate to use the term 'bachelor.' We need to think hard about what being a bachelor implies, and what implies that someone is a bachelor. There may be nothing in the least obvious about any of that. But, if you know the meaning of 'bachelor,' it is all a priori accessible. My suggestion in the case of desirability is just the same. To find out what it means to say that something is desirable you need to think hard about what being desirable implies, and what implies that something is desirable: indeed, you need to think about all the different ways in which it is appropriate to use the term 'desirable.' And when you do, though there will be nothing obvious about it, my hunch is that you will see that saying of an act that it is desirable simply amounts to saying that it maximises happiness and minimises suffering."

Cog sat back, evidently pleased with the look of surprise that had come over Noncog's face as he had been talking. He knew that in Noncog's view he was naive when it came to philosophising about evaluative discourse, but he had given the issues some thought, and he had come to lunch this day ready to do battle.

"All right, all right," conceded Noncog. "What you've said makes a lot of sense. I'll give you that it is possible – barely possible, mind you, but still possible – that it is a contradiction to say that an act maximises happiness and minimises suffering but isn't desirable, and that in order to find out whether it is or it isn't we need to think hard about all the different ways in which it is appropriate to use the term 'desirable.' But here's where I think you're on shaky ground. It is precisely because of what evaluative judgements imply that I find the idea that an evaluative judgement is the expression of a belief about the way things are naturalistically so utterly implausible. Indeed, it is precisely because of what evaluative judgements imply that I am inclined to deny that there are any evaluative beliefs at all."

"I see!" said Cog. "Now that is a much more interesting objection. It doesn't depend on silly views about how an a priori accessible truth is supposed to be obvious. So, tell me, what exactly do evaluative judgements imply that makes you think that there are no evaluative beliefs?"

"Well," began Noncog, "when someone makes an evaluative judgement this implies that they are disposed to act accordingly, at least other things being equal. To fail to appreciate this is to fail to understand that what is being made is an *evaluative* judgement. But if an evaluative judgement were the expression of a belief then there couldn't be any such necessary connection between evaluative judgement and motivation. Belief and desire are, after all, distinct existences, which means that they *are not* necessarily connected. If, on the other hand, evaluative judgements are not expression of beliefs, but are rather expressions of our motivational states themselves – that is, our desires – then there is no problem at all in seeing why, in order to understand what an evaluative judgement is, we need to see that evaluative judgements are necessarily connected with motivations. For while it is true that belief and desire are distinct existences the bottom line is that the psychological state expressed by an evaluative judgement is one and the same as the motivational state with which the judgement is necessarily connected. What is impossible for cognitivists to accommodate is therefore easy for non-cognitivists to accommodate. The conclusion I draw is that we should give up the idea that evaluative judgements are expressions of beliefs. We should hold that they express our motivational states instead: that is, our desires."

"What an elegant argument!" said Cog, genuinely impressed. "I honestly hadn't thought of that!" Noncog raised his eyebrows at his friend's frank admission of ignorance. It was the best-known argument for non-cognitivism in the literature, but not only had Cog not been convinced by it, he hadn't even heard of it! Cog apparently didn't notice the raised eyebrow, however, as he continued on, repeating Noncog's point for his own benefit. "There does appear to be a conceptually necessary connection between evaluative judgement and motivation, and that does seem to be inconsistent with my suggestion that an evaluative belief is simply a belief about the maximisation of happiness and the minimisation of suffering."

"Too right it appears inconsistent!" continued Noncog, annoyed. "There is no necessary connection at all between someone's believing an act to have the property of maximising happiness and minimising suffering and that person's being motivated to maximise happiness and minimise suffering. Someone could have the belief but lack the desire altogether, or even have the belief and have an aversion to maximising happiness and minimising suffering. In fact, people have just these combinations of psychological states all the time. Remember again the deontologists!"

"I take your point, Noncog! I take your point!" said Cog, trying to calm what he perceived as his friend's enthusiasm. "Remember it was me who said that it may not be obvious what we mean by the words we use. My hunch was wrong, I admit it. So let me rethink my suggestion a little. . . . Yes, now I see what I should have said. I should have said that for an act to be desirable is for it to have the property of being an act that we really desire ourselves to perform. What misled me, I think, is that the only acts that have this feature, as it happens, are those that maximise happiness and minimise suffering. That's the act that it seems to me we really desire ourselves to perform. So let's suppose from here on that I say that that's my official suggestion: when you say that an act is desirable you are expressing your belief that the act has the property of being an act we really desire ourselves to perform. Surely you'll agree that, at the very least, there is a necessary connection of sorts between my believing an act to be of a kind such that we really desire ourselves to perform acts of that kind, and my being motivated to perform acts of that kind. But the property of being an act that we really desire ourselves to perform is a perfectly naturalistic feature. What's wrong with this?"

Noncog rolled his eyes. "Can't you see for yourself? For one thing, though there is a necessary connection of sorts, it is a necessary connection of entirely the *wrong* sort. I didn't say that there is a necessary connection between *true* evaluative judgements and motivation. The necessary connection that exists holds whether the evaluative judgement is true or false. But what you've just said entails at best that there is a necessary connection between true evaluative judgements and motivation. If I falsely believe that we really desire ourselves to perform some act – if, say I don't really desire myself to perform it – then I am hardly going to be motivated to perform it, am I!? More tellingly though, it simply isn't true that desirable acts are those that we really desire ourselves to perform. Sometimes acts are desirable and yet we really *don't* desire ourselves to perform them, and other times we really do desire ourselves to perform acts that are not desirable. Remember once again the differences between the deontologists and the utilitarians. So the analysis is just obviously hopeless as an analysis."

"I take both your points, especially the last one," admitted Cog. "So let me rethink the analysis again. I need to spell out what I mean when I say that an act is one that we really desire ourselves to perform. What I have in mind is that the acts that we really desire ourselves to perform are those that we would desire ourselves to perform if we were to think things through carefully. As we think things through carefully we will acquire information and thereby notice various internal tensions in our desiderative profiles. We will get rid of certain old desires and acquire new desires in the attempt to come up with a more informed and coherent set of desires, a set on which we could all converge. That's what I meant when I talked of the acts that we really desire ourselves to perform. Wouldn't an analysis along these lines accommodate both the points you've just made? After all, if I believe that we would desire ourselves to perform an act of a certain kind if we had thought things through carefully, so coming up with a more informed and coherent set of desires, then, whether my belief is true or false, there would certainly be some internal psychological pressure on me to desire to perform that act. For suppose I retain the belief that an act is one that we would desire ourselves to perform if we had thought things through carefully, and yet I don't desire to perform it. My overall psychology would then be in a state of disequilibrium or incoherence. So here is a necessary connection we can posit: whenever I believe that we would desire ourselves to perform an act of a certain kind if we had thought things through carefully, so coming up with a more informed and coherent set of desires, provided my overall psychology isn't in a state of disequilibrium or incoherence, I am motivated to perform that act. That looks like a necessary connection between a belief, whether it be true or false, and a motivation, of just the kind that you are after. So haven't I done the job you said was impossible? Haven't I specified the content of an evaluative belief entirely in naturalistic terms, and haven't I explained why there is a necessary connection of the sort you believe there to be between someone's having that belief and their being motivated?"

Noncog, who had been trying to look like he was listening attentively but who in fact had decided halfway through that the suggestion wasn't going anywhere shook his head. "I can see what you're trying to get at," he said. "But while what you have suggested is an improvement, I don't think that either part is right. Let's start with the analysis. Your suggestion is that desirable acts are all and only those that we would desire ourselves to perform if we had thought things through carefully, so coming up with a more informed and coherent set of desires. But I can remember lots of occasions on which I formed desires to do things after thinking things through carefully and yet where what I ended up desiring to do wasn't desirable – something I soon subsequently realised, often with just a little more thought! So I think that the analysis is still hopeless, as an analysis. And for this reason I think the other part of what you said is incorrect too. Because the belief is about something utterly without normative significance, there is no disequilibrium or incoherence involved in believing that an act is one that we would desire ourselves to perform if we had thought things through carefully, so coming up with a more informed and coherent set of desires, and yet not desiring to perform that act. What you have described is more like a situation in which I firmly believe that we would all desire ourselves to perform a particular act if we were to read a novel, or watch a movie, or talk with a friend, and yet do not desire to perform that act. Just as in the latter cases there is no disequilibrium or incoherence involved, so in the former case there is no disequilibrium or incoherence involved either."

"I do see the problem," agreed Cog, earnest as ever. "But what if I suggested that desirable acts are all and only those that we would desire ourselves to perform if we had thought things through carefully, so coming up with a more informed and coherent set of desires, for as long as it takes to settle on a stable set of desires? Wouldn't that meet both your points?"

"I don't think so," said Noncog, shaking his head again. "A belief with that content isn't about something with any normative significance either. I know from my own case that certain desires that are a very, very stable feature of my psychology, and which cohere well enough with each other, are simply desires that I have been left with from a time, long, long ago when I used to reflect on my desires and change them in a manner like the one you describe all the time. The reason why they are a stable feature of my psychology is that I became so bored with the constant pattern of reflection and desire-revision, reflection and desire-revision, reflection and desire-revision that I couldn't bring myself to reflect any more. I am therefore quite sure that I would change my desires if I reflected some more. But so what? I would simply acquire desires that I would in turn get rid of if I was to reflect even more. What a bore!"

Cog didn't much appreciate the overtly dismissive tone of that last remark. But he let it pass. "It seems to me that you've misunderstood my suggestion," he said. "When I said that desirable acts are all and only those that we would desire ourselves to perform if we had thought things through carefully, so coming up with a more informed and coherent set of desires, for as long as it takes to settle on a stable set of desires, I meant the desires in question to be stable because they were immune to change via

366

more reflection. In other words, I meant them to be part of a *maximally* informed and coherent set of desires. All you have pointed out is that we might come to have a stable set of desires for a completely different reason – because we find rational reflection boring, say – which is true but irrelevant."

"A *maximally* informed and coherent set of desires! These desires that are part of the maximally informed and coherent set: they are, I take it, just those desires, whatever they happen to be, that a person who is good will have. Isn't that right? Isn't that secretly what's been guiding you all along, especially when you spoke of us all converging on the same desires? So now we've moved right on over to the other horn of the dilemma, just as I said we would at the outset. You've made a first-order moral claim: people who are good will all have the same desires. Maybe this is true, I really don't know. But whether it is true or not, note that it most certainly isn't an analysis of what it is for something to be desirable. It presupposes an understanding of what it is for someone to be good."

"Hang on," retorted Cog, "that all seems a bit swift! As it happens, I do think I could explain what a 'maximally' coherent set of desires is in purely naturalistic terms. But it also seems to me that we needn't bother getting in to all of that. Maybe I'm wrong. Maybe I'm not smart enough to think of the precise form of words required to state the naturalistic analysis I'm convinced that there is in a way that makes it immune from your counter-examples. But even if you are right about that surely you have to agree that that tells us more about the relative powers of you and me than it tells us about the possibility of a naturalistic analysis. What does seem especially significant, to me at any rate, is the *progress* we have already made. It seems to me that that progress itself gives us inductive grounds for *optimism* about the analytic project I said I could carry off. I admit that I haven't yet come up with a naturalistic analysis of desirability which secures the relevant necessary connection with motivation, and I admit that I mightn't be up to the task of coming up with an analysis that is immune to counter-example from you either. But surely you must admit that I have given you good reason to think that there is such an analysis, and that the analysis will be along the lines already sketched. What I have said is intrinsically plausible, after all; and, besides, every time you come up with a counter-example, I come up with an amendment which makes the analysis immune to it, so making the general form of the analysis seem even more plausible."

Noncog guffawed. "This is incredible! I was about to suggest that without going any further surely you would have to agree with me that the *lack* of progress we have already made gives us inductive grounds for *pessimism* about the analytic project you said you could carry off. For not only have you not yet come up with a naturalistic analysis of desirability which secures the relevant necessary connection with motivation, you must surely admit that I have given you good reason to think that no such analysis is possible: every time you come up with an amendment to your analysis in light of a counter-example I produce, I come up with yet another counter-example! You don't ever make the bump in the carpet go away, you just move it around."

Cog stopped dead in his tracks. "I hadn't actually thought about it that way," he admitted.

Noncog smirked. Cog looked across at him and saw the smirk. His disdain registered immediately, and Noncog pulled himself together. He liked Cog well enough. He knew it was wrong of him to think Cog ridiculous for failing immediately to grasp a point that was so familiar to someone like himself, who had been thinking about these issues for years.

"The fact is, Cog," said Noncog in an attempt to bring the whole issue to a close, "you've simply demonstrated how right I was when I posed the original dilemma at the outset. All you have succeeded in doing is coming up with false claims about naturalistic equivalents, or else you have gone over to making a first-order moral claim."

"I really hadn't thought about it in the way you've just suggested," said Cog. "I'll have to think about it. But maybe you are right." Then, after some further thought, he added, "But look Noncog, can we change tack a little? While we were talking I kept on wondering how you yourself think that your own boo!–hooray! theory of evaluations enables you to capture the necessary connection between evaluative judgement and motivation. Would you just remind me?"

Noncog felt himself in the ascendancy. He leaned forward. "Unlike you I don't have any problem at all explaining the necessary connection between evaluative judgement and motivation because I say that when we call something desirable we are *expressing* our desires, not saying that we have them. It is exactly as if we said 'Hooray!' for the thing in question. There is thus no *connection* with motivation for me to explain. Evaluative judgements are a *direct* expression of our motivational states, not expressions of beliefs which then have to stand in some normative relation with them."

"I see the general idea," said Cog, "and I can see why you think this is an explanation in a broadly naturalistic spirit. Desires are certainly naturalistic states. But just as you haven't been allowing me to get away with saying that an evaluative belief is a belief with some naturalistic content or other, whichever content it is which is such that a belief with that naturalistic content has the right sort of connection with a motivational state – and quite rightly so, I might add! – I wonder whether you would mind saying a little more to convince me that you really have told me, in naturalistic terms, precisely *which* desires you think an evaluative judgement is an expression of. Earlier, when you explained what the necessary connection between evaluative judgement and motivation amounts to, you said that if someone makes an evaluative judgement then this implies that they are disposed to act accordingly, *at least other things being equal.* I assume that the 'other things being equal' clause is in there for a reason. So tell me why it is there, and convince me that your suggestion that evaluative judgements express desires really does capture the necessary connection, so understood."

"Well," said Noncog, "for one thing, when someone judges it desirable to do something, they do not reveal any failure to understand that they are making an evaluative judgement if they do not have an *overriding* desire to act in that way. All that is required is that they have *some* desire to act in that way, a desire that may be overridden by another, stronger, desire to do something else instead. This is consistent with my suggestion because I have simply said that an evaluative judgement expresses a desire, not that it expresses an overriding desire. That's one thing the 'other things being equal' clause captures."

"I see," nodded Cog, "but surely that is not all that the 'other things being equal' clause is supposed to capture. Remember I suggested earlier on that what explains the necessary connection between evaluative belief and motivation is the fact that it is a conceptual truth, given the way I defined the content of an evaluative belief, that those whose overall psychology is in a state of equilibrium or coherence will desire to do what they believe they would desire themselves to do if they had a maximally informed and coherent set of desires. When I said that I was struck by how commonsensical the idea really was. After all, it is a commonplace that when (say) someone suffers from a deep depression then they may have no desire at all to do what they judge to be desirable. They see all the good to be done, but have no inclination to pursue it. It would be quite incredible to suppose that they temporarily fail to understand that they are making an evaluative judgement when they judge something desirable or worth achieving! Indeed, one of the more depressing aspects of depression is the fact that the value of the things that leave you unmoved is especially vivid to you. (I speak from experience!) Now, as I see things, this is best explained by a lack of overall coherence or equilibrium in the depressive's psychology. Clearly you don't like my explanation. But, however you want to explain it, I assume that you will at least agree with me that something along these lines is required to explain the depressive's ability to make moral judgements while remaining unmoved, and I assume further you will want to explain it by appealing to the idea of other things not being equal. Someone who makes an evaluative judgement has some motivation, though not necessarily an overriding motivation, at least absent the effects of depression and the like."

Noncog began to get a little irritated. "Yes, of course. I meant the 'other things being equal' clause to capture cases of depression, and weakness of will, and all sorts of other similar psychological maladies as well. I just didn't think to mention them because I took it for granted that we would take cases like that as read. The idea is that someone who makes an evaluative judgement is motivated accordingly, absent the effects of depression, weakness of will, and the like: that is, absent any of the causes of practical irrationality. I suppose I should have said this all along."

Now it was Cog's turn to lean forward. "But surely you can see that this means that your official story about what an evaluative judgement is is in error. Your official story is that the psychological state expressed by an evaluative judgement is one and the same as the motivational state with which the judgement is said to be necessarily connected. Yet this cannot be true if someone who *lacks* that motivational state – someone who is depressed, and so has no desire at all to do what he judges desirable – can still make an evaluative judgement. For such a person has no motivational state to express."

Noncog blushed. He hadn't seen this one coming, but the point was so obvious now it had been made that he was embarrassed at the way in which it so decisively undermined his official statement of his position.

"I take your point," Noncog said, trying to mask his embarrassment at having been undone by Cog, a complete newcomer to the field. Cog continued on in the same manner.

"So it turns out that you too are obliged to explain the *connection* between the psychological state that you think we are in when we are disposed to make an evaluative judgement and a motivational state. Evaluative judgements *are not* direct expressions of our motivational states," he said, poking the table with his index finger as he said "are not" just for added emphasis, "but rather are expressions of states which have to stand in some normative relation with our motivational states."

"I guess that sounds right," Noncog agreed reluctantly.

"Okay. So now let me tell you my hunch, Noncog," said Cog with an air of supremacy. "My hunch is that you yourself are going to be as vulnerable as you think I am to the dilemma you posed at the outset. For you now have to tell me what naturalistic state it is that we are in when we are disposed to make an evaluative judgement. But when you attempt to do so either you will succeed in characterising a state in purely naturalistic terms, but (by your standards) it will be incredible to suppose that a state so characterised is a state such that, whenever we are in it we are disposed to make an evaluative judgement, or else you will only ever succeed in making (what by your standards is) a first-order evaluative judgement. That's my hunch."

"I don't see how that's supposed to follow from what we've just said," Noncog protested nervously.

"Well let me explain it to you," said Cog. "You've just conceded that to say that people are in a psychological state that disposes them to make an evaluative judgement is to make a claim that entails a *normative* claim. Those who are in such a state *should* be motivated accordingly, in the sense that they must be suffering from some sort of practical irrationality if they aren't, and so liable to the relevant sort of normative criticism that that form of practical irrationality enjoins. By your own lights, then, I just don't see how you are going to be able to analyse in purely naturalistic terms what that psychological state is. For that would be, in effect, to provide a naturalistic analysis of the relevant normative claim, and so a naturalistic analysis of just the sort that I said I could provide and whose impossibility you take yourself to have demonstrated." Cog sat back in his chair, evidently pleased with himself. "So. Just go ahead and tell me which naturalistic state you think I am in when I am disposed to make an evaluative judgement. It will be plain enough which horn of the dilemma you're impaled on."

"Okay," Noncog replied, unconvinced by what Cog had just said, but desperately trying to work out what would be going on a few moves further on in their argument, just to make sure that he was right not to be convinced. "Just give me a chance to rethink my suggestion a little . . . Yes . . . now I see what I should have said. I should have said that when someone judges an act desirable they express their desire that they have a desire to act in that way. And I should have added that when we imagine away the effects of weakness of will, depression, and the like, we are to imagine someone who first-order desires what they desire themselves to desire. If I'm not mistaken, this accommodates your point.

371

After all, I can have a desire to have a desire to act in a certain way without desiring to act in that way. This is what the depressive can still have. What his depression saps is his first-order desire. So when we imagine away the effects of weakness of will, depression, and the like, we imagine him desiring what he desires himself to desire. This is why it is a necessary truth that someone who makes an evaluative judgement is motivated, absent the effects of depression, weakness of will, and the like."

"Good try," said Cog, patronisingly. "I can see what you're trying to get at, but while what you have said is an improvement, I don't think that either part of what you have said is right. Let's start with the new analysis of what it is to make an evaluative judgement. Your idea is that when someone judges something desirable they express their desire that they desire that they act in that way. But what's so special about our second-order desires that makes them what gets expressed in an evaluative judgement? After all, it is quite possible to desire that I have a desire to act in a certain way and yet to desire that I *not* desire to desire that I act in that way. So, in this case, why say that it is my *second*-order desire that gets expressed in an evaluative judgement, and not my contrary *third*-order desire? Or, for that matter, why not say that it is my *fourth*- or *fifth*-order desire, if I happen to have one? Your choice of the second-order is entirely arbitrary, as would be the choice of a third- or a fourth- or a fifth-order desire as well. They're all entirely arbitrary. A second-order desire isn't a desire to desire something that has any special normative significance, and neither is a third- or a fourth- or a fifth-order desire either. It therefore follows that the second part of what you say is implausible as well. For your suggestion that weakness of will is a matter of our first-order desires being contrary to our second-order desires is only as plausible as the idea that second-order desires are what get expressed in our evaluative judgements: that is, that they have some special normative significance. Without that idea in place, what you have offered is simply implausible as a story about the nature of weakness of will. There is no normative requirement that someone first-order desires what they second-order desire."

Noncog paused and thought for a moment. "What if I suggested that when we judge acting in a certain way desirable we are expressing our *highest* order desire that we act in that way. The highest level is not an arbitrary choice. Wouldn't that meet both your points?"

"I really don't think so," said Cog, "because as far as I can see our highest-order desires do not necessarily have any normative significance either. Indeed, quite the opposite is sometimes the case. I remember once sitting on a selection committee. A very good friend of mine had applied for the job. I thought long and hard about the merits of the various candidates, desperately wanting to come up with the conclusion that my friend was the best choice. But in the end I had to admit that someone else, Bloggs, was better. Though I decided that the desirable thing to do was to give the job to Bloggs, I desperately wanted to think otherwise! I wanted to judge it desirable to give the job to my friend. In this case, whatever order of desire you say I expressed in my judgement that the desirable thing to do was to give the job to Bloggs, you'll have to admit that I clearly had an even higher-order desire that I not have that desire. What this shows, I think, is that if an evaluative judgement expresses an n-order desire at all, then it must be at least possible for me to have a contrary n+1-order desire, and for that contrary n+1-order desire to be, by hypothesis, a desire for something without normative significance. Since that n+1-order desire could be the highest-order desire I have, it follows that an evaluative judgement can't be the expression of an agent's highest-order desire. Nor can it be the expression of a first-order desire either – that's what cases of depression show – and nor can it be the expression of any of the orders of desire in between, because they are all entirely arbitrary. The only conclusion to draw is surely that an evaluative judgement isn't the expression of any desire at all."

Noncog didn't much appreciate the dismissive tone of that last remark. But he let it pass. "It seems to me that you have misunderstood my suggestion," he said. "When I said that our evaluative judgements express our highest-order desires I meant that they express that order of desire with which we identify ourselves, or which we can stand behind with integrity. All you have pointed out is that if the relevant order of desire for an agent is n, then he might have an n+1-order desire with which he does not identify, or which he cannot stand behind with integrity, which is true but irrelevant."

"The order of desire with which we identify ourselves, or which we can stand behind with integrity! Now you've moved over to the other horn of the dilemma. You have evaluated the desires in question, not given me a naturalistic description of them."

"Hang on," retorted Noncog, "that all seems a bit swift! As it happens, I do think I could explain what it is to identify ourselves with an order of desire, or to stand behind it with integrity, in purely naturalistic terms. But it also seems to me that we needn't bother getting in to all of that. Maybe I'm wrong. Maybe I'm not smart enough to think of the precise form of words required to state the naturalistic analysis in a way that makes it im-mune from counter-example. Maybe you're right and if I went on trying to precisify my analysis you could go on putting up counter-examples forever. But even if you are right about that surely you have to agree that the progress we have already made gives us inductive grounds for optimism about the analytic project I said I could carry off. I admit that I haven't yet come up with a naturalistic analysis of the psychological state we are in when we judge something desirable which secures the relevant necessary connection with motivation, but surely you must admit that I have given you good reason to think that there is such an analysis, and that the analysis will be along the lines already sketched. What I have said is intrinsically plausible, after all; and, besides, every time you come up with a counter-example, I come up with an amendment which makes the analysis immune to it, so making an analysis of the general form I have been suggesting even more plausible."

"This is like déjà vu!" guffawed Cog. "I was about to ask you whether you wanted to stop going on as well, but I was going to cut the discussion short for exactly the opposite reason. I was going to say that without going any further you would surely have to agree with me that the lack of progress we have already made gives us inductive grounds for pessimism about the analytic project you said you could carry off. For not only have you not yet come up with a naturalistic analysis of the psychological state we are in when we are disposed to make an evaluative judgement which secures the relevant necessary connection with motivation, you must surely admit that I have given you good reason to think that no such analysis is possible: every time you come up with an amendment to your analysis in light of a counter-example I produce, I come up with yet another counter-example! As you yourself said just a few moments ago, "You don't ever make the bump in the carpet go away, you just . . .""

"You're begging the question!" yelled Noncog. "That's not the standard of analysis you wanted to apply when *you* were trying to give *your own* naturalistic analysis of what it is for something to be desirable earlier!!"

"No I'm not, you are!" Cog yelled back. "I'm just applying the standard of analysis that *you* wanted to apply in *your objections* when I was attempting to give that analysis!!"

And then, as if in a moment of pure unadorned insight, they both looked at each other, their frowns turned to smiles, and they said in unison, "Wait a minute!"

"Something has gone badly wrong here!" ventured Noncog. "Maybe we're both guilty of begging the question!" They sat back in their chairs.

"Let's retrace our steps," suggested Cog. "Earlier on I appealed to an inductive argument of exactly the kind you have just given. My claim

374

then was that, though I hadn't already done so, I'd at least given you good reason to think a naturalistic analysis of what it is for something to be desirable is available. Now you want to appeal to an inductive argument of just that kind in order to show that, though you haven't done so yet, you've at least given me good reason to think that a naturalistic analysis of the psychological state that we are in when we are disposed to judge something desirable is available. It seems, then, that our respective attempts at analysis are on all fours. Either we have both succeeded or we've both failed."

"That sounds right," said Noncog.

Cog paused for a moment, and then a smug look began to appear on his face. "So this leaves us with only two options," he said. "Either we should agree that a naturalistic analysis is possible in both cases, or we should agree that a naturalistic analysis is possible in neither case."

"Right," agreed Noncog.

"So let's begin with the idea that we have inductive reason to suppose that a naturalistic analysis of both evaluative content and the psychological state we are in when we are disposed to make an evaluative judgement is possible," suggested Cog. "What's the upshot then?"

"The upshot then, I guess," answered Noncog, "is that we are each able to say why there is a necessary connection between evaluative judgement and motivation. You tell a cognitivist story, a story according to which an evaluative judgement expresses a belief with a content characterisable in purely naturalistic terms (though you don't actually tell us what those naturalistic terms are), and then, given this analysis, it looks plausible that someone who has a belief with this content will have a corresponding desire, at least absent a certain sort of incoherence or disequilibrium in their overall psychology. I, on the other hand, tell a non-cognitivist story, a story according to which an evaluative judgement expresses a higher-order desire characterisable in purely naturalistic terms (though I don't actually tell you what those naturalistic terms are either), and then, given this analysis, it looks plausible that someone who has such a higher-order desire will have a corresponding first-order desire, provided they have first-order desires with which they identify."

"That would be very bad news for you, Noncog!" Cog replied, just a little too enthusiastically. "If a naturalistic analysis of the *content* of evaluative judgements is possible which can explain the connection between evaluative judgement, construed of as a belief, and a motivation, then why on earth would anyone want to bother with giving a non-cognitivist analysis of the psychological state that we are when we make an evaluative judgement, requiring as it does that they engage in the fruitless task of trying to explain the meaning of conditional statements like 'If it is desirable to do such-and-such, then so-and-so will know all about it'? As I understand it, your official story about the meaning of 'It is desirable to do such-and-such' suggests that the conditional statement means 'If hooray for doing such-and-such then so-and-so will know all about it' which makes absolutely no sense at all. But I'm yet to see you come up with any other interpretation of the conditional statement that does any better than this. What I want to know is why anyone would bother engaging in this task if they could opt for a cognitivist analysis of the content of evaluative beliefs instead, and so give the conditional statement its literal interpretation? Interpret it as meaning 'If such-and-such is something that we would desire ourselves to do if we had a maximally informed and coherent set of desires then so-and-so will know all about it' and our problems are over. Evaluative sentences *appear* truth-assessable because evaluative sentences *are* truth-assessable. I can see why you might have thought yourself forced to give such a non-cognitivist treatment of the meaning of conditionals with evaluative antecedents if you thought that only a non-cognitivist analysis of evaluative judgement could explain the necessary connection between evaluative judgement and motivation. But if, as we're supposing, that isn't the case, then I just don't see any reason to bother."

Noncog had started wincing at Cog's first mention of conditional statements like "If it is desirable to do such-and-such, then so-and-so will know all about it." In the heat of the argument he had forgotten all about the depressing week he had had, trying to come up with an account of what such statements could possibly mean. "Maybe so," Noncog agreed, "maybe so. But if neither of us grants that inductive grounds have been provided for thinking that a naturalistic analysis is possible then it seems to me that the shoe is most definitely on the other foot."

"What? I thought you thought that on the other horn of your original dilemma we both only ever succeed in making first-order evaluative claims," Cog retorted, eyebrows raised. "How do I come out looking worse than you if that's the case?"

"Well I've changed my mind about the other horn of the dilemma," Noncog snapped. "Let's say I agree with you that to say of people that they are in a psychological state that disposes them to make an evaluative judgement is to say something that entails a normative claim: they should be motivated accordingly, in the sense that they must be suffering from some sort of practical irrationality if they aren't, and so are liable to the relevant sort of normative criticism that that form of practical irrationality enjoins. When we say of them that they are in a psychological state that disposes them to make an evaluative judgement it thus follows that we additionally hold them to certain standards, and by my non-cognitivist lights what this means is that we express certain additional attitudes of desire and approval of our own towards their being motivated to do what they judge to be desirable. I admit that this forces me to agree that there will always be an expressive remainder in any attempt I make to say which desires get expressed when we make evaluative judgements. But this seems to be neither here nor there if my aim is not to provide a naturalistic analysis of the state that we are when we are disposed to make an evaluative judgement, but the more modest one of telling a naturalistic story about the nature of evaluative judgement. For one thing, it is quite clear that the story I have just told is still naturalistic. Every single evaluative judgement we make expresses a desire of some sort or other, it is just that in order to say which desires these are we have to express further desires. More importantly, though, it is abundantly clear why, given this story, evaluative judgement displays the necessary connection we both agree it displays with motivation. What I don't see, Cog, is how as a cognitivist and a naturalist you can say anything at all to explain the failure of a naturalistic analysis. What naturalistic story can you tell about the content of evaluative judgements? The only thing you can say, surely, is that if a naturalistic analysis of desirability is impossible, then desirability itself must be a further property *over and above* all of the natural properties there are. You would therefore be forced to reject the naturalistic commitments we both agreed to be non-negotiable at the outset. So if the upshot is that a naturalistic analysis of neither evaluative content nor the psychological state that we are in when we are disposed to make an evaluative judgement are possible then that is very bad news for you. For you will have to admit that there is really an extra spooky non-natural property of desirability! So much for your naturalism!!"

But Cog hadn't flinched. "I don't think so," he said calmly. "I've been inclined to rethink the other horn of the dilemma as well. Think of an analogy. There is a debate in the philosophy of mind as to whether mental states are just physical states. One strategy of argument, aimed at showing that they are just physical states, is to provide an analysis of mental states in purely physical terms: that is, to spell out what 'desire' and 'belief' mean in terms that don't mention any mental states at all, but which only mention physical states. If such an analysis is possible, then it is clear that mental states are just physical states. This is the project in which analytic functionalists like David Lewis are engaged. It is this sort of analysis that I have been trying to provide for evaluative terms: an analysis of evaluative terms in naturalistic terms. But, in the philosophy of mind case, there are other philosophers who deny that such a physicalistic analysis of mental state terms is possible. They think that any plausible account of what 'desire' and 'belief' mean would have to spell out the meaning of desire and belief in terms of other mental states. But – and here is the important part – they don't think that any anti-physicalist consequences follow from this. All that follows, they say, is something about mental *language*. The meaning of mental *language* cannot be captured in purely physical terms. But mental language is still just a language that we use to describe a purely physical world, and they demonstrate that this is so by showing how, on their view, the mental still supervenes on the physical, and by showing how, given this supervenience of the mental on the physical, they can identify mental states with physical states. They confirm their physicalistic credentials by arguing that the mental is still nothing over and above the physical, so undermining the claim that there are any extra spooky mental properties and relations floating over and above the physical properties and relations. The failure of analytic reduction, they tell us, is purely an artefact of mental language vis-à-vis physical language. It seems to me that as a cognitivist and a naturalist in the realm of the evaluative I might say something quite similar to this. Even if a naturalistic analysis of the meaning of 'desirable' in purely naturalistic terms isn't possible – that is, even if the analogue of David Lewis's project in the case of evaluative terms isn't successful – I might say that this simply shows something about evaluative language. So what if we can't spell out the meaning of an evaluative term like 'desirable' without introducing other evaluative terms? So long as I can show how I can hold that the evaluative supervenes on the natural none the less, and so long as I can demonstrate that evaluative features are just naturalistic features, I will have confirmed my naturalistic credentials. I will have shown that the evaluative is nothing over and above the natural. I will have shown that there are no extra spooky evaluative properties and relations floating over and above the natural properties and relations. The failure of reduction is purely an artefact of evaluative *language* vis-à-vis naturalistic *language*. The language is still all descriptive of a purely naturalistic world. And once I have explained that, I will be free to tell the story I have already told about the necessary connection between evaluative judgement and motivation. Those who believe that they would desire to act in a certain way in certain circumstances if they had a maximally informed and coherent set of desires will desire to have a corresponding desire provided their overall psychological state tends toward coherence and equilibrium."

"Okay, okay, so maybe it is a stand-off even if a naturalistic analysis of both evaluative content and of evaluative judgement is impossible," Noncog conceded begrudgingly.

"No, no, no, it's no mere *stand-off*!" Cog continued, getting haughtier by the minute. "For think again about what we've established. Either we can give a naturalistic analysis of the psychological state that we are in when we are disposed to make an evaluative judgement or we can't. As we saw a minute ago, if we can then, by that same standard of what it is to give an analysis, you'll have to agree that we can give a naturalistic analysis of the content of evaluative claims as well. We will then both have succeeded in giving a naturalistic explanation of the necessary connection between evaluative judgement and motivation. But once this is agreed it turns out that there is simply no reason to opt for your non-cognitivist explanation, obliging us as it does to engage in the fruitless task of coming up with a non-cognitivist explanation of why evaluative sentences appear to be truth-assessable. We can just opt for the cognitivist explanation instead, and explain that appearance in the most straightforward way possible: evaluative sentences appear truth-assessable because they are truth-assessable. If, on the other hand, we can't give a naturalistic analysis of the psychological state that we are in when we are disposed to make an evaluative judgement, then, even if you're right that you can still tell a non-reductive naturalistic story about the desires that we express, and in this way explain the necessary connection between evaluative judgement and motivation, you will have to agree that I can tell a similar non-reductive naturalistic story about the content of evaluative claims, and similarly explain the necessary connection between evaluative judgement and motivation. So it turns out that we will still have no reason to opt for your non-cognitivist explanation, obliging us as it does to go on to engage in the fruitless task of coming up with a non-cognitivist explanation of why evaluative sentences appear to be truth-assessable. It is thus no mere *stand-off*, Noncog. It turns out that we have a decisive reason to favour cognitivism over non-cognitivism, no matter which way we adjudicate the debate over the possibility of naturalistic analyses."

Cog kicked back on the rear two legs of his chair, throwing his napkin onto his plate as he did so. Noncog watched him rock back and forth, and then looked down at the remnants of his fish and chips. Cog's air of self-satisfaction was apparent. Noncog found it thoroughly annoying, so annoying that he wasn't able to think clearly about what he should say next. He began to pick at what was left on his plate with his fork. Though he was trying to look like he was intent on finding a last morsel to eat, the fact was that he was playing for time, something which was evident to Cog, who continued to rock back and forth on the rear two legs of his chair, waiting to see what his friend would come up with in response. Several seconds passed. Noncog ate the last mouthful of food he had managed to accumulate onto his fork. Then, in a moment of pure inspiration, he put his fork down and fixed his eyes on Cog, the perfect response having occurred to him.

"Booooooooo!!!"

NOTE

Conversations with Simon Blackburn, Frank Jackson and Philip Pettit at ANU in 1996 provided much of the stimulus for this paper. Though all of us are naturalists, we offer very different accounts of the evaluative. Jackson and Pettit are cognitivists. They offer a naturalistic analysis of the content of evaluative claims in their "Moral Functionalism and Moral Motivation," *Philosophical Quarterly*, XLV, (1995) pp. 20–40. Though I am a cognitivist, too, I argue that we cannot provide a naturalistic analysis of the content of evaluative claims of the kind Jackson and Pettit prefer. The argument appears in my *The Moral Problem* (Oxford: Blackwell, 1994) pp. 44–56. My own view is that we should give a non-reductive analysis of the content of evaluative claims (pp. 151–77, pp. 182–4). I argue that such an analysis is all we need in order to identify evaluative features with natural features (pp. 184–6). Simon Blackburn defends non-cognitivism in his *Spreading the Word* (Oxford: Oxford University Press, 1984), Chapter 6, and *Essays in Quasi-Realism* (Oxford: Oxford University Press, 1993). He explains why he doesn't like views of the general kind that Pettit and Jackson defend, and that I defend, in his "Circles, Finks, Smells and Biconditionals," in James Tomberlin, ed., *Philosophical Perspectives: Volume VII, Philosophy of Language* (Atascadero: Ridgeview Press, 1994) pp. 259–79. Whether or not he should accept a naturalistic analysis of what it is to make an evaluative judgement was the topic of some of our conversations. Though, as I said, those conversations provided much of the stimulus for writing this paper, the content of the paper and the content of those conversations bear very little resemblance to each other (thank goodness!). An early version of this paper was very profitably discussed with graduate students at The University of Michigan, Ann Arbor, when I visited as their James B. and Grace J. Nelson Philosopher-In-Residence. Later versions were presented at Davidson College, East Carolina University, Macquarie University, the University of Nebraska at Lincoln, the University of North Carolina at Chapel Hill, and Monash University. The paper was also presented as the Carswell Lecture at Wake Forest University. I would like to thank all those who participated in these very useful discussions. Comments received from Dorit Bar-On, Robyn Ferrell, Lori Gruen, Dale Jamieson, Robert Mabrito, Douglas Maclean, Peter Menzies, Thad Metz, Lee Overton, Geoffrey Sayre-McCord, Daniel Stoliar, and Mark van Roojen have been especially helpful.

Index

A priori truth 271, 294, 361–362
Action 2, 146–153, 155–176
    and desires 147
    "arational" 8, 158
    Explained by emotion 158–161
    Explained by evaluative beliefs 8, 163–170
    Explained by friendship 161–163
    Explained by justifying reasons 174–175
    Explained by self-control 170–174
    explanation of 7–8, 34–38
    For the sake of/out of explanations 161
    Humean explanation of 155–176
    motivated by belief 147–150
    "normative story" 147, 152–153
Advice model 3, 18–20, 46–47
    and deliberation 41
Agent-neutral principles 93, 305–312
Agent-relative principles 93, 305–312
Amoralists 284
Anti-rationalism 107, 139–140
Autonomy 109

"Belief-identity thesis" 275
Belief-set

minimally extended and maximally coherent 48–49
Beliefs 136
    and desires 53, 142, 144
    and evaluative judgement 298–300, 362
    as causes of action 34–38
    as motivating states 147–150
    capacities of believers 85–89
    evaluative 8, 36–38, 95, 97, 106, 109, 129, 141, 163–169, 170
    motivated 148
    norms governing 85–88
    "quasi-belief" 138
    responsibility for 85–92
"Besires" 144, 147
Blackburn, Simon 232, 243, 244, 260, 319
Block, Ned 125
"Blockhead" 125
Brink, David 259, 260, 261, 281, 342

Capacities 6, 120
    and recklessness 126–128, 133
    and responsibility 128
    "constituted" 122
    rational *see* Rational Capacities

Cognitivism 11, 343, 349–354, 358,
        375–376, 377–379
    and Certitude 352–353
    and Importance 352
    and Robustness 353
Coherence 4, 23, 53, 55, 96, 130, 203,
        267–273, 301–303
    and beliefs 267–269, 270–271, 302
    and desires 267–273, 303
    and evaluative judgements 302–303
    and full rationality 303–305
    and justification of belief 23
    and justification of desires 22–25
    and rationality 267–273
Colour 197–198, 199, 237–243
    and the explanatory test 237–239
    dispositional account of 101–102,
        240–242, 255
    phenomenology 246
Commensurability 308–310
Compatibilism 105
Competence (conceptual) 52
    and Incoherence Argument 52
Compulsion 5, 57, 70, 71, 100, 115, 131
Conceptual analysis 199–200, 338
Convergence (in desires of rational
        agents) 3, 34, 93, 112, 204, 205,
        264–265, 312–314
    and error theory 11, 205, 312
    and full rationality 27–28, 312–314
    and non-relative conception of
        reasons 27
    and preferences 31
    and relative conception of reasons 26
    "convergence requirement" 333–334
Copp, David 259, 261, 265
"Could" claims 7, 69, 115–128, 133
Counterfactuals 102
    and ability to do otherwise 90–92
    and capacities 124–126

Dancy, Jonathan 7, 8, 146–153, 174–175
Davidson, Donald 5, 57, 151, 156
Deliberation 21, 62–66
    and full rationality 63
    and imagination 22
    and systematically justifiable desires
        22–25
    connection to action 34–38, 63–65
Desirability 40, 129, 272, 274–279
Desire set (maximally informed,
        coherent and unified) 23, 25, 38,
        48, 54, 202, 205, 263, 267–273,
        350, 367
    and convergence 27
    parallel with belief-set 48–49
Desires 45, 136, 354
    and beliefs 137–139, 141, 142, 156
    and evaluative judgement 58, 363
    and phenomenological
        considerations 164
    and rational capacities 128–133
    Extrinsic 74–75
    Intrinsic 74–75
    Motivated 149
    Of fully rational counterpart 44–45,
        51–52
Determinism 7, 90, 92, 118
"Direction of fit" argument 136, 140
Dispositional analysis 240–242, 253–254
    and platitudes 242, 248
    and rationalism 253–254
Dispositional theory of value 9, 11–12,
        17, 40, 84, 93–98, 168, 317
    account of freedom and
        responsibility 84–104, 105–109,
        110
    and coercion 332
    and cognitivism 297, 298–305
    and explanation of action 168
    and internalism 331–334, 339

and realism 297, 312–314
and relativism 297, 305–312,
    316
Dispositions 101
    cognitive 68
    "constituted" 121
    "finkish" 120
"Divergence miracle" 90, 118
Dreier, James 322, 341

Egocentric Value 307–310
Emotions
    and explanation of action 158–161
    and practical irrationality 22
Error Theory 10, 181, 234, 254–255,
    312, 333
Evaluative belief 36–38, 95, 97, 106,
    109, 129, 141, 360
    and explanation of action 8, 163–170
    and motivation 141, 364
    as distinct from desires 166–169
Evaluative experience 246–248
Evaluative judgement 362–363
    and belief 362
    and cognitivism 343, 349–354
    and desire 363
    and higher-order desires 371–373
    and motivation 347–348
    and non-cognitivism 343, 354–357
    belief-like features 345, 346, 348,
        352–353
    connection with motivation
        304–305
    desire-like feature 346–347, 352
    expressing both desires and beliefs
        343–344
    truth of 225–229
Example model
    and evaluative beliefs 37
Explanatory test 237–239, 256

Expressivism 181–182, 188–190, 336
    and internalism 319–322
    and Open Question Argument
        194–196
Externalism 41, 201–202, 318, 319
    and evaluative beliefs 37

Fact-value gap
    and supervenience 222–224
First-order desires 105
Fischer, John 115
Frankfurt, Harry 6, 85, 105–109, 115,
    119, 261
Free Will 7, 117
Freedom
    ability to do otherwise 90–92, 101
    and dispositional theory of value
        97–104
    and responsibility 6–7
    problem cases 98–104
Full Rationality 38, 44–45, 47–48, 76,
    93, 140, 263–267
    and conflicting reasons 266–267
    and coherence 267–273, 295,
        303–305
    and convergence 27–28
    and desires 17
    and internalism requirement 18,
        20–34
    and true beliefs 265–266
    connection between deliberation
        and action 63–65

Geach, Peter 321
Generalism 221–222
Griffin, James 10, 208, 218–223, 226,
    229

Harman, Gilbert 237, 255, 326–331, 341
Hart, H.L.A. 282

Higher-order desire 106, 261, 371–373
Hookway, Christopher 243
Hume 34, 128, 139, 148, 153, 247
    explanation of action 146, 147, 149,
        155–176 (see also Humeanism)
        146, 147, 149, 155–176
    theory of motivation 7, 136–143,
        148
Humean conception of reasons 26
"Humeanism" 146, 147, 149
    and "acting out of friendship" 161
    and emotion 158–161
    and evaluative beliefs 163–170
    and justifying reasons 174–175
    and self-control 170–174
Hursthouse, Rosalind 8, 158

Imagination 22, 24–25
Incoherence Argument 4, 43–54
Indirection 49–51
Internal Reasons 3, 17
    de dicto 30
    de se 30, 31
Internalism 9, 12, 17–39, 165, 166, 190
    and expressivism 188–189, 319–322
    and realism 202–205
    and relativism 204–205
    Dispositional theory of value
        331–334, 339
    Moral Platonism 334–336
    Moral Relativism 326–331
    Speaker Relativism 322–326
    See also Practicality Requirement
Internalism Requirement 18–39, 94–95,
    97
    Advice model 18
    and evaluative beliefs 36–38
    Deliberation and action 34–38
    Example model 18–20
Irrationality 5, 45–46, 47–48, 50–51

Is/seems distinction 240, 241, 243,
    248
    and representational content of
        experience 246

Johnston, Mark 101, 120
Justification 202, 203
    and convergence 263
    of belief 23
    systematic justification of desires
        22–25

Kant 109, 139
Kennett, Jeanette 5, 113
Korsgaard, Christine 17, 19, 94

Lewis, David 6, 90, 118, 378
Libertarianism 118
Lobel, Arnold 81

Mackie, John 10, 234, 237, 249–251,
    298, 334
McDowell, John 10, 234–237, 238–242,
    335
Mele, Alfred 171
Meta-ethics 8–9, 343
Minimalism 184–188
Moore, G. E. 192, 193, 210
Moral facts 9
Moral perception 248
Moral problem
    first-order 292
    meta-ethics 260–262
Moral Problem, The 11, 43, 54, 259, 262,
    263, 276, 282, 291
Moral facts 9
    as primary qualities 10, 335
    as secondary qualities 10, 335
Moral knowledge 336
Moral Platonism 334–336

Moral Realism 9–11, 181–206
  a priori/a posteriori 196–199
  and convergence 312–314
  and minimalism 184–188
  and relativism 204–205
  and semantic ascent 182–184
  naturalistic *see* Naturalistic Moral
    Realism
  non-naturalistic 193–194
Moral relativism 326–331
  and coercion 328–329, 331
  "inner" versus "outer" judgements
    326, 329–330
Moral requirements
  and amoralists 284
  and etiquette 282–283
  as normative reasons 280–291,
    292
Moral skepticism 292
Moralists 284–285
Motivating reasons 1, 7–8, 136, 137,
    139, 140, 146–152, 153, 262
  as belief-desire pairs 146, 156
  as explaining actions 60
  connection to normative reasons
    59–62, 66, 262
  for action 146–153
  Humean account 60
Motivation
  and Certitude 348
  and Importance 347
  and Robustness 348

Natural properties 209–222
  and empirical regularities 210–213,
    215–217
  and particularity 214
  definition 209–222
Naturalism
  evaluative 213, 223–224

Naturalistic Moral Realism 190–192,
    193, 196–206
  a posteriori 196–199
  externalist 201–202
  internalist 202–205
Neutral value 307–310
Newcomb's Problem 54
Nihilism 181–182, 194
Non-cognitivism 12–13, 182, 260, 299,
    304–305, 343, 354–357, 363,
    375–376, 379
  and Certitude 354, 356
  and connection between values and
    actions 357
  and features of evaluative judgements
    354–357
  and Importance 354, 356
  and motivation 368
  and Robustness 354
Non-relative conception of reasons
    27–28, 30, 32–33, 40
  de dicto 30
  de se 30
Normative ethics 338
"Normative story" 8, 147
Normative reasons 2–4, 76, 262–263
  Advice model 3
  and compulsion 70
  and desires 64–65
  and dispositional theory of value 61
  and Incoherence Argument 43–47
  and orthonomy 77
  and recklessness 70
  and self-control 66
  as justifying actions 60
  as moral facts 280–291
  Competence with concept of
    277–279
  Connection to motivating reasons
    59–62, 66

Normative reasons (*cont.*)
Example model 3
Objectivity of 279–280
Practicality of beliefs about 273–279

Objectively prescriptive values 234, 235, 334
as primary qualities 236
as secondary qualities 236–237
Objectivity of values 234
and dispositional analysis 253–254
and explanatory test 237–239
and phenomenology of moral experience 243–248, 253
and rationalism 253–254
as primary qualities 236
as secondary qualities 236–237
as "there to be experienced" 236, 243–248
requirements of reason 249, 250–253
Open Question Argument 13, 192–200
and a posteriori equivalence 196–199
and conceptual analysis 199–200
and expressivism 194–196
Orthonomy 74, 77–78, 81, 109

Parfit, Derek 29
Particularism 221
Pettit, Philip 7, 54, 136–143
"Phenomenological thesis" 235
Phenomenology 243–248
of colour experience 246
of evaluative experience 246–248, 253
Platitudes
and dispositional analysis 242, 248–249
and evaluative concepts 247, 253

Platts, Mark 8, 163–165, 169
Possible worlds
and "could" claims 90–92, 118–120, 122–124
Practicality Requirement on Moral Judgement 43, 285
and moral virtue 286–289
see also Internalism
Pre-emptive Causation 100–103
Primary qualities 235–236, 335
Psychologism 147

Rational capacities 115, 116–128
and counterfactuals 123–124
and desires 128–133
and recklessness 126–128
Rationalistic conception of self 109
Rationalism 139–140
and disagreement 252
and error theory 254–255
and phenomenology of moral experience 251
and platitudes 251
Rationality 4, 76
full *see* Full Rationality
instrumental 73, 74–75, 81
Ravizza, Mark 115
Rawls, John 23, 302
Realism
and convergence 312–314
Reasons 139–140, 150, 151
agent-neutral 29
agent-relative 29
and convergence 27
and dispositional theory of value 93
and "normative story" 8
connection to fully rational desires 17
for action, 156
internal 3

justifying 174–175

motivating *see* Motivating Reasons

non-relative conception 27–28, 30, 32–33, 40

normative *see* Normative Reasons

of etiquette 282–283

psychological states as 8, 150–152

relative conception 25–33

Recklessness 56–57, 70, 114, 120, 126–128, 133

Reflection 107–108

Reflective Equilibrium 23, 230

Relative conception of reasons 25–33

Relativism 11, 204–205, 297, 300–301

and universalisability 306–311

Representation 243

and experience of colour 239

and experience of moral values 246–248

representational content of experience 243, 246

Responsibility 6–7

and capacities 128

and dispositional theory of value 97–98

for belief 84–110

problem cases 98–104

Rightness

and desires of fully rational agents 51–52

Sayre-McCord, Geoffrey 259, 261, 267

Schafer-Landau, Russ 4, 43–54 (incoherence argument)

Secondary qualities 235–237, 238–239, 335

as dispositions 238–239

phenomenology 239

Self-control 5–6, 59, 66–70, 73–83, 100, 103–104

and weakness of will 56–71

as disposition to have certain thoughts 80

as explanation of actions 170–174

as non-actional 6, 67–69, 79–81

capacity for 68

diachronic 78–79, 82

paradox of 66, 73, 171

synchronic 79–80, 81, 82

Self-effacement 41, 55

Speaker relativism 322–326

Stocker, Michael 2, 8, 142, 161

Supervenience 10, 191, 194, 208–231, 378

and conceptual truth 218

and empirical regularities 210–213

and fact/value gap 222–224

intra-world 213–215

inter-world 213–215

realism/irrealism 223

relevance constraint 218–222

supervenience claim 217

Svavarsdóttir, Sigrún 301

Systematic justification 22–25

and convergence 263

Trying 73

Universalisability 306–311

Utilitarianism 50

Value 141

As objectively prescriptive *see* objectively prescriptive value

Dispositional theory 9, 11–12, 17, 40

Generalism 221–222

Particularism 221

Prudential 216, 233

Van Inwagen, Peter 89
Virtue 286–289
   and rejection of practicality
      requirement 286–287,
      288–289

Wallace, R. Jay 293
Watson, Gary 6, 19, 56, 72, 107,
   114

Weakness of Will 5, 56–59, 71, 115
   and compulsion 58
   and rational capacities 131–134
   and recklessness 58
Wiggins, David 231
Willing 105
Williams, Bernard 2, 17, 18, 20–22, 24,
   25–33, 300
Woods, Michael 59